Introduction

There is something about Mary that has stubbornly resisted the best efforts of scholars over the last three decades to offer a more balanced historical account of her life and achievements. The fundamental problem is that her reign is deeply intertwined with two stories that are fundamental to English national identity and history: the Reformation and the British Empire. On one hand, penal laws introduced against Catholics during Elizabeth's reign and not repealed until the nineteenth century, and the direct military threat to her from the papacy, produced religious polemic and political propaganda that forged a powerful and lasting association between the patriotic and the anti-papal and anti-Catholic, which has shaded all too easily into the anti-Spanish and anti-Marian.[1] Linda Porter's lively biography concludes that the 'blackening of Mary's name began in Elizabeth's reign and gathered force at the end of the seventeenth century, when James II compounded the view that Catholic monarchs were a disaster for England. But it was really the enduring popularity of John Foxe which shaped the view of her that has persisted for 450 years… vilification of Mary has obscured the many areas of continuity between her rule and those of the other Tudors.'[2] Spain was the country that came to embody this objectionable papistry most fully; at the forefront of converting millions in the New World, its monarchs 'Catholic', presenting the greatest direct military threat to England – embodied in the attempted invasion by the Armada in 1588 – and less independent from Rome than France, while many other parts of Europe were riven by their own sectarian conflicts. The Black Legend of an intellectually enervated, repressive and superstitious religion underlying the tyrannous and cruel oppression of indigenous peoples around the world under the Spanish Empire first emerged in England towards the end of Elizabeth's reign and was consolidated in the eighteenth century, when Britain justified its own imperial adventures through negative exemplification, in contrast to Spain:[3]

English Protestants and nineteenth century English liberals gladly accepted the 'Black Legend', depicting Philip as a 'monster iniquity', which had been created by William the Silent's *Apologia* (1580). This hostile presentation of Philip can be traced in all the Protestant historians of the sixteenth and seventeenth centuries, and then in Robert Watson's *History of the Reign of Philip II* (1777) and through the influential works of the nineteenth century such as those of J. A. Froude, J. L. Motley and W. H. Prescott.[4]

The problem with Mary is in many ways a problem with Philip. It is true that '[b]ecause of her marriage to the Spanish Habsburg Philip, Mary also became the godmother of the association between popery and arbitrary (foreign) power', but this *ex post facto* construction dates from long after their reign.[5] The Marian period thus has the misfortune of lying right across the two major fault lines in England's story; an indigenous religion recognised in the creation of a national Protestant church and divergence from European historical tradition.

The culturally inflected nature of Mary I's historical reputation is nowhere more apparent than in the contrast between her place in British history and in other European traditions. Perhaps unsurprisingly, in Spain, whose capital has a tube station named after her (no such honour is accorded her here), she is renowned as pious and wise, something underlined by the assertion in María Jesús Pérez Martín's 2008 biography that she was 'the most majestic of English queens'.[6] The frame for understanding her as a historical figure is apparent from chapter headings that take us from her 'duro calvario' to 'Gólgota', echoing Christ's passion, reinforcing her saintliness and the providential significance of her sufferings. While this work is overly reliant on nineteenth-century sources like Agnes Strickland's *Lives of the Queens of England*, it does make an important contribution to rehabilitating Mary, exposing the 'systematic blackening of the memory of the deceased'; Pérez Martín hopes the biography will 'break down the wall of hate erected against Mary Tudor'.[7] In his follow-up to his Yale biography, part of Penguin's Monarchs series, John Edwards expresses the hope (like Pérez Martín) that Mary's motto, *veritas temporis filia* [truth is the daughter of time], will prove prophetic in her case and that the truth about this queen will out, despite centuries of accretions, building on the efforts of her half-sister's Protestant establishment to entomb her within their religiously inspired opprobrium.[8] Pérez Martín is clear that Mary was forced to combat 'the fanaticism and intransigence of radical Reformers' from the first and is still locked in that conflict; a reversal of the familiar tale.[9]

Just how religiously controversial the events of the Tudor period carried on being into the twentieth century can be judged from the fact that as late as 1970 members of the British Council of Protestant Churches, led by their general secretary, the Reverend Brian Green, mounted a protest against a public act of penance by 300 Catholics for the burning of Protestants under

Mary and Philip

Manchester University Press

STUDIES IN EARLY MODERN EUROPEAN HISTORY

This series aims to publish
challenging and innovative research in all areas
of early modern continental history.
The editors are committed to encouraging work
that engages with current historiographical
debates, adopts an interdisciplinary
approach, or makes an original contribution
to our understanding of the period.

SERIES EDITORS
Joseph Bergin, William G. Naphy, Penny Roberts and Paolo Rossi

Also available in the series

Full details of the series are available at www.manchesteruniversitypress.co.uk

Mary and Philip

The marriage of Tudor England and Habsburg Spain

ALEXANDER SAMSON

Manchester University Press

Published by Manchester University Press
Altrincham Street, Manchester M1 7JA, UK
www.manchesteruniversitypress.co.uk

British Library Cataloguing-in-Publication Data is available

ISBN 978 1 5261 4223 8 hardback
ISBN 978 1 5261 6024 9 paperback

First published by Manchester University Press in hardback 2020

This edition published 2021

The publisher has no responsibility for the persistence or accuracy of URLs for any external or third-party internet websites referred to in this book, and does not guarantee that any content on such websites is, or will remain, accurate or appropriate.

Typeset by Servis Filmsetting Ltd, Stockport, Cheshire

Contents

List of plates

List of abbreviations

AGS	Archivo General de Simancas
APC	*Acts of the Privy Council, New Series*, vols 4–6, ed. John Roche Dasent (London: HMSO, 1892–3)
BL	British Library
BNE	Biblioteca Nacional de España, Madrid
Cal. Dom.	*Calendar of State Papers, Domestic: Edward VI, Mary, Elizabeth I, and James I*, 12 vols (London: 1856–72)
Cal. For.	*Calendar of State Papers, Foreign: Edward VI, Mary, Elizabeth I*, 25 vols (London: 1861–1950)
Cal. Scot.	*Calendar of State Papers, Scotland*, vol. 1, *1547–63*, ed. Joseph Bain (London: HMSO, 1898)
Cal. Span.	*Calendar of Letters, Despatches, and State Papers, Relating to the Negotiations Between England and Spain*, vol. 1, ed. G. Bergenroth (London: Longman, Green, Longman & Roberts, 1862), vols 11–13, ed. Royall Tyler (London: HMSO, 1916–54)
Cal. Ven.	Brown, Rawdon, ed., *Calendar of State Papers and Manuscripts, Relating to English Affairs etc., Venetian*, vols V–VII (London: Longman & Co. 1873–90)
CODOIN	*Colección de Documentos Inéditos para la Historia de España*, ed. Fernando Navarete, 113 vols (Madrid: 1842–95)
CPR	*Calendar of Patent Rolls: Philip and Mary*, 4 vols (London: HMSO, 1936–9)
Grey Friars Chronicle	*Chronicle of the Grey Friars of London*, Camden Society 1st ser., no. LIII (London: J. B. Nichols and Son, 1851)
Letters and Papers	*Letters and Papers, Foreign and Domestic, Henry VIII*, 21 vols (London: HMSO, 1864–1920)
LMA	London Metropolitan Archives
Machyn's Diary	Nichols, John Gough, ed., *The Diary of Henry Machyn,*

	Citizen and Merchant Taylor of London 1550–1563 (London: Camden Society, 1848)
ODNB	*Oxford Dictionary of National Biography*, online version available at www.oxforddnb.com/
Rutland Papers	William Jerdan, 'Device for the Coronation of Henry VII', *Rutland Papers*, Camden Society Old Series 21 (London: Camden Society, 1842)
TAMO	Foxe, John, *The Unabridged Acts and Monuments Online* (1563 edition) (HRI Online Publications, Sheffield, 2011). Available from: www.johnfoxe.org [Accessed: 26th August 2015]
Tower Chronicle	Nichols, John Gough, ed., *The Chronicle of Queen Jane and of two years of Queen Mary and especially of the Rebellion of Sir Thomas Wyat*, Camden Society XLVIII (London: The Camden Society, 1850)

Mary, despite the fact that they were joined by 200 Anglican counterparts in a gesture of reconciliation. Green apparently stated that '[r]eparation towards the dead is not sufficient. Reparation toward God is needed. In other words, the Roman Catholic Church has not changed its doctrines.'[10] Indeed, in popular culture these negative, anti-Catholic associations abound to this day. In a review of Trevor Nunn's film *Lady Jane* (1985), starring Helena Bonham-Carter, one reviewer described Mary as 'Edward's half-wit sister', picking up on Geoffrey Elton's infamous assessment of the first Tudor regnant queen as rather stupid.[11] More recently, in Shekhar Kapur's two films on 'good queen Bess', *Elizabeth* (1998) and *Elizabeth: the Golden Age* (2007) – some of the most widely disseminated public representations of Tudor history – the image of Mary and Philip reinforces many of the myths that recent historical work has overturned. Their varying historiographical fortunes are encoded aesthetically in casting Kathy Burke as Mary I, opposite Cate Blanchett's Elizabeth. In the first film, a hysterical and neurotic Mary moves around a dark, torch-lit world, with her brooding, uncomfortable consort clearly disinterested in her. This reflects the claim made by Sir Francis Hastings in 1598, in *A Watchword to all religious true hearted Englishmen*, that the marriage 'could not drawe the least sparke of true loue from him to this noble Queene, who so louingly made choice of him to be her husband'.[12] Mary is still seen largely as a tragic figure, on the basis of the idea that Philip was unenthusiastic about their marriage and for this reason largely absent. The BBC History website describes her as '[c]hildless, sick and deserted by Philip'.[13] The problem is that there is no evidence to support this idea. The representation of Philip by Jordi Mollà in the second film is very much in keeping with the idea of the king blinded by religious zealotry, but as John Guy, for example, has argued, the Philip of this period was a Renaissance prince, rather than the Counter-Reformation fundamentalist of legend, an impression confirmed in Geoffrey Parker's recent biographies. Although of a precocious religiosity, all the evidence supports a vision of a pragmatic and tolerant ruler, sensitive to the problems presented by cultural and religious difference, who for a year between 1550 and 1551 'ate and drank, danced and jousted, hunted and talked with Lutherans, and his surviving letters to Lutheran rulers from this period exude warmth'.[14] In representations of the reign in the half-century after its end, there is little of the image that has come down to us. In plays by Thomas Heywood (*If you know not me you know nobody* (1605)) and Thomas Dekker, John Webster (*Sir Thomas Wyatt* (1607)), it is Philip who saves Elizabeth from Stephen Gardiner's plot to have her put to death. Mary is represented in the latter play with a nun's wimple, praying:

I haue forsaken for a rich prayer Booke.
The Golden Mines of wealthy India, ...

This little volume inclosed in this hand,
Is richer then the Empire of this land.[15]

The sacramental focus of her piety positioned her deliberately in relation to the critical doctrinal issue underlying the Reformation.[16] The personal and theological were inextricably intertwined for Mary, who was the more intransigent, principled and less pragmatic of the two monarchs, although not noted for her piety until after 1547 and the persecution she suffered under Edward.[17] Criticising her zealous religiosity only makes sense because she chose the 'wrong' religion. Moreover, these criticisms were not true of either monarch in this period. The most striking example of the persistence of negative judgements of Mary is the London Dungeon's exhibition 'Bloody Mary: Killer Queen', complete with the smell of burning flesh, whose advertising was actually banned for being too frightening: depicting a seated queen who transforms into a screeching zombie. By contrast, in Radio Televisión Española's major series *Carlos Rey Emperador* (2015), continuation of the hugely successful *Isabel* (2012), Mary I, played by Ángela Cremonte, is presented as self-possessed and powerful, the political and aesthetic equal of her husband. The series reflects the uncomfortable confusion of the sexual and political in dynastic politics and explores a series of questionable commonplaces from the writing about their co-monarchy, from his unhappiness with the marriage contract to her unreciprocated devotion to him.[18]

Much recent writing on Mary has returned to critique the judgements of nineteenth- and twentieth-century historians that have led here, but seem to continue to haunt the present, without our being able to fully exorcise them.[19] More sympathetic assessments of Marian England originally appeared in the nineteenth century, from the Catholic John Lingard and Agnes Strickland, the latter denounced as a 'papistical sympathiser'.[20] Lingard, the first historian to consult original documents in Simancas and the Vatican, is simultaneously and unsurprisingly sceptical about the notions of an indigenous antique church, a papacy encroaching on English sovereignty and the Reformation as a movement of national liberation, characteristic of mainstream historical tradition. The tendency to study British history in contrast to European history has entrenched the nationalist and isolationist bias implicit in Protestant historiography. Lingard and Strickland overturned the image of Mary I as a cruel tyrant (Bloody Mary). But to explain without condoning the burnings, they emphasised her personal misfortunes and minimised her agency. James Anthony Froude's characterisation of Mary's rule as a 'barren interlude' has been perhaps the most influential of all. As late as 1970, E. H. Harbison concurred: the 'reign of Mary has been called a "barren interlude" in Tudor history, and so it undoubtedly was'.[21] Froude's Mary was hysterically deranged if not mad, desolated by Philip's departure and her failed pregnancies.[22] At the beginning of the twentieth century Albert Pollard, influenced by Froude, wrote '[s]terility was the conclusive note of Mary's reign':

> in default of royal or ministerial leadership there could only be stagnation... the whole nation malingered in diverse degrees. Debarred from the paths it wished to pursue, it would not follow in Mary's wake. A blight had fallen on national faith and confidence, and Israel took to its tents.[23]

He claimed 'a dim consciousness that their affairs were being administered, and their resources exploited, in Philip's interests estranged the English people from the Spaniards and from Mary's rule': in spite of attempts to prevent 'Philip from converting his titular dignity to anti-national purposes... no safeguards could control Mary's affection for her Lord, or compel her to follow the wishes of her privy council'.[24] For the first time since 'England had attained to national consciousness', it was controlled by a foreigner.[25] As we will see, the issue of whether Philip obtained real power and authority in England goes on being controversial. There is a delicious irony in the fact that it was precisely Froude's historical judgement of Philip II as 'the personification of the intolerant spirit of Catholic Europe' that provoked Julián Juderías at the beginning of the twentieth century to write the book often taken to have coined the term 'Black Legend': 'the iniquitous legend created around Philip II seems fine to him [Froude], because it is aimed at discrediting Catholicism'.[26] The image of an emotionally hysterical queen beset by tragedy exculpates the Tudor monarch, in order to reassign agency and blame to Catholics and foreigners.

Froude's and Pollard's language closely echoed each other's, in its providentialism and imagery of infertility. The judgement that in terms of our nation's destiny 'Mary's reign had been a palpable failure' relies on seeing the Reformation as a form of manifest destiny.[27] According to these whiggish interpretations, 'Mary represented the failed past, while the Protestant Henry VIII and Elizabeth I stood for the glorious future'.[28] In 1950, Stanley Bindoff judged the Marian 'interlude': '[p]olitically bankrupt, spiritually impoverished, economically anarchic, and intellectually enervated, Marian England awaited the day of its deliverance'.[29] Geoffrey Elton's assessment of Mary in 1977 was no better, describing her as 'arrogant, assertive, bigoted, stubborn, suspicious and (not to put too fine a point upon it) rather stupid... devoid of political skill, unable to compromise, set only on the wholesale reversal of a generation's history'.[30] For him it was truly a barren interlude: 'positive achievements there were none'.[31] In their major reassessment of the mid-Tudor period in 1980, Jennifer Loach and Robert Tittler described the reign of Mary I as bedevilled by 'the liberal and Protestant shibboleths of the Asquithean era'.[32] Despite the wealth of subsequent academic scholarship 'the basically Whiggish and ultimately Protestant view of things is still a potent influence', albeit in diluted, residual and secularised form.[33] The trouble with Mary and what makes the Marian period fascinating are two sides of the same coin.[34] The official view of the British past is built around an understanding of the Reformation in which Mary is necessarily antipathetic; an investment in the image of the Tudors riding on the back of popular anti-clericalism and turning their backs on a papacy which had systematically encroached and trespassed on the liberties and independence of the English church and state during the medieval period. The concept of the Reformation as a movement of national liberation, restoring England to an original sovereign independence and laying the foundations for the nation's 'divinely appointed role as the "elect nation", destined to lead Protestantism in the old world of Europe and in the new world of the widespread colonies abroad', makes any recuperation of Mary atavistic.[35] Many scholars have begun to question this picture and, while there is still a certain cautiousness about lauding England's first regnant queen, the woman who blazed a trail for her half-sister, that achievement is increasingly recognised.

Mary's childlessness was linked from the period itself to the Catholic restoration, stillborn as a result of her death.[36] Eamon Duffy has criticised the connection of Mary's 'bitter preoccupation with the past and her tragic sterility', which rest on the notion of the Catholic church as 'backward-looking, unimaginative and reactionary'.[37] In polemic and anti-monarchical writing, Mary's gender and natural body were consistently attacked. Anthony Gilby, in *Admonition to England and Scotland to call them to repentance* (Geneva: 1558), claimed that England had been desolated by 'one crafty Gardiner, whose name was Stephen, having wolf-like condition, [who] did maintain many a wolf, did sow a wicked seed in the garden, and cherished many weeds to deface the vineyard. And his said Marie, who after was his mistress, now married to Philip.'[38] In the first year of her reign she had been subject to rumours that she was carrying Gardiner's illegitimate child.[39] Arguments that in marrying Mary gave up her most powerful propaganda tool, chastity, and exposed herself to vilification on the grounds of her sexuality, are highly paradoxical, apparent from their being supported by noting the invocation of her purity by her supporters in the absence of alternative 'Catholic' female iconography: 'long after her marriage, Marian propaganda still needed to hark back to a lost virginity', on her death 'the poet George Cavendish still praised her accession as a virgin':[40]

> To a virgin's life which liked thee best
> Professed was thine heart, when moved with zeal

And tears of subjects expressing request,
For no lust but love for the common weal,
Virginity's vow thou diddest repeal.[41]

In Pole's oration at Westminster prior to the reunification with Rome, the legate described how Mary 'being a virgin, helples, naked, and unarmed prevailed, and had victory over tyrauntes'.[42] Mary's image has always been caught uncomfortably between the poles of the virginal and saintly and the dangerously sexualised. The housewifely or matronly has been almost entirely displaced by the image of an unnatural stepmother or a sexual betrayer and whore. Even the biblical and mythological figures with which she was compared by the Genoese community in London at the time of her coronation, Judith, Tomyris and Pallas Athene, were ambivalent sexually, either aggressive viragos or symbolic, as the tag beneath Pallas Athene on the triumphal arch stated, of 'invincible manly virtue'. Seeing Mary's childlessness as the key to her failure is not without irony. She is most often denigrated through on-going and wilfully unfavourable comparison to her sister Elizabeth, who similarly failed to provide an heir, but is not cast as a failure as a queen: 'virginal Elizabeth and her impenetrable realm become naturalized as the satisfying consequence of, as well as contrast to, Catholic decay, which was fated to be superseded'.[43] Anna Whitelock's sympathetic biography begins with the emblem of Mary and Elizabeth's joint tomb in Westminster Abbey, '[p]artners both in throne and grave, here rest we two sisters, Mary and Elizabeth, in the hope of one resurrection', noting how symbolically Mary is buried beneath: for Whitelock she was 'a complex figure of immense courage and resolve'.[44] At the outset of her reign Elizabeth's virginity was more likely to have been seen as monstrous and anomalous, because in Tudor times marriage was considered to be the natural state for non-religious women. Mary, more than Elizabeth, can be rightly celebrated for her chastity and virginity, qualities highly prized in women in the era. A whiff of scandal surrounded Elizabeth on more than one occasion. It is clear the moniker acquired in her later years, the Virgin Queen, would have appeared risible in the 1550s. As Paulina Kewes has shown, there were many continuities between the reigns of the Tudor half-sisters,[45] not least in their struggles to find an iconography of female power to legitimate their rule. The very different expectations in England and Spain of female rule and rulers may, then as now, have muddied the waters about how the marriage should be read. Spain had the outstanding example of a regnant queen in Mary's grandmother, Isabel la Católica, as well as a long history of regnant and ruling queens, and female members of the royal dynasty pressed into service to govern distinct territories in the absence of male dynasts; from Philip's sister Juana, who ruled Spain in his absence, having been recalled weeks after being widowed and giving birth to her first child, to Charles' aunt, Margaret of Austria, and sister, Mary of Hungary. Isabel's marriage to Ferdinand II of Aragón was consciously emulated in the contract and treaty of Philip and Mary.[46] By 1523, the dynastic problem that would assail England for the rest of the sixteenth century, brought to an end only with the accession of the Stuarts in 1603, was clear: Catherine's inability to give Henry a longed-for, legitimate male heir. Catherine responded by preparing her daughter Mary for rule, commissioning humanist educational treatises from her countryman Juan Luis Vives.

David Loades, the most important modern historian of Marian England, someone whose many works necessarily influence anyone writing on this subject, agrees that 'the picture painted by Froude and endorsed by Pollard was a grotesque caricature'.[47] But he remains 'unrepentantly sceptical of the attempts which are sometimes made to claim that Mary's death at the relatively early age of forty-three deprived England of a great catholic queen'.[48] The grounds for his position are that her reign 'did not command the same consensus of support as that of Elizabeth – or even the level achieved by Henry in the last years of his life'.[49] The comparison to two monarchs who reigned for over three decades is telling, however. Who would doubt that Mary would have forged doggedly ahead into old age, had disease not cut her reign short? A growing number of scholars have offered more positive readings. John Edwards, whose brilliant biography has restored Mary and her reign to its European context, both in a political and a religious sense, making fuller use than anyone previously of Spanish archives and sources, concludes that 'her personal and specific contributions to her country's history went well beyond institutional efficiency and continuity... she was an active cultural patron... gave vital help to Oxford and Cambridge... and although her restoration of the link with Rome seemed to end with her death, it has never left the ecclesiastical, or even secular, agenda'.[50] Most importantly, he recognises that the marriage was 'an epoch-making strategic alliance for England, with a major European power'.[51] England's profound entanglement with Spain throughout the sixteenth century, for better or for worse, hinges on this alliance.

The visual emblem that perhaps best summarises the argument of this book is the *Queen Mary Atlas*, produced by Diogo Homem in 1558–9, probably commissioned by Mary for Philip, to appeal to his well-known fascination for geography. The Iberian peninsula and British Isles are depicted together on the opening map. To the left of the Tudor armorial device a blank space lies, where Philip's coat of arms has been scratched off (see Plate 1).[52] Mary's premature death forced Homem to rededicate the atlas to another royal patron, but its original context is clear. This historical vandalism is the first act in a centuries-long campaign to obscure the Spanish marriage and erase the memory of England's Spanish king. It is a palimpsest of the attempt to set England apart from Europe and its Spanish past. The atlas contains a unique depiction of Pizarro's soldiers in Peru, and across its pages consistently emphasises Spain's global importance, undermining Portuguese claims to the Spice Islands in the far east by prominently situating Spain's coat of arms there. France is depicted surmounted by an open, non-imperial crown, dismembered in accordance with the belligerent objectives of the Anglo-Spanish axis that declared war in 1557.[53]

David Loades wrote in a review of historiography and research on the period: 'Philip as king of England remains a shadowy figure, and his relationship with Mary appears less straightforward the more it is investigated'.[54] The marriage of Philip and Mary has been interpreted by historians as underlying her ultimate failure as a queen: the 'Spanish marriage was unpopular' and 'did nothing to help Mary'; although royal authority weathered this particular storm and proved 'effective even in the hands of a woman of no political experience', 'the extent to which her Catholicism was an asset or liability will continue to be debated'.[55] This book aims to open up a space for alternative interpretations of the Spanish marriage, not by making a claim for its unqualified success, but rather by showing the fundamental lack of evidence for judging it, as all too often it has been judged, in personal terms.

In terms of contemporary expectations of dynastic alliances, and given the European political context, it is hard to see the alliance as anything other than a success. Panegyric and pamphlets about the marriage swept Europe in a slew of celebratory publications that outshone anything produced for a domestic audience. Importantly, according to a wealth of recent research, far from failing 'to discover the Counter Reformation', 'the Marian church "invented"' it.[56] Clerical education and recruitment, restocking parishes and churches with liturgical objects, preaching, along with a 'formidable body of catechetical and hortatory material making a positive case for catholicism' made considerable strides towards the wholesale reversal of the previous twenty years' radical religious changes and were fundamentally reflective of what most people wanted.[57] Remarkable work has been done on the hugely influential figure of Bartolomé Carranza, who composed a monumental new catechism with which to complete the re-Catholicisation of England. It is telling that the Great Bible of 1539 was never officially withdrawn and remained in parishes throughout the period.[58] Repugnant as the burnings were, although perhaps inevitable in the Europe of the period (Philip's government in the Low Countries burned a similar number over a slightly longer period), even they achieved the policy's intention, with the numbers defiantly refusing to conform, especially among social elites, tailing off by the end of the reign.[59] Two further books on the Marian church demonstrate how fruitful an area for recent research this area has been.[60] The epithet 'bloody' was not applied to Mary until 1658, of course, a century after her death, and only gained currency in the reigns of Charles II and James II.[61] One of the most positive aspects of reconsiderations of her reign is the move away from the dour and isolated figure towards the enthusiastic hunter, dancer, lover of cards and gambling, jewellery and fine clothes, the accomplished musician and linguist, the humanist engaged in theological discussion with intellectuals at her court such as Cardinal Reginald Pole. At least in popular culture, Mary will probably go on being someone we love to hate, a villain. But this tells us more about historical writing and its relationship to national identity than it does about her or her reign.[62]

Philip was not an absolutist ruler; rather, he faced the monumental task of ruling a global empire, whose composite monarchies made him more used than English monarchs to negotiating complex legal, political, social and cultural differences. The affability and courtesy that he displayed, judicious use of self-fashioning in portraiture and courtly displays, his clothing, patronage of books, maps and other objects, did win him widespread acceptance, even popularity among his English subjects. The generous pensions he distributed among privy counsellors and went on paying into the Elizabethan period oiled the wheels. One of the central contentions of the argument is that the Hispanophobia that so many have seen as defining the reign was ultimately political, more concerned with jealousy born of intensely personal relationships than some form of patriotic resistance. It was driven by a need to ensure the English part of the new Anglo-Spanish global empire got its fair share. Elizabeth Russell has suggested that in England the 'allegation of insuperable domestic opposition and strong anti-Catholic and anti-Spanish feeling' was specifically exploited by Mary to obtain greater concessions from the imperialists over the treaty of alliance, by exaggerating the weakness of her position.[63] We might question similarly how disinterested was what William Paget, First Baron Paget reported to the bishop of Arras, during negotiations in Brussels on 14th November 1554, concerning the weakness of the government and divisions in the Council over Pole's coming to England:

> It seemed to him that the only way to correct this evil, given the Queen's gentle character and inexperience in governing, would be that the King should take over the task himself with the assistance of the best qualified Englishmen in Council... At the same time, it must be remembered that the English had a natural hatred for foreigners and were not without some hostility towards Spaniards. These feelings were much stronger among the people than among the nobility.[64]

This representation was flattering of Philip's authority, while underlining the need for the best qualified to represent him, presumably including Paget himself. The allegation of xenophobia and hostility to the Spanish was laid at the door of the people rather than the nobility. But in reality much of the tensions between groups when Philip came to England originated from the precincts of the palace itself. Documents written by Philip himself demonstrate that not only did he have no sinister or hidden intentions but more importantly he felt insulted by the suggestion that *his* wars had resulted in specie being exported from England: 'I did not wish to have a single *real* from this kingdom, but have spent there the amount you well know'.[65] England gained immeasurably from the presence of Philip on her shores, in terms of science and navigation, experiencing cultural marvels from the Tunis tapestries to the paintings of Titian, witnessing the magnificence and style of Europe's most prestigious court as well as providing the military experience of the last major entanglement in a war on the mainland, with the successful siege of Saint Quentin.

John Guy has written recently that far from 'sterility being the keynote of this decade... many fertile and enduring reforms were discussed or initiated in the 1550s. Among the most significant was the switch in the theory of taxation.'[66] In addition one might point to the reform of the navy, overseas exploration, the restoration of the church, the recoinage, a thriving and vibrant court culture and the stability of the regime in the face of both famine and epidemic disease. Mary's own musicianship and patronage of court musicians supported the careers of the most outstanding composers of her age, including Thomas Tallis and Willian Byrd. Penry Williams has commented, in relation to the debate about Mary's Catholicism, that the 'one thing that can be said with certainty about England in 1558 is that it was not yet Protestant'.[67] Perhaps the most outstanding example of the new vision of Mary, as humanist princess, courageous and successful queen, is Judith Richards' magisterial biography that argues that 'she ruled the country with some success at a very difficult and divided time'.[68] It may or may not be true that '[i]n terms of her own ideas and purposes, Mary Tudor was a failure, and nothing can conceal that fact'.[69] But given what Mary did achieve in the short time given to her, she is a figure who deserves to be celebrated.

Too much of Mary's posthumous reputation has been based on the perceptions and reports of foreign ambassadors; especially the imperial envoy, Simon Renard, who Philip's court sidelined as soon as the match had been concluded.[70] The fact that Renard's intelligence came largely from Mary herself should arouse suspicion. The transition between the reigns of Charles V and Philip II was the central fact of European politics in this period, brilliantly contextualised in Mia Rodríguez Salgado's broad, synoptic study of the polycentric empire.[71] The Habsburgs were well used to balancing the competing demands of their different kingdoms. The multilingual, composite nature of the Habsburg monarchy has furthermore posed linguistic and physical difficulties to scholars working on the period. The sources are dispersed through archives all over Europe – Brussels, Paris, Vienna, Rome, Madrid, Simancas – leading to a misleading reliance on Victorian translations and summaries of documents calendared by Royall Tyler and others. The danger of this is pointed out in a number of instances where fundamental mistranslations have formed the basis for significant historical distortions.

The Spanish sources for this period suffer by comparison as a result of the loss of Philip's chancellery documents on the return to Spain, meaning that the Spanish side is less well-documented than others. The most frequently used source on the marriage and co-monarchy of Philip and Mary is the group of documents collected together by Cesare Malfatti in *The Accession, Coronation and Marriage of Mary Tudor as related in Four MSS of the Escorial*.[72] These derive from two extant volumes, manuscript copies of contemporary materials that the royal chronicler Florián de Ocampo gathered together during his lifetime; *Noticias de varios sucesos acaecidos, 1521–1558*.[73] Ocampo's function as royal historian included the compilation and gathering together of written records on the events of the day. They date roughly from the time of his release from his ecclesiastical duties in 1555.[74] They provide a fascinating insight into Ocampo's correspondents and sources of information, his prioritisation of materials and equally the problems they posed for him if they were ever to be redeployed in a contemporary imperial chronicle. The miscellanies were interspersed with what look like *relaciones*, brief notices about important events. For the year 1548, there were accounts of the movements of the Turkish fleet, its assault on Malta, letters from Rome, personal letters from courtiers and news from the sessions of the Council of Trent. However, for the historian the more interesting material is that which fills the gaps; highly specific and personal first-hand accounts of a myriad of incidents from the Mediterranean to England, by a set of informants and correspondents, some of whom had Zamoran connections, others of whom had an unknown relationship with Ocampo. His local contacts provided him with rich sources of information. He obtained copies of a letter sent from Vélez-Málaga to the Zamoran *corregidor* Francisco Carrillo, and another from the bishop of Zamora to his brother Alonso del Aguila about his journey to Germany in the company of Maximilian, king of Bohemia, as well as Diego de Azevedo's fascinating account of the arrival and wedding of Philip to Mary for his wife back in Zamora.[75] Azevedo arrived in England before Mary's entry into the city, writing to his wife on 1st August from London. His account, found in Ocampo, has not been cited before in any of the major accounts of the marriage. He later served as Philip's *caballerizo mayor* and remained at post in England probably until 1557, when we know he returned to Spain from the last letter in the volume from Hernando Delgadillo, a source in Valladolid, who wrote: 'a post passed through Salamanca with the news of Don Diego de Azevedo's disembarkation; the archbishop of Toledo and Regent Figueroa also arrived with the fleet'.[76] Ocampo had also managed to acquire transcriptions of letters from Juan de Barahona, now in the library at El Escorial.[77] The second set of sources is reprinted in the great nineteenth century *Colección de Documentos Inéditos para la Historia de España (CODOIN)*.[78] These require an important caveat. They are mostly by Philip's favourites, Ruy Gomez da Silva and Juan de Figueroa, who inevitably provided positive assessments of the king's statesmanship, as power slowly slipped from his father Charles V's grasp. Tensions between the emperor and his son had been apparent for years and this was the moment when Philip began to seize the reins of power. Their highly positive accounts of England need to be read in light of the fact that these men were themselves attempting to displace an old guard of Charles' servants, headed by the duke of Alba, so inevitably underlined their master's political success and competence.

This book emphasises the fundamental nature of commercial and economic links between England and Spain throughout the sixteenth century and how the marriage fitted into a set of strategic interests central to both countries that had been reflected by dynastic marriages stretching back into the medieval period and Eleanor of England's (1161–1214) marriage to Alfonso VIII. In tracing how Philip and Mary's marriage came about, it challenges the notion that Charles' concessions came as a surprise to Philip, given the presence of his familiars and favourites at the courts in Brussels and in London throughout the period of negotiations. Furthermore, the treaty closely followed precedents he and his advisors would have been familiar with. The infamous *ad cautelam* document he drew up as he signed the matrimonial capitulation may have had as much to do with the realistic prospect that he might find himself trapped in an infertile marriage. With only one living heir, he needed a spare. If Mary had lived as long as Elizabeth, their marriage might have lasted over twenty years. This book focuses on the ways in which ceremony and material culture, particularly dress, were used to ameliorate the legitimate anxieties about Philip and Mary's co-monarchy in practice and underline Mary's continuing precedence, contrary to typical expectations of a woman in marriage. Her coronation and accession were hailed by many observers as nothing short of miraculous. Nevertheless, it is clear that she was well prepared to mount a bid for the throne and had been prepared for rule both through her education and early experience, and through being one of the richest magnates and land owners in the realm. The problem of female rule is considered in depth, both in terms of legislation like the 'Act for the Queen's Regal Power' and how aspects of the treaty responded to problems with the political law in relation to women. In terms of dynastic politics, she negotiated for herself a glittering match with the most powerful prince in Europe, in the face of first domestic opposition and then a potentially serious rebellion. The book explores the analogy between the Wyatt and *comuneros* revolts, both of which produced a rash of political writing around legitimate authority and the limits of royal power. By going back to many of the original Spanish documents, it challenges a series of distortions that have grown up around the marriage and its alleged success or otherwise. Fundamentally, it is demonstrated that there was no abrogation of English sovereignty as a result of the marriage, but that the marriage catalysed an incipient constitutionalism.

Detailed analysis of the provisions of the treaty demonstrates how closely they followed the example set by Philip's grandparents, the Catholic monarchs Ferdinand and Isabella, and how the Marian exiles continued to allege insuperable domestic opposition, based on deep-rooted xenophobia and Hispanophobia. This historiographical assumption is challenged in an exploration of what Englishmen might have thought of the Spanish in 1554, the extent to which the Black Legend had reached their ears from the Low Countries. There is no doubt that Protestants throughout Europe were intensely aware of the reputation of the Spanish kingdoms in both Italy and Germany. Their propaganda repeated verbatim the denunciations by Luther of Charles V's troops in the Holy Roman Empire. This book also unpicks the association between the marriage and malign Catholic and foreign influence. Firstly, it discards the assumption that Catholic restoration was antipathetic to the majority of English subjects, and secondly, it shows that the careful negotiation of reconciliation by Philip meant that the English church's independence from the papacy was assiduously maintained and enshrined in statute and the holders of ecclesiastical property assured in their possession of dissolved monastic lands. Philip and Mary's role in the government of England is analysed to show that both were involved in making fundamental decisions. Mary was not overawed by her husband, nor was Philip uninterested in the government of his newly acquired kingdom. There were numerous startling cultural achievements also associated with the marriage, not least the first Spanish-English language-learning textbook and dictionary.

First and foremost, this book seeks to highlight the positive achievements of the reign and offer a balanced assessment of the glittering dynastic union of England and Spain, which for a time sat at the heart of early modern Europe.

Notes

1 Perhaps the most influential text linking Catholicism and the unproductive in the twentieth century is Max Weber, *The Protestant Ethic and the Spirit of Capitalism*, trans. Talcott Parsons (London: Routledge, 1992).

2 Linda Porter, *Mary: The First Queen* (London: Portrait, 2007), p. 418.

3 There is a brilliant account of the definition, birth and development of the Black Legend in Italy, the Low Countries and Germany in Antonio Sánchez Jiménez's *Leyenda negra: la batalla*

sobre la imagen de España en tiempos de Lope de Vega (Madrid: Cátedra, 2016). See the discussion of Robert Watson's *The History of Philip II* (London: Strathan and Cadell, 1777), note 4.

4   Edwin Jones, *The English Nation: The Great Myth* (Thrupp: Sutton Publishing, 1998), p. 190.

5   David Loades, *Mary Tudor: The Tragical History of the first Queen of England* (Richmond: The National Archives, 2006), p. 8.

6   María Jesús Pérez Martín, *María Tudor: La gran reina desconocida* (Madrid: Rialp, 2008), pp. 499–500: 'la más majestuosa de las reinas inglesas'.

7   Pérez Martín, *María Tudor*, p. 867: 'sistemático ennegrecimiento de la memoria de la difunta' and 'ayudar a romper ese muro de odio erigido contra María Tudor'.

8   John Edwards, *Mary I: The Daughter of Time* (London: Allen Lane, 2016), p. 79.

9   Pérez Martín, *María Tudor*, p. 510: 'el fanatismo y la intransigencia de los radicales reformistas'.

10 Reported in '300 Catholics make penance for deaths', *Los Angeles Times*, 26th January 1970, p. A10.

11 Barbara Lovenheim, 'Nunn's story: a challenge in *Lady Jane*', *Los Angeles Times*, 17th February 1985. See Alex von Tunzelman's rightly corruscating review of this 'simpering romance', awarded a D+ for History, *The Guardian,* 26th August 2010: www.theguardian.com/ film/2010/aug/26/reel-history-lady-jane-grey [Accessed 30th October 2014]. Full quote from Elton is given in the text relating to note 30.

12 Sir Francis Hastings, *A Watchword to all religious true hearted Englishmen* (London: Felix Kingston for Ralph Jackson, 1598), sig. G3r.

13 BBC, 'Mary I (1516–1558)', www.bbc.co.uk/history/historic_figures/mary_i_queen.shtml [Accessed: 30th October 2014].

14 Geoffrey Parker, *Imprudent King: A New Life of Philip II* (London: Yale University Press, 2014), p. 40. The other, lengthier tome is *Felipe II: La biografía definitiva* (Madrid: Planeta, 2010).

15 Thomas Dekker and John Webster, *The Famous History of Sir Thomas Wyat*, ed. John Farmer (Amersham: Tudor Facsimile Texts. 1914), sigs A3r–A4v.

16 On Lord Morley's gift 'An Account of the Miracles Performed by the Holy Eucharist', see Lorraine Attreed and Alexandra Winkler, 'Faith and forgiveness: lessons in statecraft for Queen Mary Tudor', *Sixteenth Century Journal* 36 (2005), 971–89. Also discussed extensively in *'Triumphs of English' Henry Parker, Lord Morley Translation to the Tudor Court: New Essays in Interpretation*, ed. Marie Axton and James Carley (London: British Library, 2000).

17 John Guy, 'Conference style' review of *Talking Peace 1604* exhibition and Rosemary Mulcahy, *Philip II of Spain: Patron of the Arts*, *Times Literary Supplement*, 10th September 2004, p. 17.

18 www.rtve.es/alacarta/videos/carlos-rey-emperador/carlos-rey-cap16/3455288/   [Accessed: 5th February 2019].

19 See Anna Whitelock, 'Mary Tudor: the first queen of England' in Liz Oakley-Brown and Louise Wilkinson, eds, *The Rituals and Rhetoric of Queenship: Medieval to Early Modern* (Dublin: Four Courts, 2009), pp. 59–60; Thomas Freeman, 'Inventing Bloody Mary: perceptions of Mary Tudor from the Restoration to the twentieth century' and Judith Richards, 'Reassessing Mary Tudor: some concluding points' in Susan Doran and Thomas Freeman, eds, *Mary Tudor: Old and New Perspectives* (New York: Palgrave Macmillan, 2011), pp. 91–100 and 206–24.

20 Richards, 'Reassessing Mary Tudor', p. 207.

21 E. H. Harbison, *Rival Ambassadors at the Court of Queen Mary* (New York: Books for Libraries Press, 1940, repr. 1970), Preface, p. vii.

22 J. A. Froude, *The Reign of Mary Tudor* (London: Continuum, 2009), p. 15. Consternation at the nineteenth-century Catholic revival influenced his writing; see Ciaran Brady, *James Anthony Froude: An Intellectual Biography of a Victorian Prophet* (Oxford: Oxford University Press, 2014).

23 A. F. Pollard, *The History of England From the Accession of Edward VI to the Death of Elizabeth (1547–1603)*, The Political History of England, 12 vols (London: Longmans, Green and Co., 1915), vol. 6, p. 172.

24 Pollard, *The History of England*, vol. 6, p. 158.

25 Pollard, *The History of England*, vol. 6, p. 158.

26 Julián Juderías, *La Leyenda Negra: Estudios acerca del concepto de España en el extranjero* (Madrid:

Editora Nacional, 1960), p. 234: 'la personificación del intolerante espíritu de la Europa Católica' or 'la leyenda inicua creada en torno a Felipe II le parece bien, porque va encaminada a desprestigiar al catolicismo'.

27 Pollard, *The History of England*, vol. 6, p. 173.

28 Jones, *English Nation / Great Myth*, p. 226.

29 S. T. Bindoff, *Tudor England* (London: Penguin, 1950), p. 182.

30 Geoffrey Elton, *Reform and Reformation: England 1509–1558* (London: Edward Arnold, 1977), p. 376.

31 Geoffrey Elton, *England under the Tudors* (London: Longman, 1964), p. 214.

32 Jennifer Loach and Robert Tittler, eds, *The Mid-Tudor Polity c. 1540–1560* (London: Macmillan, 1980), p. 1.

33 Jones, *English Nation / Great Myth*, p. 239.

34 Elizabeth Russell, 'Mary Tudor and Mr Jorkins', *Historical Research* 63 (1990), 263–76, p. 263.

35 Jones, *English Nation / Great Myth*, p. 192.

36 Thomas Betteridge, 'Maids and wives: representing female rule during the reign of Mary Tudor', in Doran and Freeman, eds, *Mary Tudor*, p. 139.

37 *London Review of Books*, 7th February 2008, p. 27.

38 Anthony Gilby, *Admonition to England and Scotland to call them to repentance* (Geneva: 1558), sigs Iiiii, Iiiii v, reprinted in John Knox, *The History of the Reformation of Religion within the Realm of Scotland* (Glasgow: J. Galbraith and Co., 1761), p. 459.

39 Kirk M. Fabel, 'Questions of numismatic and linguistic signification in the reign of Mary Tudor', *Studies in English Literature* 37 (1997), 237–255, p. 244. See John Strype, *Memorials especially Ecclesiastical*, 3 vols (London: S. Richardson, 1721), vol. 1, p. 456.

40 Glyn Redworth, 'Matters impertinent to women: male and female monarchy under Philip and Mary', *English Historical Review* 112 (1997), 597–613, p. 599.

41 Untitled poem by Cavendish in Emrys Jones, *The New Oxford Book of Sixteenth-Century Verse* (Oxford: Oxford University Press, 1992), p. 132.

42 John Elder, 'Letter describing the arrival and marriage of King Philip, his triumphal entry into London, the legations of Cardinal Pole, etc.', Appendix X in J. G. Nichols, ed., *The Chronicle of Queen Jane and of two years of Queen Mary and especially of the Rebellion of Sir Thomas Wyat*, Camden Society XLVIII (London: The Camden Society, 1850), p. 157, conventionally known and cited henceforth as *Tower Chronicle*.

43 Sabine Lucia Miller, 'Ageing out Catholicism: representing Mary Tudor's body', in Oakley-Brown and Wilkinson, eds, *Rituals and Rhetoric*, 238–51, pp. 242 and 247.

44 Anna Whitelock, *Mary Tudor: England's First Queen* (London: Bloomsbury, 2009), pp. 1 and 4.

45 Paulina Kewes, 'Two queens, one inventory: the lives of Mary and Elizabeth Tudor' in Kevin Sharpe and Steven Zwicker, eds, *Writing Lives: Biography and Textuality, Identity and Representation in Early Modern England* (Oxford: Oxford University Press, 2008), 187–207.

46 Alexander Samson, 'Power sharing: the co-monarchy of Philip and Mary', in Anna Whitelock and Alice Hunt, eds, *Tudor Queenship* (New York: Palgrave MacMillan, 2010), 159–172, pp. 161–3.

47 David Loades, *The Reign of Mary Tudor: Politics, Government and Religion in England 1553–1558* (2nd edn, London: Longman 1991), p. x.

48 Loades, *The Reign of Mary Tudor*, p. x.

49 Loades, *The Reign of Mary Tudor*, p. x.

50 John Edwards, *Mary I: England's Catholic Queen* (London: Yale University Press, 2011), pp. 348–9.

51 Edwards, *Mary I*, p. 346.

52 British Library Add. Ms. 5415 A.

53 See Peter Barber, *The Queen Mary Atlas: Commentary* (London: Folio Society, 2005), pp. 45 and 63–4. Homem had fled to England in 1544 and appears to have remained until 1559 when the atlas was probably completed.

54 David Loades, 'The reign of Mary Tudor: historiography and research', *Albion* 21 (1989), 547–58, p. 556.

55 Loades, 'Historiography and Research', pp. 556–7.

56 Eamon Duffy, *Fires of Faith: Catholic England under Mary Tudor* (London: Yale University Press, 2009), pp. 1 and 207.

57 Duffy, *Fires of Faith*, p. 78.

58 See the fascinating collection of essays on his legacy in John Edwards and Ronald Truman, eds, *Reforming Catholicism in the England of Mary Tudor: The Achievement of Friar Bartolomé Carranza* (Aldershot: Ashgate, 2005), and esp. David Loades, 'The English Church during the reign of Mary', p. 41.

59 Duffy, *Fires of Faith*, p. 7.

60 William Wizeman, *The Theology and Spirituality of Mary Tudor's Church* (Aldershot: Ashgate, 2006) and David Loades, *The Religious Culture of Marian England* (London: Pickering and Chatto, 2010).

61 Freeman, 'Inventing Bloody Mary', p. 81.

62 We might see as a sign that this is shifting the fact that 'A Wicked History' ends with a chapter entitled 'Wicked?', and states 'Mary was said to be a kind and generous woman': Jane Buchanan, *Mary Tudor: Courageous Queen or Bloody Mary?* (New York: Franklin Watts, 2008), p. 119. Or the 'Thinking Girl's Treasury of Dastardly Dames' book by Gretchen Maurer on *Mary Tudor: 'Bloody Mary'* (Foster City, Cal.: Goosebottom Books, 2011), which ends with a section, 'Good Queen Mary?' that describes her as 'brave, truthful and compassionate... Her entire family had blood on their hands, yet their nicknames are not at all bloody like Mary's', p. 26.

63 Russell, 'Mary Tudor and Mr Jorkins', p. 271.

64 *Calendar of Letters, Despatches, and State Papers, Relating to the Negotiations Between England and Spain*, vols 11–13, ed. Royall Tyler (London: HMSO, 1916–54), 13, pp. 88–9 (hereafter, *Cal. Span.*).

65 Parker, *Felipe II*, p. 307: 'Yo no he querido aver un real dese reyno, sino gastado en él lo que vos sabéis'.

66 John Guy, *The Oxford History of the Tudors and Stuarts* (Oxford: Oxford University Press, 1996), p. 263.

67 Penry Williams, *The Later Tudors* (Oxford: Clarendon Press, 1996), p. 465.

68 Judith Richards, *Mary Tudor* (London: Routledge, 2008), p. 11.

69 Loades, *Mary Tudor*, p. 8.

70 The lack of preparation by the ambassadors was a cause of consternation amongst Philip's entourage, Figueroa writing to Granvelle the day after the wedding: 'aunque no querría culpar a nadie, los embaxadores... ninguna cosa tenían proveyda de lo neçesario'; transcribed in María Pascual Ortega, 'El matrimonio entre Felipe II y María Tudor en la correspondencia de Granvela', unpublished PhD thesis (University of Valencia, 2017), p. 303, from Biblioteca del Palacio Real MS II 2285, fols 70–1. See David Loades, *Intrigue and Treason: The Tudor Court 1547–1558* (London: Pearson, 2004), p. 180.

71 Maria Rodríguez Salgado, *The Changing Face of Empire: Charles V, Philip II and Habsburg Authority, 1551–1559* (Cambridge: Cambridge University Press, 1988).

72 Cesare Malfatti, ed. and trans., *The Accession, Coronation and Marriage of Mary Tudor as related in Four Manuscripts of the Escorial* (Barcelona: Sociedad Alianza de Artes Graficas y Ricardo Fontá, 1956).

73 Escorial Manuscript V.ii.4, mostly in the hand of Florián de Ocampo, item 39 – 'Nuevas de España, guerras de Siena y Francia, Relaciones de la ida a Inglaterra del Principe D. Felipe y su casamiento con la reina Doña María. Año 1554', fols 439–56, at fols 444–9 is 'Relación del viaje del Principe D. Felipe cuando se fue a casar a Inglaterra', by Juan de Barahona, published in *Colección de Documentos Inéditos para la Historia de España*, ed. Fernando Navarete, 113 vols (Madrid: 1842–95) (hereafter: *CODOIN*), vol. 1, pp. 564–74. There is also the anonymous printed account of her coronation, *La coronacion de la inclita y serenissima reyna doña Maria de*

Inglaterra, que oy reyna bienauenturadamente en aquel reyno: con todos los autos, solenidades y cerimonias que se hizieron el dia de su coronacion y la manera como fue jurada y alçada por reyna en primero de octubre, año de mil y quinientos y cinquenta y tres años (n. p., n. s., 1553) between fols 436–8. Then Real Biblioteca del Monasterio de San Lorenzo de El Escorial V.ii.3, item 43: 'Relación de las cosas de Inglaterra en tiempo de sus reyes Enrique VIII y Maria, su hija', fols 483–8, handwriting Antonio Gracián.

74　There are extensive discussions of provenance and composition of these manuscripts in Georges Cirot, 'Florian de Ocampo, chroniste de Charles-Quint', *Bulletin Hispanique* XVI (1914), 307–36, who usefully discusses the main manuscript sources and other extant letters; and Marcel Bataillon, 'Sur Florian Docampo', *Bulletin Hispanique* 25 (1923), 33–59.

75　He is mentioned in Malfatti, *Accession, Coronation and Marriage of Mary Tudor*, p. 145: 'A cinco de agosto sus magestades salieron de aqui [Windsor Castle] y mandaron por don Diego de Açeuedo que quedase aqui a recoger todos los cauallos y la gente española de la corte por que por los castillos donde yban no abia aposentos para todos los cortesanos'. He was *caballerizo mayor* to Philip.

76　BNE MS 9937, fol. 212v: 'pasó un correo para Salamanca con la nueva de como es desembarcado Don Diego de Azeuado, viene en esta armada el Arçobispo de Toledo, y el Regente Figueroa'.

77　BNE MS 9937, fols 126–54. These letters were reprinted by Malfatti, *Accession, Coronation and Marriage of Mary Tudor*.

78　See note 73 for citation.

1

Prenuptial

Economic exchange

The longevity and significance of trade and economic relations between England and Spain leading up to the early modern period can be gauged from the large volume of treaties in the British Library's Cottonian collection. Dating back to an agreement between Henry III and Castile in 1252 that preceded the marriage of Edward I and Eleanor of Castile, half-sister of Alfonso X 'el Sabio' (the Wise), the collection contains successive confirmations of English merchants' privileges in Castile in 1351, 1362, 1366, 1391 and 1409, and in Aragón in 1374 and 1387. The volume culminates with the Treaty of Medina del Campo of 1484 and the commercial agreement reached by the Catholic Monarchs and Henry VII in 1489; preliminary to the 'Tractatus matrimonii inter Arthurum principem Wallice et Catherinam filiam Ferdinandi regis Castiliae Ferdinandus et Helizabet' of 1st October 1497. Dynastic marriages bound shared economic interests with ties of blood and kinship, from Eleanor of England and Alfonso VIII in 1170 to Edward I and Eleanor of Castile in 1254 to Arthur and Catherine of Aragón in 1501. In February 1496, the year the Spanish Infanta Juana married Philip the Handsome, a major treaty for commerce, the 'Intercursus Magnus', had been concluded between England and the Netherlands, closing the circle of shared commercial interests. All three trade agreements were renewed under the treaties with which the volume closes; the 'Amicitia inter Henricum et Phillippum' of 1505 and 'Tractatus inter Henricum Septimum Regem Angliae et Phillipum regem Castilae' of the following year.[1] English merchants had possessed equal terms of trade with Castilian subjects since Edward IV's alliance with Castile in 1467, which had also extended the protection of subject status to Castilians in England. A treaty of 1482 with Guipúzcoa made depredation subject to compensation; a provision prefiguring Medina del Campo, which attempted to make international trade agreements binding with pre-agreed sanctions for breaking their terms. Medina del Campo stated that individual infractions were not to undermine the treaty itself (clause 14) and that letters of marque were only to be issued if redress from the relevant sovereign was refused (clause 15). Henry VII established a guild in the precincts of Blackfriars, specifically for 'strangers corvyours' from Spain or the Low Countries, 'The Fellowship of the Blessed Trinity'. When Henry VIII passed an act in 1513 against alien cordwainers buying uncurried leather, within a year 'The Fellowship', with whom Charles V stayed during his visit to England in 1522, managed to procure an act excepting those born in the realms of the emperor and prince of Castile.[2]

Mercantile exchange between England and the Iberian peninsula had cultural and technological, as well as economic aspects. The Henrician court poet John Rastell, adapter of Fernando de Rojas' La Celestina (1499),[3] was a friend of the most prominent English merchants trading out of Seville: the brothers Robert and Nicholas Thorne, and Roger Barlow, who had accompanied Sebastian Cabot on the first voyage to the River Plate in 1526,[4] and included his experiences in the first English translation of a Spanish navigational treatise, Martín Fernández Encisco's Suma de Geographia (1519), dedicated to Henry VIII around 1541.[5] Barlow's approach to the king aimed to secure backing for an expedition to find the Northwest Passage to the Spice Islands, the Moluccas; a dream that Martin Frobisher followed in his three voyages in 1576, 1583 and 1585. English merchants enjoyed privileges in Sanlúcar de Barrameda, along with official protection from the dukes of Medina Sidonia, for most of the sixteenth century.[6] Men like Thomas Malliard, Robert Thorne, Barlow and Thomas Bridges were all well established in Seville by the early 1520s, enriched by their involvement in sugar refining, the Indies trade, local viticulture and soap manufacturing. After Malliard's death in 1522 his Spanish mistress Beatriz challenged his will, which left the bulk of the estate to a brother living in England. By claiming to be his wife, she persuaded a court to replace his executor, Roger Barlow, with Pedro López de Herrera, whose kinsman Sancho de Herrera was supposed to have married Malliard and Beatriz's daughter, Ana. Pedro and Sancho were members of a local family that owned the four smaller Canary Islands. To meet a legal requirement and be allowed to participate in the Indies trade Roger Barlow had worked with a Spanish merchant, Luis Fernández, in exports to Santo Domingo, while he and Robert Thorne used another man, Juan de Marcia, trading soap, wine, tallow and flour with the colonies. English involvement in the Atlantic slave trade dated back to at least 1490, but it was their share in the soap factory of Triana that was probably central to the financial success of this group.[7] Robert Thorne's will, like Malliard's, sought to bypass a Spanish mistress, Ana García and their son Vicente, by leaving her £50 on condition that she renounced their claim to the rest.[8]

The Low Countries were Spain and England's biggest wool export market and Spanish merchants often returned to the Iberian peninsula through London, Southampton or Bristol with English cloth, wheat and cereals.[9] The greatest threat to this trade was French and Scottish privateering. A petition by Antwerp merchants on 7th September 1551 estimated that their losses to pirates during the previous eight to ten years stood at 1.6 million Holland pounds.[10] Piracy was an occupational hazard; however, its intensity and victims often followed the fault lines of underlying political tensions. By 1534, the Reformation in England had begun to have a measurable impact on commercial relations. John Mason, later secretary to the older Sir Thomas Wyatt and then William Paget, noted in a letter from Valladolid to Thomas Starkey at Padua:

> ii marchawnts browght hyther off lat a follyshe booke agaynst the Pope and wer taken therewith, and thers goodds all confiskyd, and theyr bodyes in dawnger off buraning, if we had not made for them great frinds and intreatance.[11]

He described the people as 'tractable inowgh'. In 1539, the merchant Thomas Pery did public penance along with four other English merchants (John Robyns, Harry Hollande, Robert Asorgante[?] and William Alcat) in Triana (site of the soap factory), after a visit from a priest who had spotted a church bell amid a recently-arrived cargo from England in the warehouse he used in Ayamonte on the banks of Guadiana. Interrogated in Seville by the magistrate, Pero Díaz, Pery countered the accusation that he and his king were not good Christians asserting 'hys grace hym selfe dowthe dayly here masse and praise gode within hyse owyn chapill… and confissyth hym self and recevyth hys makr yerly acording to the laws and costom of awr holly mother churche': pressed further over whether he thought it good that Henry 'is pope within his ryme', the merchant reasoned 'many other docters which be taking for gret lernyde men and they do declare that all that hys grace hathe downe he maye do hit be the atoryte of holly scryptuore'.[12] The merchant's naivety, attempting to exculpate himself by engaging in theological debate, led him to be tortured. Central to the Spanish attitude to Henry's actions was the notion that he was a 'tyrant' acting from his own 'will' rather than conscience. By this point Henry VIII had reversed the theological experiments of the previous six years with his restatement of his church's doctrinal orthodoxy in the Act of Six Articles.

Earlier in the 1530s, in the context of the Boleyn marriage, the imperial ambassador Eustace Chapuys had counselled Charles V against mistreating English merchants in Spain and the Low Countries: 'for they will be instrumental in maintaining and fostering the goodwill and affection of the people to Your Majesty'.[13] He argued against prohibiting England's trade with Spain or the Low Countries: such a confiscation of English merchants' goods would be counterproductive, whereas a papal interdict against Henry would turn the Council and people against the Boleyns. Spanish merchants and artisans in London were uniquely exempted from the assessment of a contribution towards the costs of Anne Boleyn's coronation and from swearing the oath of obedience to the Succession Act which made it law.[14] The deterioration of Anglo-Habsburg commercial relations after the Boleyn marriage was halted by a treaty in June 1542, which renewed the exemption of English merchants from a prohibition on the export of goods from Spain in foreign ships when Spanish vessels were available; an exemption originally granted at the time of Henry's betrothal to Catherine. It had been suspended by Mary of Hungary in retaliation against Henry VIII's Navigation Act of 1540, which had made rates for aliens and subjects the same only if they transported goods on English ships.[15] Nevertheless new duties and depredations continued to spark conflict. Deteriorating Anglo-Spanish trading relations culminated in the despoliation of the ship *San Salvador* returning from Santo Domingo laden with silver, gold, pearls and sugar by Robert Reneger in 1545. In retaliation Philip seized English merchants' goods in Andalusia, breaking the terms of Medina del Campo that insisted on prior arbitration (clause 12), a provision that had been reiterated only a year or so earlier by Charles V and Henry VIII in an agreement signed in February 1543.[16] This agreement was explicitly renewed by the marital alliance of Philip and Mary in 1554. The treaties between the Low Countries and England of 1543 and 1546 served as templates for the commercial aspects of the later marital alliance.[17] One of the most important aspects of these agreements was the establishment of direct travel between England and Spain by sea, without the need to travel overland through France.[18]

The Reneger incident is revealing about the importance of Anglo-Spanish commerce and good political relations to both sides. A letter from the customs house in Seville (Casa de la Contratación) to Philip, echoing Chapuys' earlier appeal, outlined their opposition to any confiscation of English goods:

> if they embargo goods, the English will not come to trade as they are accustomed to because it was they who principally bought the greater part of the wines and oils from these towns and if they do not do it great damage will ensue not only for the royal revenues but also for the subjects and people of these regions who live and survive from their harvests so if your majesty were well served you might order the suspension of the embargo.[19]

Since the English were the biggest buyers in the region, reprisals were damaging ultimately to Spain's own interests. By the 1560s 40,000 of the 60,000 butts of wine produced in the Sanlúcar region were being exported to England and the Netherlands, as well as 2,000 foals of thoroughbred Arabian horse stock from Castile and Aragón.[20] According to the Venetian ambassador, Soranzo, in 1554 English merchants 'export annually from five to six thousand weight of unwrought tin, and to the value of 100,000 ducats in the wrought metal, the greater part to Spain'.[21] English merchants' special privileges in the region were renewed again by the duke of Medina Sidonia in 1566.[22]

Political prelude: the early 1550s

The crucial nature of the economic and commercial exchanges between England and Spain throughout this period did not go unnoticed by their rulers. In a letter of 5th October 1551 to Antoine Perrenot Granvelle, bishop of Arras, the regent of the Netherlands, Mary of Hungary, drew attention to the centrality of Anglo-Habsburg relations in neutralising the French threat and keeping the seas of the Channel open. After the duke of Northumberland's alliance with the French, she speculated that 'the possession of one port there, if we managed to seize one, would enable us to protect our shipping'.[23] Invading England would 'deprive the French of the use of English harbours, lacking which they are unable to keep up a dangerous fleet' and could be secured with the marriage of the princess Mary to one of 'three persons who might try their fortune, conquer the country, and marry our cousin':[24] the King of the Romans, Ferdinand (Charles' brother), Dom Luis of Portugal, or Adolf, duke of Holstein (the third son of King Frederick I of Denmark, who had been partly brought up by Philip, Landgrave of Hesse). Not only would it protect Habsburg commercial interests, but as a supplementary benefit it was 'a task so good as the restoration of an important kingdom to the fold of the Church'.[25] Charles V's seventeenth-century biographer Fray Prudencio de Sandoval pointed to 'the free trade and commerce that his subjects would have with the kingdom of England, from which great benefits could ensue because of their nearness'.[26] The memorandum about the marriage prepared by Philip in the autumn of 1553 focused on the strategic and political advantages of protecting commerce with the Low Countries: 'his Majesty has negotiated this marriage... for the preservation and extension of the territories of his Majesty and the universal peace of Christendom and principally for the great advantage to these kingdoms [the Low Countries], their peace and tranquillity, from a union with that kingdom'.[27] Mary of Hungary's 1551 plan was the second occasion the imperialists had sought to use Mary, who had been coming under increasingly ferocious pressure from the regency council to conform to the Edwardian religious settlement, to safeguard English neutrality.

A year earlier an attempt had been made to spirit Mary physically out of the country to the safety of Antwerp, after which 'the English believed his Imperial Majesty, once he had her in his court, would marry her to the Prince of Spain' and 'wage war against the English for her'.[28] On 30th June 1550, two imperial ships had appeared off Maldon in Essex, three miles downstream from Woodham Walter where Mary was staying. Jean Dubois, secretary to the recently recalled ambassador Van der Delft, and then to his replacement Jehan Scheyfve, disembarked and was conducted to Mary. She played for time in a series of highly staged scenes, with Rochester convincing Dubois that the guard had been reinforced at Maldon and that his ship was in imminent danger of being confiscated. In the end he departed without her and by 13th July the Council had sent Sir John Gates into Essex with a troop of horse 'to stop the going away of the Lady Mary'.[29] This incident has been reinterpreted recently as demonstrating Mary's acumen in manipulating conventional expectations of women and using her household servants, like the Treasurer Sir Robert Rochester in this case, to deflect blame for decisions that clearly were ultimately her own, rather than weakness and indecision.[30] Despite her pleas for imperial assistance, she must have realised that fleeing to the Netherlands was political suicide and a land invasion of England quixotic. In the memorandum of political advice to Philip from his father dated 13th January 1548, the 'Augsburg Testament', Charles V advised his son against acting 'without first seeing there is a solid foundation and opportunity, that it is supported by the Empire and that the French are impeded through the English or in some other way'.[31] England was a critical counterweight in Habsburg international political strategy against Valois France throughout the sixteenth century. On 28th January 1552, the emperor responded from Brussels to the queen dowager's suggestion for securing 'some strong place there for the protections of navigation and commerce'.[32] These exchanges underline that throughout the 1550s England was considered crucial in consolidating Habsburg dominance in northern Europe, ultimately through a dynastic marriage to Mary. Mary of Hungary had originally suggested in her letter of October the year before that in order to consolidate relations 'it would be necessary to have an intelligent ambassador there, such as Renard'.[33] In the event, the imperial evoys sent to England shortly before Edward VI's death on 6th July 1553, with a brief to negotiate a marital alliance with Mary, were indeed headed by Simon Renard.

A few months before the July embassy, on 28th April 1553, the then imperial ambassador in London, Jehan Scheyfve, had reported rumours spread by Northumberland about possible dynastic matches including Mary: to cement a fresh Anglo-Imperial alliance 'the King is said to be about to marry one of the King of the Romans' daughters, and the Prince of Spain the Princess of England'.[34] A possible marriage of Mary to Philip repeatedly surfaced in the thinking of political actors from 1550. Mary was well used to being a pawn in international diplomacy, having been betrothed while still a child to both the French Dauphin, Francis III of Brittany, son of Francis I, and later Charles V himself. Henry VIII's will (30th December 1546) subjected her right of succession to the stipulation that she 'shall not marry nor take any person to her husband without the assent and consent of the privy counsellors'.[35] The possibility of her accession on the death of her brother without issue placed her at the centre of European politics. As his health deteriorated, Edward VI's 'Letters Patent for the Limitation of the Crown' disabled Mary and Elizabeth 'to aske, claime, or challenge the said imperiall crowne' precisely on the grounds that:

> should [they] then happen to marry with any stranger borne out of this realme, that then the same stranger, havinge the governmente and the imperiall crowne in his hands, would rather adhere and practice to have the lawes and customes of his or their owne native countrey or countreyes to be practised or put in use within this realme, then the lawes, statutes, and customes here of longe time used, wherupon the title of inheritance of all and singular our loving subjects doe depend, which would tende to the utter subversion of the comon-welth of this our realme, which God defend.[36]

A fundamental threat to property rights, inheritance patterns and English law followed inexorably from the accession of a regnant queen. This would become a common thread in discussions before the marriage took place. The papal emissary Giovanni Francesco Commendone, sent covertly to England to reopen diplomatic relations between England and the papacy, claimed that Edward VI 'drew up his will 21st June disinheriting both sisters under pretence that they might bring foreigners into the Realm, with the danger of introducing new laws and new orders of living'.[37] Northumberland likewise spread panic, manipulating and playing upon the fear of a 'stranger borne out of this realme' obtaining dominion through a dynastic marriage to Mary, a notable reversal of plans being made just two months earlier. During the succession crisis Northumberland spread rumours in Norfolk and Suffolk that Mary's flight from him was a prelude to a foreign invasion from the Low Countries in support of her claim: 'making it known to everyone that her Highness had gone towards the counties of Norfolk and Suffolk which are towards the coast facing Flanders with the intention of creating unrest in the realm and wars and to effect the entrance of strange nations to defend what she pretends against the Crown'.[38] The popular xenophobia stirred up by Northumberland to sell the 'limitation' cast a long shadow over Mary's whole reign. However, these anxieties were well understood and an inevitable part of the dynastic landscape of Europe.

Charles V's brief to his new ambassadors in England, Jean de Montmorency, sieur de Courrières, Jacques de Marnix de Sainte-Aldegonde, sieur de Thoulouse, and Simon Renard, who were despatched on 23rd June 1553 and who arrived on 6th July, displayed a similar awareness of the inevitable problem of xenophobia in the context of a female accession. He proposed they should 'tell them that our solicitude for the good administration and government of the kingdom causes us to consider that she [Mary I] had better contract an alliance with some Englishman', and so 'reassured of our intentions they may be less accessible to the schemes of the French and cease to dread having a foreigner, loathed as all foreigners are by all Englishmen, for their king'.[39] Renard concurred with this, agreeing that 'while the Duke of Northumberland lived the very fear of a foreign match was enough to cause several vassals to follow his faction and rise against the Queen's person and rights'.[40] The political problem of a regnant queen alienating the crown through a future foreign succession sharpened the need to assuage indigenous sensibilities. The ambassadors' principal strategic concern, as outlined in their brief, was to counter French machinations and safeguard the friendly relations that 'commercial interests render... desirable'.[41] England continued being key to Spanish/Habsburg strategy to protect commercial, economic and political hegemony.

Although the marriage has often been presented purely as the initiative of his father, Philip's intimate servant Diego de Azevedo, one of his *mayordomos*,[42] was in England throughout the period, writing to his wife at Zamora on 2nd August 1553 that 'the king of England died, they say the duke of Northumberland and French ambassador killed him with poison. After he died, this Northumberland with favour and encouragement from the king of France forced them to cho[o]se a son of his as king.'[43] Philip's well-informed envoy had access to Mary and Renard even before her coronation. Renard wrote to Philip on 6th September that 'don Diego will fill your majesty in on the occurrences of this kingdom'.[44] Azevedo wrote a detailed eye-witness account of the queen's entry into London on 1st August to his wife in Zamora.[45] Juan Hurtado de Mendoza, according to his letter from London on 19th March 1554, had been summoned before Mary because he was Azevedo's nephew, and in their interview the queen specifically mentioned 'Don Diego, whom she seems to like': it is worth citing the end of this letter, where Hurtado de Mendoza recorded that as he took his leave and responded to her comment that it was a good time to go to Spain, he retorted that it was '[a] better time to come from Spain to England': counter to her reputation as a dour or even melancholic figure, Mary 'laughed till she spluttered'.[46] In England Azevedo served as Philip's *caballerizo mayor* [master of the horse] and remained at post there probably until 1557, when we know he returned to Spain.[47] Shortly after the marriage, Philip and Mary left Diego at Windsor 'to gather together the horses and Spanish courtiers because in the castles where they were going, there were not sufficient number of lodgings for all the courtiers'.[48] Other Spanish subjects were almost certainly in England in the autumn, using back-door channels to communicate with the queen. Diego de Mendoza apparently held several meetings with Mary's favourite Susan Clarencius in the house of a London alderman, perhaps her nephew Humphrey White, and passed on a Latin letter for the queen.[49] What is clear is that it is misleading to suggest that Philip was uninformed or excluded from negotiations, in which his father inevitably took a lead.

The rumours Azevedo reported that Edward VI had been murdered and the succession altered by the Protector in collusion with the French ambassador egged on by Henry II, are corroborated in several sources, including the Protestant Robert Parkyn's 'Narrative of the Reformation': 'the wherof [Edward's illness] was thrugh poosonyng', at least that was what 'the common voce... spreddde abrode amonge people'.[50] During the succession crisis rumours circulated of a French fleet lying off Brittany ready to support Northumberland's bid for the crown. If Henry II had moved against Mary supported by troops from Scotland, then the seas might have closed permanently to the commerce and trade that linked together the two halves of Charles' empire. The heir to the Scottish throne, Mary Queen of Scots, had grown up at Henry's court and was betrothed to the dauphin. In the face of the pro-French alliance entered into by the Protector in 1551, recovering England had become the central strategic priority for the Habsburgs. As late as 1583, after the repulse of an Anglo-French force from the island of Terceira in the Azores, the royal secretary Mateo Vázquez wrote to Philip II that to 'have the sea under our control is, as Your Majesty knows, most important for the affairs of the Low Countries'.[51] Philip became king of England to secure and retain the wealthiest and most troublesome part of his dynastic inheritance, the Low Countries.

'Womanly daring': Mary's accession

Recent writing on Mary's accession has foregrounded her cultivation of local allies and championing of traditional religion, to supplement earlier insistence on Tudor legitimism. The affinity and baronial household gathered around her during Edward's reign, following a massive bequest of land, titles and property in her father's will, played a crucial role in her road to the throne. Conservative religion, along with popular sympathy for her unjust treatment and persecution from the time of her parents' divorce, were also significant. Another factor may of course have been active dislike of the duke of Northumberland. Many no doubt did not embrace the possibility of Mary's accession, but even her antagonistic faith did not outweigh an illegal alteration of the succession and usurpation of the Tudor line.

Jeri McIntosh has shown how Mary became one of the wealthiest people in England in 1547, with only six peers and the king exceeding her income of £3,819 per annum.[52] Mary sent out circular letters demanding loyalty from local gentry and nobles on 9th July 1553, within hours of her receiving definitive confirmation that the king was dead. Her sudden turning back from London and carefully planned route through Suffolk, Cambridgeshire, the Thames Valley, East Anglia and Norfolk following intelligence from court informants, demonstrates that her bid for the throne had been planned, reliant on effective spies at court and that it mobilised nobles and landed gentry located around lands and houses she had inherited six years previously.[53] It was a moment for which she had been waiting and preparing.

On 4th July 1553 she 'set out secretly from Hunsdon' in Hertfordshire, moving to Sawston Hall in Cambridgeshire, the home of a Catholic ally, John Huddleston.[54] (Sawston was later partially burned down in revenge by Northumberland's troops.) Two days later her party moved on to Hengrave Hall, the residence in Suffolk of John Bourchier, second earl of Bath. Her party then reached Lady Burgh's residence, Euston Hall near Thetford, on the 8th, where 'she was told of the king's death by Robert Reyns, her goldsmith, newly returned from the City', and on 'this account she stayed there no longer, but hurried on to her house at Kenninghall'.[55] The news was confirmed by Dr John Hughes there and according to the chronicler Robert Wingfield Mary then decided to challenge the duke of Northumberland for the throne:

> this attempt should have been judged and considered one of Herculean rather than of womanly daring, since to claim and secure her hereditary right, the princess was being so bold as to tackle a powerful and well-prepared enemy, thoroughly provisioned with everything necessary to end or to prolong a war, while she was entirely unprepared for warfare and had insignificant forces.[56]

This underlines the dramatic nature of her decision, with her household servants probably numbering no more than sixty, of whose principal members – Robert Rochester, Edward Waldegrave, Francis Englefield, Henry Jerningham and her secretary John Bourne – only one was a knight.[57] On the 9th she wrote to the council in London, commanding obedience and instructing them to proclaim her queen.[58] Simultaneously letters were sent out 'in all directions to draw all the gentlemen of the surrounding countryside to do fealty to their sovereign'.[59] Sir Edward Hastings was ordered to support her in Middlesex and Buckinghamshire.[60] Within three days, she had been joined by her recent host John Bourchier, earl of Bath, Sir Thomas Wharton, Sir John Mordaunt, Sir Richard Southwell, Sir William Drury, Sir Edmund Peckham, Thomas

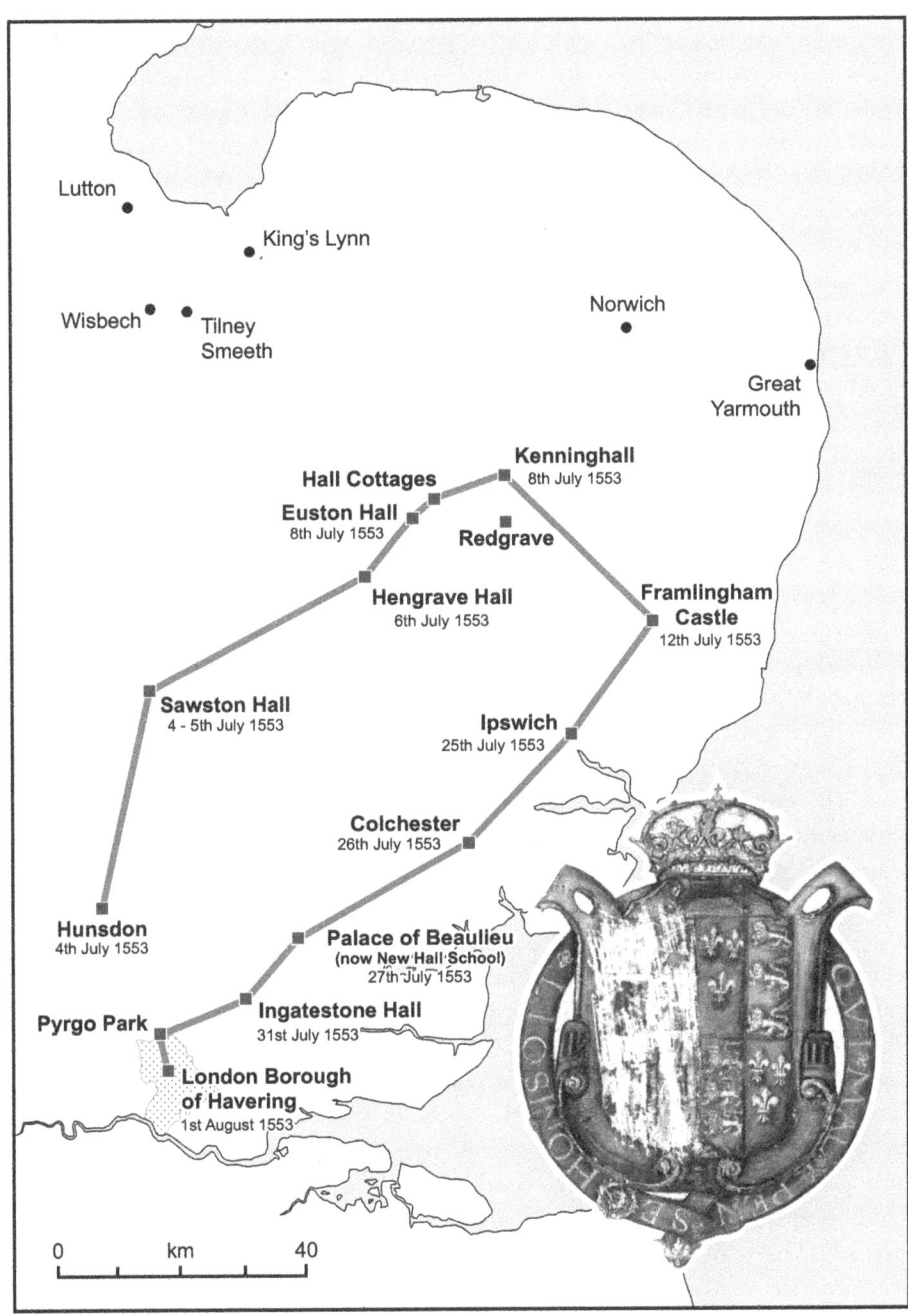

Lutton

King's Lynn

Norwich

Wisbech Tilney
Smeeth

Great
Yarmouth

Kenninghall
8th July 1553

Hall Cottages

Euston Hall
8th July 1553

Redgrave

Hengrave Hall
6th July 1553

**Framlingham
Castle**
12th July 1553

Sawston Hall
4 - 5th July 1553

Ipswich
25th July 1553

Colchester
26th July 1553

Hunsdon
4th July 1553

Palace of Beaulieu
(now New Hall School)
27th July 1553

Pyrgo Park

Ingatestone Hall
31st July 1553

**London Borough
of Havering**
1st August 1553

0 km 40

Diogo Homem, *Queen Mary Atlas* (1558). Detail.

Morgan, Richard Freston, Ralph Chamberlain and Robert Strelley (husband of her gentlewoman of the privy chamber Frideswide). Sir John Huddleston, while on his way to Mary, stumbled across Henry Radcliffe, one of the sons of the earl of Sussex, carrying letters to London from his father. He was conveyed to Mary and soon the earl of Sussex, who was Sir Thomas Wharton's brother-in-law, had also joined her. On the 12th she moved over the Suffolk border to the castle of Framlingham (see Plate 2), joined by Sir Thomas Cornwallis.

That day Norwich, which had refused to open its gates to her messengers on the 11th, became the first town to declare for Mary.[61] On the 15th Henry Jerningham heard of six warships lying off Great Yarmouth, sent by Northumberland to prevent her escaping to the continent. The town committed itself to Mary after its municipal representatives witnessed her proclamation in Norwich. By the time Jerningham arrived in the town, the captains had rowed back to their ships, but 'the marynours axed maister Gernyngham what he wolde have, and wether he wolde have their captaynes or no; and he said, "Yea marry." Saide they, "Ye shall have theym, or els we shall throwe theym to the bottom of the sea"'.[62] The ships furnished Mary's swelling ranks of supporters with ordnance. Areas around her Hunsdon residence from Berkshire to Buckinghamshire and Oxfordshire provided substantial numbers under Sir Thomas Wharton, Sir Edmund Peckham and Lord Hastings, who was said to have added a force of four thousand from Middlesex and Buckinghamshire, a clear exaggeration.

The fact that within days of her letters she had been joined by gentry, with armed and provisioned retinues in some cases, even before she had sent to be proclaimed in London, provides powerful evidence to support the suggestion 'that Mary had lined up her loyal followers in readiness in these areas… well before Edward's death'.[63] Recent writing has underlined that her success rested on a 'household affinity that was augmented through regional and familial connections and increasingly defined by its Catholic allegiance'.[64] Northumberland left London through Shoreditch on the 13th and reached Cambridge three days later with a sizeable force of about three thousand. At 7pm the same day, i.e. the 16th, the gates of the Tower of London 'upon a sudden was shut, and the keyes caryed upp to the quene Jane'.[65] Two days later a dozen Privy Councillors slipped away from the Tower to the earl of Pembroke's London residence, Baynard's Castle, between Blackfriars and St Paul's.[66] There they were joined by the mayor and aldermen of London. A proclamation of Mary was drawn up and two heralds were despatched the next day, the 19th, around 6pm to St Paul's Cross in Cheap to read it out. According to Commendone, the covert papal emissary in England, Arundel had argued at this meeting that:

the forces of this Crown will fail, owing to such dissension, which will ultimately bring into the country foreign armies, and we may expect to find ourselves at the mercy of foreign soldiers, with our properties, our children and wives, with the complete ruin of our nobility.[67]

Contested successions were always dangerous times. There is an irony in the fact that both sides employed the same argument, the spectre of foreign invasion, in favour of and against Mary's accession. From Cambridge, Northumberland had travelled to Bury St Edmunds, a mere twenty-four miles from Framlingham, unaware of what was happening in London. Disunity in his army led to the defection of Lords Howard and Grey, and when on the 18th he moved towards Mary's army, news of the earl of Oxford's defection reached him through Henry Gate. He retreated to Bury and then back to Cambridge, where he learned on the 19th that London and the Council had proclaimed Mary in his absence. Northumberland published the Council's proclamation himself the next morning.

Lord Paget and the earl of Arundel arrived at Framlingham on the 20th with a letter of submission from the Council and a copy of the London proclamation. Arundel was sent to Cambridge the following day to arrest Northumberland, whose army had already begun to disperse and who had already been belatedly surrounded and incarcerated by the mayor. Contemporary chroniclers claimed perhaps unsurprisingly that her victory reflected her popularity among the people. Despite what historians have suggested, that she lacked the 'common touch' of Elizabeth, there is no doubt she was popular throughout her life. The Spanish observer Antonio de Guaras claimed with literarily inspired hyperbole: 'it is wondrous the love that this people bear towards this Lady, they certainly offend God in it for they neglect to worship him and adore her instead'.[68] As we have seen, though, the notion that Mary was carried to the throne by widespread popular acclamation or 'through some national act of judgement' in favour of Tudor legitimism cannot explain the highly localised but effective mobilisation in areas where she had landed influence. Her provincial rising against central government relied on middle-ranking gentry, a number of whom had connections with the fallen Catholic Howards, dukes of Norfolk, whose lands Mary had been gifted in 1547. Thomas, third duke, was among the first political prisoners released by the queen following her entry into London.

Robert Tittler and Susan Battley have shown how at King's Lynn, Yarmouth, the village of Lutton in the Lincolnshire fens, Wisbech and Tilney Smeeth, in marshy areas to the south and south-west of King's Lynn, the picture was more complex. These areas bordered Mary's land holdings to the north. During that summer severe drought throughout Norfolk and Suffolk sharply affected the fenlands, which depended on central and eastern parts of the counties for food, which was being rapidly siphoned off to supply Mary's army. Although by the 20th Mary's bid for the crown had been successful and Northumberland was in custody, rioting broke out in Wisbech, a town where one of Northumberland's sons had stayed. Lutton in Lincolnshire was besieged by disgruntled countrymen around the same time and following an unfortunate order for further purveyance in Suffolk, Cambridgeshire and Norfolk on the 29th, violence broke out again in several parts of the fens. Sir Edward Beaupre in a letter to Henry Bedingfield as late as 7th August claimed that five thousand malcontents were planning to raise their standard in Tilney Smeeth, apparently supported by soldiers recently assembled by the bishop of Ely, the evangelical Thomas Goodrich, who was replaced by Thomas Thirlby in 1554.[69] The balance of religion, fealty and economics was delicate and highly localised.

Another factor behind Mary's successful mobilisation of areas around her landed holdings may have been the brutal suppression of Kett's rebellion by Northumberland in 1549. This had persuaded him to take the field in person: 'because that he had atchieved the victory in Norfolke once already, and was therefore so feared, that none durst lift up their weapon against him'.[70] Fear may have driven Norfolk towns into the arms of the Marians. But this cannot account for her proclamations' success elsewhere, in defiance of the government. Her local support was not just that of an 'out' faction, excluded from the patronage of the regency government, although it was Catholic and conservative in character: 'activists in Mary's coup were Catholic nobles and gentlemen'.[71] In Norfolk, of fourteen magnate families the two who backed her (Sir Henry Bedingfield and Sir Robert Southwell) were both strongly Catholic. Jennifer Loach noted:

> The list of those swearing loyalty to Mary during these early days, like the list of those receiving rewards for service at Kenninghall and Framlingham, contains catholic name after catholic name... when in 1561 Dr Sanders composed a list of catholic gentlemen who were suffering as a result of the accession of a protestant monarch it bore an uncanny resemblance to the earlier list of those rewarded in 1553: Browne, Waldegrave, Hastings, Sir Thomas Wharton, and Sir Thomas Mordaunt. No nobleman sympathetic to protestantism supported Mary, and most of those who came to her aid were committed catholics. Thus the Earl of Derby, for example, had opposed the religious changes of Edward's reign, Lord Dacre, who marched south to join Mary, had voted in the House of Lords against the 1549 Prayer Book and was to remain a catholic in Elizabeth's reign, and Lord Windsor, who assisted Hastings in proclaiming Mary in Buckinghamshire, had persistently voted against the religious innovations of the previous reign. Thomas West, Lord Delaware, had opposed the Edwardian Prayer Books as he had earlier opposed the dissolution of the monasteries. The

Earl of Bath, although he played little part in public affairs in Edward's reign, had voted against the bill for the marriage of priests.[72]

The coup's popular character ('noblemen's tenauntes refused to serve their Lordes agaynst quene Mary'),[73] and the role of traditional religion were clearly significant; however, many Protestants of all degrees supported Mary, not Northumberland. Municipal elites also played a key part. Ultimately, though, support from within Edward's Privy Council itself was decisive, as the scale of opposition in the provinces persuaded peers to desert Northumberland.[74]

Although the struggle centred on East Anglia, the region of Mary's affinity, it had enjoyed key backing elsewhere; in Oxfordshire (where Sir John Williams proclaimed Mary), Buckinghamshire (where Sir Edward Hastings and Edward Baron Windsor did the same) and the Thames Valley: 'the queen learnt from her scouts, who were ranging far and wide, that the people of Buckinghamshire, Oxfordshire, Berkshire and Northamptonshire were in arms and supported her cause'.[75] In other parts of the country, the earl of Oxford, John de Vere (allegedly persuaded by his household servants),[76] Richard Rich, Henry Stanley, fourth earl of Derby, William Dacre (in the north), Sir Thomas Cheney and Sir John Gage all marshalled support.[77] In Wales where Mary had resided as princess of Wales from 1525–33 in Denbigh and Beaumaris, the Northumberland adherents Ellis Price and Richard Bulkeley declared Lady Jane Grey queen and Mary a traitor. Their proclamation was quickly reversed and the 'lies of Beaumaris' were denounced by the bard Siôn Brwynog: for the country 'wished for its welfare', 'judging her to be Queen'.[78] Others welcomed the 'genial Queen from the heart of Gwynedd with her fortunate face' (a reference to Mary's beauty) and the 'silencing [of] those Saxons'.[79] Welsh support of the Tudors had been powerfully reinforced by Mary's viceregal court's eight-year stay there.

In London on the 19th, in contrast to the silent reception of the heralds for Jane, Mary's proclamation was joyously received: 'bonefires weare without nomber, and what with showtynge and crienge of the people and ringinge of the belles, theare could no one heare amoste what another sayd, besides banketyngs and synging in the street for joye'.[80] Another anonymous London chronicle recorded similarly 'the Joye whereof wonderfull for some caste money abrod, & some made bonfyars thorowe the whole cyte: the prayses were geuen to God in the churches with te deum & orgaynes, belles ryngynge & euery wher the tables spredd in the stretes, meate & drynke plentye, wyne geuen ffrely of many men'.[81] The ringing of bells was of course a symbolically Catholic form of celebration. Bells had been exported and taken down since the 1530s.[82] Although Guaras' witty and ironic literary allusion comically exaggerated the people's love, English sources bear out his reading of the public mood.[83] Diego de Azevedo, Philip's chamberlain, who was in London at this time, described Mary's victory in a letter to his wife:

> all the principal men of the kingdom went to acclaim her, and from there she came at the pace of a concertina, and put together shortly more than thirty thousand men, and with them came back to London. Knowing this everyone in the kingdom rose up for her and they imprisoned the Duke of Northumberland, and the newly elected king and queen and the rest of those who favoured them and the Queen Mary (of England) enters today as I write or tomorrow into London, where she will be sworn in and cut the heads off them all, except the queen, who was chosen, they say she has taken pity on this; and the queen and kingdom are all at peace. These events seem incredible and I believe they could happen nowhere else. The queen is *exceedingly pious and for this reason God has favoured her*. The first thing she has to do is restore Catholicism to the way it was, there will be little to do in relation to this because the majority of the heretics were only heretics out of fear of the King and Protector and not of their own free will. These have all been very prosperous happenings for his Majesty and the best of all is that he is well and dispatching business.[84]

Azevedo's parting remark suggests that he had travelled from Brussels to London, having had an audience with the emperor, who had been suffering from debilitating depression and gout during this period. Mary's accession was for him embedded in a providential narrative about the Hispanic monarchy. His appraisal of the religious situation is also fascinating, framing the problem of schism as political rather than religious, 'heretics' apostate from fear not free choice. His reading is corroborated by the form of the popular celebrations. After her proclamation in London on the 19th, 'that same nyght had the [most] parte of London *Te Deum*, with bone-fyers in every strete in London, with good chere at every bone[fyer], the bells ryngynge in every parych cherch'.[85] The return of traditional religion was joyfully celebrated.

At Ipswich Mary was presented with a golden heart inscribed 'the heart of the people', while staying at the chronicler Robert Wingfield's house. She visited her palace of Beaulieu near Colchester, and then Sir William Petre's residence, Ingatestone Hall in Essex (see Plate 3), Pyrgo and then Havering, before finally making her royal entry into London on the evening of 3rd August 1553: the 'nomber of velvet coats that did ride before hir, as well strangers as others, was 740; and the nomber of ladyes and gentlemen that folowede was 180'.[86] She was accompanied by her half-sister Elizabeth 'and a grette company of ladys wyth hare', the guard and 'after them Northampton and Oxfordshire men, and then Buckinghamshire men, and after them the Lordes' servants; the whole nomber of horsemen weare esteemed to be about 10,000'.[87] A central place was given to the men from the counties, who had been key to her success. At Whitechapel 'the mayer with the aldermen reseved hare, and he delyveryd hare the swerd, and she toke it to the erle of Arendelle, and he bare it before hare, and the mayer the masse [mace]'.[88] From there she continued down to Aldgate, which 'was goodly hangyd with clothes, banners, and stremers, and syngers, and goodly aparelde alle the way downe to Ledynhalle... on the one syde the crafftes of London with-in raylles in their best aparalles and clothe hangynge before them'.[89] At the Tower three political prisoners were symbolically released: Thomas Howard, duke of Norfolk, Edward Courtenay, marquis of Exeter, and Stephen Gardiner, bishop of Winchester. The conservative Howard had been imprisoned when it had become clear that Henry VIII was dying; a victim of the reformed faction which came to power with Edward's accession. He remained in prison throughout the young king's reign. Courtenay's father had fallen foul of Henry's decision to eliminate all living members of the Plantagenet line in 1538 and had spent most of his life in prison. Gardiner had been committed to the Fleet on 25th September 1547, for his protest at the issuing of the *First Book of Homilies* on 31st July.

In spite of the general welcome of religious reaction in the capital, committed evangelicals were bold enough at first to attack the new regime. On 13th August Gilbert Bourne, a chaplain of Edmund Bonner, bishop of London, was 'pullyd owte of the pulpyt by vacabonddes, and one threw hys dagger at hym' in the course of a sermon at Paul's Cross: five days later the queen issued her first proclamation, for 'avoiding the inconvenience and dangers that have arisen in times past through the diversity of opinions in questions of religion'.[90] At the next Paul's Cross Sunday sermon, 200 guards were present. Her proclamation asserted: 'her majesty being presently by the only goodness of God settled in her just possession of the imperial crown of this realm... cannot now hide that religion, which God and the world know she has ever professed from her infancy hitherto'.[91] Summoned for her dissident celebration of Mass under Edward, her retainers processed through the streets of London prominently displaying the rosary. Despite this she minded 'not to compel any her said subjects thereunto, until such time as further order, by common assent, may be taken therein':

> seditious and false rumours have been nourished and maintained in this realm by the subtlety and malice of some evil-disposed persons, which take upon them, without sufficient authority, to preach and interpret the word of God after their own brain in churches and other places, both public and private, and also by playing of interludes, and printing of false fond books and ballads, rhymes, and other lewd treatises in the English tongue, concerning doctrine in matters now in question and controversy touching the high point and mysteries of Christian religion.[92]

Print culture and the transnational nature of book circulation posed major challenge by the 1550s to political authorities everywhere, especially with the increasing use of the vernacular and proliferation of different forms: 'interludes... false fond books and ballads, rhymes, and other lewd treatises'. Stephen Gardiner, the new Lord Chancellor, claimed in a letter from prison to Lord Protector Somerset: 'I was never author of any one thing, either spiritual or temporal; I thank God for it', a dubious claim on the part of the author of *De vera obedientia* (1535), cornerstone of the Royal Supremacy.[93] The proclamation reinforced the proper subordination of God's word to political authority. Although Mary nominally rejected the Supremacy, she invoked it in enacting all the initial religious changes of her reign.[94] This was the 'monarchical republic' of Mary I. One of the early court entertainments of her reign, *Respublica*, 'dramatizes the paradox, or perhaps the perfectly acceptable balance, of a divinely ordained queen whose power is negotiated and limited by parliament'.[95] Mary's power over the church of England remained as full as her predecessors' and even after reunification, legislation specifically prevented its abrogation by Rome. To see the Marian period's religious settlement as a foreign imposition is to ignore the evidence of popular support and the innovative and progressive nature of the Catholic restoration. Mary's reign began with an explicit acknowledgement of the problem posed to authority by the rapid expansion of the international book trade and vernacular print culture.[96] Vernacular religious material and translation had become readily available to the unschooled under Edward with the Prayer Book. The publication of primers became the major priority for Catholic reformers seeking to turn the tide of religious innovation and forge a new consensus.[97]

Coronation

The imperial ambassador Simon Renard requested holy oil for Mary's coronation ceremony from the bishop of Arras, Antoine Perrenot de Granvelle, secretary of state to Charles V, because papal censure rendered the kingdom's oil unhallowed. The bishop sent three phials from Brussels, with a wild boar from Mary of Hungary for the celebrations.[98] The oil was used again at Elizabeth's coronation in 1559, despite the fact that she felt it was 'grease and smelt ill', while John Coke dismissed the superstition altogether: holy oil was no more than Spanish 'oyle olyve... very good for salettes'.[99] As was customary on the eve of a coronation, she created fifteen Knights of the Bath, who 'according to thorder every man to bere unto the quenes Ma.tie. at her fyrst course a dyshe of mete'.[100] She was decorously represented by Arundel at the actual bathing ceremony itself. At 1pm on 30th September, Mary left the Tower and proceeded to Whitehall along the traditional route with 'many pagenttes in dyvers places as she came by the wey in London, with alle the craftes and alder-

men'.[101] Preceded by knights, bishops and judges, her council, the knights of
the Bath, the marquis of Winchester bearing the mace, and the earl of Oxford
the sword, she proceeded, according to the Tower chronicler,

> sytting in a charret of tyssue, drawne with vj. horses, all betrapped with redd vel-
> vett. She sat in a gown of blew velvet, furred with powdered armyen, hangyng
> on hir head a call of clothe of tynsell besett with perle and ston, and about the
> same apon her hed a rond circlet of gold, moche like a hooped garlande, besett
> so richely with many precyouse stones that the value therof was inestymable; the
> said call and circle being so massy and ponderous that she was fayn to beare uppe
> hir hedd with hir handes; and a canopy was borne over the char.[102]

The coronation device of Henry VII preserved in the Rutland Papers specified
that a king should wear 'a long goune of purpur velwet, furred with ermyns
poudred' and travel beneath a canopy of bawdkyn cloth of gold; identical to
the description in the herald's account. The queen consort (in Henry's case)
was to wear 'a round cercle of gold' and travel in a litter.[103] Mary was a hybrid
mixture of elements belonging to kings and consorts. In contrast to the *Tower
Chronicle*, the official records describe her wearing white cloth of gold, the
prescribed dress of a queen consort.[104] Unfortunately Renard's account of
3rd October for Philip omits to mention what she was wearing, although the
ambassador noted that Mary's champion entered on a Spanish horse.[105] Judith
Richards has argued that the contradictions in the accounts of her appearance,
whether as 'a queen *qua* royal wife dressed in white cloth of gold or a monarch
dressed in blue or purple velvet', reflected uncertainty about Mary's position
and authority, the unprecedented accession of a regnant queen mirrored in
the heterogeneous combination of ritual and ceremonial elements, confusing
spectators as to what they had actually seen.[106]

   She was followed by Elizabeth and Anne of Cleves in a second chariot and
then by forty-six gentlewomen. The streets were gravelled and railed on one
side 'to the intent that the horsys sholde not slyde on the payene mente nor the
people shold not be hurte by the said horsys'.[107] The crafts and aldermen stood
within the rails and on every side the windows and walls of the streets through
which the procession passed were 'garnisshed with cloth Tapistry Arras cloth
of gold and cloth of Tesshew with quishiones of the same garnished with
stremers and baners as Richely as myght be devysed'.[108] There were 'in many
placis ordained goodly pagents and devissys and therin goodly great melydy
and eloquent speeches of nobyll historis treatinge the joyfull comminge and
recepte of so noble a quene'.[109] There is no published extant English account of
the pageants and coronation, although there were accounts published abroad
in Spain and Italy.[110] The coronation was an event celebrated largely on a
European stage and strangers were well represented among its makers.

The Genoese triumphal arch at Fenchurch Street bore two inscriptions: 'To Mary, famous queen, constantly pious, on receiving the crown of the British Empire and the palm of virtue, the Genoese, happy about the public wellbeing, render the desired veneration' and 'Virtue has won, Justice reigns, truth triumphs, piety is crowned, the health of the republic is restored'.[111] The Florentine triumphal arch at Gracechurch was graced by three female icons: Pallas Athene above the inscription *Invicta virtus*, Judith *Patriae liberatrici*, and Tomyris *Liberatis ultrici*.[112] Allusions to Judith's triumph over Holofernes (who the 'Almighty Lord brought... to nought by the hand of a woman'[113]) and the victory of Tomyris over all-conquering Cyrus, were topical, a month after the execution of Northumberland: both women had decapitated the defeated.[114] The analogy between Mary's victory over Northumberland and Judith's salvation of the Hebrews from bondage to Nebuchadnezzar figured her rise to power as reflection of a biblical prototype. Holofernes asserts in the apocryphal story, 'who is God but Nebuchadnezzar'.[115] Other contemporary female rulers invoked Judith to bolster their political authority.

Isabelle d'Este commissioned Andrea Mantegna's *Judith and Holofernes* (1492), which depicted the biblical heroine as an icon of chastity and classical restraint, simultaneously clothed in signifiers connoting rule (see Plate 5). She turns aside serenely, dropping the bearded head of Holofernes, whose foot is visible through the tent flaps, into a bag held by a servant. The sandals and dress are classical. The purple toga (symbol of imperial authority in the Roman Empire), sword and suggested diadem transform a figure of piety into a political blazon for its patron. The painting was an appropriation of the biblical Judith to create a prototype of early modern political womanhood. Nicholas Harpesfield's sermon in October 1553, *Concio quaedam admodum elegans,* similarly compared Mary to Judith,[116] and later another biblical heroine, Deborah. While Marian exiles compared her to Jezebel and Athalia, Deborah was unique as a Christian role model of female power and authority.[117] Unsurprisingly, she also figured prominently in early celebrations of Elizabeth, including in her coronation oration.[118]

On 1st October, Mary travelled by barge to Westminster and the Parliament building. There she appareled herself in 'her parlement robes of crymsyn veluit under a rich canapye of Bawdkyn... with iiii stauis and iiii belles of syluer according to the old precydoure borne by the barouns of the v ports'.[119] She then proceeded to the church for the coronation. She 'lay prostrat' on a velvet cushion before the altar, while the oration *Deus humilium* was said over her, a formula identical to that of Edward VI's coronation: then 'shall the King falle groveling before the Awltare, and over him tharchebushope shall saye Collet *Deus humilium*'.[120] The ceremonies reproduced almost exactly those of her predecessor; retaining changes which had been made to the forms

employed by Henry VII and VIII. However, there were two significant changes
to the Edwardian ritual. At the suggestion of Stephen Gardiner, Mary had
studied the wording of the coronation oath. A minor emendation was made
to the first section, 'Will ye grawnte to kepe to the people of Englande and
others your realms and dominions the lawes and liberties of this realme and
other your realmes and domynions?', with the insertion of the words 'the just
and licit laws of England'.[121] Gardiner's refusal to promulgate the *First Book of*
Homilies in his diocese rested on its illegality according to legislation that was
only subsequently repealed. The change here protected Mary from violating
her oath by not upholding Edwardian religious statutes. These cavils exposed
a constitutional contradiction. Although unrepealed pre-Reformation legislation could have been cited to make a case against Edwardian innovations, how
did invoking unrepealed statutes affect the status of existing law? This paradox
of the Tudor constitution was given substance in the contradiction between
Henry VIII's Third Succession Act (1544), which made its own 'interruption,
repeal, or annulment' high treason, and his Bill for Wales (1543), which
provided for its modification by letters patent. These contradictory statements called into question the relative status of statute law and monarchical
authority.[122]

The second change was that while Mary 'promised and sware upon the
sacrament lyinge upon the aulter in the presences of all the people to observe
and kepe' her oath, Edward had sworn on the bible by the 'Holy Evangelistes
by me bodily towched apon this Holy Awltare'.[123] The development of the
coronation oath from the late fifteenth to the mid-sixteenth century is a fascinating gauge of political and religious changes, with the diminishing role of the
clerical estate and the kingly Saint Edward the Confessor, alongside a growing
subordination of law to religious principle. Below is Henry VII's oath, with the
Edwardian version Mary used set out in square brackets:

> Wole ye graunte, and kepe, to the peple of England, the lawes and customes
> to them as of old rightfull and devoute Kinges graunted, and the same ratefie,
> and confirme by your oth, and specially' the lawes, customes, and liberties,
> graunted to the clergie and peple by your noble predecessor and glorious King
> Saynt Edward? [Will ye grawnte to kepe to the people of England and others
> your realmes and dominions the lawes and liberties of this realme and others
> your realmes and dominions?]

> I graunte, and promitte.

> Doe ye graunte the rightfull lawes and customes to be holden, and promitte ye,
> after your strenght and power, such lawes as to the worshippe of God shalbe
> chosen by your peple by youe to be strenghted and defended? [Do ye grawnte
> to make no newe lawes but such as shalbe to thonour and glory of God, and to

the good of the Commen Wealth, and that the same shalbe made by the consent of your people as hath been accustumed.]

I graunte and promitte.[124]

The allusion to Edward the Confessor in the original oath, alongside the use of his crown in coronation ceremonies, emphasised dynastic continuity and dated the lineal descent of English kings to before the Norman Conquest. Although the excision of the Anglo-Saxon king and Catholic saint (canonised in 1161) was respected by Mary, the Confessor's shrine at Westminster Abbey was restored on her orders in 1556 and his crown still played a prominent part in her coronation ritual.[125] Laws relating to the 'worship' of God, chosen by the people, were reframed in relation to the 'honour and glory' of God and good of the commonwealth. The alterations to the last section reconfigured relations between the sovereign, clergy and people in keeping with the theocratic political ideology developed to underpin the Supremacy. The sovereign was no longer merely custodian of law, but a lawmaker. In the first half of the sixteenth century diagnoses of social ills increasingly focused on the opposition between private and common good.[126] The changes to the coronation oath were significant, not because Edward swore to observe them, but because Mary, after closely examining them, did so too with the exception of minor emendations. She did not reject the political ideology associated with the Supremacy, although she might object to the use of the title. Her vision of royal authority was essentially the same as that of her two predecessors. She made it clear to Cardinal Pole's secretary Henry Penning 'fervently that she did not believe herself called by God'.[127] Mary was in no sense a theocrat.

Following the oath 'her grace was neweley appareled' in crimson velvet with a 'mayntell of Crymsyn velvit bordered with Ermyn with buttons and tasiles of sylke and golde for the same In which robes she resevyd hir oyntementes' and then 'her grace was broughte to the aulter where at she offered the Soward that she was gyrt with all by the said bushop of Wynchester and after was redemid agayne by thearl of Arundell Lord Stewarde [...] who bare the same sowarde before her grace'.[128] Mary was the first ever anointed female sovereign and received the sword, symbol of rule, representing justice, but also kingly prowess and strength. The implicit extension of a claim to *imperium* in her oath was taken even further in the unprecedented nature of the crowning itself. Edward VI received one crown, while she in imitation of her great uncle Charles received three:

the byshop of wynchester and the duke of Norfolk brought unto her highnes iii corownes to wyt/one kinge Edwards crowne *the other the imperiall crowne of this realme of Englande* the thyrd a very riche crowne the which was made purposefely for hir grace.[129]

Mary was the first English monarch to be crowned with a triple crown and the first to wear the imperial crown which had been commissioned by Henry VIII, first mentioned in an inventory of 1521. The third crown was commissioned specifically by Mary, underlining that the appropriation of imperial iconography was entirely intentional. The imagery of the triple crown originated in the three-tiered papal tiara which represented the universal, catholic jurisdiction of the pope, and had been appropriated by Charles V for his entry into Bologna to be crowned Holy Roman Emperor in 1530. This ritual object inspired Ibrahim Pasha, the powerful grand vizier of the Ottoman Empire, to commission a four-tiered ceremonial helmet-crown from Venice for Süleyman the Magnificent's triumphal march on Vienna as part of their military campaign of 1532, in a self-conscious game of one-upmanship. It advanced a symbolic counterclaim for Süleyman as 'imperator del mondo'.[130] Mary's borrowing from Habsburg symbolism reflected her dynastic affiliations, but also more importantly advanced her own imperial authority.

The gesture was alluded to in European accounts, published rapidly soon after; the first in Rome, *Coronatione de la serenissima Reina Maria d'Inghilterra faltta il di primo d'Ottobre MD.LIII* (Rome: Antonio Blado, 1553) and then in Castile in the spring of the following year, *Coronacion de la Inclita y Serenissima reyna Maria de Inglaterra* (Medina del Campo: March, 1554). The Castilian account, part of the campaign to promote the marriage, described Mary as 'de treynta y ocho años: y hermosa sin par', the tag used of the beautiful heroine Oriana from the romance of chivalry *Amadís de Gaula*:

> the Anointing began and she was anointed on the chest, back, forehead and temples, and afterwards they dressed her in a surplice of white leather and they girt her with spurs and sword like a knight and they put in her hand the royal sceptre of a king and then a staff that is customarily given to queens which had on the top a dove and finally they gave her a large gold orb and crowned her with three crowns. One for the kings of England, another for France and one for Ireland, and then they dressed her in another crimson mantle different from the first although it was the same velvet and lined with ermines.[131]

The last part, describing her clothing, accords exactly with the heralds' manuscript. The crowns are assumed, however, to represent the three kingdoms of the Tudors as opposed to being an appropriation of imperial/Habsburg iconography. Again the gender confusion of a queenly coronation is apparent, with Mary being given symbolic objects pertaining to both a king and queen. She is girt with spurs and a sword 'como a los caualleros' [like a knight], given the sceptre of a king but then a staff customarily given to queens. She is a representational hybrid, king and queen, male and female.[132] Mary's investiture as a knight with 'spurs' and 'sword' was inevitably dissonant.

The Cornishman, John Colwyn, on Christmas Eve 1553 amidst rumours of a Spanish invasion, voiced the opinion that '[w]e ought not to have a woman to bear the sword'.[133] In 1555 Myles Hogherde's tract *Certayne questions demaunded* similarly questioned 'whether the expres word of god in the xxii chap. of Deut. forbyd a woman to beare a sworde, or weare spurs, as kyngs do in theyr creacion, or to weare any other weapon, or apparell of man', a claim reiterated in later gynophobic polemic.[134] Her creation was a travesty. The unsettling nature of a regnant queen's coronation was reflected in both the heralds and Castilian accounts lingering on moments when the discordance between a ceremony tailored for a king and its performance by a regnant queen were most apparent. Identical concerns about a sword of state being born before a woman had surfaced when Mary's grandmother Isabel, queen of Castile, had been crowned in Segovia in the absence of her husband Ferdinand almost eighty years earlier.[135]

After the anointing and crowning, Mass was performed 'with great solemnity, her majesty kneeling the whole time with sign of great devotion and piety'.[136] As the most important queenly virtue, her exemplary piety was emphasised, with the prospective marriage months away and reconversion the essence of the English mission. Finally the assembled company did homage to Mary I. Gardiner on behalf of the spiritual Lords swore: 'I shallbe fathfull and trew... I shall do and truly knowlige the servys of the landes which I cleme to holde of yow as in the right of youre churche as god shall helpe me', an acknowledgement that church lands were held mediately from the crown. The wording here was unchanged from the oath taken by Henry VII. The church had never been recognised as possessing seisin or *plenum dominium* in its ecclesiastical properties in England. A representative of each rank of the temporal Lords then swore on behalf of their peers: 'I N. become your lyege man of lyfe and lynne and of all erthly worship and faith and al truth shal beare unto to you to lyue and dye with you agaynst all manner of foke so god helpe me and all halowes'.[137] After doing homage, they kissed her left cheek. Then Mary changed again and at 4pm she departed to Westminster for a banquet, 'having in hir hande a cepter of golde, and in hir other hande a ball of golde, which she twirled and tourned in hir hande as she came homewarde'.[138] At the feast Mary, Elizabeth, Gardiner and Anne of Cleves, all seated at one board, were served with over 312 dishes. A total of 7,112 were offered to the company as a whole of which 4,900 are described in the records as 'waste'.[139]

The magnificence of the coronation figured prominently in the Castilian account which put a figure on what it had cost:

it is known certainly that they spent on the coronation at her majesty's cost more than 100,000 ducats. And it is not so much the sum spent that gives pause for thought but rather the ordering of time and ceremonies well carried out, all ordered and provided for with great prudence and council in such a way that this kingdom and magnanimous queen have given most ample material for writers who wish to record it.[140]

An identical figure was given in the Roman tract of 1553. Despite the prompt, no English writer took advantage of this 'ample material'. While Spanish audiences prepared for a blossoming political romance figured in terms of their favourite chivalric literature, the bestseller *Amadís*, the anomalous and exotic accession of an unmarried queen provoked profound anxieties in England, all the more in the face of a foreign marriage whose spectre and threat to English sovereignty had already been rehearsed and catalysed throughout the succession crisis. Confusions as to how Mary was dressed, whether she was given symbolic objects belonging to a king or queen, on the day of her coronation, mirrored uncertainty about how to represent their unprecedented regnant queen.

Notes

1 BL MS Cotton Vespasian C xii. The negotations between Edward IV and the Basque provinces are contained in this volume. On the background to this trade to 1485, see the indispensable Wendy Childs, *Anglo-Castilian Trade in the Later Middle Ages* (Manchester: Manchester University Press, 1978), especially chapters 3, 'Complementary markets I: England's exports to Castile' and 4. 'Complementary markets II: England's imports from Castile', pp. 71–148.

2 William Page, ed., *Letters of Denization and Acts of Naturalization for Aliens in England, 1509–1603* (Lymington: Publications of the Huguenot Society of London, 1893), vol. 8, pp. vi–ix.

3 Fernando de Rojas, *La Celestina* (1st edn, Burgos: Fadrique de Basilea, 1499). Rastell was married to Thomas More's sister, while his daughter Joan married the poet and dramatist John Heywood. He attempted to dip his toe in the water of maritime discovery in 1517: see Richard Axton, ed., *Three Rastell Plays: Four Elements, Calisto and Melebea, Gentleness and Nobility* (Cambridge: Brewer, 1979), p. 6. Rastell's version, *The Interlude of Calisto and Melebea*, (pp. 69–96) was printed *c.* 1525 and has been associated with Juan Luis Vives' presence in England on six occasions between 1523 and 1528.

4 Sebastian Cabot's biography is instructive. Leading voyages of discovery from Bristol from as early as 1504, he worked for Henry VIII until around 1522, when he moved to Spain to undertake his famous exploration of the River Plate as a *piloto mayor* of the Casa de Contratación. By 1547 he had returned to England, while continuing to enjoy his Spanish titles and pension. He attempted unsuccessfully to rejoin imperial service in 1553, and was involved in the Willoughby, Merchant and Borough expeditions that led to the foundation of the Muscovy Company. Borough of course brought back Martin Cortés' *Arte de navegar* to be translated by Richard Eden, the first navigational treatise printed in English.

5 Roger's brother was the bishop of St David's, William Barlow: Gustav Ungerer, *Anglo-Spanish Relations in Tudor Literature* (Madrid: Francke Verlag Berne, 1956), p. 31. See also the fascinating account of this text and its history in Heather Dalton, 'Fashioning new worlds from old worlds: Roger Barlow's *A Brief Summe of Geographie, c.* 1541', in Lisa Bailey, Lindsay Diggelmann and Kim Phillips, eds, *Old Worlds, New Worlds: European Cultural Encounters c. 1000–1750* (Turnhout: Brepols, 2008), 75–97.

6 Specific recognition was granted in 1517 by Alonso Pérez de Guzmán along with land on which to build a chapel to St George; see Pauline Croft, *The Spanish Company* (Chatham: London Record Society, 1973), p. vii.

7   An invaluable source for all of the issues discussed here is Gustav Ungerer, *The Mediterranean Apprenticeship of British Slavery* (Madrid: Verbum, 2008), esp. chapters 1– 4 and 7. Heather Dalton, '"Into speyne to selle for slavys": English, Spanish, and Genoese merchant networks and their involvement with the "Cost of Gwynea" trade before 1550' in Toby Green, ed., *Brokers Of Change: Atlantic Commerce and Cultures in Pre-Colonial Western Africa*, Toby Green, ed., British Academy Proceedings Series (Oxford: Oxford University Press, 2012), 91–123.

8   The sparse bibliography on Anglo-Spanish trade and economic relations in this period has been brilliantly added to recently by Heather Dalton: see 'Fashioning new worlds' and, for this paragraph, 'Negotiating fortune: English merchants in early sixteenth-century Seville', in Caroline Williams, ed., *Bridging the Early Modern Atlantic World: People, Products and Practices on the Move* (Farnham: Ashgate, 2009), 57–73; and, crucially, *Merchants and Explorers: Roger Barlow, Sebastian Cabot and Networks of Atlantic Exchange, 1500–1560* (Oxford: Oxford University Press, 2016).

9   Gordon Connell-Smith, *Forerunners of Drake: A Study of English Trade with Spain in the Early Tudor Period* (Westport, Conn.: Greenwood Press, repr. 1975), chapters 1 and 2.

10 James D. Tracy, 'Herring wars: the Habsburg Netherlands and the struggle for control of the North Sea, ca. 1520–1560', *Sixteenth Century Journal* XXIV:2 (1993), 249–73, pp. 256 and 262.

11 BL MS Cotton Vespasian C XIII, fol. 328v, 3rd July 1534. Both Starkey and Mason were pro-tégés of Thomas Cromwell. The address on the letter makes it clear Starkey was staying with Reginald Pole at the time. This and manuscripts below are transcribed in Henry Ellis, ed., *Original Letters Illustrative of English History; Including Numerous Royal Letters: From Autographs in the British Museum and one or two other Collections*, 2nd ser., 4 vols (London: Harding and Lepard, 1827), vol. 2, pp. 59, 146 and 148.

12 BL MS Cotton Vespasian C VII, fols 91–95, 92v, 93r. This volume consists of 'Actas inter Angliam et Hispaniam 1516–1588'.

13 *Cal. Span.*, IV(2) (1531–3), no. 1058, pp. 631–2.

14 An anonymous Spanish chronicle recorded: 'Cromwell sent a gentleman to tell them not to summon the Spaniards and these returned to their houses. All the other foreigners were summoned, but what they swore need not be told, only that the Spaniards were free': *Chronicle of King Henry VIII of England*, ed. Martin A. S. Hume (London: George Bell and Sons, 1889), p. 38. Elsewhere, the chronicler praised Henry VIII: 'good King! how liberal thou wert to everyone, and particuarly to Spaniards!', *ibid.*, p. 127. One of the originals is BNE MS 18408. There is a bibliographical description of the eleven extant codices with this text in the edition by Mariano Roca de Togores, Marqués de Molina, *Crónica del Rey Enrico Otavo de Inglaterra* (Madrid: Alfonso Durán, 1874), Appendix X, pp. 449–67. The exemption is at *Cal. Span.*, IV(2) (1531–3), no. 1073, p. 682. Chapuys wrote later: 'now they want to subject all foreigners to payment; but this time, as far as I can gather, Spaniards are to be exempted which is no doubt a compliment paid to *our nation*': *Cal. Span.*, V(1) (1534–5), no. 58, p. 164. The ambassador himself, as a subject of Charles from the Low Countries, would not have been exempt. See Connell-Smith, *Forerunners of Drake*, pp. 102–3.

15 *Letters and Papers, Foreign and Domestic, Henry VIII*, 21 vols (London: HMSO, 1864–1920) (hereafter, *Letters and Papers*), xvii, no. 440, *Cal. Span.*, I (1485–1509), no. 380, p. 318 (granting English merchants equal terms of trade); nos 405, p. 337 and 438, p. 366. See Connell-Smith, *Forerunners of Drake*, pp. 128–9.

16 Connell-Smith, *Forerunners of Drake*, chapters 6–8. The 1543 agreement is in *Letters and Papers*, xviii (I), no. 144.

17 National Archives, SP 11/1/20, pp. 6–7. See below.

18 A. M. Kinghorn, *The Chorus of History: Literary-historical relations in Renaissance Britain 1485–1558* (London: Blandford Press, 1971), p. 78.

19 Connell-Smith, *Forerunners of Drake*, transcribed in Appendix D, p. 244. Original at Archivo General de Indias, Contratación, leg. 5103: 'como se enbargan los bienes de los dichos yngleses no vienen a contratar como solian porque ellos principalmente conpraban todos los

mas de los vinos y azeytes de todos estos pueblos y al no hazerse el mucho daño que se rrecibe asy en las rrentas rreales de su magestad como sus subditos y los destos pueblos que biben y se valen de sus cosechas y si vuestra alteza fuese seruido podria mandar suspender el enbargo'.

20 Peter Edwards, *The Horse Trade in Tudor and Stuart England* (Cambridge: Cambridge University Press, 1988), pp. 40–1. Joan Thirsk, *Horses in Early Modern England: for Service, for Pleasure, for Power*, The Stenton Lecture 1977 (Reading: University of Reading, 1978), p. 26. On the Eastern associations and trade in horses in the period, see Lisa Jardine and Jerry Brotton, *Global Interests: Renaissance Art between East and West* (London: Reaktion, 2000), p. 145 and on exports see Hugh Johnson, *The Story of Wine* (London: Mitchell Beazley, 1989), p. 173.

21 Rawdon Brown, ed., *Calendar of State Papers and Manuscripts, Relating to English Affairs etc., Venetian*, vols V–VII (London: Longman & Co. 1873–90) (hereafter, *Cal. Ven.*), VI, p. 543.

22 English merchants' involvement with the Atlantic trade continued to be highly significant throughout the sixteenth century. England's trade with Morocco was 'a natural extension of the existing trade with Spain' and involved backing from Spanish merchants working with the Ostrich and Lambert families: see T. S. Willan, *Studies in Elizabethan Foreign Trade* (Manchester: Manchester University Press, 1959), p. 95. The fullest account of the initial voyage is by James Alday, once a servant of Sebastian Cabot.

23 *Cal. Span.*, X, pp. 378–9. Queen Dowager to the Bishop of Arras, 5th October 1551.

24 *Cal. Span.*, X, pp. 378–9. Queen Dowager to the Bishop of Arras, 5th October 1551.

25 *Cal. Span.*, X, pp. 378–9. Queen Dowager to the Bishop of Arras, 5th October 1551.

26 Fray Prudencio de Sandoval, *Historia de la Vida y Hechos del Emperador Carlos V*, 3 vols, (Madrid: Atlas Ediciones, 1955–6), p. 432: 'el trato y comercio que ternían sus súbditos y vasallos libremente con el dicho reino de Inglaterra, de que se podía seguir mucho beneficio por la vecindad que tienen'.

27 Archivo General de Simancas (hereafter, AGS), Secretaria de Estado, E807, fol. 20: 'su mt. ha tractado de casarme paresciendole ser cosa mui necesaria para la conseruacion y augmento de los estados de su mt. y la vniersal paz de la xpiandad y principalmente por lo mucho que conuiene a estos reinos la vnion de aquel reino con ellos para su quietud y sosiego'. See also David Loades, *The Reign of Mary Tudor: Politics, Government and Religion in England 1553–1558* (2nd edn, London: Longman 1991), p. 67.

28 *Cal. Span.*, X, p. 145. On this incident see David Loades, *Mary Tudor: A Life* (Oxford: Basil Blackwell, 1992), pp. 156–7.

29 *Cal. Span.*, X, p. 136.

30 Jeri McIntosh's reinterpretation of this scene is entirely convincing: see her *From Heads of Household to Heads of State: The Preaccession Households of Mary and Elizabeth Tudor, 1516–1558* (New York: Columbia University Press, 2009), Appendix C: Mary's Aborted Flight, 1550s, pp. 231–6.

31 BNE MS 1167, fol. 275r. *Lecturas Varias, escripturas a Carlos V por el Almirante*: 'sin ber primero que aya buen fundamento y oportunidad y que sea con el fauor y asistencia Delymperio y que franceses fuesen ympedidos con yngleses o de otra manera'. There is a critical edition of Charles' earlier advice: Rachel Ball and Geoffrey Parker, eds, *Como ser rey. Instrucciones del Emperador Carlos V a su hijo Felipe. Mayo de 1543* (New York: HSA, CEEH, CSA, 2014).

32 *Cal. Span.*, X, p. 447. Emperor to Queen Dowager, 28th January 1552, Brussels.

33 *Cal. Span.*, X, pp. 378–9. Queen Dowager to the Bishop of Arras, 5th October 1551.

34 *Cal. Span.*, XI, p. 36. Jehan Scheyfve to the Emperor, 28th April 1553, London. [Vienna Imperial Archive E. 20].

35 *English Historical Documents*, Vol. V. *1485–1558*, ed. C. H. Williams (London: Eyre and Spottiswoode, 1967), pp. 456–7.

36 *Tower Chronicle*, p. 93.

37 Cesare Malfatti, ed. and trans., *The Accession, Coronation and Marriage of Mary Tudor as Related in Four Manuscripts of the Escorial* (Barcelona: Sociedad Alianza de Artes Graficas y Ricardo Fontá, 1956), pp. 5 and 10.

38 Real Biblioteca del Monasterio de San Lorenzo de El Escorial MS V. ii. 4, fol. 424r: 'haziendo a todos saber que su Alteza se hauia ydo hazia las prouincias de Norfolc y Sofolc que estan hazia las partes maritimas de la banda de Flandes con intencion de poner el Reyno en trabajos y guerras y hazer venir a estrangeras naciones a defender lo que ella pretende contra la Corona'.

39 *Cal. Span*, XI, p. 64.

40 *Cal. Span*, XI, p. 338, Renard to the Emperor, 6th November.

41 *Cal. Span*, XI, pp. 62–3.

42 Claire Cross, David Loades and J. J. Scarisbrick, eds, *Law and Government Under the Tudors* (Cambridge: Cambridge University Press, 1988), p. 190.

43 BNE MS 9937: Florián de Ocampo, *Sucesos Acaecidos, 1550–1558* and *1521–1549*, 'Relaçion enbiada por Don Diego de Azeuedo a su muger llego a Çamora en 2°. de Agosto de 1553', fols 97r–99r: 'El rey de Inglaterra morio, dizen que le mataron con ponçoña el Duque Barinque, que era protetor, y el embaxador de francia. Luego que murio, este Barinque con favor, y calor del Rey de francia hizo elegir por Rey a un hijo suyo'.

44 AGS E 807, fol. 15.

45 BNE MS 9937: 'Relaçion enbiada por Don Diego de Azeuedo', fols 97r–99r.

46 *Cal. Span.*, XII, p. 162. Mendoza to Arras, 19th March 1554, London. Original is in Biblioteca del Palacio Real, Granvelle.

47 BNE MS 9937, fol. 212v: letter from Hernando Delgadillo in Valladolid to Florián de Ocampo. He arrived with Bartolomé Carranza and Don Juan de Figueroa; see *Introduction*, p. 14.

48 Malfatti, *Accession, Coronation and Marriage of Mary Tudor*, p. 145.

49 *Cal. Span.*, XII, pp. 179–80.

50 A. G. Dickens, ed., 'Robert Parkyn's Narrative of the Reformation', repr. in *English Historical Review* 52 (1947), 58–83, p. 77.

51 See Geoffrey Parker, *Philip II* (London: Sphere Books Ltd, 1979), p. 56.

52 See McIntosh, *From Heads of Households to Heads of State*, p. 132 and Appendix A: Henry VIII's Will and The Bequests to Mary and Elizabeth, 1547; see also chapter 4. 'Accomplishing the Female Accession: The Succession Crisis of July 1553 and Its Aftermath', pp. 148–93; Paulina Kewes, 'The exclusion crisis of 1553 and the Elizabethan succession', in Susan Doran and Thomas Freeman, eds, *Mary Tudor: Old and New Perspectives* (New York: Palgrave Macmillan, 2011), pp. 49–61; Charlotte Merton, 'The women who served Queen Mary and Queen Elizabeth: ladies, gentlewomen and maids of the Privy Chamber, 1553–1603', unpublished PhD thesis (Cambridge University, 1992); Anna Whitelock, 'In opposition and in government: the household and affinities of Mary Tudor, 1516–1558', unpublished PhD thesis (Cambridge University, 2004), chapter 3. 'The Succession Crisis, July 1553', pp. 112–36; Anna Whitelock and Diarmaid MacCulloch, 'Princess Mary's household and the succession crisis, July 1553', *The Historical Journal* 50 (2007), 265–87.

53 Sir Anthony Browne had been imprisoned for hearing Mass in Mary's household in March 1551, yet was equerry and Knight of the Bath to Edward. Another figure who enjoyed favour from both was Sir Thomas Wharton.

54 The house can be glimpsed in the background of the portrait of Edward VI, who spent time during his childhood and much of 1546 there; see Karen Hearn, ed., *Dynasties: Painting in Tudor and Jacobean England 1530–1630* (New York: Rizzoli, 1995; Peterborough: Rate Publishing, 1995), p. 50.

55 Diarmaid MacCulloch, 'The *Vitae Mariae Angliae Reginae* of Robert Wingfield of Brantham', *Camden Miscellany* XXVIII, 4th ser. (London: Royal Historical Society, UCL, 1984), p. 251. See also Loades, *Mary Tudor: A Life*, pp. 174–5 and H. F. M. Prescott, *Mary Tudor* (London: Eyre & Spottiswoode, 1953), pp. 165–9.

56 MacCulloch, 'The *Vitae Mariae Angliae Reginae*', p. 252.

57 Robert Rochester was Edward Waldegrave's uncle. Waldegrave's wife Laura was the daughter of Robert's brother John. Rochester may have been brought up in the household of the

Earl of Oxford, John de Vere, whose support was crucial to Mary during the succession crisis.

58 A copy is in East Suffolk Record Office, Ipswich EE2/E/3, fol. 26v; see Whitelock, 'In opposition and in government', p. 124, note 49.

59 MacCulloch, 'The *Vitae Mariae Angliae Reginae*', p. 253. William Cecil drew up a list of those likely to support Jane in July 1553, BL Lansdowne MS 103, fol. 2v.

60 Letters to Marian supporters: BL Lansdowne MS 1236, fol. 29. Mary's holograph letter to Sir Edward Hastings, Inner Temple Library, MS 538/47, fol. 13 is reproduced in Mortimer Levine, *Tudor Dynastic Problems, 1460–1571*, Historical Problems Studies and Documents no. 21, ed. G. R. Elton (London: George Allen and Unwin Ltd, 1973), p. 170.

61 MacCulloch, 'The *Vitae Mariae Angliae Reginae*', pp. 252–6; *Tower Chronicle*, pp. 4–5; Loades, *Mary Tudor: A Life*, pp. 176–8 and *The Reign of Mary Tudor*, pp. 18–19; and Jennifer Loach, *Parliament and the Crown in the Reign of Mary Tudor* (Oxford: Clarendon Press, 1986), pp. 2–3.

62 *Tower Chronicle*, p. 8.

63 Robert Tittler and Susan Battley, 'The local community and the crown in 1553: the accession of Mary Tudor revisited', *Bulletin of the Institute of Historical Research* 57: 136 (1984), 131–9, p. 132, note 5, and David Loades, *The Tudor Court* (Totowa, NJ: Barnes & Noble Books, 1987), p. 159.

64 Whitelock, 'In opposition and in government', p. 117.

65 *Tower Chronicle*, p. 9.

66 The earls of Bedford, Arundel, Pembroke, Shrewsbury and Worcester, Lords Paget, Darcy and Cobham, Cheyne, Cheke, William Paulet and Sir John Mason. This building burned down in the Great Fire of London.

67 Malfatti, *Accession, Coronation and Marriage of Mary Tudor*, p. 15.

68 Real Biblioteca del Monasterio de San Lorenzo de El Escorial MS V. ii. 4, fol. 427r: 'es de marauillar el amor que este pueblo tiene a esta Señora que cierto offenden a nuestro Señor en ello porque le dexan de querer y la adoran'. In *La Celestina* (1499), Calisto affirms to Sempronio that he has ceased to be a Christian, in order to become a Melibean, a devotee of his lady.

69 Tittler and Battley, 'Local community and the crown', pp. 132 and 136–9.

70 *Tower Chronicle*, p. 5.

71 Christopher Haigh, *English Reformations: Religion, Politics, and Society under the Tudors* (Oxford: Clarendon Press, 1993), p. 205.

72 Loach, *Parliament and the Crown*, pp. 6–9. The list of Mary's supporters is at BL Lansdowne MS 156, fols 90–94.

73 Loach, *Parliament and the Crown*, p. 8.

74 See the discussion in Alice Hunt, *The Drama of Coronation: Medieval Ceremony in Early Modern England* (Cambridge: Cambridge University Press, 2008), pp. 115 and 119.

75 MacCulloch, 'The *Vitae Mariae Angliae Reginae*', p. 260.

76 Edward Windsor was married to John de Vere's daughter. See *Oxford Dictionary of National Biography*.

77 Loades, *The Reign of Mary Tudor*, p. 19.

78 Glanmor Williams, 'Wales and the reign of Queen Mary I', *Welsh History Review* 10:3 (1981), 334–58, p. 336.

79 Williams, 'Wales and the Reign of Queen Mary I', p. 336.

80 *Tower Chronicle*, pp. 11–12. This section of the narrative is supplied from Ralph Starkey's Collections, BL MS Harleian 353, p. 139. This account is confirmed by *Machyn's Diary*: John Gough Nichols, ed., *The Diary of Henry Machyn, Citizen and Merchant Taylor of London 1550–1563* (London: Camden Society, 1848).

81 Charles Lethbridge Kingsford, ed., *Two London Chronicles from the Collections of John Stow*, Camden Miscellany XII (London: Camden Society, 1910), p. 27. Antonio de Guaras recorded: 'arrojauan quasi todos los bonetes al ayre perdidos y todos los que tenian dinero en

sus bolsas los arrojauan al pueblo. Otros siendo hombres de autoridad y viejos no se podian contener echando de si sus ropas saltando y baylando como si estuuieran fuera de seso. Otros yuan corriendo por las calles en donde hauia houido noticia desta tan grande nouedad gritando' [transported, they almost all threw their hats in the air and all those who had money scattered it among the people. Others, being ancient men of authority, could not contain themselves, tearing off their clothes and dancing as if mad. Others ran through the streets where the news of this great novelty had reached, shouting], Real Biblioteca del Monasterio de San Lorenzo de El Escorial MS V. ii. 4, fols 426r–v.

82 See text relating to note 12 above.

83 The firmly Protestant Richard Taverner perhaps in the hope of keeping his position at court addressed to Mary *An oration gratulatory made upon the ioyfull proclayming of the moste noble princes Quene Mary Quene of Englande* (London: John Day, 1553), BL C.12.b.21.

84 BNE MS 9937: 'Relaçion enbiada por Don Diego de Azeuedo a su muger llego a Çamora en 2°. de Agosto de 1553', fols 97r–99r: 'La Infanta Maria hermana del Rey muerto, sabida la muerte de su hermano, se fue al [...], y alli se fueron para ella todos los mas principales del reyno, y de alli se vino al paso de concetayna, y hizo muy breuemente mas *de treinta mil hombres*, y con ellos se vino la buelta de Londres. Sabido esto por los del reyno, todos se alçaron por ella, y tomaron en prision al Duque Baurique, y al rey, y ala reyna nuevamente eligidos, y alos demas que eran en su favor y la Reyna Maria (digo de Inglaterra) entra oy dia, que esta escribo, o mañana en Londres, a donde luego sera jurada, y cortara las cabecas a todos, ecepto ala reyna, que fue eligida, que desta dizen que auido piedad; y la reyna, y el reyno queda todo pacifico. Por cierto que parescen cosas increybles estos acontecimientos, los quales yo creo que no pueden acaecer en ninguno reyno. *La reyna es cristianissima, y asi la ha ayudado Dios*: lo primero que haze es tornar la fe Catholica en su ser, como de antes: tendra poco que hazer en ello, porque los mas de los erejes, lo eran mas de miedo del Rey, y Protetor, que de sus voluntades. Prosperos sucesos han sido todos para su Mag. y el mas prospero es que tiene salud y trata negocios.'

85 *Chronicle of the Grey Friars of London*, Camden Society 1st ser., no. LIII (London: J. B. Nichols and Son, 1851) (hereafter *Grey Friars Chronicle*), p. 78.

86 *Tower Chronicle*, p. 14.

87 *Grey Friars Chronicle*, p. 81, and *Tower Chronicle*, p. 14. Henry Machyn put the figure at 3,000.

88 *Grey Friars Chronicle*, p. 81.

89 *Grey Friars Chronicle*, p. 82.

90 *Grey Friars Chronicle*, p. 83.

91 Paul Hughes and James Larkin, eds, *Tudor Royal Proclamations*. Vol. 2, *The Later Tudors (1553– 1587)* (London: Yale University Press, 1969), vol. II, p. 6.

92 Hughes and Larkin, eds, *Tudor Royal Proclamations*, vol. II, p. 6.

93 John Foxe, *The Unabridged Acts and Monuments Online* (1563 edition) (Sheffield: HRI Online Publications, 2011) (hereafter, *TAMO*), Book 4, p. 798. Available from: www.johnfoxe. org/index.php?realm=text&gototype=modern&edition=1563&pageid=798 [Accessed 26th September 2016].

94 After Henry had licensed the printing of the Great Bible, he responded to anxieties about its accessibility to those who 'taking and gathering divers Holy scriptures to contrary senses and understanding, do wrest and interpret and so untruly allege the same to subvert and overturn as well the sacraments of Holy Church as the power and authority of princes and magistrates, and in effect generally all laws and common justice': 'Limiting Exposition and Reading of Scripture', April 1539, in Hughes and Larkin, eds, *Tudor Royal Proclamations*, vol. I, pp. 284–6.

95 The Reformer Richard Taverner's oration on the proclamation of Mary insisted on the 'warrant of Parliament'; see Alice Hunt, 'The monarchical republic of Mary I', *Historical Journal* 52 (2009), 557–72, p. 567.

96 See my 'Culture under Philip and Mary I', in Sarah Duncan and Valerie Schutte, eds, *The Birth of a Queen: Essay on the Quincentenary of Mary I* (New York: Palgrave MacMillan, 2016), 155–78.

97 Edmund Bonner's *An honest godlye instruction and information for the tradynge, and bringinge vp of children, set furth by the Bishoppe of London co[m]maundyng all scholemaisters and other teachers of youthe within his diocese, that they neither teach, learne reade, or vse anye other maner of A B C, catechisme or rudimentes, then this made for the first instruction of youth. Mense Ianuarij. 1556. Cum priuilegio ad imprimendum solum* (London: Robert Caly, 1555) and *A profitable and necessarye doctrine with certayne homelies adioyned thervnto / set forth by the reuere[n]d father in God, Edmunde Bishop of London* (London: John Cawood, 1555), although the latter was probably by Nicholas Harpsfield and Henry Pendleton.

98 Rosalind K. Marshall, *Mary I* (London: HMSO, 1993), p. 85.

99 See Dale Hoak, 'The coronations of Edward VI, Mary I, and Elizabeth I, and the transformation of the Tudor monarchy', in C. S. Knighton and Richard Mortimer, eds, *Westminster Abbey Reformed, 1540–1640* (Basingstoke: Ashgate, 2003), 114–51, p. 137.

100 *Machyn's Diary*, p. 45 and note on p. 334, and College of Arms MS WB I 7, fol. 65v. They were the earls of Devonshire and Surrey, Lords Berkeley, Bergavenny, Lumley, Mountjoy and Herbert of Cardiff, Sir William Paulet, Sir Hugh Rich, Sir Henry Clinton, Sir Henry Paget, Sir Robert Rochester, Sir Henry Jerningham, Sir Henry Parker and Sir William Dormer. The latter's daughter Jane Dormer, one of Mary's ladies-in-waiting, later married the duke of Feria and led six Catholic ladies into exile on the accession of Elizabeth. An eighteenth-century copy is also found at BL Harleian MS 6166, fols 67–8.

101 *Grey Friars Chronicle*, p. 84. The order of procession is set out in Society of Antiquaries MS 123, item 3.

102 *Tower Chronicle*, p. 28.

103 William Jerdan, 'Device for the Coronation of Henry VII', *Rutland Papers*, Camden Society Old Series 21 (London: Camden Society, 1842) (hereafter, *Rutland Papers*), pp. 4 and 6.

104 A full account is at BL Royal Appendix 89, fols 93–105: 'The manner of the ceremony of the coronation of the late quene Mary'.

105 AGS, E 807 fols 3r–v, Spanish translation of French original on previous folio: 'yua en vna litera descubierta, y con vn palio de brocado seguianla dos carros y en el vno yuan las señoras elisabeth, y de Cleues y en el otro algunas damas de la Corte, todas las calles estauan entapiçadas y sembradas de muchas yeruas y flores y con muchos arcos triunfales... en vn cadahalso que estaua hecho para este effecto, en el qual se mostro a todo el pueblo, al qual se significo la dicha coronaçion preguntandoles sy les era agradable, y la queria por reyna y todo respondieron que sy... le puso el cetro y vara de justiçia con el globo y espueblas y espada y se le tomo el juramento acostumbrado'.

106 Judith Richards, 'Mary Tudor as 'sole quene'?: gendering Tudor monarchy', *The Historical Journal* 40 (1997), 895–924, pp. 900–3.

107 College of Arms MS WB I 7, fol. 66r.

108 College of Arms MS WB I 7, fol. 66r.

109 College of Arms MS WB I 7, fol. 66r.

110 The best secondary source for Mary's coronation and its historical context is Hunt, *The Drama of Coronation*, chapter 4, '"He hath sent Marye our soveraigne and Queene": England's first queen and *Republica*', 111–45, for details of publications, note 37. A detailed comparison of Tudor coronations is found in Hoak, 'Coronations', and Sarah Duncan's account of gender and symbolic aspects of ceremony in *Mary I: Gender, Power, and Ceremony in the Reign of England's First Queen* (New York: Palgrave MacMillan, 2012), chapter 2, 'The Coronation of a Queen', 21–36 and note 75.

111 College of Arms MS WB I 7, fol. 66r: 'Mariae Reginae inclytae constanter piae coronam britanici Imperii e palmar uirtutis accipienti Genuenses publica salute laetantes cultum optatum tribuunt' and 'Virtus superauit, Justitia dominatur, veritas triumphat pietas coronat salus Reipublicae restituitur'.

112 Malfatti, *Accession, Coronation and Marriage of Mary Tudor*, pp. 32 and 115.

113 *The Apocrypha*, based on the 1611 version (London: Cambridge University Press, rev. 1895), Book of Judith: XVI.6, p. 168.

114 Judith Richards, '"To promote a woman to beare rule": talking of queens in mid-Tudor England', *Sixteenth Century Journal* 28 (1997), 101–121, pp. 108*ff.* A psychoanalytic interpretation would probably begin by looking at beheading as symbolic castration.

115 See the Catholic priest Leonard Stopes' lines 'Our Iwell oure joye, our Judith doutlesse / The great Holofernes of hell to withstand...' in *An Ave Maria in Commendation of oure most vertuouse Queene* (London: Richard Lant, 1553?).

116 Nicholas Harpesfield in his *Concio quaedam admodum elegans, docta, salubris, & pia magistri Iohannis Harpesfeldi, sacre Theologiae baccalaurei, habita coram patribus & clero in Ecclesia Paulina Londini 26 Octobris. 1553* (London: John Cawood, 1553), sig. A3. A list of other texts availing themselves of this comparison is found in Duncan, *Mary I*, p. 196, note 51, drawing on John King, *Tudor Royal Iconography: Literature and Art in an Age of Religious Crisis* (Princeton, NJ: Princeton University Press, 1989), p. 219.

117 Jennifer Loach, 'The Marian establishment and the printing press', *English Historical Review* 101 (1986), 135–48, p. 140.

118 Hoak, 'Coronations', pp. 139–40.

119 College of Arms MS WB I 7, fol. 69r. In the *Rutland Papers'* description of the 'Device for the Coronation of Henry VII', it was specified that he should go 'vndre a ceele, or canape, of cloth of gold bawdekyn, with iiii staves and iiii bellis of siluer and gilt, the same to be born by the Barons of the v ports', p. 10.

120 Roche Dasent, John (ed.), *Acts of the Privy Council*, vols 4–6 (London: HMSO, 1892–3), n. s. II (1546–7), p. 30.

121 *APC*, n. s. II (1546–7), pp. 30–1. Reprinted in *English Historical Documents*, Vol. 5, *1485–1558*, no. 45 (i), p. 467. See also Marshall, *Mary I*, p. 85.

122 Levine, *Tudor Dynastic Problems*, pp. 161–2.

123 College of Arms MS WB I 7, fol. 69r and *APC*, n. s. II (1546–7), p. 31.

124 *Rutland Papers*, p. 14, and the text in brackets from *APC*, n. s. II (1547–50), pp. 30–2, reprinted in *English Historical Documents*, Vol. 5, *1485–1558*, no. 45 (i), p. 467. Another absence from the later ceremony is a section dealing with the ecclesiastical estate: Henry VII swore to 'in asmoche as I may be reason and right, by Godds grace defend youe, and eurich of youe, Bishoppes, and Abbot thorough my realme', etc.

125 Marshall, *Mary I*, p. 128.

126 The dichotomy is central in political texts like Thomas Starkey's 'A Dialogue between Pole and Lupset' (*c.* 1529–32), ed. T. F. Mayer, Camden Society 4th ser., XXXVII (London: Royal Historical Society and UCL, 1989); Sir Thomas Elyot's *The Boke Named the Gouernour* (London: Thomas Berthelet, 1531); John Ponet's *A Shorte Treatise of politike pouuer, and of the true Obedience which subiectes owe to kynges and other ciuile Gouernours, with an Exhortacion to all true naturall Englishe men* (Strasbourg: heirs of W. Köpfel, 1556); and Sir Thomas Smith's *De Republica Anglorum* (1562–5, pub. 1583), ed. Mary Dewar (Cambridge: Cambridge University Press, 1982).

127 Hunt, *The Drama of Coronation*, p. 119 and *Cal. Ven.* V (1534–54), p. 430.

128 College of Arms MS WB I 7, fol. 70v.

129 College of Arms MS WB I 7, fol. 71r. My italics. See *APC*, n. s. II (1547–50), pp. 29–33.

130 Gülru Necipo_lu, 'Süleyman the Magnificent and representation of power in the context of Ottoman–Habsburg–Papal rivalry', *Art Bulletin* LXXI:3 (1989), 401–27, pp. 409–14.

131 Real Biblioteca del Monasterio de San Lorenzo de El Escorial MS V. ii. 3, fols 435v and 437r: 'se començo la vncion y fue ungida en el pecho y en las espaldas y frente y en las sienes y despues le vistieron vn roquete de cuero blanco y le calçaron vnas espuelas y le ciñieron vna espada como a los caualleros y la pusieron en la mano vn cetro real de rey y luego toro que se acostumbra a dar a las reynas que tenia en lo mas alto del vna paloma y finalmente la dieron vn pomo de oro grande y la coronaron con tres coronas. Una del rey de Inglaterra y otra de Francia y otra de Yrlanda y luego la vistieron otro manto de carmesi diferente del primero aunque era del mesmo tercioeplo carmesi y aforrado en armiños.'

132 See further discussion in Chapter 4: text relating to note 71.

133 Prescott, *Mary Tudor*, p. 225. *Cal. Dom.*, 11, 2, No. 2.

134 Myles Hogherde, *Certayne questions demaunded and asked by the Noble Realme of Englande of her true naturall chyldren and Subiectes of the same* (London: 1555), sig. Aii v. On Hogherde, see the fascinating and comprehensive assessment in J. W. Martin, 'Miles Hogharde: artisan and aspiring author in sixteenth-century England', *Renaissance Quarterly* 34 (1981), 359–83.

135 See Judith Richards, 'Renaissance queen' in Carole Levin, Jo Carney and Debra Barrett-Graves, eds, *'High and Mighty Queens' of Early Modern England: Realities and Representations* (Basingstoke: Palgrave Macmillan, 2003), p. 35.

136 Real Biblioteca del Monasterio de San Lorenzo de El Escorial MS V. ii. 3, fol. 438r: 'con mucha solemnidad estando siempre su magestad de rodillas con grande deuoccion y grandes señales de religion'.

137 College of Arms MS WB I 7, fol. 72v.

138 *Tower Chronicle*, p. 31. The banquet is described by Robert Wingfield: 'A sumptuous ancient dish was offered her after the custom and usage of kings and queens, with noblewomen serving her and with the most distinguished figures in the realm eagerly attending to their duties; indeed they performed their services assiduously according to their ancestral serjeanties assigned them by the kings of England from olden time, from which it is worth selecting one or two to record. Thomas, duke of Norfolk, exercised the dignity of marshal, perpetual and hereditary in his family; the Earl of Arundel had the custody or charge exercised by his ancestors of the coffer of gold goblets and other precious vessels; the Earl of Shrewsbury and the bishop of Durham had a valid legal claim to the duty of supporting the arms of the king or queen when they were tired from the effort of holding the orb and sceptre – the latter claimed by grant to him and his successors, the former to him and his heirs. [Edward Dymoke] sought a contest or single combat by challenging any competitor for the throne to fight: a custom, indeed, more recent than the others, for it was no older than the reign of Henry IV who drove Richard II from the throne, but nevertheless a duty of great honour and fame'; MacCulloch, 'The *Vitae Mariae Angliae Reginae*', pp. 276–7.

139 BL Add. MS 34320, fol. 97.

140 Real Biblioteca del Monasterio de San Lorenzo de El Escorial, MS V. ii. 3, fol. 438r: 'sabese por cierto que le gastaron en la dicha coronacion a costa de su magestad mas de cien mil ducados. E no es tanto de ponderar la summa del gasto quanto la orden del tiempo y las cerimonias bien hechas todo ordenado y reglado con gran prudencia y consejo en manera que este reyno y esta magnanima reyna an dado amplissima materia a los escriptores que quisiese escriuir'.

2

Contracting matrimony

The negotiations over the marriage contract and treaty reveal much about the anxieties surrounding England's first regnant queen. Nevertheless, the situation although anomalous in England was known in Europe during the period, especially in Spain, where female rule had become familiar over the previous century. Unsurprisingly, these precedents closely informed how the contract and union were framed; dealing with foreign succession, inheritance and settling the detailed political rights of each party regardless of their gender, during and after the marriage.

Marital difficulties

Antonio de Guaras, who proclaimed himself to be a servant of Mary I, in a letter addressed to the third duke of Alburquerque, Beltrán de la Cueva y Toledo, noted on 1st September 1553: 'what a great benefit would result to our Spain, halting the French if these kingdoms and those of his Majesty were one and even if it were for no other reason than to conserve the states of Flanders'.[1] The duke of Albuquerque had been a familiar figure at the Henrician court, serving against France with distinction under Henry in the Boulogne campaign in 1544. However, Guaras was cautious about the prospects for such an alliance 'because they are not great devotees of our nation they say', although 'they love his Majesty and Spain particularly for the love they bore the good Catholic queen [i.e. Catherine]'.[2] The paradoxical claim that the English loved Spain, yet were not much fond of 'our nation' encapsulates one of the central problems addressed in this book: the way English xenophobia and anti-Spanish sentiment were invoked, both at the time and in subsequent historiography, to diminish the marriage and suggest that Philip only ever occupied the throne of England in name. A regnant queen's marriage to a foreign dynast of course raised the possibility of disputed successions through the female line and the alienation of sovereignty in an unequal partnership according to the *mores* of the time.[3] Nevertheless, it is important to remember that the general misogyny of the period was qualified by fundamental hierarchies of power. Salic law in France prohibited female transmission of political claims, leading Nicholas Harpsfield, Reginald Pole's archdeacon and the biographer of Thomas More, to lambast Henrician legislation ensuring male succession in England, arguing '"[s]omewhat tolerable this talk had been in the mouth of some Frenchman"', but 'the rejection of female rule was "un-English"'.[4] Xenophobia figured on all sides of these hotly contested debates about female rule, inheritance and dynasticism.

The Venetian diplomat Michiel Soriano in 1561, in a codicil to the reign, suggested: 'no foreigner could rule this kind of people', they 'are universally partial to novelty, hostile to foreigners, and not very friendly amongst themselves'.[5] Conversely, the French ambassador François de Noailles commented in a letter on 21st July 1555 to Anne, duke of Montmorency, the general who had captured Metz two years before: '[a]ll those who have written of the complexion of insular peoples lay at their door lightness and inconstancy' but 'beyond all others those who inhabit this island have been grievously afflicted with deceit and all diversity'.[6] Environmental understandings of peoples saw the bishop of Burgos, Alfonso de Cartagena, in the context of a dispute over precedence, characterise England and Britain as isolated, insular and liminal: 'although that part of England facing France perhaps touches the furthest reaches of the seventh climatic zone, the most part of the country is outside it', 'so the island of Britain is set apart from all the world in the ocean sea and separated by the waters from it and so it seems that correctly speaking England is outside the world'.[7] In Francisco de Tamara's edition and translation of Johann Boemus' 1520 *Omnium Gentium Mores, Leges et Ritus* as *El libro de las costumbres y maneras de vivir de todas las gentes* (1556), a similarly dismissive description recorded that: 'this [island is] surrounded by the sea on all sides and in no place next to solid ground, instead it is totally set apart from our world'.[8] More importantly, however, than its liminality, kings of Castile 'were never subject to the Roman empire nor to any other', whereas 'the first king of England received the realm in tribute from the Romans' and furthermore 'all agree that just before our days the kings of England held the kingdom in fief from the Church'.[9] The first two books of Boemus' treatise had been published in England the previous year, translated by William Watreman as *The fardle of facions* (1555).[10]

The claim of papal overlordship, so vigorously contested by Tudor propagandists, had recurred repeatedly in works on precedence in the previous century. The fifteenth-century French dialogue *Le débat des héraulx d'armes de France et d'Engleterre*, product of another dispute about precedence, this time at the Council of Constance, alluded to it and was considered worth republishing in 1515 and 1520, drawing a reply from John Coke as late as 1550.[11] Simon Fish had directed Henry VIII in his *Supplicacyon for the Beggers* (1529) to consider his 'nobill predecessour king Iohn' and how 'your most nobill realme wrongfully (alas for shame) hath stood tributary (not unto any kind temporall prince, but unto a cruell deuilisshe bloudsupper dronken in the bloud of the sayntes and marters of Christ) eversins'.[12] Despite his villainous medieval reputation and part in the Robin Hood stories, King John was transformed by early Protestants into 'a proto-Protestant martyr, a champion of English integrity... a victim of the villainy of Rome', a national icon for his defiance of the papacy.[13]

Central to historically negative views of Mary is the reading of her foreign marriage and Catholic restoration as undermining English sovereignty. These two events have been yoked together to cast her reign as in some way fundamentally un-English. Repudiations of papal overlordship, however, dated back, as we have seen, to well before the Tudor period and even Alfonso de Cartagena. The opening address to Edward III's last parliament in 1377, presided over by his heir Richard II, contained a fully developed English version of theocratic royal authority: "'[p]acem super Israel*", peace over Israel, because Israel is understood to be the heritage of God as is England. For I truly think that God would never have honoured this land in the same way as He did Israel through great victories over their enemies, if it were not that He had chosen it as His heritage.'[14] The French had been recognised as 'Emperors in their own kingdom' since the 1202 Bull *Per Venerabilem* and Philip the Handsome's *plenum dominium* and imperial authority underscored by a Bull of 1311 echoed in the parliamentary address (they were 'like the people of Israel... a peculiar people chosen by the Lord to carry out the orders of Heaven'[15]): but it was not until Henry IV's reign that an English king was first depicted wearing an imperial, closed crown. Henry V was the first English monarch unequivocally depicted as possessor of imperial status. Both he and Henry VI were of course also kings of France.[16] Henry VII, whose patronage helped establish a cult for Henry VI, linked his kingship to his step-uncle, who he revered with a veneration which 'amounted almost to superstition'.[17] England's status as a papal fief was explicitly repudiated by both Henry VII and VIII as part of their cultivation of international standing and reputation.[18] In the 1501 pageant for Catherine, Henry VII was styled by his propagandists 'Most Christian King', the distinctive title of French monarchs. However, it was not until 1521 after the publication of Henry VIII's *Assertio ad Lutherum* that England's sovereign actually possessed a title to rival those of the French and Castilian monarchies, proclaiming his piety as *Defensor fidei*.

The portrayal of papal jurisdiction in England as an abrogation of the kingdom's *plenum dominium* had not been, nor would be exclusive to evangelicals, despite their identification of themselves with the Jews of the Old Testament. The notion that the Marian restoration of Catholicism meant a 'blight had fallen on national faith and confidence, and Israel took to its tents',[19] simply echoed religious exiles' understanding of their persecution under Mary as underscoring their elect status. The assumption that evangelicals were uniquely associated with the notion of England as an empire is highly selective. As those same polemicists pointed out, the definitive ideological statement of the Supremacy, *De vera obedientia*, had been written largely by Mary's Catholic Lord Chancellor, Stephen Gardiner. Neither side accepted the papal claim and Marian religious policy, as has been definitively demonstrated in recent scholarship, successfully created an indigenous, innovative Catholicism that influenced theological debates at Trent and beyond.[20] Mary's marriage potentially transformed England into an empire again by dynastically creating claims to continental possessions, like the Low Countries. It also provided a significant impetus to access to and knowledge of the New World, catalysing England's colonial ambitions.

The negotiations of the international treaty and marriage contract by which England and Spain were united and Mary I married the most powerful prince in Western Europe, registered profoundly the problems posed by a regnant queen's foreign match. Within days of Northumberland's arrest, the imperial ambassadors were blaming émigré communities for the attempt to exclude Mary. Foreign religious dissidents, who had fled to England to enjoy the relative religious freedom of her brother's evangelical regime, were immediately associated with heresy and sedition, having 'published abroad in writing that if your Majesty came to the throne you would wish to alter religion to the hurt of their consciences, marry a foreigner, change the government and ancient laws of the kingdom and introduce new customs and administration'.[21] The emperor wrote in reply to them on 23rd August that it 'is clear that the foreign refugees will oppose her as much as any other class of people, in their fear of a change of religion'.[22] Targeting them distracted from broader questions surrounding England's religious complexion after two decades of religious change. While the question of how Catholic England remained in 1553 has sharpened, few contest Christopher Haigh's conclusion that Reformations under Henry and Edward might have driven 'Catholic public worship from the churches... [but it] did not destroy essentially Catholic views of Christian life and eternal salvation': the association between English patriotism and reform would only be forged in the later decades of Elizabeth's reign.[23] Although Flemish and German exiles might have had personal and political reasons for opposing the accession of Mary, the evidence is that neither they, nor evangelicals at large, did so. Sectarian divisions had not sharpened to the extent they would later in the century.

Philip, during his journey to win acceptance for his succession in the Low Countries between 1548 and 1551, had mixed freely with Protestants and two of his court preachers from this period would later be burned for holding Reformist ideas.[24] Nor did the religious complexion of the regime prevent the Flemish evangelical printer Thomas Geminus from actively courting Philip and Mary's patronage, producing the earliest complete map of the Britain Isles in England, enshrining a Catholic vision of pre-Reformation England, omitting dioceses created since the upheavals of the 1530s. The original copper plates had been associated with the publication of Paolo Giovio's *Descriptio Britanniae, Scotiae, Hyberniae, et Orchadum* (Venice, 1548),[25] a text that had included accounts of a number of key English Catholic martyrs supplied by George Lily, including one for his friend Thomas More.[26] The plates almost certainly arrived with Reginald Pole (see Plate 4).

Following on from his original instructions, in which he had noted how 'loathed [...] all foreigners are by all Englishmen', the emperor now asked his representatives to canvas for an expulsion 'by the Parliament, which might be brought to do it because of the general hatred of foreigners'.[27] A decree to expel aliens was postponed however, they reported on 9th September, although Stephen Gardiner 'had hit upon a good device for getting the Lutherans out of the country': when 'he hears of any preacher or leader of the sect, he summons him to appear at his house, and the preacher, fearing he may be put in the Tower, does not appear, but on the contrary absents himself'.[28] The proclamation 'Ordering the Deportation of Seditious Aliens' was eventually promulgated on 17th February 1554, in the immediate aftermath of the Wyatt rebellion.

Simon Renard had been told by his predecessor Jehan Scheyfve that the English 'dreaded the rule of the Spaniards' who would 'have great difficulty in keeping possession of the Low Countries after his Majesty's death, for the King of Bohemia is loved there and his Highness and the Spaniards hated'.[29] Philip had failed to win over hearts and minds in his progress through Italy and the Low Countries four years earlier, with even his own eulogists describing how 'he displeased the natives... his Highness was excessively serious and reserved'.[30] English preference for Charles' brother, Ferdinand, king of the Romans, or his son, Maximilian, archduke of Austria, reflected the pluralism of the states they ruled, making them potentially more tolerant of and sensitive to the religiously variegated English context. Maximilian, who had become king of Bohemia in 1548, was suspected of abetting Maurice of Saxony's revolt against Charles and refused demands to deny it publicly. In Bohemia by the sixteenth century, Catholics made up only a third of the population and less than 5 per cent of the inhabitants of Prague. The king's Protestant leanings were an embarrassment to his family, and he was obliged in 1562 to swear to live and die in the Catholic faith.[31]

The papal diplomat Gianfrancesco Commendone discussed the plans for a marriage, registering the anxiety that England might be put 'into perpetual servitude, as it happens now to the Reign of Naples and all that part of Italy which is subject to the Emperor'.[32] Polemicists too availed themselves of this analogy, which formed the subject of an acerbic anti-Marian pamphlet, attributed to John Ponet, in November 1555: *A Warnyng for Englande Conteynyng the horrible practices of the kyng of Spayne in the kyngs dome of Naples and the miseries whereunto that noble Realme is brought. Wherby all Englishe men may understand the plage that shall light upon them if the kyng of Spayn obteyne the Dominion in Englande.*[33] The 'warning' underlined Habsburg expropriations in Italy, the increasing tax burden and their disenfranchisement of native-born Neapolitans. The fear of the foreign became part of broader anxieties about 'Spanish' power.

An anonymous manuscript history of England in Spanish from this period, the *Account of events in England from King Henry until his daughter Queen Mary* recorded that '[t]he inhabitants of this island naturally hate foreigners, leaving their homeland very little they are inhospitable to others there… the women are very ugly and dress and coiff themselves worse than in Flanders and in that style'.[34] Antoine Perrenot de Granvelle, bishop of Arras, admitted to his fellow ecclesiastic, the Cardinal of Jaén on 3rd February 1554, in light of the Wyatt revolt: 'the English may come with the greatest difficulty to consent to the marriage and so much more for they naturally detest foreigners'.[35] Stephen Gardiner was unaware that Renard had already proposed the match to Mary and that at a secret interview on 29th October she had vowed to accept Philip, when he asserted in a conversation (reported in a letter on 6th November) how difficult it would be 'to induce the people to consent to a foreigner, for the very name was odious to them and always had been. If the Queen were to marry his Highness, the people would never put up with the Spanish character, in which they would be imitating your Majesty's own subjects, who could never learn to bear them in Flanders.'[36] Courtiers in Brussels resented Spanish influence and there was widespread popular resentment of the *tercios* from the peninsula, who were entrusted with garrisoning border fortresses.[37] Time and again the situation in the Low Countries was invoked as a warning to England.

Renard reminded the emperor that 'as his Highness and his attendants would be unable to speak English there would be great confusion among a rough, fickle and proud people, who could neither understand nor make themselves understood in the requisite manner'.[38] It is particularly ironic that Gardiner was blamed in numerous histories and plays after Mary's reign for the Spanish marriage, given his consistent, vociferous opposition to it, in favour of Edward Courtenay.[39] At a subsequent meeting Gardiner shifted his objections onto economic grounds:

He did not know what the merchants of England would say to it, except that it was intended to enrich foreigners by opening the gates of the country to them and impoverish its unfortunate inhabitants. When the privileges of the Stillyard [Hanseatic League] were confirmed and restored to their position before the decree of suppression, the English merchants had complained and displayed dissatisfaction. I made answer that... As for the objections that might be made by merchants, I thought the alliance would mean riches and advantages for them rather than poverty, because navigation would be safer and trade freer.[40]

Mary had reinstated the privileges of the Hanse merchants just a week before in the face of bitter objections from the Merchant Adventurers, who had originally won a suspension of their privileges from Edward's regime. The change of policy appears related to her decision to marry Philip. Fundamental as we have seen to the appeal of his candidature was the strong commercial ties it secured with northern Europe's most affluent, industrial region, largest financial market and England's principal trading partner. As the queen's chaplain John Christopherson wrote after the marriage, on the enhancement of trade it promoted: 'what a benefite is it for thys realme to haue free libertie to conueye such thinges from hence thither, as we haue plentye of, & to bring in those agayne from thence hyther, that we haue nede of'.[41] Inevitably, some commercial interest groups would complain about increased competition, especially domestic artificers, seeing themselves disadvantaged by equal terms of trade.

On 11th September 1549, just months before the Anglo-French treaty, England's mercantile community had expressed their dependence on the Spanish and Low Countries trade through a triumphal arch celebrating Philip's entry into Antwerp:[42]

To the most invincible Charles, Emperor, August Caesar, and to his son the great Philip, Prince of the Spains, for his happy and wished for arrival in this city and for the perpetual constancy of the friendship and confederacy that they have had until now with the kings of England, English merchants and traders in this illustrious city, they have raised up this grandiose arch to witness their proper gratitude and joy.[43]

The arch was adorned with statues seated inside a gigantic gold scallop. At the side of the figure of Oceanus, a female figure representing the Thames and Britannia poured golden water from a pitcher: 'having respect to the ancient name that was Albion, so-called either from the giant Albion, son of Neptune, or from the abundance of white stones there'.[44] The blazon linked geography, mythical genealogy and mercantile success to the festive moment of its production. Higher up the arch were statues of 'two most illustrious figures, who were English'; the Emperor Constantine the Great, who had converted the Roman Empire to Christianity and whose *De Donatione Constantini Magni* had been exposed as a fake by Lorenzo Valla in the fifteenth century, having served as a central argument for the temporal power of the papacy for over a millennium.[45] Next to him stood his mother Helen. Constantine was in fact born in Upper Moesia (modern Bulgaria and Serbia), but had been adopted into English mythology and was specifically related to its claim to *imperium*. During Charles' visit to England in 1522, Henry had wanted him to 'know that the Tudor *imperium* predated Charlemagne, that from Constantine the Great it derived through King Arthur'.[46] Underneath Constantine and Helen were statues of Constantia and Pietas. In the context of the political tensions between the Habsburgs and the schismatic government of Edward VI, the arch was riskily contentious, alluding to the discredited prop that had been used to support the temporal power of the papacy. So it could have been read as an indirect critique of Roman superstition and gullibility or alternatively orthodoxly placing England firmly at the heart of Catholic Europe.

A painting on the panels of the arch depicted Charles V and Henry VIII 'shaking right hands in signal of perpetual frienship, concord and alliance'.[47] Inside, it contained a scene of Constantine's conversion before his victory over Maxentius 'enemy of the Christian religion' which was related to Philip: 'in likeness of whom, the prince Philip was depicted, fighting against the Turks and Moors' with Victory in his hand, foretelling 'QVO SIGNO MAGNUS VICIT CONSTANTINUS, EODEM ET MAGNUM DE BARBARIS ALIQVANDO TRIVMPHATVRVM PHILLIPUM, AIT CLOTHO' [by the same sign that Constantine the Great triumphed, so the great Philip will triumph over barbarians, according to the Fate Clotho].[48] The crusading mentality associated with *reconquista* was transposed onto the New World and on-going engagement in the Muslim Mediterranean.

Opposition to a foreign match in England was shared by a broad coalition of privy counsellors and significant members of Mary's household, including Robert Rochester, Francis Englefield and Edward Waldegrave. This group 'decided together to cause Parliament to speak to the Queen about the match, begging her not to wed a foreigner', aware 'that if no foreigner succeeds Courtenay is sure of success, as he is the only man of the blood royal in England'.[49] Parliamentary petitioners, headed by John Pollard, in a speech 'full of art and rhetoric, and illustrated by historical examples', attempted on 16th November to dissuade her from marriage outside the realm.[50] Mary was angered, responding that 'if she were married against her will she would not live three months'.[51] By December, Renard had got wind of more substantial murmuring, the first rumours about the conspiracy that would become Wyatt's revolt: 'persons have been sent out to travel about the country saying that England is to be governed by Spaniards and that the Queen is of Spanish blood'.[52] During the succession crisis, authorities at Antwerp had embargoed

English ships and confiscated merchants' goods. One correspondent noted how by this point 'the young English at Antwerp use their talk very wildly' and 'have lately had a bickering with the Spaniards, which has so tickled them that they hesitate not everywhere to express their discontentation with the whole nation'.[53] Renard had also heard of these unfolding tensions:

> The Spaniards are detested here because of the quarrel they had with the English at Antwerp, the manner in which your Majesty's own subjects complained of their arrogance, and what they did the other day at Douai, the dislike many English feel for the alliance, and especially the unfortunate stories repeated by several exiled and refugee Spaniards who reside over here.[54]

A number of Spanish Protestants and *conversos* had emigrated to northern Europe to escape persecution, while discontent with the Spanish presence in the Low Countries was a forerunner of the Eighty Years War. Protests about Spanish 'arrogance' ironically mirrored the reception of Flemings and Netherlanders in Spain when Charles had first travelled to take possession of his new kingdom in 1516. The miraculous dynastic good fortune of the Habsburgs presented the recurring problem of foreign successions in many of the realms they ruled. The resemblances between the Wyatt and *comunero* revolts reveal how international dynastic politics and local particularities inevitably came into conflict.

Contracting matrimony

Charles V played little or no part in the actual discussions that led to the marriage contract/treaty. The emperor had been incapacitated by melancholy, gout, catarrhs and haemorrhoids for most of 1553, following the disastrous reversal of Metz, gifted by Maurice of Saxony to the French king the previous year. In September Francisco Duarte reported the emperor's

> haemorrhoids swell and torment him with so much pain that he cannot move without great emotion and tears and these things together with the passions of the spirit which have been great and [qu]otidian have changed his condition and the good grace and affability he used to have and caused in him so melancholy a humour that they say he is pensive and cries often and for long periods of time so earnestly and with such shedding of tears as if he were a small child… [and] he does not wish to hear about business nor sign the little that is dispatched, I understand he spends day and night adjusting and synchronising his clocks, which are many, they are what matter most to him.[55]

Earlier in the summer Edward's ambassadors had been turned away and Carlos' isolation was such that he only saw a small group of his bedchamber.

Negotiations were conducted through envoys sent by Granvelle, with legal advice from councillor Viglius, and overseen by Mary of Hungary.[56] The imperial secretary Francisco Eraso confirmed on 12th December from Brussels to Philip that his father was suffering from 'weakness, [and] loss of appetite' and lamented that among the envoys 'for our sins there will be no Spaniard, given that I attend much to the nation's honour, in order that the business may be done as one might wish and so I have written to Juan Vázquez that he relate everything to your Highness'.[57] All three envoys, Jean de Montmorency, sieur de Courrières, Lamoral, count of Egmont, and Philip Negri were natives of the Franche-Compté in the old dukedom of Burgundy. When they arrived in England, the Grey Friars chronicler described them coming 'in the name of the hole howse of Bowrgone'.[58] Stephen Gardiner extracted an agreement to have the treaty ratified by Charles, Philip and the Estates General of the Netherlands. However, he failed to get the supplementary articles incorporated into the formal treaty or to have Philip's procuration worded 'per verba de futuro' which would have made the treaty contingent on Philip's landing in England to take the oath 'per verba de praesenti'.[59]

Eraso referred to English changes to the treaty: 'although they have come back with two or three changes they are unimportant and his Highness grants them willingly' and Charles three days later confirmed to Renard 'in so far as the changes they have made to our clauses to avoid becoming embroiled in disputes with them and more importantly because we have not found anything unreasonable in the changes, it has seemed better to accept them without alteration, as you can declare to them with our other ambassadors as soon as they arrive, we are hurrying their departure as much as possible'.[60] Initially Philip received instructions from Brussels on 26th December that 'you will be espoused by words of the present or future, in whatever case is necessary'.[61] The suggestion that the prince insisted that the marriage be concluded 'per verba de praesenti' before he went to England, rests on an inaccurate translation in the nineteenth-century *Calendar*. On 21st January 1554, the emperor wrote soothingly: 'the articles were seen to be so just and reasonable that the capitulation was at once agreed to, and has been sent to me signed, so that I may ratify it, as I now have done'.[62] He then asked Philip to ratify it with two powers: 'one so that the espousal can take place *per verba de praesenti*, and the other *de futuro*, it seems they are still insisting on the latter: because they hope that when with the blessing of our Lord, you are married, you will swear and approve the capitulation and to respect the laws and customs of that land. But the said Queen confidently assures us that it will be effectuated in secret according to our will (and we hold it certain)'.[63] While the first person plural ('our will, desire or wish') might refer to Charles, to his son or to both, it is undoubtedly not Philip's insistence alone. An adjunct to the document stated that the count of Egmont was going to travel to Spain after the espousal 'por palabras de futuro', next to which in the margin Philip has written in his own hand: 'may this ratification of the capitulation be signed because I granted it and taken with the Marques de las Navas who a package will reach with all the despatches for his majesty' and it is signed playfully 'yo el rey' [I, the King]. As I have argued elsewhere Philip readily agreed to this looser wording despite the Wyatt rebellion being at its height at that very point.[64]

Gardiner's proposal to have the treaty ratified in the Netherlands and tensions over the more or less binding form of the oath, all suggest the extent to which the Spanish marriage had been conceptualised and negotiated as an Anglo-Netherlandish political arrangement. In late November, long before the finalisation of the terms, Mary of Hungary (preparing the ground for the treaty's ratification in the Netherlands) detailed the territorial splits that were embodied in the treaty if the marriage were to produce children:

> His Majesty had often considered how difficult it would be for them to hold out for a lengthy period against France and Germany unless they found support elsewhere, and the present war had made this quite clear. But now that God, in His divine bounty, had in a miraculous manner, as all knew, called to the throne of England his cousin, the Lady Mary, his Majesty had seen that it would be well for her on all accounts to marry, and had bethought him that the best way of making these countries safe would be to marry her to our Prince. The kingdom was very near, and if the marriage were blessed with children it would be possible to give them England and the Low Countries, leaving the Spanish dominions, the Italian states and the adjacent islands to the son of the first marriage. This would protect both countries and drive the French from the Ocean, which would be the best possible means of encouraging commerce, the foundation of the Low Countries' prosperity, and hold the French perpetually in check... Even if there were no children, the marriage would serve, as long as it lasted, to enable the Low Countries to send through England to Spain for help as often as need might arise.[65]

The agenda and political expedients the marriage served, adduced in the diplomatic correspondence of the autumn, are restated. It protected the Low Countries economically and strategically from the threat of both France and Germany, since with England's friendship the maritime link between Spain and the Netherlands could not be closed for either commerce or military aid. The Low Countries inheritance, however, was to be permanently alienated from the Spanish crown by the treaty.

Much has been made of the marginalisation of the Spanish from the negotiation of the treaty, in line with the sentiment expressed by Eraso. Nevertheless, Philip maintained independent contacts with Mary from the moment of her accession, sending his favourite, Iñigo de Mendoza y Mendoza (after 1566 the fifth duke of Infantado) with a letter to signify his happiness at her accession and enquire after her health.[66] His *mayordomo* Diego de Azevedo left Spain on 18th May and as we saw witnessed the entry and coronation of Mary in August and September, as did Antonio de Guaras, who described himself as her servant.[67] The notion of Philip's profound unwillingness to ratify and assent to the marriage rests on two pieces of evidence. The first is one of the most unusual documents found in the Spanish archives. On 4th January, eight days before the final treaty was signed in London, he drew up an 'Ad cautelam' document releasing himself from any obligation to be bound by the treaty's terms.[68] It cast him as swearing so that the marriage might be effectuated, but against his will so that he could not be bound by terms agreed before he had seen them. *Ad cautelam* can be loosely translated 'for security' or 'as a precaution' and is a legal instrument filed in advance of a future eventuality, calling into question a court's jurisdiction to enforce a particular contract or judgement. The only other example in the Spanish archives relates to the temporary truce signed with the Dutch rebels in 1579.[69] The concern expressed in the document surrounded articles that might burden his conscience or bind his heirs to observe them. One interpretation might be to suggest that the concessions made to England were so overwhelmingly favourable as to be unacceptable in Spain. However, the contract followed closely precedents familiar in both the Low Countries and Spain, not least the example of Isabel of Castile in her marriage contract with Ferdinand.[70] Furthermore, George Everett, in the English entourage sent to Spain to ratify the treaty, attested that 'all the whole realm of Spain doth much rejoice at the marriage of their prince... [and] bear her Majesty as much good will as their own prince', while Edward Dudley wrote to the Council about a banquet thrown by the duke of Albuquerque who 'did intertyne the yerll of warcestor and also all the roest of the inglishe gentillmen in as mache as he cold devise'.[71] It seems more likely than there being insurmountable opposition in Spain to the obviously advantageous union of Atlantic powers that in an uncertain world such a document gave Philip a legal basis for acting freely, should for example an heir prove intractable in relation to Habsburg priorities or some unexpected contingency such as a military emergency require him to take men, money and arms out of England.

One further interpretation might be that it was necessary to assuage his conscience, because he was already married, to his mistress since 1545, Isabel Osorio. She later claimed, according to the chronicler Luis Cabrera de Córdoba, to be the king's wife. Far less reliably, William of Orange accused Ruy Gomez in his *Apology* of having arranged their clandestine wedding.[72] This seems highly unlikely although evidence points to a relationship that lasted from 1545, perhaps until 1552. The most probable explanation was that Philip recognised that at 37 Mary might be unable to produce an heir, but then live another twenty or thirty years as her sister did, binding him to an heirless marriage. It offered a get-out clause, far short of expedients to which Henry VIII had resorted.

The second reason for alleging that Philip was reluctant to undertake the marriage was the delay between the settling of the legal formalities and his departure for England. The betrothal ceremony, at which Philip was represented by Egmont, took place on 6th March. Although the English ambassadors then departed immediately for Spain, they were delayed by bad weather and did not arrive in Valladolid until 8th May. Philip left Valladolid on 16th May on a lengthy progress to the coast, during which he visited his grandmother Juana 'la Loca'. He and his son Carlos were entertained at the Conde de Benavente's villa on 3rd June, with exotic spectacles that included an elephant ridden by an African whose dress imitated 'the Indians from the parts of Africa on the Ocean sea', followed by two castles, one made of fireworks with pediments sculpted in the shape of monkeys and the other carried on the shoulders of 'some savages most graciously made with a ferocious serpent almost on top'.[73] The earl of Bedford and Sir John Mason were waiting for Philip with a second set of capitulations when he reached Santiago on 23rd June.[74] A 'Copia de la ratificación por el Príncipe Felipe de sus capitulaciones matrimoniales con la Reina de Inglaterra', signed on 25th June 1554 at Santiago de Compostela, employed the long-sought-after formula 'matrimonium uerum, purum et legitimum *per uerba de presenti* in Anglia contrahat celebretur et consumatur'.[75] The ratification of the alliance renewed the treaties of friendship between the Low Countries and England: 'effectum nouissimi tractatus arctioris amcitiae et declarationem eiusdem, de dats Apud West monsterium Anno dni. MDXXXXII. quantum ad tractatum eet Traiesti Decimo sexto Januarii Anno dni. MDXXXXVI quantum ad declarationem'.[76] The preamble explained the rationale for the supplementary *capitulos*, preventing Philip from disposing of a personal patronage in England: 'against the future dangers and inconveniences which are accustomed sometimes to arise from diversity of nations and the mixing and admission of strangers'.[77] In June in England rates of exchange were fixed and through the mayor of Salisbury wine merchants were ordered to provide wine for ambassadors who drank only that.[78] Philip's envoy, the marquis de las Navas, reached Southampton on 11th June and met Mary at Guildford on the 17th, bearing her a ring from the bridegroom.

In addition to having to arrange funds for himself in accordance with his father's instructions, by February an additional 1 million ducats were being urgently demanded in the Low Countries. Mary of Hungary, writing to Philip on 4th February, repeated this no fewer than eight times in her letter, lamenting that these obligations 'have forced you to not be able to leave to come here as you might wish, and the difficulty that is encountered in finding the money required for your coming... [however] I can assure you that if these lands are not assisted you will lose them'.[79] The delays to Philip's journey to England were in large part a result of finance. The market had been decimated by political expropriations, including 4.5 million ducats from Castile that had left it chronically short of specie and Habsburg credit in ruins. Embarrassingly, when Mary asked Charles for money in the spring of 1554, the 200,000 ducat loan arranged through Sir Thomas Gresham and the Genoese bankers, Antonio Spinola and Federigo Imperallo, to be taken up at Villálon in Spain and repaid in Antwerp, could not be fulfilled.[80] Philip wrote on 12th June that 'the 200k ducats that the most serene Queen Mary took there on exchange and sent to be paid in Genoa and that from there these funds might be provided, I have already written to Your Majesty and there is no way of being able to pay them'.[81] Having looked at alternative sources of money to complete the exchanges, given that 'no remedy for providing the funds has been found', he suggested 'sending them from the funds that don Juan de Figueroa is bearing, and as the galleys that have come do not need to return to Italy for now, it seemed that the whole half million ought to be sent, from which Your Majesty can order the payment of the said 200k'.[82] A list of the debts assigned on Castilian revenues due for immediate settlement, included in the same letter, illustrated why 'there is no order or form of completing these transactions, the consignations which might be given will be over so long a period that the interest will add up to more than the principal'.[83] The letter concluded with an acknowledgement of receipt of letters from the emperor dated 27th April and the suggestion that the sum which 'Your Majesty orders be given to the most serene Queen Mary my aunt and be situated on Medina, Valladolid and Segovia, but given that the rents in those places have already been sold, there is nowhere to assign them' be reassigned in Seville, to be discharged at the Fair in Medina del Campo.[84] The reality of these problems is corroborated by a document in Florián de Ocampo's miscellany which recorded that:

> [a]ll the prices of things have doubled from their accustomed value... there was no money in public transactions, at least gold, not even one solitary piece, given that an uncountable quantity of gold comes constantly from the Indies, all passes over to Germany, to meet the unbearable expenses of his Majesty and the difficulties that the Germans place him in.[85]

The transaction arranged by Gresham, in theory instantaneous, was held up for months and the export licence for the money to be brought out of Spain was not granted by Philip until July. The unremitting requests for another 1 million ducats were simply impossible to meet.

Philip had been forced to send after the courier carrying the power for his espousal to the Infanta of Portugal on receiving the new proposal for marriage to Mary from his father in September. He claimed that he had ended the negotiations, unsatisfied with the dowry offered. In fact England was a clearly more advantageous offer, one he accepted with enthusiasm by breaking off the negotiations with Portugal and recalling his messenger at the very last moment.[86] While the Castilian crown's cession of the Low Countries to the prospective heir of the marriage might well have given pause for thought, his father's contemporary biographer, Prudencio de Sandoval, suggested that Philip's hesitation might have had more to do with the fact that the queen was ten years older and could not unfairly be described in contemporary terms as old: 'he could feel less pleasure, because although the queen was saintly, she was old and ugly, being already thirty-eight years old, while the king was young and gallant in the extreme, no more than twenty-seven. He acted in this like Isaac, allowing himself to be sacrificed to do his father's will and for the good of the church.'[87] Even if there was a growing sense of resistance to the match in some of his language, he clearly recognised its importance. In addition to the financial problems that had to be resolved before he could depart, Philip also needed to arrange a regency government. After his sister Juana's husband João was killed in a riding accident on 2nd January and she was safely delivered of their son on the 20th, he decided to appoint her regent. Philip met her near the Portuguese border in May. Extracting his recently widowed sister from the country whose Infanta he had just spurned, ensuring her sole appointment as regent in the face of Charles' opposition and passing on his instructions occupied him until then.[88] Moreover, if he had been that reluctant, the lavish expenditure fitting out the *El Espíritu Santo* with flags and banners, chests for arms, and armour, all bearing the conjoined arms of England and Spain, is hard to explain.[89]

According to the *Tower Chronicle*, by 'the beginning of Novembre was the furst notyce among the people towching the maryage of the quene to the king of Spayne'.[90] Renard had suspected by December the existence of a conspiracy and imminence of an uprising, an eventuality being monitored by Paget's spies.[91] When the 'Earl of Egmont, Charles de Laing and Sieur de Corriers', arrived to sign the treaty on 2nd January 1554, they were received coldly by the city of London:

> the people, nothing rejoysing, helde down their heddes sorowfully.

> The day befor his coming in, as his retynew and harbengers came ryding through London, the boys pelted theym with snowballes; so hatfull was the sight of ther coming in to theym.[92]

They dined with the council on the 9th and then rode to Hampton Court on the 10th, where they hunted and where on 12th January the treaty was signed. Its contents were officially proclaimed at Westminster on 14th January 'to the Lordes, nobilytye, and gentyllmen', by Stephen Gardiner, the Lord Chancellor. He explained: Mary 'partely for the welthe and enryching of the realme, and partely for frendeship and other waighty considerations, hathe, after moche suit on his (the king of Spaynes) behalf made, determyned, by the consent of hir counsaille and nobylyty, to matche herselfe with him'.[93] The bishop of Winchester drew attention to the fact that 'she should have for her joynter xxx[ml] ducketes by the yere, with all the Lowe Country of Flanders' and that according to the terms of the marriage Philip

> would vouchsaff so to humble himself, as in this maryadge to take apon him rather *as a subject* then otherwise; and that the quene shoulde rule all thinges as she doth nowe; and that ther should be of the counsell no Spanyard, nether should have custody of any fortes or castelles; nether bere rule or offyce in the quenes house, or elswhere in all Inglande.[94]

In order to safeguard English sovereignty, the treaty had enshrined Philip's subjection: as an English subject he would be subordinate to his wife as queen. The articles were declared to the people ('the mayre, sheryfes, and diverse of the best commoners'[95]) on the following day in the belief that disseminating the favourable terms would ameliorate mistrust and suspicion of the foreign match.

On 22nd January the Privy Council commanded 'the effect of the articles of the Treaty with Spain, to be declared to the people' at Plymouth,[96] with directions to 'suppress false and seditious rumours about the Prince of Spains coming'.[97] Their sources informed them the unrest there was such that active preparations were being undertaken to resist a Spanish landing. The French ambassador Noailles had received information about agitation in Plymouth as early as 23rd December.[98] The Cornishman John Colwyn, who had objected to a woman bearing the sword, heard that 'before New Year's Day outlandish men will come upon our lands, for there be some at Plymouth already'.[99] The account of Gardiner's declaration of the terms of the marriage treaty in the *Tower Chronicle* is followed by the comment that '[t]heis news, althoughe before they wer not unknown to many… was not onely credyted, but also hevely taken of sondery men, yea and therat allmost eche man was abashed, loking daylie for worse mattiers to growe shortly after'.[100] On 6th December 1553, just before the dissolution of parliament, an anonymous member of the Commons pointed in the debate on the queen's marriage to its equivocal and uncertain status given its dual nature as an alliance between both the natural persons of the monarchs and the political estates of their kingdoms.

> In case…. the Bands should be broken between the Husband and the Wife, either of them being Princes in their own Country, who shall sue the Bands?

Who shall take the Forfeit? Who shall be their Judges? And what shall be the Advantage?[101]

As both private contract and international treaty, it created difficulties that were intertwined with the problem of the asymmetric roles and inequality of men and women in married relationships. The expectation that Philip would exercise authority as Mary's husband undermined the credibility of the articles that sought to limit his power in England as king. The fundamental problem would be enforceability.

According to the first page of the treaty of marriage, Philip was to enjoy 'ioyntely togeder with the said most noble Quene his wif, the state honour and kyngly name of the Realme and Dominions unto the said most noble Quene apperteyning And shall ayde that same most noble Quene his wif in the prosperous administration of the realmes and Dominions'.[102] A special provision followed: he 'shall leave unto the said Lady his wief Quene Mary those dispositions of all the benefits and offices, lands revenues and fruicts of the said Realmes and Dominions and that they shallbe disposed to suche as be naturalle bourne in the same', and that everything 'shallbe treated, mayntayned and used... as of olde they have been wonte to be treated there, and by the naturall bourne of the same'.[103] While being excluded from exercising independent powers of patronage with English royal lands, income or appointments, the treaty specifically envisaged his aiding Mary in the prosperous administration of the realm and enjoying the honour, title and name of king. The first clause of the additional articles, attached to the main treaty, similarly stipulated that Philip was not to 'permite admitte or receive to eny office administration or benefyce... any stranger or foreign borne'.[104] Offices, benefices and other sinecures were one of the main ways monarchs bound subjects to them; excluding him from these decisions was an attempt to prevent Philip from gaining influence and building a political power base to rival Mary's by rewarding faithful servants with key positions. The pensions and rewards he distributed to English servants were all drawn from Spanish revenues at an estimated cost of £5,600 a year.[105] The question was where the line between exercising power in name of the joint authority of Philip and Mary shaded into his doing so in his own name alone.

The treaty as a whole responded to the same perceived problem posed by common law inheritance patterns being taken to apply in the case of a regnant queen's title. Renard reported on 7th January 1554 that, according to what he had heard from 'two English lawyers', 'if his Highness marries the Queen, she loses her title to the Crown and his Highness becomes King, so that if children are born to the couple, the oldest will not be King, but his Highness will continue in that position'.[106] If women's status and estate in common law applied to Mary, then her patrimony and so patronage would pass to Philip on their marriage with both her political and property rights transferred to him to exercise in her name.[107] Even though this might be specifically provided against in the marriage treaty, custom, precedent and social expectations might undermine the treaty's contractual provisions. The problem arose from uncertainty concerning the precise relationship between constitutional and common law. The marriage confronted complex issues about the relationship between the sovereign and political estate. How was a kingdom held? If a crown was like freehold estate, then it was subject to testamentary disposition. Henry and Edward both attempted to will the crown to heirs of their chosing. When Henry had sought legal advice over Mary's betrothal to Charles V and the future status of the crown, he had been informed that it was not encompassed by the law of courtesy (according to which husbands might enjoy the political rights of their spouses although not transmit them if living offspring had been born to the couple) but that she could grant him the title and style of the political title if she chose to do so.[108]

Since the Conquest queens had been recognised as sharers in the royal power, *regalis imperii participem*, able to issue charters and take over regencies.[109] However they had never been recognised in their own right. A crowned queen regnant was unprecedented in English history. Mary was an anomaly. The *de facto* political power and patronage exercised by a small number of women by virtue of royal birth and high status contradicted the general disqualification and exclusion of women from even the most basic political privileges. As Christopher Goodman argued in 1558: '[y]f women be not permitted by Ciuile policies to rule in inferior offices, to be Counsellours, Pears of a realme, Iustices, Shireffs, Bayliues and such like: I make your selves iudges, whither it be mete for them to gouerne whole Realmes and nations?'[110] This contradiction was reflected by Juan Luis Vives' tract, the *De Institutione Christianae Feminae*, written for Mary and dedicated to her mother Catherine, in its simultaneous advocacy of female education and condemnation of women's participation in public life. He praised Catherine with her sisters for 'there were no quenes by anye mannes remembraunce more chast of bodye thanne they'.[111] The preeminent female virtue was chastity, a function of women's importance as guarantors of primogenital legitimacy. In spite of Catherine's chastity, Vives continued, 'woman's thought is swift, and for the most part, unstable, walking and wandering out from home, and some will slide by of it[s] own slipperiness, I wot not how far'.[112] His celebration of his patron as a type of domestic piety ignored the important political role that she had played, especially early in Henry's reign, when she had acted as regent while he was fighting in France, conducting a successful campaign against the Scots, which culminated in the defeat of James IV at Flodden. She was also the accredited Spanish ambassador in England.

Although *mores* and social expectations of women in the early modern period opposed their occupation of positions in the public sphere, there were numerous precedents of powerful and politically influential women, including Mary I's contemporaries Mary of Hungary, regent of the Netherlands, Philip's 19-year-old sister Juana, who became regent of Castile during his absence, and Mary of Guise, regent of Scotland. In 1560, England, Scotland and France were all being ruled by women.[113] Royal status and kinship entailed political responsibility. On setting aside her regency Mary of Hungary claimed 'given her inferiority to him in every respect, and the fact that she is a woman… a woman is never feared or respected as a man is, whatever her rank' and especially in times of war 'it is entirely impossible for a woman to govern satisfactorily'.[114] There was a contradiction between the general disenfranchisement of women and the high-ranking positions enjoyed by some by virtue of dynasticism, blood and maternity. As Mary of Hungary recognised, the martial nature of noble culture could not easily be drawn upon by a regnant queen: '[j]ustice and defense, long celebrated in the iconography of the great seal, were both seen to be dependent upon military might'.[115] The zenith of a king's representative function was as a military leader: 'as in warre where the king himselfe in person, the nobilitie, the rest of the gentilitie, and the yeomanrie is, there is the force and power of Englande'.[116] The moment when Mary was girt with sword and spurs during her coronation was dwelt on in both the heralds' account and the tract published in Castile in the spring of 1554. Once in England Philip assiduously cultivated this aspect of the kingly role, developing his martial image by promoting and participating in a series of martial entertainments from jousting to foot tourneys, indigenous *juegos de cañas* and even a proposed bullfight which never took place.[117]

The second clause in the additional articles of the treaty required Philip to extend offices in his household to Englishmen: 'the said noble prince shall receyve and admitt unto the service of his householde and courte gentlemen and yeomen of the said Realme of Englande in a convenyent nomber'.[118] Discontent among his Castilian subjects had forced Charles to make identical concessions in 1520. These two stipulations had both been echoed in the marriage contract of Philip's great-grandparents, Ferdinand and Isabella, which had stated: 'Item that none be placed in the Council of those kingdoms saving only Castilians and natural born of the same with the consent and determined deliberation of her said most serene highness… and that the placement of any officials, saving always that such are chosen by her and be natural born and not foreigners of those kingdoms'.[119] In addition Ferdinand swore on 1st October 1469 in Zaragoza: 'I will not grant favour of any kind or extent in relation to the concession of vassals, fortresses, offices, rents or rights for life or a limited period, as aforesaid, in the said kingdoms of Castile and Leon'.[120] Ferdinand

and Isabella's situation was analogous to that of Philip and Mary, except that Isabella was only an heiress to the kingdom of Castile when she married the foreign Ferdinand. Along with the condition, if no progeny resulted from the marriage, 'that Isabel may possess and hold them... after her days all those lands as much those annexed as those improved as all others may return to us and our heirs to whom by right they belong'.[121] Mary's aunt Juana, the queen unfortunately dubbed 'the Mad', succeeded her mother as queen, not her father Ferdinand, who had been the co-ruler of Castile since 1474. She ruled in her own right for a period of five years, before being slowly deprived of political authority in a conspiracy of her closest male relatives, including her father, husband and nephew – a cautionary tale for England's new queen in 1553.[122]

Surrounding Philip with English courtiers was an attempt to tie his international interests to more localised ones. It also made the match more attractive to the nobility by opening up rewarding positions in his household. But what was a 'convenyent nomber'? The interpretation of this part of the treaty became a source of significant tension between English and Spanish courtiers during Philip's time in England. One Castilian courtier complained 'we all wander around like vagabonds being unneeded'.[123] Ruy Gomez da Silva expressed the problem more tactfully in a letter to Francisco Eraso on 26th July 1554: 'another great inconvenience has arisen and that is that before his Highness arrived here they had prepared a household with officials high and low in which there are a Master of the Horse, Grand Chamberlain and Gentlemen of the Chamber and from there down all the officials and a guard of an hundred archers [who] if any of us wants to lend a hand in something, they take it ill and do not wish to allow it'.[124] On the other hand Thomas Radclyffe, Lord Fitzwalter, one of the envoys who had travelled to Spain and then became a gentleman of the king's privy chamber, complained he had so little access to the king that his fluent Spanish was getting worse. Renard reported that 'the people say the King will not be served by Englishmen although this point was settled by the articles'.[125] Tensions and jealousies between his English and Spanish households spilled over into violence in the early months of the marriage leading to a number of fatalities.

The treaty's financial arrangements granted Mary a dower of 'three score thousande pounds' at a fixed exchange rate of 'forty grots flemmyshe money the pounde'; of which two-thirds, i.e. £40,000, were to be assigned upon the realms of 'Spayne Castiel and Aragond' and the remaining third on Brabant, Flanders, Seymour, Holland and nether Germany 'in like mannier as the Ladye Margarete of England sumtyme wief and widow of the Lorde Charles of laudable memorie Duke of Burgundye'.[126] The main treaty concluded by stating that between Charles V, Philip and their successors and Mary there shall be 'an entier and syncere fraternitie unitie and most forthright confederacie forever', an accord to do 'in all thinges which to themselfe and their honour, and to the conservation and encrease of thier astats, realmes families countries Dominions and of their heirs and successours shalbe most agreable according to the strength and effort' of the Anglo-Imperial treaties concluded in 1542 and 1546.[127] These treaties were highly significant in the context of the marriage, as we have seen. Their centrality was reinforced by an anonymous Castilian account of the 'Marriage of Philip II in England, 1554, with Mary daugher of Henry and Catherine' which specifically alluded to 'the agreement made in Westminster in 1542 and treaty signed in Utrecht on 16th January 1546 be[ing] especially respected'.[128] The Italian papal diplomat Commendone's report on his secret mission also alluded to the fact that 'all agreements and conventions be confirmed which were made in the past, especially the last alliance made at Westminster the year of 1542 which was published at Utrecht the xvi January 1546'.[129] Proposals for further liturgical reform in Henrician England had been shelved when prospects of agreement with Charles over a joint invasion of France had improved on the back of the 1542 agreement: Henry had informed his bishops that there was not to be 'any other innovation, change or altera-tion, either in Religion or ceremony'.[130] By 1544, the clock had begun to be turned back with his conservative reversal of religious policy, the Act of Six Articles.

The marriage contract concluded by insisting 'the said noble Prince shall nothyng do, wherby any thing be innovate in the state and right publique or private and in the lawes and customes of the said Realme of Englande or the Dominions thereupon depending'.[131] An advice manual, probably by Stephen Gardiner, dedicated to Philip in 1555, reiterated that 'of all other things nothing generates greater hate for the prince than defying the ancient laws observed in any kingdom': 'it is an extreme grief to men of any nation or province to see other men, foreigners, possess those honours, offices and dignities which in past times their father or predecessors had enjoyed, and to see their own children deprived of them without cause'.[132] In 1510 the French bishop and Chancellor Claude de Seyssel had written '[a]ll nations and reasonable men prefer to be governed by men of their own country and nation, who share the same language as them... rather than by strangers'.[133] The reasoning enshrined in the precedent of 1609 (not repealed until 1870), by which strangers were disqualified from holding land in England, merely reformulated the terms of a debate already implicit in the treaty: without such disqualifications the 'revenues of the realm (the sinews of war and ornament of peace) should be taken and enjoyed by strangers born'.[134] The fears of the Council were visible throughout the treaty. It might seem unnecessary, but Philip was specifically prohibited from removing 'jewels and preciouse things of grete estimacion nor also shall alienate or do away any white of thapperteyning of the said Realme'.[135] Forts and frontiers were to be maintained by natural-born Englishmen. Ships, guns and ordnance were similarly not to be exported.

Suspicions of aliens were not exclusive to the English and in the context of the marriage were a response to the specific problem of female rule; a realistic expectation that a foreign dynast might attempt to appropriate a kingdom through such a marriage or inheritance transmitted through the female line. Anxieties about a female succession and foreign marriage had haunted Tudor England since before the death of Henry VIII. His third Succession Act had made the right of female heirs to succeed contingent on conciliar consent to any marriage that might take place. Similarly, here the contract stipulated that heirs female would be subject in matrimonial questions to the consent of Philip's son and heir in Castile, Carlos: 'if she take any man to husbande that is not borne in Englande or in the lower Germanye neglecting the counsaill and consent of the said Lorde Charles In that cace the right of succession shallbe and remayne to the saide Lorde Charles'.[136] Succession was central to the problem of female rule. Mary was already 37 at the time of her accession and had a history of gynaecological illness. Her decision to marry a foreign prince exacerbated problems already implicit in her gender. Death in childbirth was common and infant mortality high. In the event of a long regency following Mary's death in childbirth, it would have been impossible to curtail Philip's power.

Heirs born of the marriage were, therefore, subjected to the will of the English nobility and not Philip. Their consent was required for the residence or education of Mary's children outside England: he shall not 'carry the children that shalbe borne of this matrymonie out of the same realme of England, but shall there suffer them to be nourished and brought upp, onlie it shal otherwise be thought good to be done by the consent and agreament of the nobilitie of England' and Mary was also to remain there 'unles she her selfe desire it'.[137] The contract warned Philip not to claim any right to the throne or interfere in the succession after Mary's death:

> And in the cace that no children being lefte, the moost noble Lady the Quene dothe dye before hym The said Lorde Prince shal not chalenge unto him any right at all in the saide Kingdom but without any impedyment shal permitt the succession thereof to come unto them to whome it shall belong and appetayn.[138]

The penultimate paragraph of the main body of the treaty provided that it was

> expressly forseen and reserued about all and singuler the aboue declared cases of sucession, that whosoever he or she be that shall sucede in them, they shall have to ensure the said Realmes lands and Dominions whole and entire thier privileage righte and customs, and the same realmes and Dominions shall

administer and cause to be administered by the naturall borne of the said
realmes and Dominions and lands and in all thinge faithfully promise thier
utilitie and quyet and in good justice and peace shal rule and nourishe them
acoording to their statutes and customes.[139]

While the fear of Mary's disenfranchisement through subjection to a foreign
husband was apparent throughout the treaty and the anti-Spanish propaganda
casting the marriage as a sexual conquest or betrayal, a despoliation and foreign
colonisation (Wingfield recorded the Wyatt rebels' allegation that they had
been 'overwhelmed by a Spanish whore'),[140] Charles brushed aside all such
quibbles as he looked forward to his abdication and retirement to Yuste,
confidently stating that 'England is also on the way to Spain'.[141]

Notes

1 Real Biblioteca del Monasterio de San Lorenzo de El Escorial MS V. ii. 4, fol. 434v: 'que
   beneficio tan grande succederia a nuestra España en detener al Frances con estar estos Reynos
   y los de su Magestad vnos y aun que no fuese por mas de por conseruer los estados de
   Flandes'. Two editions of the pamphlet by Guaras offering an account of Mary's accession and
   then coronation appeared in March 1554: *Relacion muy verdadera de Antonio de Guaras: criado de
   la Serenissima y Catholica reyna de Inglaterra: al Illustre S. Duque de Alburquerque: Visorrey y Capitan
   General del Reyno de Nauarra &c. En la qual se trata en que miserias y calamidades y muertes de grandes
   ha estado el reyno tantos años ha Como doña Maria fue proclamada por Reyna y de todos obedescida y
   de su coronacion &c.* (Medina del Campo: Mateo and Francisco del Canto, 3rd March 1554).
   The other edition was printed at Álcala by Atanasio Salzedo, who also printed one of the four
   simultaneous earliest extant editions of *Lazarillo de Tormes* in the same period.
2 Real Biblioteca del Monasterio de San Lorenzo de El Escorial, MS V. ii. 4, fol. 434v: 'porque
   no son muy deuotos de nuestra nacion segun algunos dizen' although 'tienen amor a su
   Magestad y a España specialmente por el amor que tuuieron a la buena Reyna Catholica'.
3 See the fascinating study of medieval regnant queens and their fortunes by Elena Woodacre,
   'The Queen's marriage: matrimonial politics in premodern Europe', in Jacqueline Murray,
   ed., *Marriage in Premodern Europe: Italy and Beyond* (Toronto: Centre for Reformation and
   Renaissance Studies, 2012), 29–48.
4 Cited in Margaret Sommerville, *Sex and Subjection: Attitudes to Women in Early Modern Society*
   (London: Arnold, 1995); see chapter 3, 'Exceptional Women', 40–78, p. 52.
5 *Cal. Ven.*, VII, p. 328.
6 E. H. Harbison, *Rival Ambassadors at the Court of Queen Mary* (New York: Books for Libraries
   Press, 1940, repr. 1970), p. 64, note 12. Original in *Affaires Etrangères* IX, fol. 494: 'Tous
   ceux qui ont escrit l'humeur des peuples insulaires les ont générallement blasmez de légerité
   et inconstance', but 'pardessus tous autres ceux qui habitent cette isle ont esté griefvement
   reprins de mensonge et de tout diversité'.
7 BNE MS 1091, fols 44v and 48r: 'avnque aquella parte de ynglaterra que esta fazia françia por
   ventura tañe la postrimera parte del clima seteno pero la mayor parte de ynglaterrra es fuera
   de los ssiete climas', 'assy bretaña ynsula del mar oçeano apartada esta de todo el mundo y la
   tiene la mar puesta en medio de si y del. Et assy paresçe que fablando propiamente ynglaterra
   esta fuera del mundo'. I have discussed this material elsewhere: see 'A fine romance: Anglo-
   Spanish relations in the sixteenth century', *Journal of Medieval and Early Modern Studies* 39
   (2009), 65–94.
8 Johann Boemus, *El libro de las costumbres y maneras de vivir de todas las gentes, el qual traduzia y
   copilaua el Bachiller Thamara Cathedratico de Cadiz*, trans. Francisco Tamara (Antwerp: Martin

Nutius, 1556), sig. 40r: '[e]sta es de todas partes cercada de la mar, y por ninguna parte junta con la tierra firme, mas totalmente apartada de nuestro mundo'. BNE R–13359.

9 Boemus, *El libro de las costumbres*, sigs 15r–v: 'nunca fueron subjetos al ymperio Romano ni a otro alguno', whereas 'el primero Rey de ynglaterra reçibio el Regno de los Romanos so tributo', however, 'todos concuerdan que çerca de nuestros dias los Reyes de ynglaterra tienen el Reyno en feudo de la eglesia'.

10 Johann Boemus, *The fardle of facions conteining the aunciente maners, customes, and lawes, of the peoples enhabiting the two partes of the earth, called Affrike and Asie*, trans. William Watreman (London: John Kingston and Henry Sutton, 1555).

11 John W. McKenna, 'How God became an Englishman', in Delloyd J. Guth and J. W. McKenna, eds, *Tudor Rule and Revolution: Essays for G. R. Elton from his American friends* (Cambridge: Cambridge University Press, 1982), p. 29. Charles d'Orléans(?), *Le debat des heraulx darmes de frānce et d'engleterre* (Rouen: Richard Azoult for Thomas Iaisne, 1515?) [BL C.32.g.4], another edition (Paris: widow of Jean Trepperel, 1520) and John Coke, *The debate betwene the heraldes of Englande and Fraunce, compyled by Ihoñ Coke, clarke of the kynges recognysaunce, or vulgerly, called clarke of the statutes of the staple of Westmynster, and fynyshed the yere of our Lorde. M.D.L* (London: Robert Wyer for Richard Wyer, 1550). Both dates are significant, with the Anglo-French treaty of 1514 and the Field of the Cloth of Gold in 1520 straddling the original French editions and the outbreak of hostilities in 1549 followed by an uneasy peace in 1550 coinciding with Coke's translation. It is possible that this Coke was a relation of the more famous Sir John Coke, but there is no evidence linking them.

12 Simon Fish, *A Supplicacyon for the Beggers* (London: n. p., n. d., 1529?), sig. `3v. See also Howard Norland, *Drama in Early Tudor Britain 1485–1558* (Lincoln: University of Nebraska Press, 1995), p. 189.

13 On this see David Scott Kastan, ' "Holy wurdes" and "slypper wit": John Bale's *King Johan* and the poetics of propaganda' in Peter Herman, ed., *Rethinking the Henrician Era: Essays on Early Tudor Texts and Contexts* (Urbana: University of Illinois Press, 1994), 267–82, p. 269 and Carole Levin, *Propaganda in the English Reformation: Heroic and Villainous Images of King John* (Lewiston, Maine: Edwin Mellen Press, 1988), chapter 3, 'The Creation of the Heroic Images', 55–104.

14 See McKenna, 'How God became an Englishman', p. 31.

15 See McKenna, 'How God became an Englishman', p. 26.

16 David Loades, *The Tudor Court* (Totowa, NJ: Barnes & Noble Books, 1987), p. 29.

17 Dale Hoak, 'The iconography of the crown imperial' in *Tudor Political Culture* (Cambridge: Cambridge University Press, 1995), pp. 60 and 72.

18 Walter Ullmann, 'This realm of England is an empire', *Journal of Ecclesiastical History* 30 (1979), 175–204.

19 A. F. Pollard, *The History of England From the Accession of Edward VI to the Death of Elizabeth (1547–1603)*, The Political History of England, 12 vols (London: Longmans, Green and Co., 1915), vol. 6, p. 172.

20 On these developments see John Edwards and Ronald Truman, eds, *Reforming Catholicism in the England of Mary Tudor: The Achievement of Friar Bartolomé Carranza* (Aldershot: Ashgate, 2005); William Wizeman, *The Theology and Spirituality of Mary Tudor's Church* (Aldershot: Ashgate, 2006); Eamon Duffy, *Fires of Faith: Catholic England under Mary Tudor* (London: Yale University Press, 2009); David Loades, *The Religious Culture of Marian England* (London: Pickering & Chatto, 2010); and John Edwards, *Archbishop Pole* (Farnham: Ashgate, 2014).

21 *Cal. Span.*, XI, p. 118. Ambassadors to Mary I, 24th July 1553. Vienna, Imperial Archive E. Varia, 5. Their belief that the expulsion of religious refugees should be central to Mary's strategy for consolidating her power was evident when they wrote to the Emperor a couple of weeks later, explaining '[i]t was difficult to remedy the state of religion without the (sanction of) Parliament, particularly because of the number of foreigners, Frenchmen, Germans and Flemings, exiled and thrust out of their own countries for heresy and other crimes, who fearing that if religion were restored they would be compelled to leave the country,

would do nothing except seek opportunities for troubling the Queen's reign': *ibid.*, p. 169. Ambassadors to the Emperor, 16th August 1553.

22 *Cal. Span.*, XI, p. 179. Emperor to ambassadors, 23rd August 1553, Brussels.

23 Christopher Haigh, *English Reformations: Religion, Politics and Society under the Tudors* (Oxford: Clarendon Press, 1993), pp. 222 and 289.

24 Geoffrey Parker, *Felipe II: La biografía definitiva* (Madrid: Planeta, 2010), p. 105.

25 Peter Barber, 'England II: monarchs, ministers, and maps, 1550–1625', in David Buisseret, ed., *Monarchs, Ministers and Maps: The Emergence of Cartography as a Tool of Government in Early Modern Europe* (Chicago and London: University of Chicago Press, 1992), 57–98, p. 62.

26 On this see my article 'Mapping the marriage: Thomas Geminus's *Britanniae Insulae Nova Descriptio* and *Nova Descriptio Hispaniae* (1555)', *Renaissance and Reformation* 31 (2008), 95–115.

27 *Cal. Span.*, XI, p. 179. My italics. See Chapter 1, note 39, and *Cal. Span*, XI, p. 64.

28 *Cal. Span.*, XI, p. 217. Ambassadors to Emperor, 9th September 1553.

29 *Cal. Span.*, XI, p. 228.

30 Calvete de Estrella, *El felicissimo viaje del muy alto y muy poderoso Príncipe don Phelippe*, ed. José María de Francisco Olmos and Paloma Cuenca (Madrid: Sociedad Estatal para la Conmemoración de los Centenarios de Felipe II y Carlos V, 2001), pp. 610 and 619: 'desplugó a los naturales... era su Alteza demasiado grave y desconversable'. David Loades, *Politics, Censorship and the English Reformation* (London: Pinter Publications, 1991), p. 41.

31 M. J. Rodríguez-Salgado, *The Changing Face of Empire: Charles V, Philip II and Habsburg Authority, 1551–1559*, Cambridge Studies in Early Modern History (Cambridge: Cambridge University Press, 1988), pp. 44–5, and Jean Bérenger, *A History of the Habsburg Empire 1273–1700*, trans. C. Simpson (London: Longman, 1994), p. 175.

32 Cesare Malfatti, ed. and trans., *The Accession, Coronation and Marriage of Mary Tudor as related in Four Manuscipts of the Escorial* (Barcelona: Sociedad Alianza de Artes Graficas y Ricardo Fontá, 1956), p. 38.

33 John Ponet, *A Warnyng for Englande / Conteynyng the horrible practices of the kyng of Spayne / in the kyngs dome of Naples / and the miseries whereunto that noble Realme is brought. Wherby all Englishe men may understand the plage that shall light upon them if the kyng of Spayn obteyne the Dominion in Englande* (Emden: E. van der Erve, 15–20th November 1555).

34 Real Biblioteca del Monasterio de San Lorenzo de El Escorial, MS V.ii.3, fols 486r–v, 'Relación de las cosas de Inglaterra desde el Rey Henrico hasta la Reina Maria su hija': 'Los de la Isla naturalmente son enemigicissmus de estrangeros a causa de salir muy poco de su tierra y assi acogen a otros mal en ella'; the 'mugeres son muy feas y vistense y tocanse peor que en Flandes a aquel modo'.

35 Biblioteca del Palacio Real, MS II 2318 *Correspondencia de Granvela*, fols 283v–285r: 'los Ingleses vengan con mayor dificultad a consentir el casamiento y tanto mas pues naturalmente aborrecen estangeros'. Granvelle, bishop of Arras to Cardinal de Jaén, 3rd February 1554.

36 *Cal. Span.*, XI, p. 338. Renard to Emperor, 6th November 1553.

37 Joan M. Thomas, 'Before the Black Legend: sources of anti-Spanish sentiment in England 1553–1558', unpublished PhD thesis (University of Michigan, 1984), p. 57.

38 *Cal. Span.*, XI, p. 339.

39 On the vagaries of Gardiner's reputation see Michael Riordan and Alec Ryrie, 'Stephen Gardiner and the making of a Protestant villain', *Sixteenth Century Journal* 34 (2003), 1039–63. Courtenay's mother Gertrude was Mary's bedfellow in the early part of the reign; see David Loades, *Intrigue and Treason: The Tudor Court 1547–1558* (London: Pearson, 2004), p. 146.

40 *Cal. Span.*, XI, pp. 347–8. Simon Renard to Emperor, 8th November 1553.

41 John Christopherson, *An exhortation to all menne to take hede and beware rebellion* (London: John Cawood, 24th July 1554), sig. Niii.

42 Henry Kamen, *Felipe de España*, trans. Patricia Escandón (Madrid: Siglo Venitiuno de España Editores, SA, 1997), p. 43.

43 Calvete de Estrella, *El felicissimo Viaje*, sig. 244v: 'Al Inuictissimo Carlos Maximo Emperador

Cesar/Augusto, y al Gran Phelippe su Hijo Principe delas/Españas, por su dichosa y muy deseada venida a/esta Ciudad, y por la perpetua constancia dela amis-/tad y confederacion, que hasta agora han tenido con/los Reyes de Inglaterra, los Mercaderes Ingleses y/negociantes en esta esclarecida Villa, leuantaron la/grandeza d'este arco en testimonio de su deuida gra-/tulacion y alegria'. Calvete de Estrella was Greek and Latin tutor to Philip in the 1540s.

44 Calvete de Estrella, *El felicissimo Viaje*, sig. 243r: 'teniendo respeto al nombre antiguo, que fue Albion, llamada assi, o d'el gigante Albion hijo de Neptuno, o de la abundancia, que tiene de piedras blancas'.

45 Calvete de Estrella, *El felicissimo Viaje*, sig. 243r: 'dos illustrissimas personas, que auian sido Ingleses'.

46 Hoak, 'The iconography of the crown imperial', p. 83.

47 Calvete de Estrella, *El felicissimo Viaje*, sig. 244v: 'que se dauan las manos derechas en señal de perpetua amistad, concordia y liga'.

48 Calvete de Estrella, *El felicissimo Viaje*, fol. 244v: 'enemigo dela Religion Christiana', 'a semejanca d'ello estaua pintado el Principe Don Phelippe, que peleaua con los Turcos y Moros'. The Latin is translated in the text: 'Con la misma señal, que vencio el gran Constantino, dize la Parca Cloto tambien en los tiempos venideros triumphará delos Barbaros el gran Principe Don Phelippe'.

49 *Cal. Span.*, XI, p. 333. Renard to Emperor, 4th November 1553.

50 *Cal. Span.*, XI, pp. 363–4. This incident is also detailed in Diarmaid MacCulloch, 'The *Vitae Mariae Angliae Reginae* of Robert Wingfield of Brantham', *Camden Miscellany* XXVIII, 4th ser. (London: Royal Historical Society, UCL, 1984), p. 277.

51 *Cal. Span.*, XI, p. 364. Renard to Emperor, 17th November 1553.

52 *Cal. Span.*, XI, p. 412. Renard to Emperor, 11th December 1553.

53 *Cal. For.*, 1553–58, p. 32.

54 *Cal. Span.*, XI, pp. 425–6. Renard to Emperor, 11th December 1553.

55 AGS E 98, fols 274–5, 'Memorial que embio Francisco Duarte de lo que le dixo Nicolas Nicolai, September 1553': 'las emerroidas se le hinchan y atormentan con tantos dolores que no se puede rodear syn gran sentimiento y lagrimas y estas cosas juntadas con las pasiones del espiritu. que an sido muy grandes y ordinarias le an mudado la condiçion y buena gracia que solia tener y la afabilidad y se le a todo conuertido en tanto humor malencolico que es siempre diz que esta pensatiuo y muchas vezes y ratos llorando tan de veras y con tanto derramiento de lagrimas como sy fuera una criatura', 'ni quiere oyr negocios ni firmar los pocos que se despachan, entiendo y ocupandose dia y noche en ajustar y concertar sus relojes, que son hartos, y tiene con ellos la principal quenta'. *Cal. Span.*, XI, pp. 221ff., see reference to Azevedo on p. 226.

56 Charles Weiss, ed., *Papiers d'état du Cardinal de Granvelle*, 9 vols (Paris: Imprimerie Royale, 1843), vol. 4, pp. 78, 144 and 149–51. There is interesting information about the power struggle between Renard and Eraso for control of the English mission in a letter of 3rd September 1554: *ibid.*, pp. 298–300.

57 AGS E 807, fol. 40: 'flaqueza, no gana de comer', 'por nuestros pecados no yra ningun spañol puesto que miro mucho a la honra de la nacion por como el negocio se haga sea por quiera y a Joan Vazquez scriuo que haga relacion a V. Al:'.

58 *Grey Friars Chronicle*, p. 86.

59 Thomas, 'Before the Black Legend', p. 58.

60 AGS E 807, fol. 37, no. 2 and fol. 42: 'aunque han replecado en dos o tres cosas no son de momento y su Alte. las concede de buena voluntad', 'quanto a la mudanca que han hecho nuestros puntos por no nos poner conellos en disputa y mayormente que no hauemos hallado cosa que no sea fundada en razon nos ha parescido por mejor de los aceptar sin poner alteracion alguna como vos lo podeys declarar juntamente con los otros nuestro embaxadores quando alla llegaren cuya partida apresuramos lo mas que ser pueda'.

61 AGS E 98, fol. 374v: 'estouieredes desposado por palabras de presente o de futuro que en qualquier destos casos lo haueys de hazer'.

62 AGS E 808, fol. 119: 'parecieron tan iustificados e razonables que luego se concluyo la capitulacion, es firmada, e auctorizada la han embiado para que la confirme, e ratifique, e assi lo he hecho'. *Cal. Span.*, XII, p. 36.
63 AGS E 808, fol. 119: 'el vno para que se haga el desporio por palabras de presente, e el otro de futuro que todauia parece que estan en esto vltimo: porque pretenden que al tiempo que con la bendicion de nuestro señor, os ayais de casar, jureis e aprobeis la dicha capitulacion e guardar las leyes e fueros de aquel Reyno. Pero la dicha Serenissima Reyna confidentemente asegura que en lo secreto se efectuara a nuestra voluntad (como lo tenemos por cierto)'. *Cal. Span.*, XII, p. 36. In the *Calendar* it suggests that Mary 'assures us that in secret it shall be done according to *your* desire, and we trust her word'. Philip's marginal comment: 'esta ratificacion de la capitulacion se haga porque yo la otorgue y baya con el marques de las nabas al qual alcanzaria vn correo con todos los despachos para su mt.'.
64 Alexander Samson, 'Power sharing: the co-monarchy of Philip and Mary', in Alice Hunt and Anna Whitelock, eds, *Tudor Queenship: The Reigns of Mary and Elizabeth* (New York: Palgrave Macmillan, 2010), p. 163.
65 *Cal. Span.*, XI, p. 386. 'A Proposal to be made by the Emperor to the principal Lords and members of the Council of State', 25th November 1553, Brussels.
66 AGS E 807, fol. 11.
67 AGS E 98, fols 184r and 201r.
68 AGS E 807 fol. 36. *Cal. Span.*, XII, pp. 4–6. This was enclosed with a copy of the marriage contract and witnessed by the Duke of Alba, Ruy Gomez da Silva, *et al.*, on 4th January 1554, Valladolid.
69 Personal communication with Professor Geoffrey Parker.
70 Samson, 'Power sharing', p. 161. An oppposing view is expressed by Glyn Redworth, 'A family at war? King Philip I of England and Habsburg dynastic politics' in Franz Bosbach, ed., *Prinz-Albert-Gesellschaft/Prince Albert Society* (Coburg: Prinz-Albert-Gesellschaft, 2008), 1–20, p. 5.
71 Cited by Sarah Duncan, '"He to be intituled Kinge": King Philip of England and the Anglo-Spanish court', in Charles Beem and Miles Taylor, eds, *The Man Behind the Queen: Male Consorts in History,* Queenship and Power Series (New York: Palgrave Macmillan, 2014), 55–80, p. 57. [Original: National Archives, SP 69/4/204.]
72 Parker, *Felipe II*, pp. 80–1. See also Kamen, *Felipe de España*, p. 55.
73 Andrés Muñoz, *Viaje de Felipe Segundo a Inglaterra (Zaragoza, 1554) y Relaciones Varias Relativas al Mismo Suceso*, ed. Pascual de Gayángos and Manuel Zarco del Valle (Madrid: La Sociedad de Bibliófilos Españoles, 1877), p. 45: 'los Indios de las partes de Africa del mar oceano'/'vnos saluajes graciosamente hechos con vna sierpe muy feroz quasi encima'. The three letters also printed with this volume are thought to be by Philip's steward, Pedro Enriquez. On Philip's progress and reception see Martin Hume, 'The visit of Philip II', *English Historical Review* VII (1892), 253–280 and more recently Teofilo Ruiz, *A King Travels: Festive Traditions in Late Medieval and Early Modern Spain* (Princeton, NJ: Princeton University Press, 2012), pp. 1–33.
74 Kamen, *Felipe de España*, p. 56 and David Loades, *The Reign of Mary Tudor: Politics, Government and Religion in England 1553–1558* (2nd edn, London: Longman 1991), pp. 86–7.
75 BNE MS 1029, fol. 356v.
76 BNE MS 1029, fol. 359r.
77 BNE MS 1029, fol. 363r: 'officia eiusdem Regni dominiorumque inde dependentium debeant seruari iura, priuilegia et consuetudines ipsorum; *cupientes contra futura pericula et inconuenientia quae ex diuersarum nationum comixtione et extraneorum admissione non nunquam euenire [...] solent*'. My italics.
78 *Tower Chronicle*, Appendix IX, p. 134.
79 AGS E 808, fol. 108: 'os han forçado de non poder partir para venir aca como lo podriades dessear, y la difficultad que se hallaua para la venida para proueer de dinero como se requeria', however 'os puedo assegurar que sy estas tierras de aca no son assistidas que las perdereis'. Mary of Hungary to Philip, 4th February 1554.

80 Loades, *The Reign of Mary Tudor*, pp. 148–51.

81 AGS E 98, fols 201r–v: 'los ccU ducados que la serenissima Reyna maria tomo ay acambio, y los remitio para que se pagasen en genoua, y que se proueyesen de aca los dineros, ya screuia V.M. que no hauía manera de poderse cumplir'.

82 AGS E 98, fols 201r–v: 'en ello no se a podido hallar remedio para proueerlos'/'enbiarlos delos que lleua don Juan de figueroa, y como las galeras que han Venido no han de boluer por agora a ytalia, pareçio que se deuian de enbiar en las barcas todos dU ducados, delos quales podra V.M. mandar cumplir los dichos ccU ducados'.

83 AGS E 98, fol. 202r: 'no ay orden ny manera para cumplirlos y las consignacçiones que se les podran dar seran a tan largos plazos que montar mas El ynterese quel principal'.

84 AGS E 98, fol. 203r: 'V. Magd. manda que se de ala serenissima reyna maria mi tia y se le situe en medina Valladolid y Segouia visto que en las rentas destos lugares no ay donde se pueda hazer por estar vendidas'/'ala feria de medina'.

85 BNE MS 9937: Florián de Ocampo, *Sucesos Acaecidos, 1550–1558 and 1521–1549*, fol. 94r: 'Todos los precios de las cosas llegaron a valer doblado de lo que solian... no avia dinero enlas contrataciones publicas, a lo menos de Oro, ni una sola pieza de oro, puesto que de las indias venia continuamente cosa innumerable de oro todo pasaua a Alemania, para complir los gastos incomportables de su mag. y los estrechos en que los Alemanes le ponian'. Copy of a Dutch original.

86 See David Loades, 'The Netherlands and the Anglo-Papal reconciliation of 1554', *Nederlands Archief voor Kerkgeschiedenis* 60:1 (1980), 39–55, p. 45.

87 Fray Prudencio de Sandoval, *Historia de la vida y hechos del Emperador Carlos V Máximo, fortisimo, Rey Católico de España y de las Indias, Islas y Tierrra firme del mar Océano*, ed. D. Carlos Seco Serrano, vol. 3, p. 428: 'podía sentir menos gusto, porque si bien la reina era santa, era fea y vieja, que tenía cumplidos treinta y ocho años, y el rey por extremo galán y mozo, que no pasaba de veinte y siete. Hizo en esto lo que un Isaac, dejándose sacrificar por hacer la voluntad de su padre, y por el bien de la Iglesia.'

88 Rodríguez-Salgado, *The Changing Face of Empire*, pp. 82–9. Her view is that his reluctance grew after initial enthusiasm.

89 Jesús Pascual Molina, '"Porque vean y sepan cuánto es el poder y grandeza de nuestro Príncipe y Señor": Imagen y poder en el viaje de Felipe II a Inglaterra y su matrimonio con María Tudor', *Reales Sitios* 197 (2013), 6–26, pp. 10 and 13. Original warrants to Cristiano de Amberes are at AGS CMC 1a epoca, legs1098 (for 385,000 *maravedís*) and 1184.

90 *Tower Chronicle*, p. 32.

91 David Loades, *Two Tudor Conspiracies* (Cambridge: Cambridge University Press, 1965), p. 22.

92 *Tower Chronicle*, p. 34.

93 *Tower Chronicle*, p. 34.

94 *Tower Chronicle*, p. 35. My italics.

95 *Tower Chronicle*, p. 35.

96 National Archives SP 11/2/5.

97 National Archives SP 11/2/5.

98 Loades, *Two Tudor Conspiracies*, p. 21. See *Cal. Span.*, XI, pp. 443 and 445.

99 See Anthony Fletcher, *Tudor Rebellions*, Seminar Studies in History (London: Longmans, 1968), p. 79.

100 *Tower Chronicle*, p. 35.

101 John Strype, *Memorials especially Ecclesiastical and such as concern Religion*, 3 vols (London: S. Richardson, 1721), vol. 3, p. 55. See Loades, *Two Tudor Conspiracies*, pp. 17–18.

102 National Archives SP 11/1/20, p. 1. There is a draft of the articles of marriage at BL Cotton MSS Julius F VI, fols 173–9, 'The articles of the treatie concluded for the maryage betweyne Quene Marye and the kinge of Spayne the xii of Jan:'.

103 National Archives SP 11/1/20, p. 1.

104 National Archives SP 11/1/20, p. 7.

105 David Loades, 'Philip II and the government of England', in Claire Cross, David Loades and

J. J. Scarisbrick, eds, *Law and Government under the Tudors* (Cambridge: Cambridge University Press, 1988), p. 180 and Glyn Redworth, 'Philip I of England, embezzlement and the quantity theory of money', *Economic History Review* 55 (2002), 248–61, p. 256.

106 *Cal. Span.*, XII, p. 15, Renard to bishop of Arras, 7ᵗʰ January 1554.

107 AGS E 807, fol. 3 and copy in Vienna. *Cal. Span.*, XI, p. 263, Renard to Philip, 3ʳᵈ October 1553 and p. 425, Renard to Emperor, 11ᵗʰ December 1553.

108 See Agnes Strickland, *Lives of the Queens of England from the Norman Conquest*, 8 vols (London: Henry Colbourn, 1854), vol. 3, p. 514, note 4, discussed by Charles Beem, *The Lioness Roared: The Problems of Female Rule in English History*, Queenship and Power Series (New York: Palgrave Macmillan, 2006), chapter 2, 'Her Kingdom's Wife: Mary I and the Gendering of Regal Power', 63–99, p. 69.

109 Percy Ernst Schramm, *A History of the English Coronation*, trans. L. G. Wickham Legg (Oxford: Clarendon Press, 1937), pp. 29–30.

110 Christopher Goodman, *Howe Superior Powers Oght to be Obeyd of their Subiects: and wherin they may lawfully by Gods Worde be disobeyed and resisted* (Geneva: John Crispin, 1558) p. 52, sig. Dii v.

111 Juan Luis Vives, *Vives and the Renascence Education of Women*, ed. and trans. Foster Watson (London: Edward Arnold, 1912), p. 44. It was translated into English by Richard Hyrde and first published in 1540.

112 Vives, *Renascence Education of Women*, p. 44.

113 In her *The Monstrous Regiment of Women: Female Rulers in Early Modern Europe*, Queenship and Power Series (New York: Palgrave Macmillan, 2002), Sharon Jansen argues that female rule or queenship was far less anomalous than at first appeared, and that large number of female rulers in early modern Europe should be reinserted into family trees from which they are absent.

114 *Cal. Span.*, XIII, p. 248.

115 Judith Richards, '"To promote a woman to beare rule": talking of queens in mid-Tudor England', *Sixteenth Century Journal* 28 (1997), 101–21, p. 103.

116 Sir Thomas Smith, *De Republica Anglorum*, ed. Mary Dewar (1583; repr. Cambridge: Cambridge University Press, 1982), p. 78.

117 There is a superb summary of this on-going programme of courtly entertainments by which Philip sought to marry the two courts through shared social, sporting and ritual activity in Duncan, '"He to Be intituled Kinge"', pp. 67–9.

118 National Archives SP 11/1/20, p. 7.

119 'ITEN [sic] que non pornemos algunos en consejo dessos dichos Reynos saluo castellanos y naturales de aquellos sin consentimiento e determinada deliberacion de la dicha serenissima princessa... y meta qualesquier oficiales, salvo que los tales ovieren de ser puestos por ella sean naturales y no extrangeros de aquellos', in Diego Clemencín, *Elogio de la reina Católica Doña Isabel, al que siguen varias illustraciones sobre su reinado* (Madrid: I. Sancha, 1821), pp. 578–80.

120 '[Y]o non faré merced alguna de alguna qualidad o quantidad concerniente la concession de vassallos e fortalesas e oficios e rentas de juro o de por vida o por tiempo limitado, segund dicho es, en los dichos reynos de Castilla e de Leon', Clemencín, *Elogio*, p. 582.

121 Clemencín, *Elogio*, pp. 580, 582.

122 The unfortunate story of Juana is brilliantly recounted, separating myth from what survives in the documentary record, by Bethany Aram, *Juana the Mad: Sovereignty and Dynasty in Renaissance Europe* (Baltimore, Mary. and London: The Johns Hopkins University Press, 2005).

123 Muñoz, *Viaje de Felipe Segundo a Inglaterra*, p. 91: 'todos andauamos bien vagabundos y sin hacer falta'.

124 *CODOIN*, vol. 3, pp. 526–7: 'se ha travesado otro inconveniente grande y es que antes de llegar S. A. aquí le tenian aparejada una casa con todos sus oficiales altos y bajos en que hay caballerizo mayor y camarero mayor y gentiles hombres de cámara, y de aquí abajo todos los

mas oficiales y guardia de cien archeros'/'si de nuestra parte alguno quiere meter mano en algo, tómanlo mal y no lo quieren dejar hacer'.

125 *Cal. Span.* XIII, pp. 49–50. Renard to Emperor, 18th September 1554. See Richard C. McCoy, 'From the Tower to the tiltyard: Robert Dudley's return to glory', *The Historical Journal* 27 (1984), 425–35, p. 428 and David Loades, *Mary Tudor: A Life*, (Oxford: Basil Blackwell, 1992), p. 229.

126 National Archives SP 11/1/20, p. 2.

127 National Archives SP 11/1/20, pp. 6–7.

128 BNE MS 1750: *Papeles Tocantes a Phelipe Segundo. Tomo Segundo*, fol. 93r: 'Casamiento de Phelipe Segundo en Inglaterra, año 1554, con Maria hixa de Enrique y Catalina'/'que especialmente se guardassse el acuerdo hecho en Vesmestre el año 1542 y el tratado hecho en Utrecht a 16 de hen. de 1546'. A celebratory account with a translation of the marriage treaty was published in Rome in 1554, *La vera capitulatione e articoli passati*; see Jennifer Loach, 'The Marian establishment and the printing press', *English Historical Review* 101 (1986), 135–48, p. 145.

129 Malfatti, *Accession, Coronation and Marriage of Mary Tudor*, pp. 52–8.

130 See J. J. Scarisbrick, *Henry VIII* (London: Eyre & Spottiswoode, 1968), p. 472, and Greg Walker, *Plays of Persuasion: Drama and Politics at the Court of Henry VIII* (Cambridge: Cambridge University Press, 1991), p. 204, note 73.

131 National Archives SP 11/1/20, pp. 7–8.

132 Stephen Gardiner, *A Machiavellian Treatise*, ed. and trans. P. S. Donaldson (London: Cambridge University Press, 1975), pp. 129–30 and 133. The original Italian reads 'perche trale altre cose nessuna genera magiore odio al principe, ch' il dispregiare le leggi antiche in alcuno regno osservate': *ibid.*, p. 75 (fols 76v–77r) and '[p]erche gli e un cordoglio estremo a li houmini, di qual natione o provincia che // li sono veder i altri forestieri, di posseder que' honori, officii, et dignitati che ne tempi passati lor padri o predeccessori godorno, et gli stessi lor figlioli come indigni', pp. 78–9 (fols 86r–v).

133 Noel Malcolm, 'My country, old or young?', review of Adrian Hastings' *The Construction of Nationhood: Ethnicity, Religion and Nationalism* (Cambridge, 1997) in *The Sunday Telegraph*, 30th November 1997.

134 W. S. Holdsworth, *A History of English Law*, 7th edn, 17 vols (London: Methuen & Co., 1956–72), vol. 9, p. 93. Original is at 7 Co. Rep. fol. 18b (1609).

135 National Archives SP 11/1/20, p. 8.

136 National Archives SP 11/1/20, pp. 4–5.

137 National Archives SP 11/1/20, p. 8.

138 National Archives SP 11/1/20, pp. 7–8.

139 National Archives SP 11/1/20, p. 6.

140 MacCulloch, 'The *Vitae Mariae Angliae Reginae*', pp. 273–4.

141 *Cal. Span.*, XI, p. 414. See also Harbison, *Rival Ambassadors*, p. 100.

3

Wyatt and the queen's regal power

Wyatt's revolt

A definite conspiracy against Mary I was hatched on 26th November just over a week after her rejection of the parliamentary group led by Pollard to persuade her against a foreign match.[1] Wyatt may have inherited his 'anti-Catholic and anti-Spanish' attitudes from his father, the poet, alleged lover of Anne Boleyn and Henrician ambassador to Spain.[2] However, the elder Sir Thomas Wyatt had enjoyed 'extraordinary, "inexpressible" favour' from Charles, while they had treated of a marriage for Mary with Dom Luis of Portugal in 1537–8, although his attempt to justify the Royal Supremacy had resulted in an uncomfortable audience. Wyatt's personal religious beliefs at that moment are veiled from us: although he did attend Mass occasionally.[3] In his only extant work, *A Treatise on the Militia*, dedicated to Protector Somerset in 1549 in the context of the Prayer Book rising, the younger Sir Thomas Wyatt had attacked the 'supersticious Spayniard' and 'malicious flemynge envious of our welthe', asserting 'This wot I well, that we take in hand to set up the Religion Protestantism that he the Emperor pulleth down, suerlie unto an ambicious mynd there is no better title, Then nedes of Religion as most part of men well call it'.[4] In this text he proposed the establishment of a militia in Kent, to guard against the threat of both popular insurrection and foreign invasion in a strategically sensitive county: 'the most suer and proper remedie for this headstronge mischife wouldbe to strengthen ye Kings part with a power of ye choise of his most able and trusty Subiectes, which might upon a very short warninge in a reddiness, wel armed against all sudden attemptes, either at home or abrode'.[5] Ironically, it was he who would lead just such a rising. Wyatt's reflection on military strategy in Kent along with his experience as a soldier may explain his comparative success in relation to the other three strands of the conspiracy, in which he claimed to have been a minor figure. He had served the earl of Surrey, Henry Howard's regiment of volunteers at the siege of Landrecies in

1543 and then at Boulogne in 1544, where he distinguished himself, receiving a command in the following year. The earl wrote as governor of Boulogne to Henry VIII of Wyatt's 'hardiness, painfulness, circumspection, and natural disposition to the war'.[6] Clearly, he also had an axe to grind against both the Spanish and Dutch.

There is little new to say about the Wyatt revolt, apart from recent studies of his subsequent representation in literary texts such as Thomas Dekker and John Webster's play *The Famous History of Sir Thomas Wyat* (1602).[7] The verdict of historians is divided. On one hand David Loades argues that 'the real reasons which lay behind the risings were secular and political'; it was 'anti-clerical rather than Protestant' and the rebels' 'main concern... was with the threat of Spanish domination'.[8] Against this view are those who point to the fact that the areas where it achieved greatest success coincided with places where the Reformation had taken deepest root. The rebels themselves were at pains to eschew religious motives, while the official government history by the Tonbridge schoolmaster John Proctor, printed in late 1554 and early 1555, tied the rebellion squarely to religion, comparing it with the religious wars that had desolated Germany:[9]

> With what ways of craft and subtilty she [Heresy] dilateth her dominion! and finally how, of course, she toileth to be supported by Faction, Sedition, and Rebellion! to the great peril of subversion of that State where, as a plague, she happenenth to find habitation: as well the lamentable history of the Bohemians and Germans, with all others treating of the like enterprises by heretics, as also WYAT'S late conspiracy practised with open force, doth plenteously declare.[10]

The Spanish marriage would destroy 'Protestantism that he the Emperor pulleth down', as Wyatt had written in 1549. The royal proclamation declaring 'Wyatt's Treasonable Purpose' of 1st February stated similarly that he was 'pretending thereby at the first only the misliking of the marriage lately treated upon to be concluded between her highness and the Prince of Spain', whereas he meant 'most manifestly her majesty's destruction and to deprive her grace of the crown'.[11] On the same day, in her address to the Commons at the Guildhall, Mary said: 'it appeared then unto our said council, that the matter of the marriage seemed but a Spanish cloak to cover their pretended purpose against our religion'.[12] Proctor described how Wyatt was 'fervently affected to heresy, although he laboured by false persuasion otherwise to haue coloured it'.[13] Catholic accounts of the rebellion unsurprisingly identified its causes as exclusively religious. Charles writing to Philip followed this line: 'although there has been some unquiet by the inducement of persons impassioned under the title of not wanting a foreign lord, the main foundation it is understood is religion'.[14] Under Elizabeth, however, Wyatt's son George attacked this interpretation of the rising, stressing his father's patriotism. Reformers subsequently appropriated this reinterpretation of the revolt as secular and political, since it allowed them to recover Wyatt as a patriotic hero without condoning disobedience and setting a dangerous precedent for Catholic dissidents. The representation of Wyatt's insurrection as a 'patriotic revolt' became Protestant orthodoxy. A major revolt motivated by religion would have been profoundly damaging to the Reformist cause.

Despite his insistence on its religious motives Proctor, allegedly an eye-witness at Wyatt's arraignment, standing 'not ten feet away', recorded him testifying:

> O most miserable, mischievous, brutish, and beastly furious imagination of mine! For I thought by the marriage of the Prince of Spain, this realm should have been in danger: and that I, that have lived a free born man, should, with my country, have been brought to bondage and servitude by aliens and Strangers.[15]

The Reformist *Tower Chronicle* corroborated Proctor's description of Wyatt's evidence, quoting him as affirming 'myne hole intent and styrre was agaynst the comyng in of strandgers and Spanyerds'.[16] On 22nd January his co-conspirator William Isley arrived at Ightham to declare 'the Spanyards was commynge into the realme wt harnes and handgonnes, and would make us Inglish men wondres... and vile'.[17] Wyatt's testimony that the prince of Spain would be 'the undoing of this realm for at the spring of the year such gentlemen as I with others shall be sent into France with a great power of Englishmen to enlarge his countries there and in the meantime... he shall strengthen the realm with his own nation', is particularly ironic coming from a veteran of the Boulogne campaign.[18] Popular responses echoed these fears. James Brattock, a yeoman farmer, declared Mary 'has broken her father's will for the duke of Norfolk, the Lord Courtenay and the bishop of Winchester should have remained in the Tower and she should not marry any outlandish man, wherefore she is not worthy to wear the crown'; while John Toppylow believed that, if the marriage was effected, 'we should lie in swine sties, in caves, and the Spaniards should have our houses'.[19] Wyatt's proclamation at Maidstone, insistent that the marriage 'alone' and no 'earthly cause' moved them, countered the construction in royal circular letters sent out three days earlier that the 'pretence of misliking the marriage' caused them 'to rebelle against the catholique religion'.[20] The 'propagandist strategy' of the Wyatt camp, 'to speak no word of religion, but to make the only colour of his commotion to withstand Strangers and to advance liberty',[21] successfully yoked together a diversity of discontent: those concerned about their holdings of ex-monastic property, moderates who objected to the renunciation of the Supremacy and repudiation of the Henrician settlement, bona fide religious radicals, political opportunists, malcontents, and merchants and tradesmen affected by the contraction of exports and falling domestic demand, angered at the prospect of greater Spanish competition.

The army that rallied to Wyatt's banner was only a tenth of the size of the Pilgrimage of Grace army of 1536, although the Protestant minority were strongly represented in London and the South-East, especially in towns associated with the cloth trade.[22] This was despite their successful propaganda and propagandists. In spite of the persecution Reformist texts outnumber official material in the textual remains of the Marian period by 114 titles to 93, although this simple calculus has been questioned recently by scholars.[23] As early as August 1553 leaflets were being scattered on the streets of London by these prolific and practised polemicists. One came to the attention of the imperial ambassadors, who translated and sent it back with their reports to Brussels:

> Yesterday a defamatory leaflet was scattered about the streets of town; we send a copy herewith which we have hurriedly translated: 'Noblemen and gentlemen favouring the work of God, take counsel together and join with all your power and your following. Withdraw yourselves from our virtuous lady, Queen Mary, because Rochester, Walgrave, Inglefield, Weston, and Hastings, hardened and detestable papists all, follow the opinions of the said Queen. Fear not, and God will prosper and help our holy design and intent; be assured that they have no great strength now, except two archpapists, Derby and Stourton; Arundel might be mentioned as the third, with the renegades [Sir Edmund] Peckham and [Sir William] Drury, chamberlain, who have no great power. As to the other personages in the country, of whatever condition they may be, they will assuredly prove tractable and conform to our belief, as we have seen by experience during the past seven years. But Winchester, the great devil, must be exorcised and exterminated with his disciples named above, before he can poison the people and wax strong in his religion. Draw near to the Gospels, and your guardian shall be the crown of glory'.[24]

The convoluted syntax of the second sentence of the leaflet allows it to describe Mary as 'our virtuous lady', while her household intimates are 'hardened and detestable papists all'. Religion was of crucial interest to the Habsburgs. However, we need to be careful how we gauge its significance in terms of agency. A good example of this is the case of the Kentish Protestant Sir Thomas Cawarden. Arrested by local rivals on 25th January and interrogated by Gardiner in Star Chamber, he was released on the 26th with instructions to 'be in readiness to march and set forward upon hour's warning' and letters discharging the sheriff, Sir Thomas Saunders, who was guarding Cawarden's sizeable arsenal at Bletchingley from falling into rebel hands.[25] On the 27th Thomas Howard, duke of Norfolk, rearrested him, seized his munitions and transported many of them to the Tower. Cawarden was kept in mild confinement at his Blackfriars residence, St Anne's, at the behest of the Privy Council for the duration of the crisis. Although he had fallen under suspicion for his known Protestantism and opposition to the marriage, he retained his post as Master of the Revels throughout Mary's reign, in spite of pleading illness a year later when the council requested plans for interludes, pageants and devices to celebrate Philip's arrival.[26] Whether Cawarden's arrest was motivated by justifiable suspicion (there were sixteen pieces of ordnance stored on his estate) or from personal enmity is impossible to judge.

Perhaps an even more striking example is the 'hot Gospeller' Edward Underhill, a gentleman-at-arms attending the queen on the very day the Wyatt rebels marched into London. Arrested at the outset of the reign for a polemical ballad, he had spent a month in Newgate, but by the time of Wyatt's revolt had rejoined the gentlemen-at-arms at court. In his account of Wyatt and his men marching past the gatehouse at Westminster Palace, where Mary was in the gallery, Underhill recorded how he and his company demanded 'the gates to be opened that we may go to the Queen's enemies! We will else break them open! It is too much shame that the gates should thus be shut for a few rebels! The Queen shall see us fell down her enemies this day, before her face!'[27] He remained in Mary's service for the rest of her reign, even serving at the wedding banquet the following summer. Underhill claimed 'there was no such place to shift in, in this realm, as London, notwithstanding their great spiall and search; nor no better place to shift the Easter time than in Queen Mary's Court'.[28] He continued to allow radicals to meet in his house and sealed radical books up behind a wall there.

On 1st February, at the height of the revolt with Wyatt approaching London, Mary displayed her coronation ring in an oration at the Guildhall, professing that at her coronation she 'was wedded to the realm and laws of the same (the spousal ring whereof I have on my finger, which never hitherto was, nor hereafter shall be left off)' and that although 'I cannot tell how naturally the mother loveth the child, for I was never mother of any... if a prince or governor may as naturally and earnestly love her subjects, as the mother doth the child, then assure yourselves, that I, being your lady and mistress, do as earnestly and tenderly love and favour you'.[29] An anonymous Latin manuscript account from the Real Biblioteca del Monasterio de San Lorenzo de El Escorial developed the metaphor from the Guildhall speech further: 'most dear and beloved subjects, I, by the grace of God and by your unanimous suffrages your Queen and mother (not for having borne you as my children, but full of more than motherly love towards you since the day in which you chose me as your Queen and mistress)'.[30] According to Cardinal Pole, Mary had promised, contrary to royal prerogative, 'especially not to marry without the universal consent of Parliament, when the ring which she wears was put on her finger, she purposed accepting the realme of England and its entire population as her children'.[31] The metaphor by which Mary figured her relationship to her subjects, the relation between mother and child, recurred in her rejection by Wyatt and his followers, and underlay their repudiation of her. If they were her children, then they were directly threatened by a second, foreign marriage, which might produce heirs with rival claims on her patrimony and love. Concerns about property rights being vitiated by the marriage were central to the anxieties obsessively expressed by the anti-Marian opposition.

Charles' ambassadors had been instructed in the summer of 1553 to urge Mary to show herself 'a good Englishwoman, wholly bent on the kingdom's welfare'.[32] By the following summer, after the conclusion of the marriage, the Venetian ambassador Giacomo Soranzo reported rumours and gossip that 'being born of a Spanish mother, [she] was always inclined towards that nation, scorning to be English and boasting of her descent from Spain'.[33] The later, emblematic importance of Elizabeth's virginity derived from the fact that the 'state, like the virgin, was a *hortus conclusus*, an enclosed garden walled off from enemies'.[34] The politicisation of the metaphorical language around women's bodies reflected early modern Europe's huge symbolic investment in female chastity and fidelity as guarantors of patrilinear inheritance patterns. A contemporary discussion of love suggested men 'know that they may lawfully challenge this high pris'd commoditie of love as their owne, and that they have payed for the same', but 'when this our high-pric'd Commoditie chanceth to light into some other merchants hands, and that our private Inclosure proveth to be a Common for others, we care no more for it'.[35] Anti-Marian polemic developed this imagery. Alexander Brett, captain of the Whitecoats, a company sent from London to engage Wyatt, defected with an oration in which he claimed 'yf we should be under subjection they wolde, as slaves and villaynes, spoyle us of our goodes and landes, ravishe our wyfes before our faces, and deflowre our daughters in our prescence'.[36] Brett was a business associate in the Cornish lead market of Sir Peter Carew, one of the Wyatt conspirators, and had probably been suborned by Broughton, a Scottish agent of the French ambassador Noailles.[37] His image figured the coming of the Spanish as an economic and sexual violation.

Philip was to be consistently figured as a rapist and despoiler by his opponents. Even Mary's supporter Robert Wingfield apparently endorsed the image of Spanish lust that was the corrollary of English anxieties about their disenfranchisement through the match:

> to make his faction more widely accepted, Wyatt first gave out that he had taken up arms solely for love of his country, not to harm the queen, but to hinder this marriage, lest Spaniards, *who are arrogant and indeed wanton men,*

should reduce the English nation to a base slavery, from which they shrink far more than from death.[38]

He recorded how the rebels claimed that 'they had been overwhelmed by a Spanish whore'.[39] Countering Mary's sexualisation by opponents, supporters celebrated her virginity. In a homiletic treatise that appeared a day before the marriage, again condemning Wyatt, John Christopherson exclaimed that 'the sheddynge of so pure a virgyns bloude, is of all other [acts] moste cruell and detestable'.[40] Similarly, the papal legate Pole in his oration at Westminster prior to the reunification with Rome described, as we saw, how Mary 'being a virgin, helples, naked, and unarmed prevailed, and had victory over tyrauntes'.[41] Even at the end of her reign Mary was still celebrated for a reluctantly relinquished virginity. George Cavendish claimed, as Wingfield had in his contemporary biography, that Mary had unwillingly agreed to the match for the sake of her people: 'To a virgin's life which liked thee best/ Professed was thine heart'.[42] This echoed the Guildhall speech in which Mary had explicitly disavowed carnal affection as a motive for the marriage.

In May 1554, two months before Philip landed at Southampton, a translation of a Lutheran tract, which had stirred Germany to revolt, was published that employed an identical rhetoric of rape and dispossession to that of Brett and others. Charles V's 'ayde and obedience shall serue to bring in Italianes, which shall ouerrunne his natural countrey, most shamefully defyle and abuse honest wyues, widdowes and virgyns euen before the faces of theyr husbands, parentes and frindes': its clearly false, ironic imprimatur 'at Grenewych by Conrad Freeman in the month of May MDLiiii. With the most gracious licence & priuilege of god almightie, king of heauen and earth' underlined again the connection with the international Reformist movement.[43] It made available the Lutheran discussion of the Holy Roman Emperor's subservience to the pope, which vindicated their right of resistance to his temporal authority: 'it is another thing to be a Rebel, than to be one of those, which stand in the defence of Goddes true religion and of their natural countrey'.[44] The true pastor warned that 'as for brynging Aliens into our nacion, to haue the gouernment among us, and to subuert the auncient privileges of their own natural countrey, I dare say, theyr own conscience telleth them that it is against nature'.[45] Such rhetoric shaped English responses to the Spanish marriage and furnished the rebels with a 'patriotic' rhetoric with which to articulate 'anti-Spanish sentiment', assimilating earlier Italian and German versions of the Black Legend.

Mary's representation of herself as wedded to or mother of the realm was quickly perverted by Marian exiles. In his invective the *Admonition to the Town of Calais* (1557), Robert Pownall denounced Mary as '[a]nother Athalia, that is an utter distroier of hir owen kindred, kyngdome & countrie, a hater of her own subjects, a lover of strangers & an unnatural stepdame both unto the & to thy mother England'.[46] John Ponet's anti-Marian *A Shorte Treatise of Politike Power* (1556) developed the same biblical story of Athalia as a prototype for Philip and Mary's reign:

> Quene Athalia, the woman tyranne (seing after her sonne Ahaziahu was dead, that she was childles, and past hope to haue any children) hade killed all the kynges progenye (sauing Ioas, whom Iehosaba Iorams daughter hid and get with his nource out of the waye) purposing to reigne therby in securitie, and to transpose the right of the crowne to straungers or som other fauorer of her cruel procedinges.[47]

Several of her counsellors had advocated the elimination of Elizabeth in the aftermath of Wyatt's rebellion, in spite of the fact that insufficient evidence of her knowledge and involvement had been uncovered to implicate her. The proposal of a bill allowing Mary to will the crown had of course been defeated in her second parliament. By 1556, when her phantom pregnancy failed, it was clear that Mary would not produce the Catholic heir so important to Charles V's dynastic policy. He had written to Eraso in October 1554 asking for confirmation of Mary's pregnancy, 'for it would realise our dearest wishes'.[48] As late as 1557 with the controversy provoked by the project for Philip's coronation, the concern about property rights and the despoliation of the kingdom by aliens was still alive in the imaginations of Protestant opponents of the regime. Christohper Goodman asked in his *How Superior Powers oght to be Obeyd* (Geneva: 1558): 'For do you thinke that Philip will be crowned kinge of Englande and reteyne in honor English counsellers? Will he credite them withe the governement of his estate, who have betrayed their owne? Shall his nobilitie be Spaniardes without your landes and possessions?'[49] The anxiety concerning property was made an issue precisely to reinforce the notion that sovereignty had been given up through the marriage as a consequence of Mary's problematic gender. In the same way that opponents claimed Mary was Spanish, when Philip arrived in London English supporters claimed he was English.

In a letter to the Privy Council Sir Thomas Gresham described how the exchange jumped abruptly on 15th February 1554 from 20s 6d per Flemish groat to 22s per Flemish groat when news reached Antwerp that the Wyatt rebellion had been crushed.[50] Two days earlier Renard had warned his compatriots to behave in a more circumspect way after an uncomfortable audience with a still nervous Council:

> having received a copy of the order of arrest of the bodies and goods of the English at Antwerp at the time of the tumult and recent disturbance in this kingdom I communicated to the Council of the Queen and made know the occasion, the fear in that regard and that it was not damaging to take possession

of the gunpowder those merchants and agents of her majesty had bought, which the Council took in good part understanding that if some outrage were committed on their part to her people there would be a means of avenging it in Flanders and Spain.[51]

The Brussels government's action, arresting merchants and imposing an embargo, repeated steps they had taken during the succession crisis, which in fact contravened the treaties of alliance of 1542 and 1546 and the recently signed contract. Their response was perhaps uncomfortably aggressive in relation to the internal affairs of a sovereign state but is an indication of their determination to secure Philip on the English throne.

Mary demonstrated remarkable clemency and very few of the rebels were actually executed in the aftermath of the Wyatt rebellion. Jane Grey and her husband Guildford Dudley went to the block on 12th February: the 'same day towards 9am many people noticed in the clear sky two suns with one huge iris: If it is allowed to take it as a good omen, who can prevent us from interpreting it as the foreboding of the union of the two greatest Kingdoms of Spain and England'?[52] Within two days the dismembered remains of the convicted 'wher hangyd at evere gatt and plass: in Chepe-syd vj; Aldgatt j, quartered; at Leydynhall iii; at Bysshope-gate on, and quartered; Morgate one; Crepullgatt one; Aldersgatt on, quartered; Nuwgat on, quartered; Ludgatt on; Belyngat iij hangyd; Sant Magnus iij hangyd; Towre hyll ij hangyd'.[53] The duke of Suffolk was beheaded on Tower Hill on 23rd March and his brother Thomas Grey on 27th April. Wyatt was executed on 11th April and his head set upon the gallows, from where it was stolen a week later. The same day, Sir Nicholas Throgmorton was acquitted ('wherat mayney people rejoyced'), much to the chagrin of the government, which had the jury fined and imprisoned for six months.[54] Renard, who had been relieved the previous autumn when 'French and Flemish preachers who interspersed seditious words in their sermons have been forbidden to preach',[55] reported that the proclamation 'Ordering the Deportation of Seditious Aliens' had finally been published on 17th February and 'has greatly pleased the Londoners, and the measure will rid the realm of many heretics and evil men'.[56] However, on 12th February he had written '[a] new revolt is feared because the people say so much noble blood ought not to be shed for the sake of foreigners. Many foreigners have departed, because marks were found on their houses.'[57] This passage was omitted from the Spanish translation of the document sent to Philip from Brussels.[58] Whether Wyatt was driven by concerns for English independence, religion or ambition to try and overthrow Mary, the Spanish card was played and lost:

> the limited support for the rising suggests that even in the south-east the pros-
> pects of Habsburg rule and Catholic religion were not hateful, or that, at least,

loyalty to the queen was stronger than either. There were to be scuffles in London between Spaniards and citizens, and several murders, but Philip himself was a different case. Christopher Trychay, Henry Machyn, a churchwarden at Minchinhampton (Gloucestershire), and Robert Parkyn recorded the titles of Philip and Mary with evident pride, and Parkyn thought the marriage 'was great joy and comfort to all good people in the realm'. By the autumn of 1554, three months after the marriage, Philip's stock was high and rising.[59]

Although anti-Spanish statements might figure heavily in the Protestant propaganda of the period, which (as has been alluded to) were highly effective and to a large extent overshadowed the official response, it cannot be assumed from this that these sentiments were deeply felt or widely shared by the silent majority of the English.

A queen's regal power

Even in the fifteenth century it had been believed that 'regal power is restrained by political law', as Sir John Fortescue, Henry VI's Chancellor, asserted: 'it is not a yoke but a liberty to rule a people politically, and the greatest security not only to the people but also to the king himself'.[60] Henry VIII, however, had boasted to Thomas Cranmer that he had 'no superior in earth but only God' and was not 'subject to the laws of any earthly creature'.[61] The balance in the Tudor period between an absolute royal power and political law was constantly shifting. Henry VIII's 1543 Act for Wales allowed him to 'change, add, alter, order, diminish, and reform' the legislation under his great seal and his Statute of Proclamations enjoined obedience to royal injunctions 'as though they were made by act of Parliament'.[62] A later act similarly licensed Edward VI to repeal statutes passed during his minority, while Henry VIII's three Succession Acts assumed his right to will the crown through letters patent. These same acts stated that their reform, alteration or repeal was to be considered high treason. In his opening speech to Mary's second parliament on 2nd April 1554, the Chancellor Stephen Gardiner suggested Mary be empowered by statute to will the crown: the 'bill to authorize Mary to designate her successor by her last will and testament, as the 1543 Succession Act had allowed Henry VIII to do, did not reach the floor of either house'.[63] John Ponet in *A Shorte Treatise of Politike Power* (1556) deduced that parliamentary consent was necessary to bequeath the crown, since if Henry VIII 'might do with the realm and every part thereof, what it pleased him', if he 'might do with it without consent of the Parliament: how is the Lady Mary Queen? And why might not King Edward his son... bequeath the Crown where he would, and as he did?'[64] The bill's failure 'effected... a negative form of constitutionalism' and answered the question posed by an anonymous polemicist in 1555: 'whether the Realme of Englande belong to the Quene, or to her subiectes', or 'whether the Quene of England may sell away the realme or not, to a stranger, without the consent of her commons'.[65] Mary, however, kept her promise, made in the speech at the Guildhall during the Wyatt rebellion: 'if it shall not probably appear to all the nobility and commons in the high court of parliament, that this marriage shall be for the benefit and commodity of the whole realm, then will I abstain from marriage while I live'.[66] Within ten days of opening, both houses ratified the marriage treaty.[67] In this way the alliance and treaty were unprecedentedly subject to statutory confirmation in her second parliament.

At the same time as the treaty was enshrined in statute, her parliament passed an 'Act for the Queen's Regal Power'.[68] This Act is key to understanding Marian government and Philip and Mary's co-monarchy. A detailed account of the passage of the 'Act declaring that the regal power of this realm is in the Queen's Majesty as fully and absolutely as ever it was in any of her most noble progenitors Kings of this realm' was set down by the Recorder of the City of London, William Fleetwood, in a probably 'factional' dialogue between Robert Dudley, the earl of Leicester, and his retinue riding from London to Windsor in 1575. The *Itinerarium ad Windsor* is framed by the earl's question about female rule and is lifted verbatim from the Act. Fleetwood's answer records a speech against the Act and the reasons for its drafting by Gardiner. Mary had been presented with a book in the spring of 1554 by 'the Lord Cromwell's man', which advocated she 'take upon her the title of a conqueror' so '[t]hen might she at her pleasure reforme the monasteries... and doe what she list', because the anomalous and unprecedented nature of her female monarchy excepted her from restraints expressed in precedents, customs and statutes relevant to her male predecessors: 'by the lawe she was not bound, for (said they) ther is not any statute extant, made either with or against the prince of this realm, wherein the name of queen is once expressed'.[69] Mary 'misliked it and the devisers therof' and 'bethought her of her oath that she tooke at her coronation' (i.e. to keep to the people of England and others your realms and dominions the laws and liberties of this realm), while Stephen Gardiner responded: 'I say that it is pittie that so noble amd vertuous a lady should be endangered with pernitious devises of such lewd and subtile sycophantes. The book is naught, the matter *horrendum dictu*, yea most horrible to be thought of' and so 'without any tarrying she tooke the said book and presently cast it into the fier', while the Chancellor 'devised the said act of Parliament'.[70] Far from clarifying ambiguities about Mary's position as a queen regnant of married estate and acting as a constitutional check on foreign influence by fencing in her regal authority, according to Fleetwood's account Ralph Skinner, later Dean of Durham, believed the Act was intended to allow Mary to arbitrarily extend her power:

Embassadors be come, and as we heare a marriage is intended betwene the infant or prince of Spaine (sonne vnto Charles the Emperour) and the Queene our mistris. If we by a Lawe do allowe vnto Her Majestie all such prehemi-nences and authorities in all thinges as any of her most noble progenitors kinges of England ever had, enjoyed, or used, then doe we give to Her Majestie the same power that her most noble progenitors William the Conqueror had, *who seised the Landes of the Englishe people, and did giue the same vnto straingers*; and... that King Edward the First had, who was called the Conqueror, because he conquered all Wales, who did *likewise dispose of all men's landes in Wales at his owne pleasure.*[71]

Skinner's argument runs completely against the thrust of Fleetwood's account, i.e. that Mary and her Chancellor rejected outright any attempt to extend the *lex coronae* in an absolutist direction. The parliamentary intervention revealed, nevertheless, the powerful link between uncertainty over the rights of holders of ex-monastic properties, the return of papal jurisdiction and the precise nature of Mary's authority and power in the kingdom as a married woman. The repeal of the Henrician legislation that had transformed England into an *imperium* had been anticipated since the first proclamation of her reign on 18th August. The Acts of Appeals, *Praemunire* and Submission of the Clergy had asserted that 'by dyvers and sundrie olde autentike histories and croni-cles it is manifestly declared and expressed that this Realm of Englond is an Impire, and so hath been accepted in the world', a 'Realme, recognysyng noo superior under God but only your Grace, [which] hath byn and is free from subjection to any mannes lawes but only suche as have bene devysed made and ordyned within thys Realme'.[72] By the time writs of summons were sent out for her second parliament Mary had dropped the title of Supreme Head of the church.[73] Concern over the consequences of reunification with Rome for secularised property were not confined to Protestants like Skinner, per-sisting even after the papal dispensation and statutory confirmation. Holders of ex-monastic property had needed to be reassured that a papal bull issued in 1555 only applied to the German lands.[74] That this went on being an issue is apparent from the fact that, despite assurances of a papal dispensation and statutory confirmation of holders' property, William Petre, principal secre-tary of the Privy Council, obtained through the representations of the English envoy at Rome, Sir Edward Corne, a special private dispensation confirming his and his heirs' possession of ecclesiastical property. Paul IV's bull of 28th November 1555 is a unique document, which was issued in the context of dire political and diplomatic relations between the papacy and Habsburgs and so by association England.[75] The association of Spain in England with a threatened expropriation of property by the Roman church through the marriage, and by extension foreign tyranny, was bound up with uncertainty over 'possession' never being laid to rest. Even though a political reversal was unlikely, ecclesiastical pressure might easily have been brought to bear on the many Catholic families who had along with their Protestant neighbours rushed to expand their estates and regional power and influence in the 1530s. Despite the many provisos in the marriage treaty it was only after tense negotiations in parliament in November 1554 that anxieties about what might happen were partially laid to rest.[76] The connection of the marriage with the return of papal jurisdiction was emphasised both in Habsburg propaganda and by exiled Reformist critics of the government. The Habsburgs delayed the legatine mission, detaining the cardinal at Brussels until after the wedding, in order to emphasise their role in a victorious act of salvation and reconversion. Moreover, Pole fought against the blanket absolution that Philip and his advisors, even more than Mary, were insistent on.[77] Despite this, the link between the return of a foreign, papal jurisdiction and the marriage became a central pillar of Protestant historiography of the Marian period.

In fact, no abrogation of England's constitutional sovereignty transpired under Philip and Mary, whether related to Catholic restoration, Mary's married status or the 'Act for the Queen's Regal Power'. The opposite was the case: as William Dunham expressed it, 'one of Mary Tudor's fires helped to save constitutional government for Elizabethan England'.[78] It is worth noting that the account of it, written by a Protestant, Fleetwood, in conversation with Elizabeth's favourite, Robert Dudley, offers a positive image of Mary as a conscientious parliamentary queen. According to Philip and Mary's first joint parliament Acts were not 'construed understanded or expounded to derogate, diminish or take awaye any the Lybertyes Pryvilegies Prerogatives Prehemynences Auchtorities or Jurisdiccions, or any part or percell therof, which were in your Imperiall Crowne of this Realme or did belong to yr. said Imperiall Crowne, the xxth yere of the raigne' of Henry VIII, i.e. 1529 the year divorce proceedings against Mary's mother had been initiated.[79] The Act continued 'for that the title of all Landes Possessions and Hereditamentes in this yr Maistes Realme and Doms., ys grownded in the Lawes Statutes and Customes of the same, and by yor highe Jurisdiction Aucthorities Roiall and Crowne Imperiall and in yor Courtes only to be empleaded ordred tryed and judged and none otherwise'.[80] Another statute of 1554 permitted the use of papal orders, bulls and dispensations, 'not containing matter contrarye or prejudicial to the aucthoritie, dignities, or preheminence Roial or Imperiall of the Realm, or to the Lawes of this Realm nowe being in force and not in this Parliament repealed'.[81] Philip and Mary extended and reinforced the notion of England as an empire, through both legislation and court culture, invoking the image of the closed crown repeatedly. In 1557, Philip himself was excommunicated by the rabidly anti-Spanish Carrafa pope Paul IV and severed all links between the Spanish church and Rome. Pole reassured the Venetian ambassador that he would be 'restoring to them [Alba and Philip] *in integrum* what they have forfeited, for they are deprived not only of the fiefs of the Church, which are the kingdoms of Naples, Sicily, Sardinia, England, Ireland, and so many privileges (*gratie*) in Spain'.[82] His description of England as a papal fief, from king John's humiliating thirteenth-century conflict, was precisely what exercised Reformers and Catholic patriots. The trauma of losing his mother and brother as a result of his refusal to accept the Henrician Supremacy must have coloured Pole's hard line on both ecclesiastical property and this issue. He went on to argue, nevertheless, that the duke of Alba and Philip were absolved of their duty to obey the pope, when 'he does not act as the vicar of Christ, but like sinful man',[83] an argument that would have resonated with those developed for justifiable disobedience to ungodly rulers. Cranmer, the imprisoned archbishop of Canterbury, warned Mary in 1556 from his prison in Oxford that:

> contrary to [the pope's] clayme, the emperial crowne and jurisdiction temporal of this relame is taken immediately from God... [when] the pope taketh upon him to geve the temporall sworde, or royall and Imperiall power to kynges and princes, so doth he likewise take upon hym to depose them from their Imperiall states, yf they be disobedient to him.[84]

But Philip's role in English government was not about to cease because the pope 'deprived' him of the kingdom. Nevertheless, the underlying anxiety revealed by Fleetwood's account, linking Mary's anomalous title in the crown as a married woman to the abrogation of English sovereignty implicit for Protestants in the repeal of the statutes that had constituted England as an empire enjoying *plenum dominium*, resurfaced constantly in the propaganda of anti-Marian exiles and has become a commonplace of Marian historiography.

The Act for the Queen's Regal Power has been interpreted in a variety of ways, from Jennifer Loach arguing that the 'bill is certainly a somewhat odd one, which might have been looked for in the first parliament of the reign if at all',[85] to Mortimer Levine suggesting that although 'the wording of the act indicated that it was merely confirmatory, kingly power in fact was conferred upon Mary I and future queens regnant by statute'.[86] What is clear, is that the Act responded to 'uncertainties relating to the constitutional position of a ruling queen [and] deserves greater attention than it has hitherto received'.[87] Years later, in a defence of Mary Queen of Scots following two female successions in a row, John Leslie could refer back to the 'Act for the Queen's Regal Power' as self-evident: 'all manner of the foresaide iurisdictions and other praerogatiues, and ovght to be, as fullie as wholie and as absolutlie in the prince female, as in the male, and so was yt ever deamed iudged and accepted, before the statute made for the farther declaration in that point'.[88] Earlier constitutional experts like Fortescue, however, had argued against succession through the female line, denying Edward IV's title because he 'conexeth [his descent and succession] by meanes of ij women, that is to saye Philipa and Anne [ther as n]o woman by the lawe and custom of that londe maye [or can enher]ite the crowne therof; for yt is descendable only heyres masles, and by such heyres only'.[89] He stated '[i]t is not a law or custom in our land of England that a daughter of any first-born brother should be able to or ought to challenge the inheritance of a younger brother succeeding to her father's inheritance'.[90] Like Edward IV, the Tudors derived their claim to the throne through the female line.

In Claude de Seyssel's *Monarchie de France* (2nd edn, 1541) it was argued that 'by falling into the feminine line it [the crown] can come into the power of a foreigner, a pernicious and dangerous thing, since a ruler from a foreign nation is of a different rearing and condition, of different customs, different language, and a different way of life from the men of the lands he comes to rule. He ordinarily, therefore, wishes to advance those of his nation, to grant them the most important authority in the handling of afffairs, and to prefer them to honors and profits.'[91] Although he could not advance non-English subjects, by 1555 Philip was being urged by the duke of Alba to make himself 'absolute master' of England by choosing the replacements for the ailing Stephen Gardiner: 'in that of England, for the love of God, if you wish to be absolute lord of that kingdom and rule it with your foot, they tell me the Lord Chancellor is about to die and Treasurer. They are two offices in which your Majesty must have a hand and think carefully about who to appoint and that they are not dependants of the queen.'[92] The appointments announced on New Year's Day 1556 saw Nicholas Heath, bishop of York, created Lord Chancellor and Paget, Lord Privy Seal.[93] William Paulet, whose commission had been set to expire on 23rd October, retained his post as Lord Treasurer.[94]

Doubts over Mary's constitutional position were not insubstantial and not confined to the case of breach of contract.[95] In common law, husbands gained possessions of their wives' freehold property while the marriage lasted or if a child born was born to them. By the Tudor period, the child had only to be born alive and heard to cry for a husband to hold his wife's estates after her death, by a right known as 'tenancy by the curtesy law of England'.[96] Generally, titles fell into abeyance when they passed to heirs general in the case of failure in the male line. Sometimes husbands did exercise the political privileges of their spouses during their lives, such as sitting in the Lords, by the precedent of *jure uxoris*. In 1572, Katherine Willoughby's second husband Richard Bertie brought a case before commissioners alleging this precedent in an attempt to claim the 'full political power of his wife's inheritance'.[97] Bertie claimed *he* ought to be allowed to exercise these privileges as opposed to her uncle. The court partially accepted this argument, ruling that Bertie might adopt 'the name and stile' of the title, although he could not claim a seat in the Lords. Although the issue was not clear, a husband could hold his wife's title by *jure uxoris* 'as tenant by curtesy' at least in 1572.[98] Philip and Mary's marriage treaty specifically stated that if the queen predeceased him, Philip was not by force of the marriage to be a 'tenant by courtesy of this realm',[99] repeating precisely the formula employed in the later judgment in the Bertie case. The framing of this clause by the Privy Council headed off any potential future legal challenge by Philip to exercise rights deriving from his title as king of England. The marriage contract also explicitly stated that if Mary died before him, 'he shal not chalenge unto him any right at all in the saide Kingdom'.[100] The preamble to the Act, which made the marriage alliance statute, went to great lengths to insist that Mary's power and status should in no way be diminished or compromised by marriage:

> youre maiestye as our onely Quene, shal and may, solye and as sole quene use, have, and enioye the Crowne and Soverayntye, of, and over your Realmes, Dominions, and Subiectes... in such sole and onelye estate, and in as large and ample maner and fourme... after the solemnisation of the sayde maryage, and at all tymes durynge the same... as your grace hath had, used, exercised and enioyed; or myghte have had, used or enioyed the same before the solemniza- tion of the sayde marriage.[101]

Mary was to be 'onely Quene', 'solye... sole quene'. The insistence on her sole monarchy, however, contradicted the social and cultural expectations of married women. For Mary's Catholic supporter Wingfield, her decision to marry was a 'renowned token of obedience', showing 'that the subjection of wives to their menfolk so often ordered and emphasized by St Paul and the other Apostles was held in high esteem in the queen's sacred conscience'.[102] Mary's wedding vows explicitly incorporated one of obedience, while Philip's did not. She swore 'from henceforth to be compliant and obedient to you as much in mind as in body'.[103] This unreciprocated promise existed in tension with her decisive comment to Renard the previous autumn that although she would follow 'the divine commandment, and would do nothing against his will... if he wishes to encroach in the government of the kingdom she would be unable to permit it'.[104] Secondly, while Mary endowed Philip 'withal my worldly goods', Philip merely endowed Mary with 'all my moveable goods'.[105] The notion of her 'sole' monarchy also ran counter to the notion also expressed in the treaty that Philip was to enjoy 'ioyntely togeder with the said most noble Quene his wif, the state honour and kyngly name of the Realme and Dominions unto the said most noble Quene apperteyning And shall ayde that same most noble Quene his wif in the prosperous administration of the realmes and Dominions'.[106] Although disabled from disposing of benefits, lands and revenues on his own authority, Philip was not prevented from exercising power in the name of the joint authority he shared with Mary. The alliance hinged on their personal relationship, in spite of whatever statutory guarantees were made to counter social and cultural expectations of Mary as a married woman and solve perceived problems of the legitimacy of female authority. In Spain it had been assumed that Philip 'might govern in war and supplement other things which are impertinent to women'.[107] The Act for the Queen's Regal Power responded to uncertainty about female rule and authority and was twinned with the ratification of the marriage treaty. The ratification of the marriage treaty in the 'high court' of parliament represented an intrusion into affairs which had once been exclusively a royal prerogative.

Castile had had experience of a married regnant queen, a precedent that was if anything more concerning for Philip than Mary. After Isabella's death in 1509, despite nearly thirty years at the head of the Spanish kingdoms, Ferdinand's resentment at being relegated to a mere regent led him to retire to Aragón. Following the death of Philip the Fair and on account of Juana's apparent madness, Ferdinand again assumed the regency of Castile for Juana's son Charles, in a deeply unpopular move that generated particular anxiety given his second marriage to Germaine de Foix, the niece of the king of France, Louis XII. Only the tragic death of Ferdinand and Germaine's only child, a son, shortly after birth, ensured that the kingdoms of Castile and Aragón, and so Spain, remained united. A male heir to the Aragonese throne would have taken precedence over Juana and thereby Charles. If Philip had any illusions about his future role in English politics, this example should have been enough to disabuse him about the possibilities of negotiating the treacherous waters of the 'admixture of nations'.[108]

Notes

1 David Loades, *Two Tudor Conspiracies* (Cambridge: Cambridge University Press, 1965), pp. 15–16.

2 See Patricia Thomson, *Sir Thomas Wyatt and His Background* (Palo Alto, Cal.: Stanford University Press, 1964), pp. 62–9 and 74, and Malcolm R. Thorp, 'Religion and the Wyatt rebellion of 1554', *Church History* 47 (1978), 363–80, p. 373.

3 Susan Brigden, *Thomas Wyatt: The Heart's Forest* (London: Faber and Faber, 2012), pp. 362 and 369–70.

4 David Loades, ed., *The Papers of George Wyatt*, Camden Society 4th ser., No. V (London: Camden Society, 1968), pp. 167–8.

5 BL Add. MS 62135, David Loades (ed.), *The Papers of George Wyatt*, Camden Society 4th ser., V (London: Camden Society, 1968) vol. 1, fol. 100v. Reprinted in Anthony Fletcher, *Tudor Rebellions*, Seminar Studies in History (London: Longmans, 1968), doc. 20, p. 148.

6 *ODNB*.

7 See for example Teresa Grant, '"Thus like a nun, not like a princess born": dramatic rep-

resentations of Mary Tudor in the early years of the seventeenth century' in Susan Doran and Thomas Freeman, eds, *Mary Tudor: Old and New Perspectives* (New York: Palgrave Macmillan, 2011), 62–77.

8 Loades, *Two Tudor Conspiracies*, p. 17.

9 John Proctor, a Catholic cleric, held his teaching post throughout Mary's reign. The evidence for this being an 'official' account is his appearance before the Privy Council on a summons on 21st April 1554: see *APC*, n. s. V (1554–6), pp. 12 and 13. See also J. W. Martin, 'The Marian regime's failure to understand the importance of printing', *Huntington Library Quarterly* 44 (1981), 231–247, pp. 241–2.

10 *The historie of wyates rebellion, with the order and maner of resisting the same, wherunto in the ende is added an earnest conference with the degenerate and sedicious rebelles for the serche of the cause of their daily disorder* (London: Robert Caly, 10th January 1555), sigs aviii r–v. On this text see the important article by Alan Bryson, 'Order and disorder: John Proctor's *History of Wyatt's Rebellion* (1554)', in Mike Pincombe and Cathy Shrank, eds, *The Oxford Handbook of Tudor Literature, 1485–1603* (Oxford: Oxford University Press, 2009), pp. 323–6.

11 Paul Hughes and James Larkin, eds, *Tudor Royal Proclamations*, Vol. 2, *The Later Tudors (1553–1587)* (London: Yale University Press, 1969), p. 28.

12 Foxe, *TAMO*, Book 10, p. 1442.

13 Proctor, *The historie of wyates rebellion*, sig. aviii v.

14 AGS E 808, fol. 111: 'aunque ha hauido en aquel reyno algunos mouimientos por Inducimiento de personas apasionados con titulo de que no quieren señor estrangero, el prinçipal fundamento se entiende que es lo de la religion'. *Cal. Span.*, XII, 100. Emperor to Philip, 16th January 1554.

15 Proctor, *The historie of wyates rebellion*, sig. aviii v. See William Cobbett, *Complete Collection of State Trials*, vol. 1 (London: T. Hansard, 1809), p. 862.

16 *Tower Chronicle*, p. 69.

17 National Archives SP 11/2/10.

18 National Archives SP 11/3/18 (1).

19 See Peter Clark, *English Provincial Society from the Reformation to the Revolution: Religion, Politics and Society in Kent, 1500–1640* (Sussex: The Harvester Press, 1977), p. 91.

20 *Tudor Royal Proclamations*, p. 28.

21 Proctor, *The historie of wyates rebellion*, sig. Aii v.

22 Christopher Haigh, *English Reformations: Religion, Politics and Society under the Tudors* (Oxford: Clarendon Press, 1993), Part II, 'Political Reformation and Protestant Reformation', chapter 11, 'The Making of a Minority'.

23 E. J. Baskerville, *A Chronological Bibliography of Propaganda and Polemic Published in English Between 1553 and 1558 From the Death of Edward VI to the Death of Mary I* (Philadelphia, Penn.: American Philosophical Society, 1979), pp. 6–7. There was a sharp decline in the volume of Catholic publications after 1556 and by 1558 they were producing only two titles a year. However, this does not tell the whole story: see my 'Culture under Philip and Mary I', in Sarah Duncan and Valerie Schutte, eds, *The Birth of a Queen: Essay on the Quincentenary of Mary I* (New York: Palgrave MacMillan, 2016), 155–78.

24 *Cal. Span.*, XI, 173. Ambassadors to Emperor, 16th August 1553. Transcribed in an appendix to Louis Gachard, ed., *Collections des Voyages des Souverains des Pays-Bas* (Brussels: F. Hayez, 1874–82), vol. IV.

25 William B. Robison, 'The national and local significance of Wyatt's rebellion in Surrey', *The Historical Journal* 30 (1987), 769–90, pp. 777–8.

26 W. R. Streitberger, *Court Revels, 1485–1559* (Toronto: University of Toronto Press, 1994), p. 210.

27 Edward Arber, ed., *An English Garner: Ingatherings from our History and Literature*, vol. IV (Birmingham: n. p., 1882), pp. 92–3.

28 Arber, *An English Garner*, p. 81.

29 Foxe, *TAMO*, Book 10, pp. 1442–3.

30 Cesare Malfatti, ed. and trans., *The Accession, Coronation and Marriage of Mary Tudor as related in Four Manuscipts of the Escorial* (Barcelona: Sociedad Alianza de Artes Graficas y Ricardo Fontá, 1956), p. 66.

31 *Cal. Ven.*, V (1534–54), p. 460. Pole to Cardinal Cristoforo di Monte, 8th February 1554.

32 *Cal. Span.*, XI, pp. 178–82.

33 *Cal. Ven.*, V, no. 934, p. 560. Giacomo Soranzo to Senate, 18th August 1554.

34 Peter Stallybrass, 'Patriarchal territories: the body enclosed', in Margaret W. Ferguson, Maureen Quilligan and Nancy J. Vickers, eds, *Rewriting the Renaissance: The Discourse of Sexual Difference in Early Modern Europe* (London: University of Chicago Press, 1986), p. 129.

35 Stallybrass, 'Patriarchal territories', p. 128.

36 *Tower Chronicle*, 'John Elder's Letter', pp. 38–9.

37 E. H. Harbison, *Rival Ambassadors at the Court of Queen Mary* (New York: Books for Libraries Press, 1940, rep. 1970), p. 129; Loades, *Two Tudor Conspiracies*, p. 60; and E. H. Harbison, 'French intrigue at the court of Queen Mary', *American Historical Review* 45:3 (1940), 533–51, p. 548. See National Archives E 159/334 Recognisances of the Michaelmas Term, r4.

38 Diarmaid MacCulloch, 'The *Vitae Mariae Angliae Reginae* of Robert Wingfield of Brantham', *Camden Miscellany* XXVIII, 4th ser. (London: Royal Historical Society, UCL, 1984), p. 279. My italics.

39 MacCulloch, 'The *Vitae Mariae Angliae Reginae*', pp. 273–4.

40 John Christopherson, *An exhortation to all menne to take hede and beware of rebellion* (London: John Cawood, 24th July 1554), sig. Oiii.

41 *Tower Chronicle*, 'John Elder's Letter', p. 157.

42 Untitled poem in Emrys Jones, *The New Oxford Book of Sixteenth-Century Verse* (Oxford: Oxford University Press, 1992): George Cavendish, p. 132.

43 Martin Luther, *A Faithful Admonition of a certeyne true Pastor and Prophete... translated with a Preface by M. Philip Melancthon*, trans. Eusebius Pamphilus (Greenwich [London]: Conrad Freeman [John Day?], May 1554), sig. Giii.

44 Luther, *A Faithful Admonition*, sig. Cii.

45 Luther, *A Faithful Admonition*, sig. Cii.

46 Robert Pownall, *An admonition to the towne of Callays* (Wesel?: P. A. de Zutere?,1557), fol. 1r. See David Loades, *Politics, Censorship, and the English Reformation* (London: Pinter Publishers, 1991), p. 43.

47 John Ponet, *A Shorte Treatise of politike pouuer, and of the true Obedience which subiectes owe to kynges and other ciuile Gouernours, with an Exhortacion to all true naturall Englishe men* (Strasbourg: heirs of W. Köpfel, 1556), sig. Hi.v.

48 *Cal. Span.*, XIII, p. 67. Charles V to Eraso, 1st October 1554.

49 Christopher Goodman, *How Superior Powers oght to be Obeyd of their Subjects: and Wherin they may lawfully by Gods Worde be disobeyed and resisted* (Geneva: J. Crispin, 1558), sig. g2v.

50 Raymond De Roover, *Gresham on Foreign Exchange: An Essay on Early English Mercantilism with the Text of Thomas Gresham's Memorandum for the Understanding of the Exchange* (Cambridge Mass.: Harvard University Press, 1949), p. 159. See *Cal. For.* (1553–8), p. 57, no. 150.

51 AGS E 808, fol. 93 (1). *Cal. Span.*, XII, p. 99: 'hauiendo resçebido copia del arresto hecho de los cuerpos y bienes de los Ingleses que se han hallado en eueres al tiempo del tumulto y turbaçion postrero sobre dicho en este reyno yo la comunique al consejo de la reyna y le aduerti de la ocaison del respecto que temian y que no fue dañoso por quitar estos mercaderes la poluora de cañon que la gente de la dicha señora hauia comprado, lo qual el consejo tomo a buena parte para que entendiese que si hazian de su parte algun desafuero a los suyos que tendria medios como lo vengar en flandes y en españa'. Renard to Emperor, 13th February 1554. Original is at Vienna Imperial Archive E22. The Calendar reconstructs differences between the Spanish copy and the latter: 'Your Majesty's fleet makes them suspicious because of the arrest of English merchants and their property at Antwerp and other places in the Low Countries. As soon as I heard this I went to the Council and explained that your Majesty's fleet was meant to assist the Queen and her realm, principally against the French, wherefore

there was no ground for suspicion; and that the Antwerp embargo had been decided upon in order to satisfy your Majesty's subjects, disturbed by the rumour to the effect that your ambassadors over here had been ill-treated and put to death, and by no means with the intention of acting contrary to the treaties of alliance.'

52 Malfatti, *Accession, Coronation and Marriage of Mary Tudor*, p. 73.

53 *Machyn's Diary*, p. 55.

54 *Tower Chronicle*, pp. 74–5 and *Grey Friars Chronicle*, p. 89. See H. F. M. Prescott, *Mary Tudor* (London: Eyre & Spottiswoode, 1953), p. 260 and David Loades, *The Reign of Mary Tudor: Politics, Government and Religion, 1553–1558* (2nd edn, London: Longman, 1991), pp. 82–3.

55 *Cal. Span.*, XI, p. 173.

56 *Cal. Span.*, XII, p. 109. Renard to Emperor, 17th February 1554.

57 *Cal. Span.*, XII, p. 96. Renard to Emperor, 12th February 1554.

58 AGS, E 808, fol. 12.

59 Haigh, *English Reformations*, p. 222.

60 Sir John Fortescue, *De Laudibus Legum Anglie*, ed. and trans. S. B. Chrimes (Cambridge: Cambridge University Press, 1942), p. 81. *Cf.* also William Huse Dunham, Jr, 'Regal power and the rule of law: a Tudor paradox', *Journal of British Studies* 3 (1963–4), p. 24.

61 Dunham, 'Regal power and the rule of law', p. 34.

62 Dunham, 'Regal power and the rule of law', pp. 32–6.

63 Dunham, 'Regal power and the rule of law', p. 43. See Geoffrey Elton, *England under the Tudors* (London: Longman, 1964), p. 218 and Harbison, *Rival Ambassadors*, pp. 169–70.

64 Ponet, *A Shorte Treatise of politike pouuer*, sig. Eiii.

65 Dunham, 'Regal power and the rule of law', p. 44 and *Certayne questions demaunded and asked by the Noble Realme of Englande of her true naturall chyldren and Subiectes of the same* (London: 1555), sigs Aii–Aiiii. Falsely attributed to Miles Hogherde.

66 Foxe, *TAMO*, Book 10, pp. 1442–3.

67 An Italian observer recorded: 'et chiamando il Popolo gli feci un plarlamento mostrando tutti le ragioni, quali la mouiuano a pigliari un forestieri per marito cio e il Principi di Spagna; mostrando anco la sicuri na-chi nasciua in quil Regno; facindo i Capitoli chi no era altra forla atta a diffenderi quil Regno dal Redi Francia, quali gia si come u[/r?]edeuana s'era impadronito della Scotia, chi quella del Principi di Spagna: et chi dicio non era concorsa solo in parere, ma chi il suo Consiglio era stato quello, chi per saluti della liberta del Regno sauena cosi de liberato, di chi ella si era quietata': BNE Mss 765: *Papeles de Estado*, No. 9 'Li successi nel Regno d'Inghilterra dopo la morte di Odoardo sesto fino allo arriuo in quel Regno del Serenissimo Prencipe di Spagna Filippo d'Austria', fol. 224v.

68 There have been a number of interesting discussions of queenship: see for example Theresa Earenfight, 'Without the persona of the Prince: Kings, Queens and the idea of monarch in late medieval Europe', *Gender and History* 19 (2007), 1–21 and Retha Warnicke, 'Queenship: politics and gender in Tudor England', *History Compass* 4 (2006), 203–27.

69 The Act and this text were originally discussed insightfully by J. D. Alsop, 'The Act for the Queen's Regal Power, 1554', *Parliamentary History* 13 (1994), 261–76, p. 275. The originals are at BL Harleian MS 6234, fols 10–25v and Bodleian Library MS Tanner 84, fols 201–17v. References will be to the recent scholarly edition and commentary, Charles Beem and Dennis Moor, eds, *The Name of a Queen: William Fleetwood's Itinerarium ad Windsor* (New York: Palgrave Macmillan, 2013), p. 36.

70 Beem and Moor, *The Name of a Queen*, p. 36. Alsop, 'The Act for the Queen's Regal Power', pp. 275–6.

71 Beem and Moor, *The Name of a Queen*, p. 34 and Alsop, 'The Act for the Queen's Regal Power', p. 274. My italics. The same accusation of the disenfranchisement of the English people continued to be made by anti-Marian polemicists over the next two years.

72 24 Henry VIII, c. 12 and 25 Henry VIII, c. 21, s. 1 in *Statutes of the Realm*, 11 vols (London: Dawson's of Pall Mall), vol. 3, pp. 427 and 464 respectively. See also Dunham, 'Regal power and the rule of law', pp. 30 and 34.

73 Jennifer Loach, *Parliament and Crown in the Reign of Mary Tudor* (Oxford: Clarendon Press, 1986), p. 93. However, Elizabeth I similarly gave up the title *caput ecclesiae*, the Supreme Headship, in favour of being entitled supreme governor in accordance with the Pauline injunctions against women's possession of authority in the church: see Geoffrey R. Elton, ed., *The Tudor Constitution: Documents and Commentary* (Cambridge: Cambridge University Press, 1965), p. 336.

74 *Cal. Ven.*, VI, p. 154. Pole to Morone, 9th August 1555.

75 F. G. Emmison, *Tudor Secretary: Sir William Petre at Court and at Home* (London: Longmans, 1961), p. 185. Original is in Essex Record Office D/DP F147.

76 Loach, *Parliament and Crown*, pp. 108–16.

77 John Edwards, *Mary I: England's Catholic Queen* (London: Yale University Press, 2011), pp. 142–3 and his discussion of Pole's attitudes to the possessioners in *Archbishop Pole* (Farnham: Ashgate, 2014), pp. 122–40.

78 Dunham, 'Regal power and the rule of law', p. 46.

79 1 & 2 Philip and Mary, c. 8, s. 13 and s. 24, *Statutes of the Realm*, vol. 4, pp. 246–54.

80 *Statutes of the Realm*, vol. 4, pp. 246–54.

81 1 & 2 Philip and Mary, c. 8, s. 20. *Statutes of the Realm*, vol. 4, pp. 246–54.

82 *Cal. Ven.*, VI, part ii, pp. 838–9.

83 *Cal. Ven.*, VI, part ii, pp. 838–9.

84 See John N. King, 'The royal image, 1535–1603' in Dale Hoak, ed., *Tudor Political Culture* (Cambridge: Cambridge University Press, 1995), p. 107.

85 Loach, *Parliament and Crown*, p. 97.

86 Mortimer Levine, *Tudor Dynastic Problems, 1460–1571* (London: Allen and Unwin, 1973), p. 90.

87 Alsop, 'The Act for the Queen's Regal Power', p. 265.

88 John Leslie, Bishop of Ross, *Defence of the Honour of Marie Queen of Scots* (Rheims: Jean Foigny, 1569), sigs rvi v and rvii v.

89 Sir John Fortescue, *The Governance of England*, ed. Rev. Charles Plummer (Oxford: Clarendon Press, 1885), p. 356.

90 Fortescue, *The Governance of England*, p. 75, note 4. My translation. The original Latin appears on a Close Roll from Henry's reign: 'non est consuetudo vel lex in terra nostra Angliae, quod filia fratris alicuius primogeniti fratrem juniorem patri suo succedentem haereditarie super haereditate sua possit vel debeat impetere'.

91 Claude de Seyssel, *The Monarchy of France*, trans. J. H. Hexter, ed. Donald Kelley (London: Yale University Press, 1981), p. 48.

92 *Epistolario del III Duque de Alba Don Fernando Alvarez de Toledo*, ed. 17th duke of Alba, 3 vols (Madrid: Real Academia de la Historia, 1952), vol. 1: 1536–67, p. 320: 'Lo de Inglaterra, por amor de Dios, que Vuestra Magestad quiera ser señor absoluto de aquel Reino y mandalle con el pie. Dícenme que está para morir el Canciller y Tesorero. Son dos oficios que Vuestra Magestad ha de poner de mano y mirar muy bien los que pone y que no dependan de la Reina'. Alba to Philip, 28th October 1555, Milan.

93 John Strype, *Memorials especially Ecclesiatical and such as concern Religion*, 3 vols (London: S. Richardson, 1721), vol. 3, p. 284.

94 David Loades, *The Life and Career of William Paulet (c. 1475–1572)* (Aldershot: Ashgate, 2008), p. 126.

95 Strype, *Memorials especially Ecclesiastical*, vol. 3, p. 55. Gardiner's notion that Philip undertook the marriage as a 'subject' might have answered this doubt indirectly, by suggesting that he would be under the jurisdiction of English courts in relation to breaches of the contract.

96 See Sir Frederick Pollock and Frederic William Maitland, *The History of English Law before the Time of Edward I*, 2 vols (Cambridge: Cambridge University Press, repr. 1968), vol. 2, pp. 414–18; William Holdsworth, *A History of English Law*, 7th edn,17 vols (London: Methuen & Co., 1956–72), vol. 3, pp. 185–88; and Pearl Hogrefe, 'Legal rights of Tudor

women and the circumvention by men and women', *Sixteenth Century Journal* 3:1 (1972), 97–105, p. 100.

97   J. Horace Round, *Peerage and Pedigree Studies in Peerage Law and Family History*, 2 vols (London: J. Nisbet and Co. Ltd, 1910), vol. 1, pp. 1–54, esp. 15–16. See also Sidney Painter, *Studies in the History of the English Feudal Barony* (Baltimore, Mary.: Johns Hopkins University Press, 1943), pp. 69–70; Judith Richards, '"To promote a woman to beare rule": talking of queens in mid-Tudor England', *Sixteenth Century Journal* 28 (1997), 101–21, p. 104; and Michael Graves, *The House of Lords in the Parliaments of Edward VI and Mary I: An Institutional Study* (Cambridge: Cambridge University Press, 1981), p. 10.

98   There is a long section on the 'Curtesie of England' in Thomas Edgar, *The Lawes Resolutions of Womens Rights: Or, the Lawes Provision for Woemen. A Methodicall Collection of such Statutes and Customes, with the Cases, Opinions, Arguments and points of Learning in the Law, as doe concerne Women* (London: John Moore, to be sold by John Grove, 1632). On this question see Jennifer Rowley-Williams, 'Image and reality: lives of aristocratic women in early Tudor England', unpublished PhD thesis (Bangor University, 1998), p. 73.

99   1 Mary 3, c. 2, s. 2. (April 1554) in *Statutes of the Realm*, vol. 4, part 1, pp. 222–6. See also Dunham, 'Regal power and the rule of law', p. 42.

100   National Archives SP 11/1/20, fols 7–8.

101   I Mary 3, c. 2 (April 1554) in *Statutes of the Realm*, vol. IV, part 1, pp. 222–6. See also Judith Richards, 'Mary Tudor as "sole quene"?: Gendering Tudor monarchy', *The Historical Journal* 40 (1997), 895–924, pp. 908–9.

102   MacCulloch, 'The *Vitae Mariae Angliae Reginae*', pp. 291–2. My italics.

103   '[F]utura tibi morigera & obsequiosa, tum in mensa, tum in thoro', Bodleian Library MS Wood F33, fol. 49 r.

104   *Cal. Span.* XI, p. 288. Renard to Emperor, 12th October 1553. A comment rightly cited twice by Judith Richards in her biography *Mary Tudor* (London: Routledge, 2008), pp. 145 and 157.

105   '[O]mnibus bonis meis mobilibus', Bodleian MS Wood F 33, fol. 49. See also Richards, 'Mary Tudor as "sole quene"?', p. 912.

106   National Archives SP 11/1/20, fol. 1.

107   AGS E 1498, fols 6–7, fol. 6r: 'pudiesse governar la guerra y suplir a otras cosas que son impertinentes a mugeres'. See Glyn Redworth, 'Matters impertinent to women: male and female monarchy under Philip and Mary', *English Historical Review* 112 (1997), p. 598.

108   Phrase used by the papal emissary Giovanni Francesco Commendone, sent covertly to England to reopen diplomatic relations between England and the papacy; in Malfatti, *Accession, Coronation and Marriage of Mary Tudor*, p. 58.

4

A marriage made in Heaven?

Philip left La Coruña on 12th July, with the supplication of the people that 'the sacred Empress of heaven and earth with the celestial court convey you safe and well to the new English kingdom for the augmenting of our holy Catholic faith and the good of Christendom'.[1] On the voyage from Santander he was entertained with readings from the second part of Agustín de Zárate's *Historia del descubrimiento y conquista del Peru*, which he ordered printed in Antwerp in 1555. The armada finally dropped anchor in the Solent off Southampton at 3 or 4pm on Thursday 19th July.[2]

> [T]he next morning they embarked in a barge covered in black and white cloth adorned with most rich fabrics with a brocade canopy, and twenty men who rowed dressed in green and white which is the *imprese* of the queen and they went to receive the prince accompanied by another ten ships beautifully adorned which had been prepared for that purpose by the Great Chamberlain as *mayordomo* of the Prince.[3]

On board, the earl of Arundel invested him with the Order of the Garter commissioned for him by Mary, before rowing back ashore with him in the barge. Philip then remained for three days in Southampton. On Saturday the news reached London where 'ther was great Joye & tryoumpth made... with bonffyars & ryngynge for the salffe landynge of the prynce of Spayne'.[4] In his royal apartments at Southampton, an emblem of the religious history his coming sought to reverse was prominently on display: 'a crimson and white damask cloth embroidered with flowers of gold thread and on it these words Henry by the grace of God King of England, France and Ireland, defender of the faith and Supreme Head of the English Church'.[5] Even though Mary no longer invoked the Supreme Headship, the spring parliament had again refused to rescind the title, symbolic of the religious changes that had taken place in England over the last twenty years. Philip's first act on English soil was to hear Mass.

Juan Rodríguez de Figueroa recorded in a letter written the day after the wedding that on his first public outing in Southampton: 'his appearance gave great satisfaction to the English, to whom he had been depicted as of a very different disposition and manner by the French and some others'.[6] When he went to Mass on Sunday 'there was a great crowd of people from the kingdom'.[7] Philip had many natural advantages: he was young, athletic with blue eyes or as John Elder described him: 'he is well fauored, with a brod forhead, & gray iyes, streight nosed, and mery countenance... his pace is princely, and gate so straight and upright as he leseth no inche of his higthe, with a yeallowe head, and a yeallowe berde'.[8] The question as to whether he was blonde or not is controversial, unclear in most of the surviving portraiture, but perhaps corroborated by images and descriptions of Isabella and Catherine of Aragón. But more importantly accounts all concur that this was a magisterial display of affability, grace and courtesy. Many courtiers close to him commented on the favourable impression he made. In August, Ruy Gomez da Silva reported 'they themselves say they have never had a king in England who has so quickly won over the heart of everybody' and requested Charles V's principal secretary, Francisco Eraso to exhort the emperor 'to write to his son praising him for this and persuade him to not tire of doing it'.[9] After a second Mass, on this first Sunday in England, Figueroa wrote to the emperor that 'after eating he sent Ruy Gomez to the queen and I presented her the jewels your Majesty ordered me to give her'.[10] Another account recorded more neutrally that the gift was from the prince and how much it was worth: 'the prince dispatched Ruy Gomez de Silva to the queen with a present of jewels that were worth more than 100,000 ducats'.[11] Going against his personal inclination for dining in private, Philip ate frequently in public at this time: 'he ate in public served by the officials sent by the queen, ill-pleasing the Spanish, who suspecting that it might not last long, murmured a great deal amongst themselves'.[12] The emperor had also sent 'those most beautiful tapestries representing the Tunis expedition'.[13] Figueroa noted that the queen 'was greatly delighted by them and the favour your Majesty shows in all things and of the tapestries even more, she has esteemed this favour greatly'.[14] Philip and Mary decided to leave the Tunis tapestries in London, 'because I was advised there was nowhere to hang them elsewhere where they might be appreciated, that's what the queen told me when I kissed her hands, and she asked me about them and what they were like, since they had informed her I was bringing them; and the king felt that they might be left there for now'.[15] The Tunis tapestries from Arras, setting out 'the emperoures majesties procedinges and victories againste the Turkes, as Apelles were not able (if he were alive) to mende any parcell thereof', were displayed at Whitehall, following their entry into London, along with a gold and silver organ set with jewels from the Queen of Poland.[16] They were at the time the most expensive and lavish tapestries ever made, outclassing anything in the Tudor royal collections, and would adorn Philip's royal apartments at Whitehall. Titian's *Venus and Adonis*, currently in the Prado, also arrived in London shortly afterwards, despatched by the artist in September 1554 (see Plate 6). It followed his portrait of Philip in white wolf skin, loaned by Mary of Hungary in November 1553 so his affianced could get a look at her future husband, although perhaps the portrait was not brought to England until March by Juan Hurtado de Mendoza (see Plate 7).[17] While it has been suggested that Philip was sent one of the portraits painted by Eworth, there is no evidence he ever saw an image of Mary before meeting her in July 1554 (see Plate 8).[18] These objects underlined the magnificence and wealth the marriage brought and must have impressed cultivated English courtiers with the romance of their display.

During the three days that he was in Southampton, Philip familiarised himself with the English household that since the end of May had been awaiting his arrival. Paget had been responsible for its creation, nominating Sir John Williams, Chamberlain, Sir John Huddlestone, Vice-Chamberlain, the earl of Surrey (heir of the duke of Norfolk) and eldest sons of the earls of Arundel, Derby, Shrewsbury, Pembroke, Sussex and Huntingdon, Principal Gentlemen; alongside whom served twenty-three gentleman servants, a number of yeomen and a guard of a hundred archers.[19] On 26th July, the day after the wedding, Ruy Gomez da Silva wrote to Francisco Eraso about the 'great problem' of his English household.[20] This was a recurrent theme of letters sent back to Castile: '[t]he king had a household prepared to content the kingdom, and so Englishmen serve in the major offices'.[21] An account published in Zaragoza in 1554, by a *lacayo* of Philip's son Carlos, called Andrés Muñoz, described how 'none of his servants, whether holder of preeminent office or any other, have served or serve, because the queen had a household created and ordered according to the Burgundian style'.[22] In the first of three letters, thought to be by one of Philip's stewards, Pedro Enríquez, the writer complained the 'Steward of the Prince's people has not served even in thought or taken his staff of office in hand, nor is it believed he will, nor the Treasurer nor anyone else, they could exile us all as vagabonds'.[23] According to the high-ranking Ruy Gomez da Silva, later prince of Éboli, Philip sought to resolve the problem by ordering that 'they serve together'.[24] This approach failed to mitigate the issue with his Spanish intimates being retained in the privy chamber, while English servants were limited to outer chamber duties.[25] In September, Renard warned the emperor: 'I am told that the people say the King will not be served by Englishmen although this point was settled by the articles'.[26] The outbreaks of violence between Spanish and English members of the court in the autumn, 'there are daily stabbings in the palace between Englishmen and Spaniards' as Pedro Enríquez wrote on 2nd October,[27] reflected the on-going jealous rivalries and possessiveness of competing groups of servants towards one master.[28] A solution was found in October with the division of the major offices between English and Spanish servants. On 11th January 1555, a Spaniard was hanged at Charing Cross for running through an Englishman at the court gate at Westminster while two others held the victim's arms. The accomplices were pardoned by Mary, according to Wriothesley's chronicle.[29] Machyn's Diary recorded a Spaniard being hanged for killing a servant of George Gifford in October.[30] These incidents seem to have been confined to the early part of the joint reign and were probably ameliorated to a large extent by the draconian punishments available to the commission set up by Philip and Mary to deal with such incidents.[31] More difficult to control was the massive influx of clingers-on, who travelled to service the huge Habsburg court that accompanied Philip. At the beginning of the year, he had intended to bring 3,000 people with him and 1,500 horses and mules.[32] On 12th October 1554 Francis Yaxley wrote to William Cecil: '[t]he artizans Spaniards were commanded yesterdaye to shutte up theyr shoppes, I think because by the order and lawes of the cittie they maye not open the same being not free denyzens'.[33] Renard believed 'over two thousand artisans have entered London, in defiance of the city's privileges, since the King arrived'.[34] Civic disorder and riot were frequently associated with the artisanal class and this infringement of English privileges was potentially explosive. In spite of this order and the proclamation from the spring expelling foreigners, by 1555 the mayor of London was again forced to issue an order concerning the poverty caused by the large number of strangers in London.[35]

On Monday 23th July Philip left Southampton, reaching Winchester at about 6pm. He proceeded directly to the Cathedral to celebrate Mass. One of Philip's retinue recalled in a letter of 1st August to Charles V, 'we entered the most beautiful church I have ever seen, where his majesty went in procession to the high altar, where they had set curtains and they sang the orations to him just as they might in the Cathedral in Toledo, which moved us to no little devotion'.[36] Later that evening he was brought secretly to the queen.[37] Muñoz described how:

> they walked for a goodly space through the meadows of the garden, which are very beautiful, passing over bridges, past streams and springs, it is true that it seemed as if they found themselves in one of the stories they had read in books of chivalry, in light of the beauty of the fountains, marvellous bubbling brooks and diversity of sweet-smelling flowers and trees and other lovely greenery.[38]

A passage identical to this appears in the same anonymous letter from the courtier so impressed by Winchester Cathedral, the only change being from the first person of the letter to the third person in Muñoz.[39] It is clear that Muñoz's account was based in part on the letter, a copy of which was transcribed in the historical miscellany of the contemporary chronicler Florián de Ocampo.[40] It must have been written by one of the courtiers who accompanied Philip on his first meeting Mary. Romances of chivalry were invoked throughout the Castilian accounts of the wedding, reflecting a court culture founded on books like *Amadís de Gaula*, typified in celebrations such as that at Binche, in which Philip had participated in 1549. Philip's steward Juan de Barahona described how in 1554 they had dropped anchor 'two leagues from Southampton at an island called Viqz [White] which is known by another name in *Amadis*, Insula Firme',[41] and how while on board awaiting disembarcation 'the count of Derby arrived, king of the island of Mongaza, who is crowned with a diadem of lead'.[42] In Garci Rodríguez de Montalvo's redaction of the romance, while Galvanes 'departed for the island of Mongaza, Amadis remained on the Insula Firme'.[43] Later Galvanes, while remaining a vassal, is granted the lordship of Mongaza and other islands by Lisuarte, king of Great Britain. Barahona's identification of the Isle of Wight as 'la Insola de Mongaza' and the Stanleys as the descendents of Galvanes perhaps sprang from the earls of Derby's self-authorised assumption of the title 'reges Manniae et Insularum'.[44] The courtier who conducted Philip towards his first encounter with Mary wrote similarly that the earl of Derby 'overcame in battle the rebels when they wished to besiege the queen, he is a lord who can gather together twenty thousand men and a thousand horse, and is lord of an island where he wears a crown of lead'.[45] For many of Philip's retinue, England was a place frequently imagined in their voracious consumption of romances.

After this first interview Juan de Figueroa recorded that 'all were left very happy, offering up a thousand blessings to him'.[46] On Tuesday, the following day, he 'went from the deanes house afote, where every body might see him… in a cloke of blacke cloth embrodred with silver, and a paire of white hose' to where the queen was lodging, in the adjacent palace of the bishop of Winchester, where 'the quenes majesty was standing on a skafhold, his [sic: her] highnes descended, and amiably receiving him, did kisse him in presence of all the people'.[47] They then retired to the presence chamber where 'in sighte of all the lordes and ladies, a quarter of an houre pleasantly [they] talked and communed together, under the cloth of estate'.[48] According to Figueroa there was a second private interview that evening at 10; 'he returned through the same gardens with those of his chamber and the duke of Alba and Admiral… no Englishman was present, only some ancient ladies who emerged into a chamber behind her apartments'.[49] The *ancianas* probably included Mary's favourites Frideswide Strelley, Jane Russell and Susan Clarencieux.

[H]e returned to his lodging giving order for the marriage ceremony which was to take place on the feast of Santiago, giving order for the four thousand

Spanish soldiers who had come in the armada to be conveyed to Flanders without disembarking to serve the Emperor, which when it was carried out gave great content to those of the kingdom, because they admit strangers most unwillingly.[50]

The presence of Philip's army of 4,000 soldiers and navy of more than a hundred ships just off shore, represented a radical shift in policy and was no doubt of concern in England. On 19th March, Juan Hurtado de Mendoza had been warning the bishop of Arras 'above all he must bring no soldiers'.[51] Charles V specifically ordered that the soldiers should not disembark. Mary had arrived in Winchester on Saturday 21st July and was lodged in the bishop's Palace, while Philip arrived on Monday 23rd and stayed in the Dean's house.[52]

The following morning, 25th July 1554, Philip processed to the Cathedral. According to instructions for the 'order of going to the church' Philip was 'to entre into a closett prepared for hym in the bodye of the church on the left syde of the stage which syde of the stage his nobles shall occupy'.[53] Mary arrived after him accompanied by her officials, the clergy, council and as one Spanish account commented 'a good number of well-dressed ladies venerable and young, although not especially beautiful'.[54] The queen was to repair to the church 'not led by any', processing 'unto the trauerse on the ryght side of the stage and all her nobles to stand on that syde'.[55] The careful situation of the pair on the left and right was given equal emphasis in the English heralds' account of the wedding ceremony, as well as in the contemporary Lambeth Palace Library manuscript ('allwayes the Queene on the right hand').

> First the said Church was richlie hanged with Arras and cloath of gold, and there was a stage made along the bodie of the Churche that is to saie from the west dore untill the Rode Lofte wheare was a mounte made of iiii degrees of height as large as the place wold serue. The Stage and Mounte covered with Redd saie and underneath the Rode Loft was there ii trauerses made, one for the quenes Matie. on the right hand an other for the Prince on the left side. The which places served very well for that purpose. The quier was aloft hung with rich cloath of gold, and on eche side the high Aulter was there a rich Trauers one for the queen on the right side another for the Prince on the left side.[56]

This description of the interior space of Winchester Cathedral is similar to a contemporary account of St Paul's on the day Mary's mother Catherine of Aragón had wed Prince Arthur. It seems likely that Mary was self-consciously repeating and commemorating the earlier Tudor diplomatic success in her own wedding.[57] The raised walkway, platform or *stage* constructed in the Cathedral, where the ceremonies and rituals were performed, heightened Philip and Mary's visibility, offering it up to the gaze of a loyal public and as propaganda for their co-monarchy, by furnishing material for numerous

celebratory accounts published abroad.[58] Another little known piece of literary culture associated with the wedding is the lengthy neo-Latin poem
Philippeis, seu, in nuptias divi Philippi (1554) by the foremost Dutch humanist
after Erasmus, Hadrianus Junius, who spent at least six months in England
around the wedding and dedicated the poem eventually published in London
on behalf of the 'Republic of Letters or Republic of Poetry'. Receiving only
thirty-six gold crowns in recompense, his next publication was dedicated to
Mary I alone.[59]

The focus in English and to a lesser extent Castilian accounts on Philip's
situation on the left and Mary's situation on the right underlined Philip's
anomalous occupation of the place traditionally reserved for a royal consort
in relation to a king. Their respective statuses as encoded in the physical
space of the Cathedral reversed traditional gender hierarchies. Andrés Muñoz
attempted to explain the inferiority of Philip's ceremonial position, elaborat-
ing on the fact that, in the church, Philip's 'part was silvery white and that of
the Queen gold... This concerning precedence must be so because he has still
not been crowned'.[60] During the feast following the ceremony concern over
precedence again surfaced in Muñoz's account: 'the queen was seated in the
superior chair and preceded his Majesty in all the service even in the silver,
because the place of his Majesty was white and that of the queen gold'.[61] When
Philip and Mary made their London entry on 18th August, accounts again make
it clear that Mary once more occupied the dominant male position: they rode
through London, 'the quene of the right hande, and the king of the left'.[62]
The positioning of Philip and Mary in the cathedral was designed to underline
Mary's continuing precedence over Philip as England's sovereign, even in
the context of her marriage to him, by placing her in the space traditionally
reserved for a king and Philip in that of a queen consort. The symbolic nature of
the spaces they occupied in Winchester Cathedral and for their London entry
was a coded response to the political anxieties concerning Mary's authority as
a married woman.

The clothing they wore on their wedding day was another important
part of this symbolic negotiation of power relations. Dress in the early modern
period was crucially a form of investiture, from the robing of the monarch at a
coronation to servants' liveries, the regalia of guild membership, to gifts or the
inheritance of items of clothing. The royal couple 'went dressed almost identi-
cally in cloth of gold, well embroidered. His Majesty wore the outfit the queen
had sent him, a suit more in the style of over there, than of Spain, and a chain
encrusted with beautiful jewels'.[63] The queen provided Philip with clothing for
his first two important, public, ceremonial engagements in England: his entry
into Winchester and the wedding itself. Their identical outfits on their wedding
day served to identify them visually, as they were united in matrimony. It was

a visual emblem of political union. Philip also wore the Order of the Garter: '[t]he King went forth that day in white shoes, doublet and hose, with the Garter of the Order of St George, with a French-style brocade suit with many stones that the queen had sent him the night before and with a sash in the same style as the suit, worn according to the custom of that land'.[64] Philip's dress represented a major concession to the sensibilities of his hosts. The dominant style at the English court at this time and that favoured by Mary was French. The Venetian ambassador Soranzo observed that the queen's favoured outfits consisted of 'a gown and boddice, with wide hanging sleeves in the French fashion'.[65] This may explain why Pedro Enríquez commented representatively of Mary that 'she dresses very badly'.[66] Juana the Princess of Portugal, Philip's sister and regent of Spain in his absence, sent Mary headdresses and dresses. Ruy Gomez da Silva hoped that by wearing them 'she would look less old and skinny'.[67] While Philip was dressed up in clothes and jewels given to him by the queen, Mary was clothed in symbols drawn from Habsburg iconography.[68] For the wedding, she wore a piece of jewellery in which were set two diamonds, one a gift from Philip in June, the other from Charles, previously set in the ring given to his wife the Empress Isabella in 1525, after he had broken off his engagement to Mary: 'a diamond mounted on a setting in the form of a rose, with a huge pearl hanging down onto the chest'.[69] This must be the jewel worn in the portraits by Anthonis Mor and Hans Eworth from her reign (see Plates 8 and 9). The pearl is popularly believed to be 'La Peregrina', famously given to Elizabeth Taylor by Richard Burton.

At her coronation the previous year, there was confusion in the accounts between the customary purple velvet of a king at his coronation and the white cloth of gold associated with the coronation of a queen consort.[70] The fact that both of them wore white cloth of gold to the wedding ceremony may be intended to suggest an analogy between that event and a coronation or investiture for Philip. At the same time, his wedding outfit transformed Philip into a royal consort. More importantly still, the bridegroom was dressed as an Englishman, his English-style clothing crucial in paving the way towards his acceptance as king of England. His clothes were a negotiation of national particularities, as well as international politics, an example of what Daniel Nexon has dubbed multivocal or polyvalent signalling; a crucial legitimation strategy, appealing to different, heterogeneous audiences through messages that attributed 'shared (but inconsistent or incompatible) identities and values to imperial authorities'.[71] According to the imperial ambassador Simon Renard the closing of the spring parliament after the ratification of the marriage treaty had witnessed emotional scenes: '[w]hen the Queen made her speech, she was interrupted five or six times by shouts of God save the Queen! and most of those present were moved to tears by her eloquence and virtue'.[72] In the same despatch he sent a copy of the 'genealogical tree that has been published here to show that his Highness is no foreigner, but an offshoot of the House of Lancaster. When Paget heard that the Chancellor had devised it, he said it was being done in order to give his Highness a right to the throne.'[73] Another aspect of the carefully stage-managed process by which Philip might come to be accepted in England was emphasising his genealogical links with English royalty.

For the marriage, the scholars of Winchester Cathedral posted celebratory verses on the doors of cathedral and palace, echoing the work of Gardiner's genealogical device, publicising Philip's descent from Edward III:

> There is no boy to call Mary mother and to call you,
> Philip, father, but he will be given (if Christ grants it);
> Be born, great boy, to be written of in the small world,
> Let our page be signed with your name.
> The Devil old enemy of mankind did not wish
> That the English Queen Mary marry *English* Philip
> And that the royal stock return to its source,
> But God, the provident hope of the English did wish it.[74]

The process of Philip's naturalisation initiated by Gardiner's device was continued in the scholars' verses through their allusion to his English lineage. This Philip was the 'English Philip'. Shortly after the marriage one Castilian account reported: 'The English spread abroad their great contentment of having seen and dealt with the King and so they tell us that he is English and not Spanish'.[75] Documents in the Winchester College archives reveal that Philip and Mary visited the school and rewarded those responsible for the celebratory verses with lavish gifts: Philip gave over £10, while Mary provided £6, of which 'Purdie' received two shillings for 'writtinge the verses dedicated', while 'Shellye' who delivered them to their highnesses got twelve pence. A further sum of £6 appears to have been distributed among thirty of the older scholars, again for their poems. Entries in the bursar's accounts reveal that extra brewing had been ordered in preparation for the wedding and that the fields around the school had tents pitched, perhaps to stable the large number of horses or even courtiers themselves from Philip's large following.[76] The warden from 1542, John White, a client of Gardiner's, had been preferred to the bishopric of Lincoln in 1554 and eventually succeeded his master at Winchester from 1556 until 1560, its last Catholic bishop. His famous painted ceiling and a stone fireplace at the College are also perhaps associated with the marriage. The vignettes of a female Tudor and Spanish male head may represent Philip and Mary, while banners with 'vive le roi' were an appropriate way of celebrating a new king alongside carved initials in a fireplace that may stand for Philipus

Rex.[77] New College Oxford, where White was a fellow from 1534, had been founded by William Wykeham in the reign of Edward III, the common royal ancestor foregrounded in Philip and Mary's entry into London. New College proved remarkably resistent to the Reformation under Elizabeth, with the shadow cast by Gardiner and White.[78] White delivered the famous and oft-quoted funeral sermon after Mary's death.

Mary's continuing precedence over Philip had been repeatedly emphasised in the marriage contract signed in January and then enshrined in statute by the 'Act for the Queen's Regal Power' in the spring parliament of 1554. Their positioning in relation to each other, the fact that Mary occupied the dominant (male) position on the right-hand side, Philip's visibility to the 'people', his jewel-encrusted garter and English clothes all sought to allay the underlying concerns about the position of a married, regnant queen. They were essential elements of Philip's diplomatic cultivation of his new subjects. Nevertheless, there were discordant aspects of Philip and Mary's representation in their wedding (and later entry). After the marriage rites were concluded, for example, their joint style declared in Latin and English gave him the expected precedence over his queen: 'Philip and Marie, by the grace of God king and quene of England, Fraunce, Naples, Hierusalem, and Irelande, defenders of the faith, princes of Spain and Secyll, archdukes of Austria, dukes of Millan, Burgundy, and Brabant, counties of Haspurge, Flaunders, and Tirol'.[79] Philip's precedence here was critical, since it would have circulated more widely than accounts of the marriage or the act of Parliament that sought to hedge in Mary's constitutional position as a regnant queen. It had been the subject of wrangling during the negotiations and in exactly the same way as with Philip and Mary's great-grandparents Ferdinand and Isabella, the king's name went first regardless of his constitutional position. We can see the influence of their joint style as far away as rural Devon. In 1558 the parish priest of Morebath, Christopher Trychay, dated an entry in the parish accounts 'yn the 5th and 6th yere of the rayne of Kyng Phelippe and quyne Maryes gracyus mageste'.[80] This represents the most widely disseminated form of recognition of Philip and Mary's co-monarchy and the acceptance of Philip's precedence in their joint style in many ways contradicts other aspects of the ceremony and thinking about the marriage.

Other echoes of the precedent set by Ferdinand and Isabella can be found in the images of Philip and Mary's co-monarchy that appeared on the coinage. In Castile and León the heads of both Catholic monarchs appeared, whereas in Aragón and its kingdoms the bust was almost always just of Ferdinand. An instruction sent to Toledo on 23rd May 1475 following the agreement of the *Concordancia* ordered their names, titles, busts, arms and initials to appear on coinage: on the *doble castellano (excelente)* 'their bodies or figures seated', on the *medio y cuarto de castellano* 'their profiles regarding each other', while silver *reales* had their conjoint royal arms.[81] Even after his wife's death Ferdinand's image continued to appear on all the coinage throughout the Spanish kingdoms. The iconography of shared monarchy that began to appear on English coinage from September 1554 combined elements from the earlier Spanish coins, with Philip and Mary in profile looking at each other, their joint arms and a floating crown above their heads. This almost identical image was seized upon by pamphleteers, who interpreted the floating crown as a symbol of the destruction of England's discrete sovereignty. One pamphleteer complained that it signified 'geving to the prince of Spayne (under the name of king) as much auctorite, as if he were king of England in dead. As ye may see... by the quoynid mony going abrode currant.'[82] Another pamphlet claimed 'the prince of spain hath optainid to have the name of the king of England and also is permittid in our english coins to join our english armes with the armes of spain and his fisnamy the quenes, the crowne of England being made over both ther heds in the midest, and yet upon nether of them both'.[83] Anne Hooper wrote to Bullinger on 11th April 1555 from Frankfurt: '[y]our Rachel sends you an English coin, on which are the effigies of Ahab and Jezebel'.[84] In the context of Mary's promotion of plans for Philip's coronation from Christmas 1556, the image which appeared on coins and charters reversed the respective positioning of Philip and Mary, with Philip now situated on Mary's right. This reversed the precedence that was constantly noted in accounts of the marriage and their royal entry into London in August. The crown that symbolised their co-monarchy represented a genuine sharing of power. The positioning of the two below the floating crown denoted the relative ascendancy that one enjoyed over the other. As the reign progressed Philip edged his way into the symbolically superior position. In terms of the position she occupied in relation to Philip, Mary was first a king and then a queen. Even if she had eventually managed to have Philip crowned, there can be no doubt that she would have continued to reign as she had for the majority of the time, as Philip like his father progressed around the Habsburgs' multinational empire.

Revealingly, the first occasion on which their respective positioning was reversed came in the wake of Mary's phantom pregnancy. She was described on 27th November 1554, appearing at Whitehall 'in the chamber of presence': 'the Quene sat highest, rychly aparelid, and her belly laid out, that all men might see that she was with child. At this parliament they did laboure to haue the kyng crowned and some thought that the Quene for that cause, dyd lay out her belly the more. On the right hand of the Quene sat the king.'[85] The *Dynasties* exhibition argued that the vogue for portraits of pregnant women in the seventeenth century arose from the desire to have a keepsake of a beloved partner, who was about to run a very real risk of death in childbirth. Was

Mary's gesture a message to her councillors and parliament that were she to die in childbirth, her desire was that Philip rule in her stead? Nevertheless, with her in the higher chair the tableau sent out a mixed message. Even though the arrangements between Philip and Mary might have been seen in exclusively Anglo-Burgundian terms – negotiated as they were by Simon Renard and Perrenot Granvelle and ratified in the Low Countries, not Spain – all of the clauses in the 'Capitulación' of the Catholic monarchs discussed here were echoed if not repeated in Philip and Mary's treaty and marriage contract.[86]

The representational strategies of the two monarchs reveal how ceremony and dress responded to the political difficulties presented by the Spanish match. They maintained a fine balance between the need for the Habsburgs to see the marriage as a successful and essential part of their imperial policy in Europe and assuaging English anxieties and uncertainties concerning the unprecedented marriage of a regnant queen and whether this would in practice affect Mary's position and the precedence over Philip as repeatedly emphasised in the positioning of the couple. In addition, the concern, particularly but not exclusively of Protestants, was that the repeal of Reformation legislation seen as key to England's *imperium*, might pave the way for the expropriation of the monastic lands in their hands, but also see England itself transformed into a satellite of a foreign empire. The different views as to why or whether the Act for the Queen's Regal Power was necessary ignore the fact that it responded to a contemporary division within the political nation between those who, like Lord Paget, saw potential advantages in their mistress's incorporation within the most powerful dynasty in Europe and those for whom this meant the end of their 'empire' and identity as God's chosen people. The Act aimed to placate those elements, whether 'patriotic', anti-Spanish or Protestant, who saw the marriage as inimical to their political, economic and religious interests. It is now widely accepted that England was a Catholic country in 1553. Nevertheless, if Philip had had realistic aspirations of remaining king of England after or in the event of Mary's death, he was fully aware of the need to gain the acceptance of a significant sector of the political nation. To this end, as soon as he arrived, he began distributing generous gifts and pensions drawn from Spanish revenues to important courtiers and gentlemen, some of whom continued to receive them long after his reign in England ended.[87] Eventually such patronage would have created a powerful faction in favour of Philip, the king, but in the end time and Mary's health were not on his side.

The clothes the royal couple wore, their symbolic use of the space in Winchester Cathedral, the wording of their vows and order of the ceremony, as well as their positioning in relation to each other for their London entry, its pageants and tableaux all encoded both negotiations and tensions between English and Spanish aspirations for the marriage and the problematic nature of Mary's female rule. The choice of Winchester itself for the wedding, with its long-standing association with royal ceremonial, must also have been significant beyond its strategic situation near the coast and Philip's navy. Gender inversions were offset against traditional images of obedience and female subordination to male authority. The focus in accounts on details like Philip not possessing a sword of state, his clothes and his situation in the space reserved for a queen consort demonstrates their careful awareness of the intense significance of symbols in the political and personal negotiations of Philip and Mary's relationship. What is clear is that Philip was expected by Londoners to take up the reins of power and fulfil the role of king of England in both a titular and a real sense.[88] The picture of implacable anti-Spanish opposition undermining any chance Philip had of achieving power in England needs to be reassessed in the light of evidence from the wedding and entry and closer attention to evidence of a Catholic faction, typified by men like Wingfield, who were not as unrepresentative as has been claimed. Religious opponents sought to relate the match to an abrogation of English sovereignty, by playing on anxieties about seisin in property related by analogy to the fear of a Habsburg claim to the English crown and the return of papal jurisdiction abrogating England's tortured path to claiming *imperium*. The wedding ceremony and entry to London constantly reinforced Mary's precedence, even while subversive images of Philip taking control and righting gender relations thrown off-balance subsisted alongside them. What the law could not legislate for was the reality of a personal relationship. Whether Mary was ultimately an unnatural stepmother or a wife and mother to her people, whether she was a king or a queen, whether Philip was ultimately Spanish or English, a victorious bridegroom or despoiler and rapist, largely depended on the political, religious and cultural allegiances of their viewers. One side of that divide has loomed far larger in histories of their reign.

Notes

1 Andrés Muñoz, *Viaje de Felipe Segundo a Inglaterra (Zaragoza, 1554) y Relaciones Varias Relativas al Mismo Suceso*, ed. Pascual de Gayángos and Manuel Zarco del Valle (Madrid: La Sociedad de Bibliófilos Españoles, 1877), p. 63: 'la sagrada Emperatriz imperio de cielo y tierra, con la corte celestial te lleve con bien y a saluamento al nueuo reino Ingles para augmente de nuestra santa fe catholica y bien de la cristiandad'.

2 There are at least four Italian accounts of Philip's journey and arrival; one in Dutch; another in German; and one in Portuguese. See Jennifer Loach, 'The Marian establishment and the printing press', *English Historical Review* 101 (1986), 135–48, p. 145; Corinna Streckfuss, '"Spes maxima nostra": European propaganda and the Spanish match' in Alice Hunt and Anna Whitelock, eds, *Tudor Queenship* (New York: Palgrave MacMillan, 2010), Appendix A, pp. 251–2; on the Italian accounts see M. J. Bertomeu Masiá, 'Relaciones de sucesos italianas sobre la boda de Felipe II con María Tudor', *Cartaphilus* 5 (2009), 6–17; and on the Castilian sources for the marriage Sheila Himsworth, 'The marriage of Philip II of Spain with Mary Tudor', *Proceedings of the Hampshire Field Club* 22 (1962), 82–100.

3 BNE MS 1750: *Papeles Tocantes a Phelipe Segundo. Tomo Segundo*, No. 7. Casamiento de Phelipe Segundo en Inglaterra, ano 1554, con Maria hixa de Enrique y Catalina, fols 89*ff.*, 94v: 'la mañana siguiente se embarcaron en un vaso cubierto de tela negra y blanca adornado por de dentro riquissimos paños con un dosel de brocado, y veinte hombres que remaban vestidos de verde y blanco que es la empresa de la Reyna y fueron a receuir al Principe acompañados de otras diez naues muy bien entapizadas que auia preuenido para el efeto el gran Ciamberlan como mayordomo del Principe'.

4 Charles Lethbridge Kingsford, ed., *Two London Chronicles from the Collections of John Stow*, Camden Miscellany XII, 3rd Ser. (London: Camden Society, 1910), p. 37.

5 BNE MS 1750, fol. 95r: 'un paño de Damasco carmesi y blanco con flores de oro texidas y en el estas palabras. Henricus Dei gratia Anglie, Francie, et Hibernia Rex, defensor fidei, et *caput supremum ecclesia Anglicanae*'. My italics. See also Martin Hume, 'The visit of Philip II', *English Historical Review* VII (1892), 253–80, p. 267.

6 *CODOIN*, vol. 3, pp. 520–1: 'Satisfizo muy mucho su *vista* a los ingleses, que se le tenian pintado de muy diferente disposicion y manera los pintores de Francia y de otras partes algunas'.

7 *CODOIN*, vol. 3, p. 521: 'hubo mas concurso de gentes del reino'.

8 John Elder, *Copie of a Letter Sent into Scotlande (1555)* (Amsterdam: Theatrum Orbis Terrarum, fac. edn, 1971), sig. Fv r.

9 *CODOIN*, vol. 3, p. 531: 'ellos mismos dicen que nunca han tenido Rey en Inglaterra que tan presto les haya ganado los ánimos á todos'/'que escribiere á su hijo de loalle de esto y persuadille que no se canse de hacello'.

10 *CODOIN*, vol. 3, pp. 520–1: 'despues de comer envió á Rui Gomez á la Reina, é yo le presenté las joyas que V. M. me mandó entregar'.

11 BNE MS 1750, fol. 95v: 'el Principe despachado a la Reyna al señor Ruy Gomez de Silua con un presente de xoyas, que valian mas de cien mil ducados'.

12 BNE MS 1750, fol. 95v: 'comió en publica seruido de los oficiales que le auia embiado la Reyna, con mala satisfaccion de los Españoles, los quales sospechando no durasse mucho, murmurauan harto entre ellos'.

13 *Cal. Ven.*, V, no. 898, p. 511. Marc'Antonio Damula to Doge and Senate, 17th June 1554.

14 *CODOIN*, vol. 3, p. 521: 'se holgó mucho con ellas y la merced que V.M. en todo le hace, y de la tapicería mas, la cual ha estimado en gran manera'.

15 *CODOIN*, vol. 3, pp. 521–2: 'porque fuera de allí fuí avisado que no habia donde la colgar para que bien se muestre, y así me lo dijo la Reina cuando le besé las manos, y de suyo me preguntó por ella y que tal era, que le habian avisado que la traia; y al Rey le ha parecido que se estuviese allí por el presente'.

16 *Tower Chronicle*, p. 152. See also Rosalind K. Marshall, *Mary I* (London: HMSO, 1993), p. 126.

17 Charles Hope, 'Titian, Philip II and Mary Tudor', in Edward Chaney and Peter Mack, eds, *England and the Continental Renaissance: Essays in Honour of J. B. Trapp* (Woodbridge: Boydell and Brewer, 1990), 53–65. See John Edwards, *Mary I: England's Catholic Queen* (London: Yale University Press, 2011), p. 179.

18 Lorne Campbell, *Renaissance Portraits: European Portrait-Painting in the 14th, 15th and 16th Centuries* (London: Yale University Press, 1990), p. 197.

19 David Loades, *The Tudor Court* (Totowa, NJ: Barnes & Noble Books, 1987), p. 161.

20 *CODOIN*, vol. 3, pp. 526–7, 530: 'inconveniente grande'. Cited below, Chapter 7, note 185.

21 BNE MS 9937, fol. 126v: 'Tenia casa puesta al rey por el contentamiento del reyno, y asi sirven los ingleses [en] los oficios mayores'.

22 Muñoz, *Viaje de Felipe Segundo*, p. 77: 'ningun criado de los suyos, así en los oficios preeminentes como en los demás, no le han seruido ni sirven, porque la Reina le tenia hecha y ordenada la casa al uso de Borgoña'. Original: *Sumario y verdadera relación del buen viaje que el invictissimo Príncipe de las Españas don Felipe hizo a Inglaterra, y recibimiento en Vincestre donde caso y salio para Londres* (Zaragoza: Esteban Nagera, 1554).

23 Muñoz, *Viaje de Felipe Segundo*, 'Primera Carta', p. 96: 'Mayordomo de los del Príncipe ni por pensamiento ha servido ni tomado baston en la mano, ni se cree que lo tomarán, ni el Contador

ni los demas, que á todos por vagabundos nos pueden desterrar'. Pedro Enríquez de Guzmán de Acevedo y Toledo (Zamora, c. 1525–Milan 1610), was a soldier, counsellor and governor of Milan. Son of Diego Enríquez de Guzmán and Catalina de Toledo y Pimentel (a sister of the duke of Alba, who was both brother-in-law and uncle of Pedro Enríquez). He participated in the campaign led by Alba against Paul IV in 1559. He married Juana de Acevedo after this point; see *Diccionario Biográfico Español* (Madrid: Real Academia de la Historia, 2009–13).

24 *CODOIN*, vol. 3, p. 527: 'sirvan juntos'.

25 Loades, *The Tudor Court*, p. 57.

26 *Cal. Span.*, XIII, p. 60. Renard to Emperor, 18th September 1554.

27 Muñoz, *Viaje de Felipe Segundo*, 'Tercera Carta', p. 118: 'hay cada día en palacio cuchilladas entre ingleses y españoles'.

28 For further details see *Calendar of Patent Rolls: Philip and Mary*, 4 vols (London: HMSO, 1936–9) (henceforth, *CPR*), vol. 2, pp. 242–3 and vol. 3, p. 112; David Loades, *The Reign of Mary Tudor: Politics, Government and Religion in England 1553–1558* (2nd edn, London: Longman 1991), pp. 215–16 and 220 and *APC*, V, p. 65. For Spaniards attacking Londoners, see *CPR*, Philip and Mary, vol. 2, p. 243.

29 Charles Wriothesley, *A Chronicle of England during the Reigns of the Tudors*, ed. William Hamilton, Camden Series 20 (London: J. B. Nichols, 1877), p. 125.

30 *Machyn's Diary*, p. 72.

31 Headed by Briviesca de Muñatones and Sir Thomas Holcroft; see Muñoz, *Viaje de Felipe Segundo*, 'Tercera Carta', p. 118. See also Loades, *The Tudor Court*, p. 26.

32 AGS E 808, fol. 12.

33 BL MS Lansdowne 3, fol. 92. See Loades, *The Reign of Mary Tudor*, p. 160.

34 *Cal. Span.*, XII, p. 96. Renard to Emperor, 13th February 1554.

35 William Page, ed., *Letters of Denization and Acts of Naturalization for Aliens in England 1509–1603* (Lymington: The Publications of the Huguenot Society, 1893), vol. 8, p. xxx. See licence to grant letters of denization, Pat. 2 and 3 Philip and Mary, p. 3 and *Cal. Dom.*, XII, p. 37.

36 BNE MS 9937, fol. 130r: 'entramos por la mas hermosa Iglesia que yo he visto jamas, y asi fue su mag. con la procession al altar mayor, donde le tenian puestas unas cortinas, y alli le cantaron sus oraciones como lo pudieran hazer en la Iglesia mayor de Toledo, que no movio a poca devoçion'.

37 *Tower Chronicle*, 'John Elder's Letter', pp. 139–40.

38 Muñoz, *Viaje de Felipe Segundo*, p. 70: 'anduvieron un buen rato por las praderías del jardín, que son muy hermosas, pasando por buenas puentes de arroyos y fuentes, que cierto al parescer parescia que se hallaban en algo de lo que habían leído en los libros de caballerías, segun se les representó aquella hermosura de fuentes, y maravillosos arroyos vertientes, y diversidades de olorosas flores y árboles, y otras lindezas de verdura'.

39 BNE MS 9937, fol. 130: 'Anduvimos un buen rato por las praderias del Jardin, pasando por buenas puentes de ryos y fuentes. y cierto a mi vez, paresçio que me hallaba en algo de lo que avia leydo en los libros de cavallerias'.

40 BNE 9936 (covering the period 1521–49) and 9937 (1550–58). These two miscellanies were copied by Juan Páez de Castro, Philip's confessor, and then passed on to his successor as royal chronicler Ambrosio Morales. These copies are the sources for Malfatti's edition.

41 Cesare Malfatti, ed. and trans., *The Accession, Coronation and Marriage of Mary Tudor as related in Four Manuscipts of the Escorial* (Barcelona: Sociedad Alianza de Artes Graficas y Ricardo Fontá, 1956), p. 139: 'dos legoas de Antona que se llama ysla de Viqz que por otro nombre la llama *Amadís* la ynsula firme'. Barahona was probably a relation of Antonio Barahona, described as a chronicler of Charles V and author of a text *Rosal de la nobleza de España* of which there is a seventeenth-century copy in the BNE, and a genealogy of the nobility of Baena. This may explain how the letters ended up in the miscellanies of Florián de Ocampo, Juan Páez de Castro and Ambrosio Morales.

42 Malfatti, *Accession, Coronation and Marriage of Mary Tudor*, p. 141: 'llegó el conde de Arbi, Rey de la Insula de Mongaza, el cual se corona con corona de plomo'. See also the ver-

sions reprinted in Fernando Díaz Plaja, *La Historia de España en sus documentos: El siglo XVI* (Madrid: Instituto de Estudios Politicos, 1958), p. 381, and in *CODOIN*, vol. 1, pp. 564–74.

43 Garci Rodríguez de Montalvo, *Amadís de Gaula*, ed. Juan Manuel Cacho Blecua, 2 vols (Madrid: Cátedra, SA, 1991), vol. 2, pp. 973 and 1023: 'partió de la Ínsola Firme para la ínsola de Mongaça, como oído avéis, Amadís quedó en la Ínsola Firme'.

44 See Glyn Redworth's article 'Nuevo mundo u otro mundo?: conquistadores, cortesanos, libros de caballerías y el reinado de Felipe el Breve de Inglaterra', in *Actas del I Congreso Anglo-Hispano*, 3 vols (Madrid: 1994), vol. 3, 113–25, p. 122.

45 BNE MS 9937, fol. 133r: 'vencio la batalla delos rebeldes quando querian cercar ala reyna. esse es un Senor que todas las vezes que quiere junta veintemill hombres, y mill cauallos, y es señor de un isla donde se pone una corona de plomo'.

46 *CODOIN*, vol. 3, p. 522: 'todos quedaron con gran contentamiento y dándole mil bendiciones'.

47 *Tower Chronicle*, 'John Elder's Letter', pp. 139–40.

48 *Tower Chronicle*, 'John Elder's Letter', pp. 140–1.

49 *CODOIN*, vol. 3, p. 523: 'volvió por los dichos jardines con los de su cámara y Duque d'Alva y Almirante... no estando inglés alguno presente, sino algunas ancianas damas que con ella salieron á una sala detrás su aposento'.

50 BNE MS 1750, fol. 97r: 'volvió a su alojamiento dando orden para las cerimonias del matrimonio, que se auia de hacer el dia de Santiago dando orden que los quatro mil españoles que auian venido en el armada, sin saltar en tierra de aquel Reyno fuessen lleuados a flandes, en seruiçio del emperador su Padre, como se puso en execución de lo que quedaron muy contento los del Reyno, por que de mala gana admiten estrangeros en él.'

51 *Cal. Span.*, XII, p. 161. Mendoza to Arras, 19th March 1554, London.

52 Lambeth Palace MS 285, fols 39v–40r. This account confirms that the cession of Naples was announced by Juan de Figueroa immediately before the ceremony with a patent 'fayre sealed inclosed in Syllver & gylt', as well as the contract being publicly presented 'the full conclusion of the same as may appeare by this Instrument in parchment sealed with a Greate Seale contayninge by estymacion 12 leafes'.

53 Bodleian Library MS Wood F33, fol. 47.

54 *CODOIN*, vol. 3, p. 523: 'buen número de damas ancianas y mozas, poco hermosas, bien aderezadas'.

55 Bodleian Library MS Wood F33, fol. 47.

56 College of Arms MS WB., fols 157r–58r. This is the best extant transcript. It dates from the seventeenth century and was made by the herald William Le Neve. It is reprinted in John Leland, *De rebus Britannicis collectanea* (1774: repr. Farnborough, fac. edn 1970).

57 'Also from the west dore of Powles was made a scaffold Rayled vpon both sides vnto the Queere dore, and the Rayles couered wt Rede worsted, the which scaffold was man height from the ground', from Kingsford, *Chronicles of London*, p. 249. This is an edition of BL MS Vitellius A XVI.

58 See Chapter 5, note 21.

59 Chris Heesakkers, 'The ambassador of the republic of letters at the wedding of Prince Philip of Spain and Queen Mary of England: Hadrianus Junius and his *Philippeis*', in Rhoda Schnur, gen. ed, *Acta Conventus Neo-Latini Abulensis: Proceedings of the Tenth International Congress of Neo-Latin Studies* (Tempe: Arizona Centre for Medieval and Renaissance Studies, 2000), 325–32, pp. 329 and 332.

60 Muñoz, *Viaje de Felipe Segundo*, p. 75: 'parte era plata blanca y la de la parte de la Reina era dorada... Esto del preceder debióse de hacer porque aún él no estaba coronado'.

61 BNE MS 9937, fol. 133v: 'la reyna se asento en la silla mayor y precedio asu mag. en todo el servicio hasta en la plata, porque estava ala parte de su mag. blanca. y dela otra parte dela reyna dorada'.

62 *Tower Chronicle*, 'John Elder's Letter', p. 146.

63 BNE MS 9937, fol. 132v: 'yvan vestidos casi de una manera de tela de oro muy bien bordado.

encima. y su mag. llevava una ropa que la reyna le avia embiado, que tirava mas al traje de aca, que al de españa, y un collar muy excellente de piedras'.

64 BNE MS 9937, fol. 127r: 'salio el Rey aquel dia de blanco, Calças Jubon y cuera, y la Jarretierra, y horden de San Jorge puesta, con una ropa francesa de brocado con muchas piedras que la reyna le enuio la noche antes. y su mag. con una saya dela manera dela ropa, vestida ala usança dela tierra'.

65 *Cal. Ven.*, vol. VI, p. 533.

66 Muñoz, *Viaje de Felipe Segundo*, 'Segunda Carta', 106: 'viste muy mal'.

67 *CODOIN*, vol. 3, p. 530: 'se le pareceria menos la vejez y la flaqueza'. Ruy Gomez da Silva to Francisco Eraso, 29th July 1554, Winchester.

68 See Hilary Doda's fascinating essay 'Lady Mary to Queen of England: transformation, ritual and the Wardrobe of the Robes' on Mary's sartorial choices in Sarah Duncan and Valerie Schutte, eds, *The Birth of a Queen: Essay on the Quincentenary of Mary I* (New York: Palgrave MacMillan, 2016), 49–66.

69 Muñoz, *Viaje de Felipe Segundo*, p. 74: 'un diamante tabla engastado a manera de rosa, con una gruesa perla que colgaba en los pechos'.

70 See Judith Richards, 'Mary Tudor as "sole quene"?: Gendering Tudor monarchy', *The Historical Journal* 40 (1997), 895–924, pp. 898–902.

71 Daniel Nexon, *The Struggle for Power in Early Modern Europe: Religious Conflict, Dynastic Empires and International Change* (Princeton, NJ: Princeton University Press, 2009), p. 114.

72 *Cal. Span.*, XII, 242. Renard to Emperor, 6th May 1554.

73 *Cal. Span.*, XII, p. 242.

74 'Deest puer, at dabitur (Christo donante) Mariam/Qui vocitet, matrem, teque, Philippe, patrem;/Nascere magne puer parvo scribendus in orbe,/Nomine signetur pagina nostra tuo.// Nubat ut Angla Anglo Regina Maria Philippo,/Inque suum fontem Regia stirps redeat,/Noluit humani generis Daemon vetus hostis,/Sed Deus Anglorum provida spes voluit'. The original is at BL Royal MS 12 AXX, and reprinted in *Tower Chronicle*, 'John Elder's Letter', pp. 173–4. My translation and italics.

75 BNE MS 9937, fol. 126v: 'Los Ingleses publican gran contento de aver visto y tratado al Rey. y asi nos dizen que es Ingles y no español'.

76 Winchester College Archives, Liber Albus 22992, fol. 186v. See also Account Roll 22210. I would like to thank Suzanne Foster for her enormous generosity in helping me to find these items.

77 On the ceiling, now in the Westgate Museum, see Elizabeth Lewis, 'A sixteenth century painted ceiling from Winchester College', *Proceedings of the Hampshire Field Club Archaeological Society* 51 (1995), 137–65.

78 Patrick McGrath, 'Winchester College and the old religion in the sixteenth century' in Roger Custance, ed., *Winchester College: Sixth Centenary Essays* (Oxford: Oxford University Press, 1982), 229–80, p. 231.

79 *Tower Chronicle*, 'John Elder's Letter', p. 142.

80 Eamon Duffy, *The Voices of Morebath: Reformation and Rebellion in an English Village* (London: Yale University Press, 2001), p. 169.

81 Antonio and Pío Beltrán, 'Numismatica de los Reyes Católicos' and Pío Beltrán Villagrasa 'Bibliografia numismatica de los Reyes Catolicos' in *Instituciones economicas sociales y politicas de la epoca Fernandina*, J. Vicens Vives, *et al.* (Zaragoza: Institución 'Fernando el Católico', n. d.), 223–42: 'sus bultos (o figuras) sentados'/'sus bustos mirandose'.

82 *A Supplicacyon to the quenes Maiestie* (Strasbourg: W. Rihel, 1555), sig. Cviii r. The relationship between political discourse and the coinage in mid-Tudor England is fascinatingly explored in Jennifer Bishop, 'Currency, conversation and control: political discourse and the coinage in mid-Tudor England', *English Historical Review* 131 (2016), 763–92.

83 See Richards, 'Mary Tudor as "sole quene"?', p. 915. See also *The lamentacion of England* (Germany?: n. p., 1557), p. 10., i.e. Philip and Mary.

84 See Rev. Hastings Robinson, ed., *Original letters relative to the English Reformation*, 2 vols (Cambridge: Cambridge University Press, 1846), vol. I, p. 115.
85 BL MS Harleian 419, fol. 132.
86 M. Weiss, ed., *Papiers d'état du Cardinal de Granvelle*, 9 vols (Paris: Imprimerie Royale, 1843), vol. IV, pp. 78, 144 and 149–51. There is interesting information about the power struggle between Renard and Eraso for control of the English mission in a letter of 3rd September 1554, pp. 298–300.
87 On those distributed on his arrival see Loades, *The Reign of Mary Tudor*, p. 158.
88 See Chapter 5.

5

Royal entry: London, 18 August 1554

Major public events at the outset of Philip and Mary's reign were carefully cho-
reographed opportunities to promote a vision of a harmonious new political
order, while assuaging English fears about an alienation of sovereignty through
the marriage. The entry into London, however, did not do this.[1] It sought
by contrast to underline the importance of the internationalism of the new
government and the city's place at the centre of the international connections
and networks the marriage facilitated and on which its trade, commerce and
mercantile activity depended. Foreign merchant communities were centrally
involved in the planning and funding of the entry, while the city authorities
regardless of their personal religious allegiances needed to impress their new
king, also the ruler of their two largest export markets. In this sense it picked
up where Mary's London entry the previous autumn had left off: the 'pageants in honor of the new queen were clearly dominated by the presence of
strangers'.[2] Philip and Mary's London entry on 18th August 1554 has been read
predominantly through the prism of an anecdote recounted in John Foxe's *Acts
and Monuments*, which retold how the bishop of Winchester, Stephen Gardiner,
on passing the first pageant in Gracechurch Street, noticed an image of Henry
VIII holding a book with the words *Verbum dei* written on it. According to
the *Tower Chronicle* Gardiner, who was also Mary's Lord Chancellor, immediately summoned the unfortunate artist responsible and berated him 'with
ville wourdes calling him traytour, askte why and who bad him describe king
Henry with a boke in his hand, as is aforesaid, thretenyng him therfore to
go to the Flete'.[3] Tellingly, this passage was crossed out in the manuscript
and does not mention Mary, although she was depicted alongside her father
and brother, Henry VIII and Edward VI. The *Acts and Monuments* version has
Gardiner insisting to the painter that instead of showing Henry 'delivering the
same book (as it were) to his son king Edward, who was paynted in a corner by
him... hee shoulde rather haue put the booke into the Queenes hand (who was
also paynted there)'.[4] For John Foxe, this was the only significant aspect of the

city of London's welcome for the royal couple, as he continued: 'I pass ouer
and cut of other gaudes and Pageants of pastime shewed unto him in passing
through London... hauing other graver thinges in hand'.[5] The story and its
retellings have broader and more complex implications for the understanding
of Philip's relationship with his new subjects than Foxe's dimissal allows. The
incident undoubtedly reflected religious tensions, but it has come to symbolise
more widely the unacceptability in England and particularly London of Philip
and the marriage through their implicit association with an allegedly unpopular
Catholic restoration.

The image described in Foxe and the *Tower Chronicle* of Henry VIII recalls
and perhaps even visually echoed the title page of the 1539 *Great Bible* (based
on the Holbein-designed Coverdale bible of 1535). This iconic image of the
new theocratic order inaugurated by the Henrician Reformation, with king
handing bible and *verbum Dei* to his nobility and clergy, who in turn expound
it to the people, was the work of Richard Grafton and Edward Whitchurch,
assisted by the then King's Printer, Thomas Berthelet. Grafton and Berthelet
both figured among the four aldermen charged in May 'to sett furthe there
devyses and opynyons for suche pageantes and other open demonstracions of
ioye as they should thynke meate to be made and sett furythe when the Cyte
at the comynge of the kynge of Spayne'.[6] Grafton and Whitchurch had been
firmly associated with evangelical publishing, producing six editions of the
Great Bible in the two years succeeding the *princeps*, as well as numerous other
religious texts including the first edition of the *Book of Common Prayer* in 1549.
Berthelet had printed Tyndale's *Institution of a Christian Man* in 1537 and was
the King's Printer throughout the crucial period 1530–47, a mantle he had
passed on to Grafton during Edward VI's reign. Gardiner was not merely
being oversensitive. The image reflected the vision of two men deeply invested
in the religious changes of the previous two decades and an important segment
of London's educated elite. Whether or not the painting was 'agaynst the
quenes catholicke proceedinges',[7] it certainly possessed a powerful personal
resonance for both Grafton and Berthelet. Grafton had been removed from his
post as the King's Printer and imprisoned for a month at the outset of Mary's
reign as a result of publishing the proclamation of Lady Jane Grey as queen. For
these Protestant printers, the bible was their business. It, like the entry, was
a space where commerce and conscience overlapped. Grafton served in the
November parliament which revived the heresy laws, and became the Warden
of the Grocers' Company in June 1555. He was briefly imprisoned again, by
Gardiner, in the Fleet for allowing the children in the Royal Hospitals, of
which he was Treasurer-General, to learn from an English primer as opposed
to a Latin one.[8] While there was principled opposition to what Philip represented, there were also important economic considerations at work for

the city, which made accommodation the only possible strategy. While the tableau had provocative aspects noted by the sharp-eyed bishop of Winchester, it was not representative of the entry as a whole, which also offered a series of images that were fulsomely supportive of the co-monarchy and Philip's authority in England. Unsurprisingly, neither the Catholic Scot John Elder's *Letter Describing the Arrival and Marriage of King Philip, His Triumphal Entry into London, The Legation of Cardinal Pole, &c.*,[9] nor the anonymous Italian pamphlet *La solemne et felice intrata* make any reference to it.[10]

Despite the fact that the pageants were dismantled within two days ('[a]t the Courte yt was agreed that the Chamebelyn shall cause all the Cyties pageauntes to be taken downe with conveynyente spede'[11]), the artist was forced to alter the image and 'paynted him shortly after, in the sted of the booke of *Verbum Dei*, to have in his hands a newe payre of gloves'.[12] These lines are again crossed out in the *Tower Chronicle*. In Foxe, the painter 'fearing lest he should leave some part either of the book, or of the "Verbum Dei", in king Henry's hand, he wiped away a piece of his fingers withal!'[13] The exact nature of Henry VIII's historical reputation during the reign of his eldest daughter is a complex question. She never completed the tomb he had planned for himself, although initially there was no overt attack on his memory.[14] Although Mary did not use the title, constitutional historians have been fond of pointing out that she and then her husband Philip were both *de facto* Supreme Heads of the Church of England. In Philip's chamber in Southampton, a tapestry had already alluded to the relationship between religious and secular power in England; a balance perhaps not unwelcome to a monarch who had problems of his own with the papacy and only subsequently became associated with the more 'fanatical' aspects of Catholic reform: 'a cloth of purple and white damask, with flowers picked out in gold thread and the words, Henry by the grace of God King of England, France and Ireland, defender of the faith, and supreme head of the Church of England'.[15] England had been ruled over by two adolescents and a woman since Henry's death. Did Philip dare to dream that one day he might fill those capacious greaves?

David Scott Kastan has argued that 'divergent vectors of power' were apparent in Philip and Mary's London entry with 'a Catholic Queen bringing her Spanish husband into a protestant and xenophobic capital'.[16] The varied interests at work in the staging of an entry – national, international, commercial, religious, political and cultural – were, indeed, particularly apparent in this international event. There is no evidence that seriously calls into question Philip's belief that he had been welcomed into London 'with universal signs of love and joy', as he wrote to his sister Juana, princess dowager of Portugal and in his absence regent of Spain, from Hampton Court two weeks later.[17] Mary herself subsequently thanked the aldermen of the city for 'theire good willes and

forwardenes in makyne of shewes of honour and gladnes'[18] and Sydney Anglo
concluded that it was 'more carefully furnished and finished than its immediate
predecessor'.[19] The joyful reception of Philip has more than anything else to
do with the inevitable commercial advantages of political stability and unity;
England and its most important trading partner, the Low Countries, being
ruled over by the same monarch. The organisers of the entry were aldermen,
for the most part deeply immersed in international trade, specifically that with
the Low Countries where Philip had been sworn in as Charles V's successor
five years earlier in 1549. It seems unlikely that they would sabotage their own
chance to impress their new rulers. More importantly, London was Catholic.
On Mary's arrival after her accession, icons of the Virgin and images of saints
had appeared in the windows of houses along the route. In 1551, to garner
support, she and her followers had ridden defiantly, pointedly displaying the
rosary. A decade later, in 1561 when St Paul's steeple was burned down by a
lightning bolt, the reaction of Londoners made clear 'how many had been won
back to the Catholic Church under Mary, or indeed had never left it'.[20] The
problem posed by Philip's religion and nationality have been overstated in the
light of the sectarian polarisation that took place decades after 1554. Then,
Philip could be welcomed, bringing new opportunities, opening up markets
and new worlds to Englishmen as well as bringing back the old religion of their
forebears.

The universal emphasis on people's joy in the European accounts of the
marriage and entry may have been to counteract the shadow of vociferous
opposition to the regime embodied in the Wyatt rebellion, but equally it
reflected the complexity and divided nature of responses to the marriage.
Catholics were still a majority in England at this time and an unprecedented
female regnancy had been 'normalised' through a prestigious marriage to
Europe's most powerful and influential monarch-in-waiting. Foreign accounts
of the marriage and entry universally acknowledged the couple's initial liking
for each other and understood the marriage in the broader context of European-
wide religious and political problems, as well as demonstrating considerable
sensitivity to English fears.[21] The *Copia d'una lettera* lamented, for example,
that there were no triumphal arches in Winchester despite Philip's reception
with 'as much love as one could say'.[22] Entries combined functions from royal
progresses and civic pageants, being concerned with projecting an image of
a monarch and monarchy to a captive audience, as well as foregrounding the
importance of the city to its ruler, by underlining its civic identity, power and
wealth.[23] The Philip and Mary entry had much in common with a Lord Mayor's
Show, mirroring its processional route.[24] Eight days before the treaty was even
signed preparations began for Philip's arrival. The Court of Aldermen agreed
on 4th January, two days after the arrival of the Low Countries envoys, to 'the

garnishynge of the gates and other places of the cytie', London Bridge to 'be paynted and trymmed and all the Imagery therupon to be newlye paynted also newe agaynste the comynge in of the kynge of Spayne and that the draw brydge there be lykwyse trymmed as it was trymmed at the comynge in of the mayor'.[25] The analogy suggested here with a Lord Mayor's procession was reinforced by the route, for the most part identical today, up Gracechurch Street, left at the crossroads between Leadenhall and Cornhill, down Cheapside, past St Paul's through Temple Bar to Ludgate Hill, and along Fleet Street and then on to Whitehall.

     Although this was a common ceremonial route through the city, in contrast to the statuary that had greeted Charles V there in June 1522 (Hercules, Samson and Jason with the Golden Fleece, figures chosen as dynastic flattery), Philip was greeted instead by autochthonous figures from England's mythic past, Gogmagog and Corineus Britannus. Gogmagog, a conflation of Gog and Magog, was a frequent feature of medieval *mappae mundi*. The giants' framing of the entry again played on England's chivalresque and mythical associations in the Spanish literary imagination, already called upon in the guided tour of the Round Table at Winchester (repainted by Henry, with King Arthur's portait bearing an uncanny resemblance to his own face, originally to impress Charles) and legible in the frequent literary allusions in Spanish accounts to the world of *Amadis*. According to John Elder, the giants at the draw-bridge held a tablet bearing Latin verses, translated by him:

> O noble Prince, sole hope of Caesar's side,
> By God apointed all the world to gyde,
> Right hartely welcome art thou to our land,
> The archer Britayne yeldeth the hir [sic?] hand,
> And noble England openeth her bosome
> Of hartie affection for to bid the welcome.
> But chiefly London doth her love vouchsafe,
> Rejoysing that her Philip is come safe.
> She seith her citisens love thee on eche side,
> And trustes they shal be happy of such a gide:
> And al do thinke thou art sent to their citie
> By th'only meane of God's paternall pitie,
> So that their minde, voice, study, power, and will,
> Is onlie set to love the, Philippe still.[26]

Corineus Britannus, the archer of the poem, was an ally of the Trojan Brutus, who had helped defeat the primitive giant inhabitants of Albion, among whom was the giant Gogmagog. Modern versions of these figures still guard the gates to the Guildhall in London. The statues prior to those destroyed during the blitz had stood there since 1708, when they had been carved by a Captain

Richard Saunders to renew fire and rodent-damaged wicker-and-plaster figures. These mythic guardians of the City of London's liberties dated back to
the reign of Henry V and were displayed not only in the 1554 entry but also
in Lord Mayor's Shows throughout the century. The most important early
modern version of the story derived from Geoffrey of Monmouth's *Historia
Regnum Britanniae*.[27] The Latin poem at the gates figured the relationship
between Philip and the city as a synecdoche of his relationship with Mary.
His new kingdom was a welcoming female lover. Within the providential
framework of universal monarchy, his rule in London, however, is condi-
tional; the citizenry merely 'trustes they shal be happy'. The opening tableau
is solely directed at Philip. Despite the fact that it was *his* entry, the royal
couple rode through London 'the quene of the right hande, and the king of the
left'.[28] As I argued in Chapter 4, Mary's occupation of the dominant, male,
kingly position on the right, fixed upon repeatedly in English accounts, was
a deliberate strategy to assuage English fears about the alienation of Tudor
sovereignty and power through the Spanish match.[29] It emphasised that the
marriage had not attenuated her regal authority in England; she remained sole
queen with Philip as guide. Nevertheless, in the last pageant an enthroned
virgin delivered a crown into the hands of a figure representing Philip. So the
entry culminated in a tableau representing precisely the alienation of English
sovereignty.

After the hiatus of the Wyatt revolt, preparations for the entry restarted
with the nomination on 22nd May of 'Mr Sturgeon Mr barthelett Mr Grafton
and Mr Heyworde'.[30] John Sturgeon was a Protestant friend of Hugh Latimer,
one of the first Marian martyrs, burned at the stake in the winter of 1555. On
10th September 1549 Sturgeon had headed the English mercantile community
in Antwerp which had greeted Philip on his entry into the city. Preparations for
this entry had been hurried and heavy rain led to it being cut short: 'as a result
of the continual showers, it was not possible to see many actual things... due
to the swiftness [of his arrival], there were many things of great importance
that had not been finished'.[31] Despite their not having been finished in time,
they were described in the festival book printed later as if they had been; a
caveat concerning the gulf between what actually took place during entries and
their published commemorations. According to *Le triumphe*, after the citizens
of Antwerp and merchants from Lucca and Milan came the English contingent,
followed by Spanish, Austrians and Germans:

> The said English Nation holds in this town in great reverence their superior,
> who is held for a governor, named Mr John Sturgeon, who as much for his
> great age as for the prudence of his person is reputed and held to be a man of
> great virtue, who as chief and sovereign of the said Nation brought up the rear,
> mounted on a very beautiful and triumphant English horse...[32]

A scaffold erected at the vulgarly known Meerbrugge, in the street of the tanners, displayed a series of sculptures of famous Philips, including Philip of Macedon, Philip the Apostle, Philip the Roman emperor, Philip the Bold, Philip the Good and that other Burgundian duke, Philip the Handsome, who had been married to Philip's grandmother, Juana 'the Mad'. The gallery of Philippic worthies was repeated at Cornhill in London for the second pageant although with only four of these celebrated Philips: Macedon, the Roman emperor and the dukes of Burgundy, the Good and the Bold. One suspects this may have been Sturgeon's contribution.

He was an obvious choice, having already arranged the English triumphal arch in Antwerp, participating in welcoming Philip into another European city. Royal entries were always international events, especially in important commercial cities where they mapped political geographies and patterns of trade. The English arch in Antwerp represented a personified Oceanus Britannicus, Britannia (an 'English woman in a white dress') and Constantine and his mother Helen (both reputed English in this period) above a central inscription: 'the most desired coming of he, in the hope of a lasting union between him and the King of England, held until now a breakable bond'.[33] Maritime personifications were combined with a reminder of England's centrality in the conversion of the Roman Empire to Christianity.

The aldermen were not all Protestants. Among their number was John Heywood, the Catholic court musician and entertainer. His famous epigrams and *A dialogue conteinying the number in effect of all the prouerbes in the englishe tongue* (1546, 1550) had all been published by Thomas Berthelet, who Heywood must therefore have known well, and in March 1538 he had been paid forty shillings by Mary herself for performing an interlude with the children of the Chapel Royal.[34] He addressed Mary with an oration in English and Latin at St Paul's Churchyard for her coronation procession on 1st October 1553 and was paid the princely sum of £50. William Camden and Ben Jonson recorded the contents of their witty exchanges on that occasion.[35] Heywood's pension was increased to £50 per annum in 1555 and replaced in 1558 with the grant of the manor of Bulmer in Yorkshire. In June, he withdrew from the planning committee, as a result of the demands of 'sundrye other busynes'; perhaps the composition of the ballad 'The eagle's bird hath spread his wings' or the adaptation of the elaborate allegorical poem, *The Spider and the Fly*, finally published in 1556 but perhaps begun as early as 1536.[36] Much has been made of this, along with the fact that Grafton is the only alderman named in the last entry on the preparations. But neither are necessarily significant: 'his companyons devysours of the same' were presumably the same men named on previous occasions (minus Heywood) and in the previous entry on 2nd June it had been 'Mr Barthelet and thother devasors of the Cyties pageantes shall make the merchant strangers with intende theryme selves to make pageantes prevye to the matters of the same the Cities pageants'.[37] Two days later Heywood's name appeared second on a list of citizens providing surety for a loan to the queen of 119,280 florins by Jasper Schette to be repaid at Antwerp.[38] Heywood was like Thomas Geminus, someone whose religion did not impede their professional life, his career straddling the reigns of Henry, Edward, Mary and Elizabeth.[39]

The very first pageant welcoming Philip was a triumphal arch organised by the Hansard merchants of the Steelyard, topped by a mechanical equestrian statue of the prince, which mounted and wheeled around as the procession passed by. Two female figures, one on each side, represented Castile and England. The trading privileges of the Hanse merchants had been revoked by Edward VI in 1552, after a sustained campaign by the Merchant Adventurers. Mary reinstated them a few months after her accession on 1st November. However, the Hansards complained that they continued to be disregarded. The importance of the trade to them can be seen from the fact that, despite the political instability in 1554, they exported 35,450 cloths, a figure similar to the highest achieved between 1538 and 1544. Their suspension of trade in response to the Merchant Adventurers' attacks in 1555 only applied to shipping out of England, not from the Low Countries, making it wholly ineffective. They were still in the midst of attempts to persuade English authorities to guarantee their privileges in May 1557, when a delegation headed by the 'syndic' Dr Heinrich Suderman presented credentials addressed only to Philip, outraging the Privy Council and culminating in a fiasco. William Paget, Lord Privy Seal, a former supporter of the Hansard league, berated them as Turkish, tartar and barbaric for Danzig's embargo on the export of corn to England.[40] They had attempted to curry favour with Philip too, given his dynastic links with Hanseatic towns in the Low Countries and Germany. Perhaps acting through Paget, they sponsored a city view of London, the 'Copperplate Map', three plates of which survive, incorporating panels praising the virtues of the Hanse merchants. It was calculated to appeal to Philip's well-known cartographic interest, something shared by Paget.[41]

Following the Sturgeon-inspired Philips, the figure of Orpheus reduced wild masquers dressed as lions, wolves, foxes and bears to order at Cheapside. Beneath, verses drew an analogy between Philip and the orphic origins of civility and civic harmony: 'England... Whose chiefest joye is to hear thee, Philip, speke'.[42] Foxe's hostile interpretation by contrast read the allegory as the 'English people resembled to brute and savage beasts, following after Opheus's harp, and dancing after king Philip's pipe'.[43] Here Philip and Mary no doubt admired the Eleanor of Castile Cross, newly gilded for the occasion, with images of the Virgin and Child and the resurrection.[44] At St Paul's, where they paused and heard *Te Deum* sung, a young scholar, possibly Edmund Campion, recited a Latin poem and presented Philip with a book of verse. The fourth pageant was perhaps the most significant in terms of dynastic propaganda, repeating a genealogical device that had first been used in 1501 for Catherine of Aragón's marriage procession, which alluded to the Tudor and Spanish royal families's common descent from John of Gaunt. In 1522, for Charles, trees had sprouted from the chests of both John of Gaunt and Alfonso X. John of Gaunt had mounted a military challenge for the throne of Castile in 1386 on behalf of his wife, Constanza of Castile, the last surviving descendant of Pedro I, a king murdered and usurped by his half-brother Enrique in 1369. Their daughter Catalina married the usurper's grandson and her son Juan II ruled from 1406–54. Alfonso X was Pedro I's great-great-grandfather and had signed an important alliance with Henry III in 1254.[45] In 1554 the genealogy was kingly and imperial with the family tree sprouting from Edward III, who was depicted with a 'close crowne on his head' and 'a ball imperial in his lefte' hand, 'of whom both their majesties are lineally descended'.[46] The verses underneath the device, 'Which both descended of one auncient lyne/It hath pleased God by mariage to combyne',[47] returned to a theme broached by the Winchester scholars of Stephen Gardiner in the verses they had presented to the royal couple in Winchester: 'suum fontem Regia stirps redeat', 'the royal stock returns to its source'. Replacing John of Gaunt with an English king stressed Philip's links to the English royal family. At the apex of the tree 'was a quene of the right hande, and a king of the left, which presented their majesties' and 'above that, in the heigth of al, wer both their armes joined in one, under one crown emperial'.[48] This image was repeated throughout the entry, above the Philips at Cornhill, here at the Little Conduit with children dressed as kings and queens perched in the branches detailing their descent and lastly at Fleet Street, in the final pageant, topped by a king and queen representing Philip and Mary, each handed a crown, according to Elder, by the figure of Sapientia.

Apart from the reversal in their respective positioning these images or other standardised ones like them may have been the models for Giles Godet's visualisation of Philip and Mary's co-monarchy in his *Brief Abstract of the Genealogie and Race of All the Kinges of Engalnde* (1560?), 'a magnificent woodcut', with the 'largest and most elaborate royal crest in the entire book' (see Plate 10).[49] The verses beneath the image, however, are far less obsequious than those beneath other monarchs. Philip 'raigned with hir as king, and yet was he/Not crounde, wherby no claime he could attain/She being dead of England kyng to be'.[50] But this is no more than what the image shows – Philip wears a simple open crown, while the closed imperial crown is strapped awkwardly onto Mary's headdress/wimple. This early Elizabethan representation of their co-monarchy places Philip in the superior, right-hand position. The iconography is ambiguous, however, containing a contradictory set of elements: the imperial crown perches precariously on Mary's head while Philip wears an open diadem; he holds the sword and she the sceptre; while both have their hands resting on the orb. Over both of their heads are their joint arms in accordance with the representation established in their royal entry.[51]

The image of their co-monarchy trialled in the entry began to appear on the coinage as early as September 1554. As we saw, the floating crown was seized on as a symbol of the end of English sovereignty by Protestant pamphleteers hostile to the regime.[52] A clearer image of the arms can be gleaned from Thomas Geminus's map of Spain dedicated to the royal couple in 1555 and probably displayed in the Privy Gallery at Whitehall or from the document now in the Pepys Library at Cambridge from a manuscript on salt and fisheries (see Plates 4, 4b and 11).

The way the genealogy figured in the London entry reiterated a commonplace from welcomes accorded to other visiting 'Spanish' princes. However, it was complicated by the ambiguity concerning Philip's future role as king of England. His homecoming could be read as a reclaiming of the crown itself, to which his descent might give him title. Genealogy would clearly have been key to any claim to a title to the crown. The final pageant in Fleet Street represented a king and queen encircled by the figures of Justicia, Equitas, Misericordia and Veritas 'wyth a boke in her hande, whereon was written *Verbum Dei*'.[53] The repetition of the controversial tag here orthodoxly subordinated God's word to the allegorical figure of Veritas.[54] This was the proper Catholic subordination of God's word to truth revealed by the institutional church, which had exercised Gardiner in 1546.[55] According to John Elder's letter Sapientia descended to crown both Philip and Mary; however, the verses below read 'If Wisdome then him with hir crowne endue, / He governe shal the whole world prosperously'.[56] In one of the Italian pamphlets commemorating the event, *La solemne et felice intrata*, a young virgin enthroned delivers the crown received to Philip, as the verses suggest: 'From a heaven above held up by four columns, a crown descended and received by that seated virgin, who receiving it made a show of flying to present it to the King, with these words: "Through me kings reign"'.[57] Associating Mary with the Virgin was an obvious trope and, depending on the interpretation of the seated virgin figure, might suggest either that Philip ruled only through Mary's grace and favour or that he had been divinely called to rule as king of England. Other contradictions exist between these two accounts – the equestrian statue in the Italian pamphlet becomes a painted, mounted portrait in the Scot's letter.[58] In the final pageant was an image in which Mary delivered the English crown into the hands of the foreign Philip.

The procession ended at Whitehall Palace, where the recently finished Tunis tapestries would be ostentatiously displayed; emblems of Habsburg victory in the religious conflict being waged between Catholic Christendom and the infidel Muslim East and by extension Protestant heretics. Some have argued they were shown in Winchester at the marriage or as part of the entry; however, all the evidence points to the fact that they were simply used to decorate the privy apartments, rather than forming part of any public ceremonial occasion. Symbolically, they recalled the *reconquista* of al-Andalus and the identification of Charles V as a latter-day Scipio Africanus revisiting the ruins of Carthage, from where Aeneas had sailed to found an empire.[59] Although they may 'have done nothing to allay Protestant English fears concerning the royal union's implications',[60] tapestries were ultimately domestic furnishings and in this case the most luxurious and costly objects in England, far surpassing anything possessed by the royal treasury. They were a statement underlining Philip's status but also emphasising that he was setting up home in England, decorating his quarters with the most technically sophisticated and sumptuous decorative objects yet produced. It was of course in the Privy Gallery at Whitehall that the maps of England and Spain produced by Thomas Geminus would probably have been displayed from 1555.[61] Philip took the tapestries with him when he returned to Brussels at the end of 1555.[62]

In his chronicle histories Richard Grafton did not mention anywhere the persecution and martyrdom of friends, like John Rogers, who were burned as a result of heresy laws he was involved in reviving as a member of the November parliament of 1554. As late as 1570, he recorded neutrally Wyatt's assertion that Mary would 'bring in the Pope, but also by the marriage of a straunger, to bring the Realme into miserable seruitude and bondage', and lamented that the Kentish gentleman had not 'lyued as an obedient subiect'.[63] His chronicles mentioned those executed in the aftermath of the Wyatt rebellion being displayed on gibbets 'for a terror to the common sort', but only briefly alluded to the entry he had mounted and designed for Philip and Mary, not even hinting at his own involvement, stating merely 'the Citie was bewtefied with sumpteous pagiaunts and hanged with riche and costly Silkes and cloth of golde and siluer'.[64] According to his biographer 'Mary is portayed by Grafton as a valiant and courageous woman, ardently attached to the Papacy, but never personally vindictive'.[65] Indeed, he described her as of 'inuincible heart and constancie', and merely referred the curious to 'the Monuments of the Church', to find out more about those 'in trouble for religion'.[66] In his *This Chronicle of Briteyn*, he claimed Mary 'shewed her selfe in that case more stoute then is credible' during the Wyatt revolt.[67]

The fear of overrunning by strangers, played upon in Wyatt's propaganda, appeared to have been fulfilled, according to the *Tower Chronicle*, in a passage that is again censored or crossed out, which claimed '[a]t this tyme ther was so many Spanyerdes in London that a man shoulde have met in the stretes for one Inglishman above four Spanyerdes, to the great discomfort of the Inglishe nation'.[68] Although commercial interests were clearly important and my argument here suggests that Philip was welcomed with rejoicing into the capital, this is not to ignore that there were segments of London's population vehemently opposed to the Spanish or that unsavoury incidents did take place. Commerce and the privileges granted to alien merchants were almost always at the heart of the attacks that took place throughout early modern Europe on stranger communities. They were brought there by trade and resented as a threat to native jobs and profits.

Xenophobic tensions were inevitable in an early modern city like London in these circumstances. On 31st July, a few weeks before the entry, two bakers had been punished for 'misordering a Spaniard going in the street'.[69] Mary herself felt it necessary to insist to the livery companies that they ensure their members 'use well the Spaniards'.[70] The Mercers' Company issued an order the day after the queen's letter requiring their members to refrain from deliberately throwing exrement at Spaniards in the street: 'be of honest behaviour… towards the strangers and to leave their mocking of them both in words and signs, and also the pick of quarrels, nor give any occasion of evil unto them nor cast nor throw neither in the streets nor out of their windows any manner of filth'.[71] The royal entry, like the marriage treaty, was framed by commercial interests and trade. London's civic and corporate identities were emphasised throughout. But what exactly the pageants meant is open to interpretation. They did not present a single, unified picture. By the time of the entry, Protestant figureheads like Cranmer and Latimer were already in prison. Personal friends of Grafton, like Whitchurch and Coverdale, were too. Although there had been arrests of *alumbrados* and occasional harrassment of English merchants, the first *auto de fe* involving Spanish Protestants in Spain only took place after Philip's return from England in 1559. The numbers burned that day were swelled by a papal ruling that meant the authorities were no longer obliged to accept the recantations of suspects but could go ahead with the death penalty regardless. If the English had looked to the Low Countries in 1554 as a likely model for the handling of religious difference, though, it would not have offered a reassuring picture. Although the regent Mary of Hungary had flirted with Lutheran ideas in her youth, the Netherlands possessed the harshest anti-heresy legislation and saw the greatest number of executions in this period.[72]

Notes

1 For a fuller account of the entry see my 'Images of co-monarchy in the London entry of Philip and Mary (1554)', in Jean Andrews, Marie-France Wagner and Marie-Claude Canova-Green, eds, *Writing Royal Entries in Early Modern Europe* (Turnhout: Brepols, 2013), 113–28.

2 Scott Oldenburg, 'Toward a multicultural mid-Tudor England: the Queen's royal entry *c.* 1553, *The Interlude of Wealth and Health*, and the question of strangers in the reign of Mary I', *English Literary History* 76 (2009), 99–129, p. 106.

3 *Tower Chronicle*, p. 78. The pageant is described in the following way: the 'conduit in Graciouse strete was newe paynted and gilded, and aboute the winding turred was fynely portrayed the ix wourthies and king Henry the eight and Edwarde the vj^th in their tabernacles, all in complet harnesse, some with mases, some with swordes, and some with pollaxes in their handes; all saving Henry the eight, which was paynted having in one hand a cepter and in the other hand a booke, whereon was wrytten *Verbum Dei*'.

4 Foxe, *TAMO*, Book 10, p. 1681.

5 Foxe, *TAMO*, Book 10, p. 1681.

6 London Metropolitan Archives (hereafter LMA), Repertory of the Court of Aldermen 13 (Parts 1 and 2), fol. 163v.

7 *Tower Chronicle*, p. 78.

8 See J. A. Kingdon, *Richard Grafton: Citizen and Grocer of London* (London: Rixon & Arnold, 1901), pp. 71, 73 and 75.

9 *Tower Chronicle*, 'John Elder's Letter', p. 147.

10 Sydney Anglo, *Spectacle, Pageantry, and Early Tudor Policy* (Oxford: Clarendon Press, 1969), p. 327.

11 *Tower Chronicle*, p. 79.

12 *Tower Chronicle*, p. 79.

13 Foxe, *TAMO*, Book 10, p. 1681.

14 Marcia Lee Metzger, 'Controversy and "correctness": English chronicles and the chroniclers, 1553–1568', *Sixteenth Century Journal* 27 (1996), 437–51, p. 442.

15 BNE MS 1750, fol. 95r: 'un paño de Damasco carmesi y blanco con flores de oro texidas y en el estas palabras. Henricus Dei gratia Anglie, Francie, et Hibernia Rex, defensor fidei, et caput supremum ecclesia Anglicanae'. See also Martin Hume, 'The visit of Philip II', *English Historical Review* VII (1892), 253–80, p. 267.

16 David Scott Kastan, '"Shewes of honour and gladnes": dissonance and display in Mary and Philip's entry into London', *Research Opportunities in Renaissance Drama* 33 (1994), 1–14, pp. 4–5. Sources for information about the initial preparations for the entry in City of London Record Office, rep. 13, fols 112v–113r, 118r–v, 162v, 166v, 169r, 191r–v.

17 *Cal. Span.*, XIII, p. 53.

18 LMA, Rep. Court of Aldermen 13, fol. 191r.

19 Anglo, *Spectacle, Pageantry, and Early Tudor Policy*, p. 338.

20 Susan Brigden, *London and the Reformation* (Oxford: Clarendon Press, 1989), pp. 525 and 633. See also her account of the entry, pp. 554–8.

21 Indispensable on the European dimensions of accounts of the marriage and entry is Corinna Streckfuss, '"*Spes maxima nostra*": European propaganda and the Spanish match', in *Tudor Queenship: The Reigns of Mary and Elizabeth*, ed. Alice Hunt and Anna Whitelock (New York: Palgrave MacMillan, 2010), 145–57, pp. 151–2. The brute figures are three accounts in English, seven in Italian, four in Latin, two each in Spanish, German and Dutch, and none in French.

22 *Copia d'una lettera scritta all'illustriss. S. Francesco Taverna Crancanz etc.* (Milan: F. and S. Moscheni, 1554), sig. Aii v.

23 See R. M. Smuts, 'Public ceremony and royal charisma: the English royal entry in London, 1485–1642', in *The First Modern Society. Essays in English History in Honour of Lawrence Stone*, ed. A. L. Beier, D. Cannadine and J. Rosenheim (Cambridge: The Past and Present Society, 2005), 65–94, pp. 70–4.

24 Tracey Hill, *Pageantry and Power: A Cultural History of the Early Modern Lord Mayor's Show, 1585–1639* (Manchester: Manchester University Press, 2010), p. 2.

25 LMA, Rep. Court of Aldermen 13, fol. 113r. Philip is consistently referred to as king of Spain in English documents, although his father did not formally abdicate until 1556.

26 *Tower Chronicle*, 'John Elder's Letter', p. 146. The argument also works of the Latin original, since although in Latin the words are feminine in gender, 'tota Britania', 'nobilis Anglia', the relationship represented is that of a lover.

27 See Geoffrey of Monmouth, *The British History*, trans. A. Thomson (London: William Stevens, 1842), chapter XVI, pp. 22–3.

28 *Tower Chronicle*, 'John Elder's Letter', p. 146.

29 See my 'Changing places: the marriage and royal entry of Philip, Prince of Austria, and Mary Tudor, July–August 1554', *Sixteenth Century Journal* 36 (2005), 761–84.

30 LMA, Rep. Court of Aldermen 13, fol. 163v.

31 Cornille Grapheus Greffier, *Le triumphe d'Anuers, faict en la susception du Prince Philips, Prince d'Espaign[e]* (Antwerp: P. de Lens, 1549), sig. Aii v: '(au moien d'ycelle grosse & continuelle pluye) ne a pas bien este possible veoir au vif moult de choses... au moien de laquelle celerite, a eu moult de choses de grandt consequence non du tout accompli'.

32 Greffier, *Le triumphe d'Anuers*, sig. Biii r: 'Ladicte Nation Angloise a icy en la ville en moult grandt reuerenche son superieur, lequel est tenu pour gouuerneur, nomme Monsieur Iehan Sturgion, lequel tant pour sa viellesse que pour la prudence de sa personne, est repute & tenu pour homme de grandt vertu, lequel comme chief et souuerain de ladicte Nation marchoit deriere, monte sur vng moult beau & triumphant cheual de'Engleterre...'.

33 Greffier, *Le triumphe d'Anuers*, sig. Biii r: 'la tres desiree venue d'eulx, que pour espoir de vnion pardurable, entre eulx & le Roy d'Engleterre iusqu'au present infractible entretenue'.

34 Frederick Madden, *Privy Purse Expenses of the Princess Mary* (London: William Pickering, 1831), p. 62.

35 *ODNB*.

36 John Heywood, *The Spider and the Fly* (London: Thomas Powell, 1556). On this text, see Alice Hunt, 'Marian political allegory: John Heywood's *The Spider and the Fly*', in Mike Pincombe and Cathy Shrank, eds, *The Oxford Handbook of Tudor Literature, 1485–1603* (Oxford: Oxford University Press, 2009), pp. 337–55.

37 LMA, Rep. Court of Aldermen 13, fol. 166r.

38 LMA Rep. Court of Aldermen 13, fol. 170.

39 Richard Axton and Peter Happé, eds, *The Plays of John Heywood* (Cambridge: Brewer, 1991), pp. 7–9.

40 Terence Lloyd, *England and the German Hanse, 1157–1611: A Study of their Trade and Commercial Diplomacy* (Cambridge: Cambridge University Press, 1991), p. 300. See also on this Philippe Dollinger, *The Emergence of International Business, 1200–1800*, Vol. I. *The German Hansa* (London: Routledge, repr. 1990), pp. 330–69, esp. 274, 341–2 and 346.

41 Peter Barber, 'Court and country: English cartographic initiatives and their derivatives under Henry VIII and Philip and Mary', in *Actas. XIX Congreso Internacional de Historia de la Cartografía* (Madrid: Ministerio de Defensa, 2002), 1–12, p. 10.

42 *Tower Chronicle*, 'John Elder's Letter', p. 148: 'Anglia que solo gaudet dicente Philippo'.

43 Foxe, *TAMO*, Book 10, p. 1681.

44 Brigden, *London and the Reformation*, pp. 6–7.

45 On Catalina of Lancaster's regency as queen of Castile between 1406 and 1418, see Ana Echevarria-Arsuaga, 'The Queen and the master: Catalina of Lancaster and the military orders' in Teresa Earenfight, ed., *Queenship and Political Power in Medieval and Early Modern Spain* (Aldershot: Ashgate, 2005), 91–105.

46 *Tower Chronicle*, 'John Elder's Letter', p. 149.

47 *Tower Chronicle*, 'John Elder's Letter', p. 150.

48 *Tower Chronicle*, 'John Elder's Letter', p. 150.

49 See the discussion of this text in Metzger, 'Controversy and "correctness"', pp. 443–8.

50 Giles Godet, *Brief Abstract of the Genealogie and Race of All the Kinges of Englande* (1560?).
51 For a discussion of Godet's *Brief Abstract*, see Metzger, 'Controversy and "correctness"', pp. 443–8. I would like to thank Susan Doran for originally drawing my attention to this image.
52 See the discussion in Chapter 2, text relating to note 82.
53 *Tower Chronicle*, 'John Elder's Letter', p. 151.
54 See John N. King, 'The royal image, 1535–1603', in *Tudor Political Culture*, ed. Dale Hoak (Cambridge: Cambridge University Press, 1995), 104–32, pp. 108–11 and 118–19.
55 On the problem of 'God's truth against what they call God's Word', see National Archives SP 10/1/ fol. 105.
56 *Tower Chronicle*, 'John Elder's Letter', p. 151: 'Si diadema viro tali Sapientia donet,/Ille gubernabit totum foeliciter orbem'.
57 *La solemne et felice intrata delli Serenissimi Re Philippo, et Regina Maria d'Inghilterra, nella Regal città di Londra* (Rome?: 1554), sig. A v r: 'di sopra vn cielo sostentato da quattro colonne, onde disendeua una corona riceuuta dalla detta vergine assentata, che riceuendola facea vista di volerla presentar al Re, con queste Parole. Per me Reges regnant'. See also Anglo, *Spectacle, Pageantry, and Early Tudor Policy*, p. 337.
58 On the contradiction and interpretation of these accounts see José Miguel Morales Folguera, 'El arte al servicio del poder y de la propaganda imperial. La boda del príncipe Felipe con María Tudor en la catedral de Winchester y la solemne entrada de la pareja real en Londres', *Potestas: Revista del Grupo Europeo de Investigación Histórica* 2 (1999), 165–89, pp. 186–7.
59 On this see Garcilaso de la Vega's 'Soneto a Boscán de La Goleta', analysed exhaustively by Richard Helgerson, *A Sonnet from Carthage* (Philadelphia: University of Pennsylvania Press, 2007), Part 1, pp. 3–70.
60 Lisa Jardine and Jerry Brotton, *Global Interests: Renaissance Art between East and West* (London: Reaktion Books, 2000), p. 86.
61 See my 'Mapping the marriage: Thomas Geminus's *Britanniae Insulae Nova Descriptio* and *Nova Descriptio Hispaniae* (1555)', *Renaissance and Reformation* 31 (2008), 95–115.
62 They had been sent from Brussels on 19th June and reached London on 3rd July. Willem de Pannemaeker, from the famous Flemish tapestry-weaving family who produced the Tunis tapestries between 1546 and 1554, was paid in August. See Jesús Pascual Molina, '"Porque vean y sepan cuánto es el poder y grandeza de nuestro Príncipe y Señor": Imagen y poder en el viaje de Felipe II a Inglaterra y su matrimonio con María Tudor', *Reales Sitios* 197 (2013), 6–26, p. 17.
63 Richard Grafton, *An Abridgement of the Chronicles of England* (London: Richard Tottel, 1562), sigs Yv r and Yvii r.
64 Richard Grafton, *A Chronicle at large* (London: Henry Denham, 1568), sigs Bbbbbb.iii.v and Ccccc.i.r.
65 Kingdon, *Richard Grafton*, p. 61.
66 Grafton, *A Chronicle at large*, sigs Bbbbbb.iii.v and Ccccc.iv.r.
67 Richard Grafton, *This Chronicle of Briteyn, beginning at William the Conquerour, endeth wyth our moste dread and soueraigne Lady Queene Elizabeth* (London: Richard Grafton, 1568), sig. Bbbbbb iii v, p. 1336.
68 *Tower Chronicle*, p. 81.
69 LMA, Rep. Court of Aldermen 13, fol. 190r.
70 LMA, Rep. Court of Aldermen 13, fol. 191r.
71 See Brigden, *London and the Reformation*, p. 556. See LMA, Mercers' Company, Acts of Court, ii, fol. 268v; Drapers' Company, MB 6, pp. 38–9.
72 See Jane de Iongh, *Mary of Hungary: Second Regent of the Netherlands*, trans. Herter Norton (London: Faber & Faber, 1959), pp. 85–8 and 228– 9. On heresy and burning in the Low Countries see William Monter, 'Heresy executions in Reformation Europe, 1520–65' in Ole Peter Grell and Bob Scribner, eds, *Tolerance and Intolerance in the European Reformation* (Cambridge: Cambridge University Press, 1996), pp. 48–64.

Plate 1 Diogo Homem, *Queen Mary Atlas* (1558).

Plate 2 Framlingham Castle, Norfolk and its Tudor chimneys.

Plate 3 Ingatestone Hall.

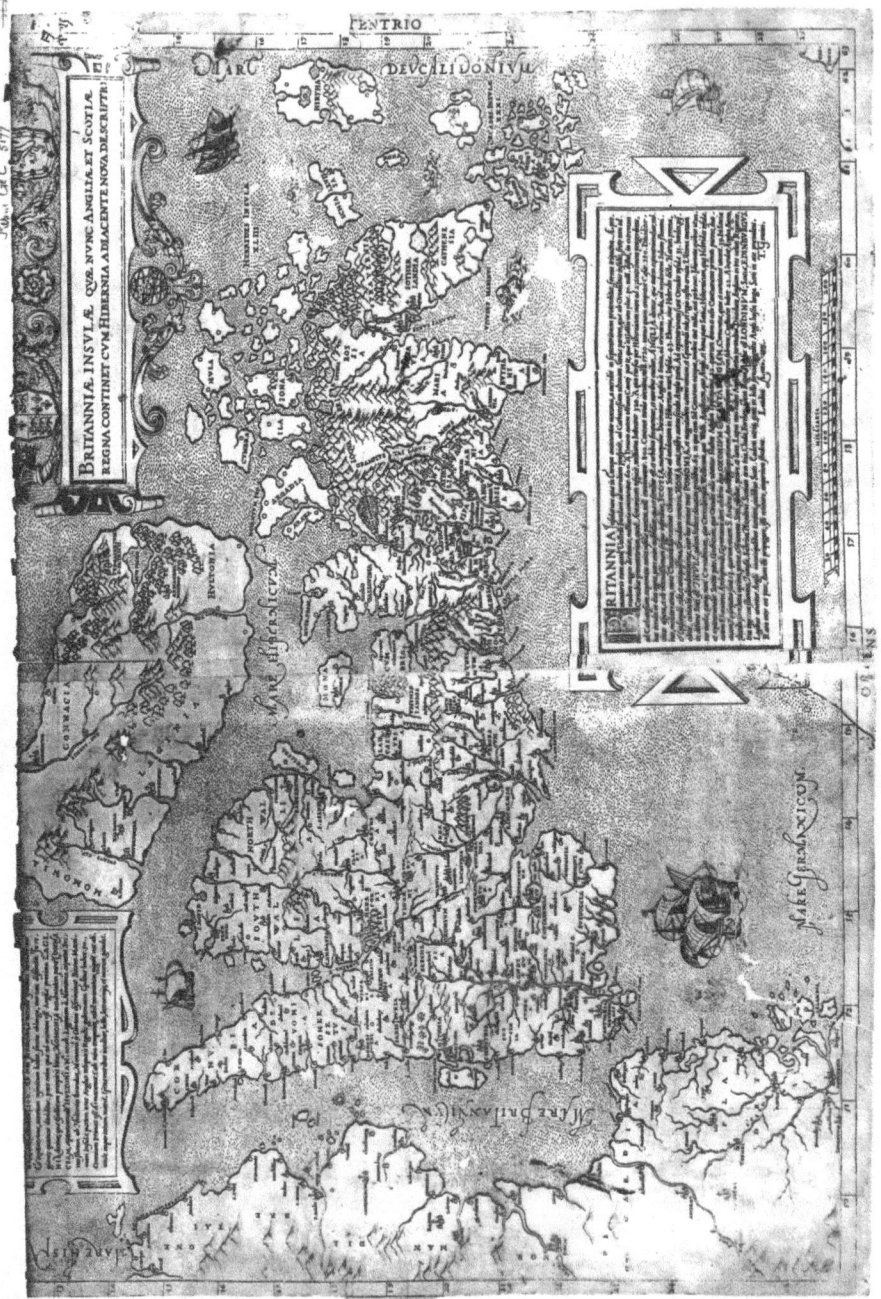

Plate 4 Thomas Geminus, *Britanniae Insulae* and *Nova Descriptio Hispaniae* (1555).

Plate 5 Andrea Mantegna / Guilio Campagnola, *Judith and Holofernes*,
c. 1495–1500. Tempera on poplar panel.

Plate 6 Titian, *Venus and Adonis*, 1554. Oil on canvas.

Plate 7 Titian, *Philip II in Wolfskin*, 1549. Oil on canvas.

Plate 8 Hans Eworth, *Mary I*, 1554. Oil on canvas.

Plate 9 Anthonis Mor, *Mary I*, 1554. Oil on canvas.

Plate 10 Anonymous, *To the reader. Beholde here (gentle reader) a brief abstract of the genealogie of all the kynges of England…* (London: Giles Godet, 1560), fol. 26.

Plate 11 Philip and Mary's coat of arms in Clement Adams' manuscript account of Richard Chancellor and Sir Hugh Willoughby's 1553 voyage to Muscovy, *Nova Anglorum per mare Cronium ad Moscovitas Navigatio, authore Clemente Adam, Regiorum puerorum institutore*. It was first printed in Hakluyt in 1589.

Plate 12(a) Grant by Philip and Mary to the widow and son of Sir Adrian Fortescue of the manors of Barton Abbots, Chipping-Sodbury, Codrington and Washbourne, Gloucestershire.

Plate 12(b) Letters Patent restoring Hemsby manor, Norfolk, to Robert and Anne Dudley, 30th January 1557 with pen and ink portraits of Philip and Mary.

Plate 13 Engraved portraits of Philip II and Mary I by Frans Huys, printed by Hieronymous Cock, 1555.

Plate 14 Gerlach Flicke, *Mary I*. Oil on canvas.

Within the image: Philippus Rex Anglorum, Princepsq Hispaniarum anno 1555.

Plate 15 Jan Cornelisz Vermeyen, *Philip II*, 1555. Etching on paper.

6

Anti-Spanish sentiment in early modern England

[A]s long as God shall preserve my master and misstress together, I am and shall be a Spaniard to the uttermost of my power...

Henry Neville, earl of Westmorland[1]

Anti-Spanish sentiment (or 'English hostility toward the objectionable character of the individual Spaniard'[2]) has been accorded a central explanatory role in the historiography of Marian England, a period traditionally read in terms of insuperable English hostility to Spain and the Spanish. This Hispanophobia meant, the argument goes, that the reign and marriage of Philip and Mary failed politically and culturally. Underlying this negative understanding of Philip and Mary's co-monarchy is an assumption that Tudor England was inexorably xenophobic, making the acceptance of a foreign (Habsburg) prince as ruler impossible. Rather, an unpopular, foreign marriage was foisted on a kingdom antipathetic to the religion and culture of early modern Spain. In this chapter, the evidence for this alleged Hispanophobia and virulent xenophobia is examined and the idea that it undermined the Anglo-Spanish alliance refuted. As long ago as 1940, it was pointed out that the Spanish marriage awaited its apologist: 'Protestants and Catholics alike have condemned it, Spaniards and Frenchmen have deplored it, and Englishmen of all shades of opinion have looked back upon it as one of the more regrettable incidents of their national history'.[3] This is that apology.

It is undeniable that the Spanish match was deeply unpopular in certain quarters, how else to explain Sir Thomas Wyatt's revolt? However, the extent and nature of the opposition is debatable. The rebellion against Mary was a tenth of the size of the Pilgrimage of Grace and a third of the size of the Prayer Book revolt. Only one of its four strands came to anything. The anti-Catholicism refined and honed by Marian exiles became a crucial aspect of the teleological history of England's rise as a nation and was made synonymous with anti-Spanish sentiment. Much of this explosion of polemic and propaganda in print, however, echoed long-standing Dutch and Italian denunciations of Spanish encroachment on and threats to their sovereign independence. The evidence of the Marian exiles needs to be contextualised in relation to a group who were the architects of radical religious reform. Examples to which historians turn of English Hispanophobia under Mary are easily confused with popular reflections on the wider sectarian struggle between Protestants and Catholics, and competing claims to define England and what it meant to be English. A number of anti-Spanish tracts from the time underlined their Catholic orthodoxy and loyalty to Mary, in order to cast the issue as exclusively one of obedience. Mary's reign was a crucial test for the first generations of English Protestants. The reversal of the palpable 'progress' made under Edward VI was a potentially serious blow to international reform and hopes of England spearheading religious reformation, something apparent from the triumphal tone of the international Catholic propaganda trumpeting news of England's reconciliation with Rome. With Elizabeth's accession the centrality accorded to England in reinvigorating reforming spirituality in the face of a corrupt and immoral papacy was reconfirmed. Under Mary, the disinheritance and exile of the central architects of the Reformation and the burning of others was made sense of by seeing persecution as a test, a paradoxical sign of divine favour and righteousness. The period between Henry VIII's creation of the Supreme Headship of the Church of England and Elizabeth's religious settlement not only saw a series of religious revolutions, but also fundamental developments in political thought and the public nature of debate. Religious polarisation under Mary was largely elite in character, embedded in a Europe-wide set of debates arising from Trent, which straddled the reign, led by intellectual luminaries. A literate and sophisticated political opposition deliberately exploiting understandable anxieties about a regnant queen and possible foreign succession made it appear that they spoke for true-hearted Englishmen. However, English fears about sovereign independence and dynastic continuity, when their aging queen married for the first time at 38, were appreciated by commentators across the political and religious spectrum. Mary's reign stimulated the production of works of political philosophy on issues from female sovereignty and dynastic succession to the origins of property rights in legitimate descent and inheritance patterns, remarkable for their radicalism and constitutionalism.

The notion of an implacably hostile English 'people', bitterly resentful of the new 'Anglo-Spanish' co-monarchy is remarkably persistent. However, it glosses over the complexity of English reactions to Spain, the Spanish and their sovereign's marriage, which varied across different segments and sectors of the population, as well as across different parts of the kingdom. David Loades finds anti-Spanish prejudice puzzling: 'it is not very easy to understand why Englishmen should have conceived a particular dislike for Spaniards by 1553, but such was the case'.[4] English experience of Spain derived from, on one hand, long-standing and important trade and economic relations embodied in the series of commercial treaties between the two kingdoms that had culminated in the Treaty of Medina del Campo. This was the harbinger of the second main source of cultural contact in the first half of the sixteenth century, dynastic links forged through Catherine of Aragón's marriage to Arthur and then Henry VIII. According to one critic 'until Mary Tudor married Philip II of Spain in 1554 Anglo-Spanish cultural relations were negligible'.[5] While it is true that there were only perhaps thirteen texts translated from Spanish available in English before this date, Catherine of Aragón had been a popular figure and her servants included a number of Spanish noblemen and women, who had remained in England, figures like María de Salinas who became the countess of Willoughby. María's daughter Katherine married the duke of Suffolk, Charles Brandon. John Skelton in 'Speke Parott' (1521) asserted that 'with Spaynyshe, my tonge can agree... With Katheryne incomporabyll, owur royall quene also,/That pereles pomegarnat, Cryste save hyr nobyll grace!/Parott *saves habeler Castylyano,*/With *fidasso de cosso* in Turke and in Thrace' (ll. 32–9).[6] The last line refers to the Turkish seizure of Thrace, and by extension the growing expansionist threat from the Ottomans in the Eastern Mediterranean, which Catherine's family were in the vanguard of containing. Her treatment by Henry VIII was understandably a major source of Spanish distrust of the English.[7] The second Anglo-Spanish marriage of the century was welcomed among London's mercantile elite, guilds and the city authorities, if the lavish nature of their royal entry is a guide. Even after the allegedly unfortunate marriage, Richard Clough wrote to England's royal financier Sir Thomas Gresham on 2nd January 1559 suggesting that a third Anglo-Spanish alliance would be for Elizabeth and the kingdom's benefit, a typically mercantile perspective.[8] Philip made the offer even before Mary was dead.

The anti-Spanish incidents on which the assertion of insuperable opposition to the match is founded were confined to London and concentrated in the precincts of Westminster at court itself. A letter from Reginald Pole to his fellow cardinal Innocenzo del Monte recorded how in a sermon preached in September Stephen Gardiner blamed Londoners, not the English in general, for opprobrious language and insults directed at the Spanish.[9] From the snowball-tossing apprentices who pelted the [Dutch] Imperial ambassadors on 2nd January 1554 to the 'blake-mor [blackamoor]' involved in a fray at Charing Cross on 4th November, tension and opposition were not predominantly anti-Spanish.[10] In contrast, in the West Country during the Wyatt revolt, Sir Peter Carew's strand of the conspiracy attempting to spread rumours about armed Spaniards appearing in the county met a lukewarm response among mercantile communities heavily invested in Anglo-Spanish trade, such as Totnes.[11]

Xenophobia and nationalism

Before considering Hispanophobia, it is necessary to examine the underlying assumption that the English were particularly hostile towards foreigners in general. On one side of this debate, some argue '[a]t one level national identity is little more than xenophobia'[12] and that 'Tudor England was a thoroughly and unapologetically xenophobic society'.[13] It is too easy to associate jingoistic elements of our own society with the past and assume it to be a national characteristic. Others counter this by pointing out the multilayered and local-ised nature of identity in the period with religion, guild, family, clientage, parish, precinct, county, trade and faction all important factors in defining a subject.[14] Any assumption of cultural homogeneity in England at this time fails to account for the 'very real diversity and the complex attitudes Tudor subjects had about that diversity'.[15] It could even be argued that 'England has been multicultural and wrestled with the central questions of multiculturalism for centuries'.[16] The issue of whether it makes any sense even to speak of national identity at all in relation to the sixteenth century remains contro-versial.[17] The views of visitors like the oft-quoted Venetian envoy Andrea Trevisano, in London briefly in 1496–7, that the English have 'an antipathy to foreigners, and imagine that they never come to their island, but to make themselves masters of it, and to usurp their goods',[18] can be easily countered by citing other commentators like Fynes Moryson, who while accepting that Europeans often complained about English 'inhumanity to strangers, because they had been ill used at Gravesend... some obscure Hosts in London, who use to entertaine and wrong st[r]angers, having otherwise never visited the Citizens of London, the Schollers of the Universities, Gentlemen, or learned men' therefore did not see that the English were 'not onely Courteous, but too much given to admire strangers'.[19] Even the emblematic instance of anti-for-eign rioting in the period, Evil May Day 1517, provoked by an inflammatory sermon, is, according to Andrew Pettegree, 'hardly indicative of a general climate of hostility'.[20] At the heart of the resentment of foreign immigrants in early modern London almost always lay economic jealousy; rivalry and competition towards a group which posed a perceived threat to native jobs and hard-won privileges. Legislation in 1523 had forced foreign masters to engage only English apprentices and limited them to two alien journeymen. All aliens in the city itself were under the purview of company wardens, with each craft appointing a substantial member of the stranger community to represent them before the civic authorities. Of course, this did not apply to the liberties beyond the city walls or outside London, although the companies did increasingly exert their influence there too. Foreigners were often highly skilled workers (brewers, dyers, lace makers, cloth workers of various kinds, printers), specifically encouraged to settle by the city authorities with a view to enriching the capital.

Defining who was foreign was also complex. The term 'foreigner' referred to Englishmen who did not possess the freedom of the city, while the words 'stranger' or 'alien' were generally used to refer to immigrants from abroad. Steve Rappaport has argued that '[a]fter decades of minimal tension between the city's free and unfree populations, protests against the illegal activities of foreigners and strangers were heard once again in the late 1560s'.[21] This suggests that problems with strangers were not a major issue under Mary, at least in an economic sense. The problems in the early Elizabethan period arose from the waves of refugees fleeing religious per-secution in France and the Low Countries and settling in London. Under Edward VI, foreign communities had acquired unprecedented concentration and visibility through the Dutch and French churches; religious refugees who were permitted to practise their own forms of reformed religion. In 1551, following two bad harvests, the city authorities had to nip in the bud a plot to attack them, after they were scapegoated for high prices and food shortages. While certain quarters did display hostility to their presence, many Londoners appreciated the economic advantages of 'offering hospitality to skilled foreigners, and others felt a genuine sympathy towards suffering co-religionists'.[22] Solidarity with brethren in Christ and support for the inter-national Protestant movement were important factors in mitigating more insular tendencies.

Although in one proclamation Mary attacked the Edwardian refugees as felons and heretics fleeing the jurisdiction of their rightful rulers and ordered their expulsion, there was no rise 'in the number of prosecutions in retailing cases, suggesting that native tradesmen who hoped... to settle old scores with alien competitors received no encouragement from the City authorities'.[23] While there is no evidence of round-ups, mass expulsions or significant num-bers leaving voluntarily, there is evidence that strangers were protected, and Londoners only cooperated with Mary's proclamation after a refugee had been interrogated by the authorities.[24] John Foxe records the martyrdom of only one stranger, a 28-year-old Flemish merchant and broker, Lyon Cawch, on 27th June 1556.[25] Similarly, although the leaders of a conventicle in the St Katherine's docks area, John Rough and Cuthbert Simson, were arrested and martyred in 1557, their host (a Dutch shoemaker known as Frog) was not even arrested.[26] Another alien, Christopher Vittels, a joiner who had settled in the parish of St Olaf's in Southwark in 1551, moved to Colchester during Mary's reign to spread the message of the Family of Love, a sect that continued to crop up in English heresy trials into the 1620s.[27] In 1556 an act forbidding freemen from employing foreigners led to a flow of petitions for exemptions.[28] Following the war with France a bill to expel denizens and other non-naturalised Francophones was defeated on 18th February 1558 by 111 votes to 106.[29] There are many types of evidence that might be used to demonstrate how representative hostility to foreigners was among the English in the period. However, whatever arguments we seek to make, two issues complicate judgement. Firstly, there is a question of interpretation: what precise mental attitude does the evidence allow us to ascribe? Secondly, the issue is always seen from the comparative perspective of the present, coloured by present-day *mores* and events in the last century that saw an apotheosis of nationalisms and their most iniquitous consequences.

The Dutch acrobat Peter, the only performer other than John Heywood named in accounts of Mary's London entry as queen, bore the arms of the City of London. Perhaps rumours of Mary's intentions to deport aliens had prompted the aldermen and city to 'showcase London's immigrants.... sending the message that Londoners were inextricably linked with the strangers living among them'.[30] During the 1550s exports of 'cloths' from London appear to have peaked at 115,200 per year, a 7 per cent increase on the previous decade. This trade grew by 116 per cent between 1500 and 1540.[31] In 1555 an abortive attempt to muscle in on the slave trade took place with the merchant John Lok bringing five black slaves back to England. Under pressure from the Spanish that year Mary banned further English involvement in the Guinean or West African trade.[32] The first three pageants of Philip and Mary's royal entry into the city were mounted by stranger communities: the Genoese, German Hanse and Florentine merchants. One of the interludes performed for the queen later in her reign, *Wealth and Health*, contained passages in French, Spanish, Latin and Dutch and featured a Flemish immigrant character, Hance Beerpot, who inhabits the St Katherine's docks, an area with a dense immigrant population.[33] The name Hance and its spelling is a pun on the Hanse merchants of the Steelyard and indicates that traditional jibes were more likely to target the Dutch than the Spanish. The trading privileges of the Hanse merchants had been revoked by Edward VI in 1552, after a sustained campaign by the Merchant Adventurers. Mary reinstated them a few months after her accession on 1st November.

Despite her proclamation, John Christopherson, the queen's chaplain, in his *An exhortation to all menne to take hede and beware of rebellion*, debunked the myth of seditious aliens:

As for straungers we nede not to feare. For yf they do any injury to any subjecte of hers, they shalbe punyshed by the lawes of thys realme, as we be. And yf they behaue them selfe gentlye, as it is very lyke that they will, we shall haue cause to love them to ioyne frendship with them, and to make muche of them. For so shall we deserue thankes both of them & at goddes hand to, who wylleth us that we offende not, or hurte anye straunger.[34]

Sir Robert Southwell, sheriff of Kent, reassured a crowd during Sir Thomas Wyatt's uprising that 'we know most certnly that there is ment no maner of evil to us by those strangers'.[35] With an immigrant population of merchants, religious refugees and strangers in London at the outset of Mary's reign that some have put as high as 12.5 per cent, 'the English more often seem to have valued and protected their immigrant neighbours... solidarity between the English and immigrants often trumped concerns about the "otherness" of strangers'.[36] One estimate suggests there were 10,000 strangers living in London at the outset of Mary's reign and around 6,000 still there at the accession of Elizabeth. By 1571 this figure had returned to 10,000 and remained constant until 1593, during a period when the city's population rose from 80,000 to around 200,000 (by 1600). As a proportion of the city's population, then, aliens declined from a peak of around 12.5 per cent in 1553 to 10 per cent in 1571 and 5 per cent in 1593.[37] Rates of naturalisation and denization were relatively low throughout the century: '[e]xcluding 1544, when 2,965 aliens were naturalised or became denizens, an average of only forty-two letters of denization and acts of naturalisation were granted each year from 1509 to 1602'.[38] Immigrants from outside the realm resident in London were mostly French, Walloon, Dutch and Flemish, with some Italians and only a handful of Spanish householders. Of the alien heads of households in London in 1571, only seventeen were Spanish. Five had arrived in the city between 1541 and 1559, nine between 1560 and 1571, three others at a point unknown. This compares with 367 from French-speaking areas and 1,102 from Dutch, Flemish or German-speaking lands, of whom 876 came from the Spanish Netherlands. By 1593, the numbers of Francophone householders had fallen by 2 to 365, while Dutch, Flemish or German-speakers had halved to 594. Towards the end of the century those of Spanish origin numbered only three. The Spanish were a practically invisible presence in London in the sixteenth century as a whole.[39]

Despite the importance of trading links with Spain stretching back centuries, the relative unimportance of Spanish merchants, factors and artisans may be reflected in the rather vague and empty nature of their characterisation before the later sixteenth century. The physician Andrew Boorde's *The fyrst boke of the introduction of knowledge. The whych dothe teache a man to speake parte of all maner of languages, and to know the usage and fashion of all maner of countreys*, dedicated

to Mary on 3rd May 1542 from Montpellier, although it was not published
until perhaps 1549, delineated the Englishman as fashion-obsessed ('aboue
al thinges, new fashions I loue well') and the Spaniard as poverty-stricken –
'[i]n dyuers countreys I do wander and peke... To get a poore lyuyng'.[40]
Unlike the lively and insulting characterisation of the Dutch as drunks – 'I am
cupshoten, on my feet I cannot stand/Dyuers tymes I do pysse vnderneath the
borde... in my felowes shoes and hose', the description of the Spaniard does
not address their 'natural disposition', but focuses exclusively on the country's
poverty and poor food.[41] Vicente Alvarez's account of Philip's journey through
Italy and Germany to the Low Countries in 1548–51, for his sister Maria of
Austria, echoes the imputation to the Dutch of drunken excess: 'some get
into such a state with the strong beer that they can not get up and so they piss
on the spot... Among the common people getting drunk is not considered an
affront.'[42] The commonplace about poor Spanish food littered English literary
sources later in the century from the 1586 translation of *Lazarillo de Tormes* to
the plays of John Fletcher.[43] Interestingly, Boorde divided up coverage of the
Iberian peninsula into chapters on Catalonia ('[t]he countres next vs al be very
bare'), Andalucia and Portugal ('the comon corse of marchaunte straungers'),
Spain ('baryn of wine and corne, and skarse of vitels'), Castile and Vizcaya
('ful of pouerte... euill fare, [and] lodgyng') and Navarre ('rude and poore,
and many theues').[44] Boorde had had an opportunity to observe the subject of
his study first-hand, when he witnessed the sixty-two-galley imperial fleet sail
from Barcelona to besiege Tunis on 29th March 1535. John Ponet in *An Apologie
fully answeringe by Scriptures and aunceant Doctors a blasphemose Book gatherid by
D. Steph. Gardiner* (1555?) described:

> a holy man named maister Doctour boord a Phisicion that thryse in the week
> would drink nothinge but water such proctour for the Papists then as Martyn
> the lawier is now? Who vnder color of uirginitie and of wearinge a shirte of
> heare and hanginge his shroud and socking or buriall sheete at his beds feet
> and mortifyeng his body and stratynes of lyfe kept thre whores at once in his
> chambre at Winchester to serue not onely him self but also to help the virgin
> preests.[45]

Ponet probably had Boorde charged with this offence shortly after becoming
Proctor in Winchester diocese in 1546, leading to the physician's committal
to the Fleet in 1547. Two years later Ponet had displaced Gardiner as bishop
of Winchester. The treatise published from continental exile was his rejoinder
to Stephen Gardiner's *A traictise declaringe and plainly prouying, that the pretensed
marriage of prestes, and professed persons, is no marriage*, which had contained a refutation of Ponet's earlier treatise against clerical celibacy by Thomas Martin,
by then an administrator for the Lord Chancellor.[46] Martin's 'whorishe and

ethnicall talke' was for Ponet unfit for the ears of our first 'virgin Queen'.[47] The allusion to the queen's virginity puts the moment of composition between the publication of Gardiner's treatise in May and the day of the queen's marriage, 25th July 1554. This gives a sense of the speed with which publication kept pace with political developments and the alacrity of responses by Reformers to what was happening, even when they were not in the country.

Thomas Wilson's *The Arte of Rhetoric* anatomised national types in highly similar terms to Boorde's. These images remained unchanged by the experience of the Marian period, a period the author spent in Italian exile, with the description identical in editions of 1553 and 1560:

> and not onelie are matters set out by descripcion, but men are painted out in their colours... The Englishman for feding, and changing of apparel: The Ducheman for drinking: The Frencheman for pride and inconstance: The Spaniard for nimblenes of body, and moche disdain: the Italian for great witte and pollicie: The Scottes for boldnesse, and the Boerne for stubbornesse.[48]

It has been argued that this demonstrates an immediate reversion to a pre-Marian view of the Spanish as known only for their 'nimblenes of body, and moche disdain'. This vision almost certainly derived from the legion of Italian sources praising Spanish soldiery. Francesco Guicciardini, for example, described them typically as 'ágiles', agile.[49] While Mary's reign was soon written about by Protestant chroniclers as a providential punishment for sin, despite her major policies – the Habsburg marriage, the Restoration of Roman obedience and the burnings – being viewed largely negatively, attitudes towards Spain did not notably harden. The marriage did not cause a violent upsurge of anti-Spanish prejudice that built through the century towards the bonfires celebrating the Prince of Wales's return in 1623 without the Spanish Infanta. Contemporary chronicles provide little evidence of negative traits being associated with the foreign interlopers: 'the demonstrable lack of hispanophobic sentiment in the latter [chroniclers Cooper, Grafton and Stow] proves that Marian anti-Spanish feeling was not more than a deliberate and opportunistic political fabrication on the part of the Protestant exiles'.[50] *Cooper's Chronicle* reported following the king's short visit in 1557 that the 'common people began to mutter and saye that kynge Phillippe esteemed not the Queene but sought occasions to be abroade and absent from hir', then towards the end of 1558 it recorded again that 'the common people whiche for the Queenes sake, fauoured kyng Phillip and the Spaniardes, at this time spake muche againste them thinkinge those paimentes to comme especially by his occasion and charges of warre'.[51] Being dragged into the war with France was something explicitly prohibited by the treaty. It underlines the economic sensitivity of the lower echelons, particularly in cities like London. Many among the nobility, however, embraced the opportunities to prove themselves in England's first European war since the Boulogne campaign of 1544–46, twenty years earlier.

In discussions of Elizabeth's marriage, many Protestants construed the Marian period as a negative *exemplum*, a warning of the dangers of foreign marriage, and emphasised its negative consequences. Discussions of the succession under Elizabeth, however, although they often referred back to the experience under Mary, drew the opposite conclusion. Towards 'the end of the sixteenth century... interpretations of Mary's rule were becoming less negative, even her religious policy being occasionally judged no more harshly than that of her father and siblings.'[52] Some like the earl of Sussex, who had served them, were unconvinced Philip had ever really posed a threat to England's sovereign independence.[53] England's involvement in the war with France and the loss of Calais, similarly often blamed on the Spanish marriage, had in fact been provoked by Henry II's continual conspiracies against the queen's life, culminating in Stafford's raid on Scarborough Castle in 1557. It was not the marriage but politics that eventually drew England into this war. Mary's devotion to Philip and affection for Spain were neither here nor there.[54] Foreign laws were not introduced under Philip and Mary and the Spanish king did not seek to interfere in Elizabeth's succession; if anything, he worked to assure it, despite complaints from some of his closest advisors to the contrary.[55] He broached the issue with Mary as early as 1557, but it was only when parliament requested her to clarify the succession that the queen finally relented (another piece of evidence showing that she was not overawed by her husband). Initially, despite the conscious attempts of the Habsburgs to exploit the impact of reunification with Rome for propaganda by identifying it with the marriage, Spain was not seen as behind the religious policies pursued in England. Thomas Brice's *A compendious register in Metre* (1559), a versified history of the Marian martyrs, does not even refer to the Spanish, referring to 'tyrannical tragedies of the unmerciful Ministers of Satan', the 'unmerciful Ministers [who] had charge of the poor sheep; who wolfishly, at their wills, devoured the same', the 'raging reign of tyrants stout', the 'tyrant's raging ire'.[56] Careful not to even mention Mary by name, the poem largely lays the blame with the Catholic clergy. Protestants under Elizabeth did come to accuse the Spanish of being behind it. These were 'straungers moste cruell, most blodie, most insufferable', but that was not until 1586.

The issue of Spain's involvement in the forging of religious policy in England is a *cause célèbre* in the new historiography. Traditionally, Alfonso de Castro's sermon on 10th February 1555 was taken as evidence that Philip opposed the English government's policy of burning heretics. To explain the delay in executing the condemned, Foxe recorded that Philip's confessor Castro 'did earnestly inuey against the bishops for burning of men'.[57] Nevertheless,

Castro was the author of two treatises about heresy and its punishment; one on its varieties and causes, *Adversus omnes haereses* (Salamanca: Michel Vascosanus, 1541), and the other on the licitude of its punishment, *De justa haereticorum punitione* (Salamanca: Joannis de Giunta, 1547). The former was reprinted at Antwerp in 1556 and dedicated to Philip, while the latter was republished in Lyons that year with a new dedication to Charles V.[58] The sermon then was probably no more than a gesture to deflect popular hostility from the Spanish.[59] The queen's confessor Bartolomé Carranza was intimately involved in pushing forward the persecuting agenda, alongside Pole and Mary herself; a fact not without irony in the light of his subsequent denunciation for heresy following the publication of a key pedagogical guide for Catholic Restoration in England, *Comentarios... sobre el Catechismo* (Antwerp, 1558), a year after his appointment to the archbishopric of Toledo.[60] Charles V had been strongly supported in his own war against Lutheran heretics by his confessor Pedro de Soto, another Dominican sent to England with Philip, who took up a chair in theology at Oxford, where he was intimately involved in the trials of Cranmer, Latimer and Ridley. There were undoubtedly differences of opinion about policy in England, from the perspective of Spanish political interests, those of the English church and those of the indigenous religious community itself, but fundamentally recalcitrant heretics had to face the death penalty. Castro had written '[t]here is another penalty, about which the Church has established absolutely nothing, since it was not appropriate that it should establish it through ecclesiastical decrees. Such is death.'[61] Instinctively, the Franciscan Castro seems to have been averse to Dominican Inquisitorial pratices, penning in 1543 a treatise in favour of teaching Latin to the indigenous peoples of the Americas.[62] There are intriguing links between Alfonso de Castro, a leading figure in the English mission, and the extant Spanish manuscript sources for the marriage, the most important of which are found in a miscellany, *Noticias de varios sucesos acaecidos, 1521–1558*,[63] a later copy of which, belonging to Ambrosio de Morales, is in the library of San Lorenzo, El Escorial. The volume was compiled by the Habsburgs' royal chronicler from 1539, Florián de Ocampo. Castro and Ocampo were both natives of Zamora born around 1495, attending and teaching at the university of Alcalá, Castro perhaps from 1507 and Ocampo from 1509. Castro had become professor of theology there by 1515, while Ocampo was *racionero* from 1519.[64] Ocampo's chronicle of Spain was first published in Zamora in 1543 and again in 1545, apparently without his permission, the latter a pirated reissue of the first edition. He was a canon of the Cathedral there.[65]

Although John Foxe has been seen as having done much to blacken the reputation of Mary, the 1563 edition of *Acts and Monuments* is not redolent with Hispanophobia and notably lacks any reference to the Spanish

Inquisition. The Holy Office only featured after a second edition of 1570, in response to the English translation of Reginaldus Gonsalvius Montanus' *A Discovery and playne Declaration of the sundry subtill practices of the Holy Inquitision of Spayne* (1568).[66] Montanus was perhaps the pseudonym of Casiodoro de Reina, an exile in England from shortly after Elizabeth's accession, who in 1557 had fled San Isidro del Campo in Seville with a group of fellow Spanish Protestants, initially to Geneva.[67] The text was explicitly framed as a supplement to Foxe: 'thou mightest vse this booke as a taste in the meane space, whiles the booke of Martires be finished', an allusion to the second edition.[68] It warned that the Inquisitorial threat extended not only to Protestants but also Catholics: 'Papist or Protestant, if thou be riche and hast any fleece, it will be all one'.[69] The Spanish Inquisition 'now brought with fire and sword into the low Countries' threatened 'sodaine imprisonment of honest men without processe of lawe, the pitifull wandring in exile and pouertie of personages sometime riche and welthy... the monstrous racking of men without order of law, the villanous and shameles tormenting of naked women'.[70] At the end of the preface, the Dutch Revolt is described as a consequence of the coming of the Inquisition to the Netherlands: those 'most duetifully obedient to their magistrats, to driue so horrible a pestilence from their countrey, haue betaken themselues to their weapons and defence of armes'.[71] The example in their neighbours' house was a warning that the tribunal did not seek reformation of religion, rather 'a straunge, vnworthie, and intollerable slauerie... outragious tyranny'.[72] The foundation of the Inquisition in Spain addressed the problem of converted Moors and Jews 'only Christians by name and for fashion sake, submitting themselues for feare and awe', a godly purpose soon perverted when rather than by 'persuasion of learning, or by charitable dealing' they sought 'to compel them by force & might... by Rackes and Torments, Chaines, Halters, Barnacles Sambenites by Fire and by Fagots'.[73] Montanus throughout the paratext invoked the concept of 'libertie' against an Inquisition seen above all to threaten secular authority and open, public representation with its secrecy.

The marginal glosses and 'declaration' that Foxe added to editions of the *Acts and Monuments* after 1570 underlined Mary's responsibility for the burnings. She

> continued more and more to reuenge her Catholicke zeale vpon the Lordes faithfull people, setting fire to theyr poore bodyes by dosens and halfedosens together. Where vpon Gods wrathfull indignation increasing more and more agaynst her, ceased not to touche her more neare with priuate misfortunes and calamities. For after that he had taken from her the fruit of children (whiche chiefly and aboue all things she desired) then he bereft her of that, which of all earthly thinges should haue bene her chiefe stay of honor, and staffe of

comfort, that is, withdrew from her the affectiō and company euen of her owne husband.[74]

The image of Mary's desolation, for she 'semed neither to haue the fauour of God, nor the harts of her subiectes, nor yet the loue of her husband', is fundamental to how she has been read ever since.[75] Even the green shoots of revisionist reinterpretations of her are overshadowed by characteristics attributed to her here; a sense of her as 'tragic', unhappily married and ultimately unpopular with her people. Although at times she was presented by some Protestants as deceived by priests, in Foxe she was a Jezebel, as the martyr Alice Driver foolhardily dubbed her before Sir Clement Higham after her arrest, leading him to cut her ears off.[76] The most striking visual symbol of this tendency is the banner on the frontispiece of Christopher Lever's seventeenth-century *The Historie of the Defendors of the Catholique Faith* with the motto 'not cruel by nature, but through the machinations of priests'.[77] After Mary's reign Protestants often sought to minimise the damage of the martyrs to her reputation by denouncing her adherence to the old faith and the burnings, while emphasising her feminine qualities of mildness, mercy and compassion and arguing she had been deluded or misled by her bishops.[78] As extremists among the Marian exiles had discovered, anti-monarchist attacks were displeasing to all monarchs, including Mary's successor, regardless of on whom they were made. The massive influence of Foxe over the centuries has almost completely obscured alternative Catholic views of the persecution, like those found in Nicholas Harpsfield, Thomas Stapleton and Robert Persons, for whom Protestants were rightly prosecuted pseudo-martyrs, largely incapable of learned disputation on the complex theological issues over which they believed themselves capable of dissent.[79]

The picture is different again if we go back to the period itself. In the final act of the apocalyptic Latin comedy the martyrologist Foxe wrote during Philip and Mary's reign, *Christus Triumphans* (Basle, 1556), the character representing the Antichrist or pope, Pseudamnus (a double joke: false lamb in Greek, damned but flying false colours in Latin), asks the whore of Babylon, Pornapolis (whore city): 'I wonder what course to follow. – Zenodore, go and soften up Dynastes with this golden rose. – You take this sword in a golden sheath to Dynamicus. – Dromo, your job is to take this linsey-woolsey pallium to Nesophilus.'[80] These topical allusions allow us to uncover something of Foxe's thinking at this point. Precisely these gifts, the golden rose and the sword in a golden sheath, had been sent by Pope Julius III to Mary and Philip on 27th January 1555. Dynastes (ruler) represented Mary, Dynamicus (powerful) Philip, and Nesophilus (island-lover) is an ironic reference to Pole, who had spent much of his life in exile from the British Isles. The 'linsey-woolsey' pallium was a pun alluding to Cardinal Wolsey, originally found in Skelton's 'Why come ye not to court?'[81] The pope is represented here attempting to manipulate the English monarchs, while Pole is condemned through association with the corrupt and worldly Wolsey. What happened shortly after this undermined the rhetorical strategy of Reformers, to blame the pope for the persecution in England, through a subtle manipulation of earthly powers, i.e. Philip and Mary. The election of the rabbidly Hispanophobic Giovanni Pietro Carafa as Paul IV on 23rd May 1555 precipitated a complete breakdown of diplomatic relations between the papacy and the Habsburgs, who launched a military campaign from Naples against the papal states and their French allies. Carafa excommunicated Philip and the duke of Alba in retaliation and recalled Cardinal Pole to Rome, rescinding his legatine mission to England on 9th April 1557 before arresting the legate's close associate Cardinal Giovanni Morone on 31st May. This caused considerable problems for the Catholic Reformation under Mary, but it also took away any sense in which the Habsburgs or English clergy might merely be puppets of the papacy and the newly established Catholic church not be a 'national' church. According to the Venetian ambassador Bernardo Navagero, Carafa described the Spanish at this time as 'heretics, schismatics and accursed of God, seed of Jews and *marranos*, scum of the earth; deploring Italy's misfortune that it was forced to serve people so vile and despicable'.[82] His hatred of the Habsburgs came from Charles V blocking his appointment to the archdiocese of Naples, held by his family for a century. This is a clue to where the Marian exiles derived much of the raw material out of which their intemperate polemics and vilification of the Spanish was constructed. If the English had little picture of the Spanish before 1554, the anti-Marian propaganda depicting Spaniards as sexually rapacious, cruel, proud and deceitful oppressors drew heavily on a series of well-established images from Italy.

As Protestants began to leave England in 1554, many would have passed through Antwerp on their way to exile in cities like Strasbourg at precisely the moment when the first edition of that infamous anti-clerical satire and Spanish Erasmian text, *Lazarillo de Tormes*, was published,[83] as well as one of the most important New World chronicles, Francisco López de Gómara's *Historia general de las Indias*, which refused to ignore the empire's worst excesses in its quest for historical authority. Hernán Cortés' chaplain after 1540 recorded at the end of his text that:

> all those who have killed Indians in that way [in the mines and pearl fisheries, or through heavy burdens], and there have been many, in fact almost all, have ended badly: in which way it seems to be that God has punished their most grave sins. I merely write, briefly, the conquest of the Indies: if anyone wishes

to see the justification for it, let them read Doctor Sepúlveda, chronicler of the Emperor.[84]

The Valladolid disputation of 1551 between Bartolomé de las Cases, the so-called apostle of the Indies, and Juan Ginés de Sepúlveda, former Latin tutor to Philip, that had followed the colonists' resistance to the imposition of the New Laws in 1542 in an attempt by the crown to bring under control the exploitation and enslavement of the indigenous peoples by conquistadors under the *encomienda* system, had centred on arguments put forward in Sepúlveda's *Democrates segundo*, a neo-Aristotelian argument that the natives were natural slaves and therefore their 'reduction' was justified.

Imperial Spain, the New World and Naples

Central to the Black Legend as it developed in the sixteenth century was a notion of Spanish tyranny, an idea powerfully crystallised in the context of the Dutch Revolt.[85] This was reinforced by British historians writing in the eighteenth century, who sought to justify empire by contrasting their enlightened colonialism with evil Spanish depredation and oppression in Latin America. The seeds of this image, however, were rooted in the Marian period and before. The eulogistic preface of Richard Eden's 1555 translation of Pietro Martire d'Anghiera's *The Decades of the newe worlde or West India, conteynyng the navigations and conquestes of the Spanyards*, which was dedicated to Philip and Mary, sought to stimulate English colonial endeavours through the emulation of Spain. This 'positive' view of Spanish colonialism contrasted sharply with the infamous denunciation of Spanish tyranny and cruelty in the New World in Bartolomé de las Casas's *Brevísima relación de la destrucción de las Indias* (1552). The first English translation of Las Casas, in 1583 as *The Spanish Colonie or Briefe Chronicle of the actes and Gestes of the Spaniards in the west Indies, called the Newe Worlde*, appeared precisely at a moment when England was slipping into war with Spain through its increasingly open support of the Dutch revolt against Spanish rule in the Low Countries. The polemical force of this account of the Indies' destruction was made ever more explicit in subsequent editions: by 1646 it was subtitled 'their unparallel'd Cruelties on the Indians, in the destruction of above Forty Millions of People'. A fresh translation appeared in 1656 by John Phillips, a nephew of Oliver Cromwell, seeking to promote a plan to establish a British colony in Jamaica. This presented itself in straightforwardly emotive terms as *The Teares of the Indians Being An Historical and true Account of the Cruel Massacres and Slaughters of above of Twenty Millions of innocent people*. Nevertheless, even at the moment when Richard Eden appeared to praise the Spanish and their demi-godlike status, his text subverted this image by alluding to the violence necessary to win and sustain an empire:

> It is therefore apparent that the heroical factes of the Spaniardes of these days, deserue so greate prayse that thautour of this booke (beinge no Spanyarde) doth woorthely extolle theyr doynge aboue the famous actes of Hercules and Saturnus and such other which for theyr glorious and vertuous enterpryses were accoumpted as goddes amonge men. And surely if great Alexander and the Romans which haue rather obteyned then deserued immortall fame amonge men for theyr bluddye victories onely for theyr owne glory and amplifyinge theyr empire obteyned by slawghter of innocentes and kepte by violence, haue byn magnified for theyr doinges, howe much more then shal we thynke these men woorthy iust commendations which in theyr mercyfull warres ageynst these naked people haue so used them selues towarde them in exchaungynge of benefites for victorie, that greater commodities hath therof ensewed to the vanquisshed then the victourers.[86]

The contradiction implicit in the notion of a 'merciful war' is compounded by its being against 'naked' people. Eden's translation of Pietro Martire, along with his previous translation from two years earlier, dedicated to the duke of Northumberland, of sections of Sebastian Münster's *Cosmographia universalis* dealing with Columbus and the earliest voyages to the New World, contained passages that delineated this darker side of imperial violence, bloody victories merely for personal glory and to amplify territorial domination. Münster's vision of Spain in the *Cosmographia universalis* reiterated descriptions from his edition of Ptolemy that had been borrowed in turn from the Spanish cosmographer Michael Servetus (Miguel Villanueva Conesa) about their deceitfulness, lack of hospitality and excessive use of make-up.[87] In *The Decades of the newe worlde*, readers learned that:

> that kynde of men (the Spanyardes I meane which folowed the Admirall in that nauigation,) was for the most parte unruly, regardynge nothinge but Idlenes, playe, and libertie: And wolde by no meanes absteyne from iniuries: Rauyshynge the women of the Ilandes before the faces of their husbandes fathers, and bretherne: By which theyr abhomynable mysdemaynour, they disquieted the myndes of all thinhabitantes.[88]

The trope of ravishing women before the faces of their husbands and fathers was a commonplace of anti-Spanish and other religious polemic. The defector Captain Alexander Brett's speech to his company of London White Coats, sent to crush Wyatt's revolt, warned that the Spaniards would 'ravishe our wyfes before our faces, and deflowre our daughters in our prescence'.[89] John Bale's translation, *A Faithful Admonition* from May 1554, of a text by Martin Luther, warned that strangers in the German lands (Italians in this case) would 'most shamefully defyle and abuse honest wyues, widdowes and virgyns euen before the faces of theyr husbands, parentes and frindes'.[90] John Bradford's *Copye of a letter* (1556) went even further, literalising this trope:

> the worst of all the companie muste haue my wife priuelie, when I am present bi: this is more vilanie, that one muste kepe the dore, will not that greue you sore, and dare not speake for your life when another hath youre wife. Perhaps the king, yet that were a noble thing. Naie perchaunce some other slaue or vile pockie knaue, this thing in dede shal make your hartes blede, when your wife bereath the marke of that nightes warke... ye perhaps with such mocks you mai both come to pockes. For fewe of them be cleane, thoughe they make lustie cheare, as Surgentes doe me tell.[91]

The obvious incorporation of a piece of doggerel verse in the letter suggests that the claim is specious. Münster, in Eden's translation, focused on slightly different features of colonial violence, underlining the desire for gold and the violence, torture and other techniques the Spanish used to extract it:

> And whereas they yet perceaued, that the Christien men entended to continue there, thei sent an ambassadour to the admiral to desyre him to restrayne the outragiousnes and crueltie of his men, at whose handes they sustained such iniuries and violence as they scarcely loked for at the handes of mortal enemies. Declaringe further, that under the pretence of seking for gold they committed innumerable wronges and mischieuous actes, spoyling in maner all the hole region: and that for the auoyding of such enormities and oppressions, they hadde rather paye tribute, then to be thus dayly vexed with incursions, & neuer to be at quiete.[92]

The tortuous logic of the passage – the natives' desire to render tribute in order to attenuate the violence being used to secure the material resources necessary to justify the 'Christien[s']' presence and ensure their continuance in that inhospitable environment – underlines the fundamental doubts underlying the justice and legality of the whole enterprise. The translation of Pietro Martire was immediately interpreted in this anti-heroic mode by the political writer John Ponet in his *A Shorte Treatise of politike pouuer, and of the true Obedience which subiectes owe to kynges and other ciuile Gouernours, with an Exhortacion to all true naturall Englishe men* (1556), which connected anxieties about the precise nature of Mary's rights within her own kingdom with arguments over the legality of property rights and ownership acquired through conquest. He conjectured, 'let vs ymagine an vntruthe, that all the subiectes goodes were the princes, and that he might take them at his pleasure', and that there were garrisons everywhere:

> so that they had not wherwith to redresse their iniuries, as nature wolde counsail them: were this a waie to make the people labour, whan others should

take the bread out of their mouthe? Wolde they desire to increace the world with children, whan they knewe that they should be lefte in worse case, than vnreasonable beastes? No surely, and that ye maie see by the worke of nature in the people of the West Indies, now called newe Spaine: who knewe of Christ nothing at all, and of God no more than nature taught them. The people of that countreie whan the catholike Spaniardes came thider, were simple and plaine men, and liued without great labour, the lande was naturally so pleintiful of all thinges and continually the trees hade ripe frute on them. whan the Spaniardes hade by flatterie put in their foote, and by litel and litel made them selues strong, building fortes in diuerse places, they to get the golde that was ther, forced the people (that wer not vsed to labour) to stande all the daie in the hotte sunne gathering gold in the sande of the riuers. By this meanes a great nombre of them (not vsed to such paines) died, and a great nombre of them (seing them selues brought from so quiet a life to suche miserie and slauerie) of desperacion killed them selues. And many wolde not mary, bicause they wolde not haue their children slaues to the Spaniardes. The women whan they felte them self with childe, wolde eat a certain herbe to destroie the childe in the wombe. So that where at the comming thider of the Spaniardes, ther were accompted to be in that countrey nine hundred thousaunt persones, ther were in short time by this meanes so fewe lefte, as Petre martir (who was one of themprour Charles the fifthes counsail there, and wrote this historie to themperour) saieth, it was a shame for him to name.

This is the frute, wher Princes take all their subiectes thinges as their owne. And wherunto at leingth will it come, but that either they must be no kinges, or elles kinges without people, which is all one.[93]

Political debates about the nature of a prince's title to a kingdom and the nature of royal dominion, whether they were analogous to rights in heritable property, had come sharply into focus in the context of England's first regnant queen and the issues this raised for laws of succession. Was it possible to will a crown or to establish a title in a kingdom by statute as Henry VIII had done? Ponet used the example of the New World to warn of the dangers that such ideas presupposed. The political authority of the Habsburgs in their Spanish kingdoms was never the same as that they exercised by proxy across the Atlantic: its legality and certain control were never so assured. The example of the New World could be used to underscore the greatness and solidity of imperial Spain, but also to undermine its very legitimacy. The Marian period provided opportunities for Englishmen to rejoin the commercial endeavours of exploiting the New World. By 1555, the Englishman Robert Thomson was in Mexico City admiring 'the streets[,] made very broad, and right, that a man being in the high place, at the one ende of the street, may see at the least a good mile forward'.[94] A little over ten years later in *A true declaration of the toublesome voyadge* (1569), John Hawkins reported how with a cargo of captured and enslaved West Africans he 'coasted from place to place makyng our traffique with the Spanyardes as wee myght, somewhat hardelye, because the kinge had straightly commaunded all his gouernours in those partes by no meanes to suffer any trade to be made with vs: notwithstanding we had reasonable trade and courteous intertainment from the Ile of Margarita unto Cartagena'.[95] His troubles only began of course after he was forced to put in on the coast of New Spain and seek permission to refit his ships from the centre of Spanish authority in the New World in Mexico City. The franchised nature of political rights and uncertain legal status of land ownership in Spanish America reveal the negotiated, contingent and flexible nature of Habsburg political thought. From the outside such elisions and improvisations could easily be read as ultimately threatening.

Hispanophobia

A remarkable feature of the exiles' propaganda was how swiftly and directly they responded to political events. One of the earliest examples of Hispanophobia in Mary's reign can be found in John Bale's *A declaration of Edmonde Bonners articles* (1554); a lengthy and intemperate attack on the architects of the Catholic restoration – 'gagling Gardiner, bocherly Bonner, and trifeling Tunstall, with other bloudy biteshepes and franticke papistes of England' like Thomas Martin and Hugh Weston.[96] It rebutted point by point the remit of the bishop of London's visitation of his diocese, which began on 3rd September 1554 and ended on 8th October 1555.[97] Bale refuted the notion of there being close dynastic bonds between England and Spain, suggesting that 'certen Genealogies of theyr lineall dissent from Jhon a Gaunt, sometime duke of Lancaster, Gardiner, White, and Harpesfeld maintaynynge the same with their flattering verses' were in fact 'the craftye conueyaunce of a Fryer that was once solde for puddynges'.[98] In relation to Bonner's ninth article that they should enquire into whether there were any foreign priests administering the sacraments, Bale rejoined:

> And as for Jack Spaniard, being as good a Christian, as is eyther Turke, Jewe, or pagane, *sine lux, sine crux, sine deus*, after the chast rules of Rome & Florence, he must be a dweller here, ye know causes whye. Than remaine there none other foreners and straungers to be loked vpon, but Duchmen, Danes, Italians, and french menne. And they for the more parte, as muche regarde the Popes priesthode, as the deuel doth holy water... the Englyshe nacyon... in thys miserable age, must come last of al and within theyr owne soyl, must be reckened inferioures to all foreners and strangers.[99]

Although clearly for Bale anxiety about property rights flowed from the Spanish marriage – '[o]ur inheritaunce is tourned to the straungers, and oure houses to the aleauntes',[100] as he wrote – the focus of his text was a polemical assault on religious conservatives and in particular the 'scismatical buggerer and biteshepe' Bonner.[101] The populace in early modern London may have demonstrated similar xenophobic tendencies to the publics in other major sixteenth-century metropolises. In the context of the Spanish marriage, this xenophobia was exacerbated by anxieties about Mary's gender and status as a regnant queen. These concerns crystallised around the political language of Marian queenship. If she was the mother of her people, as Mary had claimed to be in her great Guildhall oration, her marriage to Philip potentially turned her subjects into the unwanted sons of a first marriage (*alnados* in Spanish); marginalised, discarded or disinherited in the context of a second union. The propaganda that was employed during Wyatt's rebellion to weaken Mary's position played on fears of foreign occupation, despoliation and rape. This language was picked up on by Marian exiles on the continent to warn their fellow countrymen of the entrance of foreigners and an alien Roman religion. The corollary of this language was the sexualisation of the Spaniard. The feminisation of England in the polemics reflected apprehensions about inheritance and property, and were embodied in the image of the lustful, tyrannous and cruel Spaniard, familiar from later incarnations of the Black Legend.

The tropes of cruelty, tyranny, unbridled lust and sexual despoliation, along with racial hybridity that transformed 'the "Spaniard"... into a kind of "Europeanised" African or Moor',[102] were already fully present in Thomas Stafford's proclamation issued at Scarborough Castle in 1557, in which he asserted that he aimed to deliver England: 'from the possessyon of prowde, spytefull Spanyardes, whose Morysh maners, and spytefull condytions, no nation in the worlde is able to suffer... banyshinge and expellinge all straungers, marchauntes onlye excepted': he exhorted his fellow countrymen to resist being 'sorrowfull slaves, and carefull captyves to suche a naughtye natyon as Spanyardes, who affirme openlye, that they will rather lyve with Mores, Turkes, and Jues, than with Inglyshmen'.[103] Among the names of those taken with Stafford was a certain John Bradford, author of one of the most colourful examples of anti-Spanish sentiment, *The Copie of a Letter*, discussed below.

John Knox's infamous 1558 polemic *The First Blast of the Trumpet Against the Monstruous regiment of women* accused the Spanish of being responsible for the Cruxifixion 'for Jewes they are, as histories do witnesse, and they them selues confesse'.[104] In a marginal note he continued: '[t]he spaniardes are Iewes and they bragge that Marie of England is of the roote of Iesse'.[105] This notion probably derived ultimately from neo-Ptolemaic thought tracing Spanish descent from Japhet's son Tubal, a mythology that surfaced in Alfonso de Cartagena's

Anacephaleosis o genealogía de los reyes de España in the fifteenth century and had been reiterated by Florián de Ocampo's chronicle of 1553.[106] These histories are one potential source of ethnic jibes. The other was *estatutos de limpieza de sangre* (statutes of racial purity), which excluded descendants of Moors or Jews from church or municipal office, the most notorious of which had been introduced by Philip's tutor Juan Martínez Siliceo in 1548, sparking off a controversy that was still rumbling on when he was raised to the cardinalate in 1556.[107] Tracts written against the *estatutos* paradoxically sought to show that the entire Spanish nobility, including the royal family, descended from Jews and Moors. One of the most famous, the *Tizón de la nobleza de España*, was published in 1560. The appearance of Moorish cultural practices such as the *juego de cañas* in England with Philip's entourage underlined this multicultural past.[108]

One of the most revealing incidents of mutual cultural illegibility occurred when Mary gave audience to the duchess of Alba, María Enríquez de Guzmán. After being presented, the duchess attempted to sit on a cushion on the floor in Moorish fashion, as Spanish aristocratic women were accustomed to, where Mary, perhaps believing it to be a gesture of deference attempted to join her, but unused to the *estrado*, the queen soon needed to get up and they both ended seated on low stools.[109] There are warrants for Turkish costumes in the revels accounts; however, it is not possible to read too much into this apparent vogue for the exotic. At the jousts to celebrate Arthur and Catherine's wedding in 1501, Charles Brandon had performed in 'an oriental costume such as Sir Palomides might have worn in Malory's *Morte d'Arthur*: "the guise of a Turk or a Saracen, with a white roll of fine linen cloth about his head, the ends hanging pendant wise"'.[110] The unusual headdress would presumably also have been worn by Philip's courtiers when they took part in the *juego de cañas* in Turkish-style costumes.

Picking up on these features of Spain may have been an unintended consequence of intercultural exchange in the context of the marriage, but it is more likely that the polemicists, many of whom were not in England but rather visited or lived in Italy, picked up on early versions of the Black Legend prevalent there.[111] Perhaps they were familiar with them anyway and this was one of the factors that motivated resistance to the match, despite the many reasons in its favour. Due to the geographical proximity of Spain and Italy and the similarity of their climate, Italian commentators had been at pains to underline their national differences. The *conquistador* of Colombia, Gonzalo Jiménez de Quesada, wrote in 1567: '[a]bove all the number of nations that are spread throughout the world, this hate of Spain is most powerful amongst the Italians'.[112] Their particular hate had originated in Aragonese mercantilism in the kingdom of Naples in the fifteenth century and intensified over the sixteenth century following the sack and massacre at Prato in 1512 and of course the notorious sack of Rome in 1527. While commentators at the time were divided as to whether the Spanish had acted more barbarously than the Lutheran mercenaries or Neapolitan forces involved, in the end the sense that Italians were no longer masters of their own lands but rather their ancient civilisation, heir to Rome, was dominated by a people inferior in culture, religion and race fostered profoundly negative stereotypes and resentment.

Unfavourable judgements about Spanish government in Italy have rested on the assumption that all foreign sovereignty is *eo ipso* an unbearable imposition, inevitably exploitative, unjust and carried out in the interests of the occupying power. It was certainly true that the chancelleries in the south of Italy and Lombardy conducted their business in Spanish and in addition to large numbers of officials involved in tax collecting, numerous grants of lands and titles to members of the Spanish aristocracy were made, and moreover viceroys and other governors and officers were often Iberians. However, despite historians' tendency to accept such judgements uncritically, in fact Spanish governance in Italy was in many respects fruitful. It generally respected local laws and customs, privileges and local autonomy were preserved as were representative institutions. There are numerous testaments to the rectitude and impartiality of Spanish justice. In Naples and Sicily, the middling sort were protected from the depredations of the upper nobility and at the start of the seventeenth century the Neopolitan philosopher Campanella, in his *De Monarchia Hispanica*, even proposed replacing Italian with Spanish barons in Sicily and Sardinia:

> In such islands the barons are to be subdued more than elsewhere; since the location of the regions provides them with greater opportunity to rise up, and they are by nature more inclined to tyranny. Therefore it is better to send across barons from other nations; indeed for this purpose the Spanish are more suitable than the others, since they are placed beneath the same climate; and to them both the services and the business should be entrusted; to these transalpines are to be added, partly to do military service, partly to bear offspring.[113]

Similarly, the notion of taxation becoming unjustifiably heavy, raised disproportionately in the interest of Spanish military expansionism, is also questionable. Continuous inflation throughout the sixteenth century put pressure on the income of all western European states. Factoring in inflation, the tax burden did not increase in Sicily over the period and a similar picture seems to be the case in Naples and Milan. In Sicily taxation was agreed in a general assembly, not imposed by government, and was often considered necessary to defend against the Turks, something which was not solely in the interest of Spain but also critical for Naples and Italy as a whole, following the Turkish incursion and temporary establishment of a bridgehead at Otranto in 1480. This is not to suggest naively that Spanish imperial authority was exercised altruistically. Demographic comparisons underline the similarity between free and Spanish-dominated parts of the peninsula. According to some figures, the number of households in the kingdom of Naples, for example, doubled across the century. By comparison, in the second half of the sixteenth century the populations of the regions of Florence (excluding the city) and Siena barely grew at all, no doubt being theatres of Franco-Spanish rivalry.[114]

The form taken by the Black Legend in Italy focused on Spanish pride, excessive dignity and ceremoniousness, the introduction of corrupt social practices, and affected and courtly language, from which Italians coined the notions of *spagnolaggine*, *spagnolata*, *spagnolimso*, *spagnoleggiare*. Pietro Aretino ridiculed the Spanish *hidalgo* in his plays *L'Amor Constante* (1536) and *Gl'Ingannati* (1537). In the latter, in reply to the comment that 'although I seem ill-favoured, I am one of best, well-born *hidalgos* in all Spain', the Spanish gentleman's Italian lover replies '[a] miracle he hasn't said *Señor* or knight! Because all the Spanish who come say they are lords.'[115] While historians have lauded Fernando de Aragón for instituting the first system of resident ambassadors in Italy, he was accused of disloyalty by those with whom he conducted this diplomacy. From this the Spanish became known as masters of deceit, astuteness and perfidy. Alongside pride were racial jibes about their mixed Jewish and Moorish heritage. Francesco Guicciardini asserted 'that all the kingdom was full of Jews and heretics and most of the people were tainted by this depravity. By them were held all the greatest offices and revenues of the realm and so powerful and numerous were they that it was evident, if no remedy were taken, that in a few years all Spain would have left the Catholic faith.' Spain also gave him the impression of something African or Oriental: they are 'black in colour and small in stature, they have an innately Punic nature'.[116] These ideas about their ethnic origins arose partly from the notion of their being descendants of the Carthaginians, following Hannibal's lengthy military campaigns in the peninsula and occupation of Hispania. Most importantly, however, following expulsion in 1492, a large proportion of the Jews who had fled Spain settled in Italy. The accusation of their being *marranos* or of Jewish or Moorish blood was reinforced by Spanish dress which recalled the Moorish *chilaba* for Italians, as well as Moorish games and dances introduced into Italy by the Spanish ruling elite: '[g]rowing familiarity with Spanish customs and habits in the sixteenth century led to a burgeoning awareness of their Oriental and African heritage, reinforcing the idea that they had the same origins as Moors and Jews'.[117] The final aspect of the Italian version of the Black Legend was the association of the Spanish with sexual rapacity and prostitution in particular. This derived in part from the association of the city of Valencia with sexual licence and immorality;

an impression strengthened by the region's giving Italy two popes, Alonso de
Borja, Calixto XIII (1455–8), and the notorious Rodrigo Borja, Alexander VI
(1492–1503). A vividly salacious fictional version of this image of the Spanish
was put in print by the syphilitic priest Francisco Delicado in his *La lozana
andaluza*, published in Venice in 1528. Set in Rome leading up to the sack, the
'heroine' Lozana arrives in there in 1513 and is welcomed into a community of
converso and Jewish prostitutes and courtesans, whose ranks she joins. Shortly
after her arrival, having serviced a steward and a mace bearer, her third client
(a courier for the pope) informs her

> in all Rome I doubt you could find a man who knows more about the tricks
> whores use in their trade be they naked or fully clad. There are some whores
> who are more gracious than beautiful, and others who join the trade while little
> girls. There are passionate whores and polished whores, painted whores and
> illustrious whores, whores of reputation and those who have been condemned.
> There are Moorish whores from Zocodover Square in Toledo who ply the
> public squares, and whores who work the outskirts of the city.[118]

The name of her Neapolitan boyfriend Rampín echoes the Italian *rampino*,
which means *ardid, sutileza* [trick, ruse], linking him back to one aspect of the
negative vision of the Spanish. The Roman census of 1526–7 confirms the
impression given by the text. Of 55,035 registered inhabitants (no doubt an
underestimate) there were 1,550 prostitutes. The greatest number of foreigners in this group were Spanish (104), followed by French (59) and Germans
(52). In addition 7 were Moorish and 30 Jewish, probably most of whom were
also from Spain.[119] In 1549 three Spanish women were among the most heavily
taxed courtesans in Rome. One, Isabella de la Luna from Granada, was one of
the most famous and successful in the period and alluded to several times in
stories by Bandello. Juan del Encina's *Placida y Vitoriano*, with its Celestinesque
Eritea who boasts 'if I had a ducat for every virgin I had remade there wouldn't
be enough room to squeeze them under this roof' (ll. 697–9), was performed at
the house of the Valencian Cardinal Arborea, Jacopo Serra, before the Spanish
ambassador and Federico Gonzaga in Rome in 1513.[120] Thomas Dandelet has
underlined how the case of Spanish Rome exemplifies the power and success of
'informal imperialism', arguing that '[i]f Italians described themselves as "his-
panized" it was not from force but through choice'.[121] The Spanish conquered
Rome through patronage and left a lasting mark on the Eternal City during this
period, through their contributions to painting, music, architecture, business
and above all theology and religion.

One of the most curious aspects (for us) of Spain's image in Italy was
its association with heresy and Lutheranism. This strange notion makes more
sense though if we consider Alfonso de Valdés' *Dialogo de las cosas acaecidas en*

Roma (1529), a commissioned justification of the Emperor Charles V's actions leading up to the sack. This work of propaganda contained clearly Protestant ideas, and read the sack of Rome as a providential punishment for the failure of the papacy to embrace Erasmian reform.[122] Its ties with Protestant thought are underlined by its publication in England for the first time in 1586, accompanying the Spanish Protestant Antonio del Corro's Spanish language learning textbook *Reglas gramaticales*.[123] Alfonso's twin brother Juan de Valdés worked in Spanish Naples until his death in 1541 as a spiritual leader of a congregation of priests and socially eminent Italian intellectuals, critical of the church and influenced by Reformist ideas.[124] His activities had attracted the attention of Gian Pietro Carafa at the time, but it was a year after his death before Carafa's appointment as head of the Roman Inquisition and only in 1549 did Carafa become cardinal archbishop of Naples, although he was blocked from taking up the post by Charles V, an insult the magnitude of which can be gauged from the fact that the diocese was held by his family from 1484–1544 and then 1549–1576.[125] Valdés' *Comentarios de la Epístola a los Romanos* and *Comentarios de la Epístola a los Corintios* were published in Geneva by the Spanish Calvinist Juan Pérez de Pineda in 1556 and 1557. Another notorious case, once again pressed for by Paul IV, was that of Bartolomé Carranza, a critical figure of course in the Catholic Reformation in England, whose arrest on his return to Spain and transportation to Rome, where he languished in prison until his release in 1576, again suggested a connection between Spain and Lutheran heresy. There is a certain irony that while Spain was fighting heresy and Protestantism in the Low Countries, England and Germany, in Italy they were seen as heretics and proto-Lutherans.

There was also a version of the Legend in the German lands connected to the war against the Schmalkaldic League, 1546–52, which the emperor had been powerfully encouraged to undertake by his confessor Pedro de Soto. De Soto was sent to England in 1555 to take part in the high-profile heresy cases against Cranmer, Latimer and Ridley at Oxford, where he took up a chair in theology. By 1550, there were outposts manned with Spanish soldiers throughout Habsburg lands in the Holy Roman Empire. The German garrison at Augsburg was replaced with a Spanish one in 1551 and Granvelle declared that, without Spanish troops there, German loyalty could not be relied upon. The family compact of the same year which meant Philip would succeed Charles as Holy Roman Emperor was one of the main reasons why Maurice of Saxony returned to open rebellion in 1552. Contact between the German lands and Spain had taken place under the auspices of their shared ruler since 1519 and although there were shared enemies, personal contact through trade or culture was less significant than in the case of Italy. There was nevertheless a German infiltration into trade within the empire, largely through the importance of their bankers. A group of 150 Germans and Dutch participated in the expedition of Pedro de Mendoza to the Río de la Plata in 1535–36. The Fugger and Welser banking dynasties took over monopolies in Spain and the New World, notably the mercury mines at Almadén and the colonisation of Venezuela. Welser involvement in the New World was brought to an end by Philip II in 1556, when he took back control of the region.[126] The negative images of the Spanish in Germany originated in protectionism and military occupation. For the Protestant faction, rapacity, falsity, cruelty and immorality all became associated with Spain, by extension from the faction's contempt for the papacy. Luther frequently compared the Spanish with Turks: 'I prefer a Turkish enemy to a Spanish protector, who exercises extreme cruelty'.[127] Luther's anti-Semitism may also have influenced his hostility to the Spanish. The Hanseatic League gained partisans in the context of sectarian struggles, as merchants from different areas sought protection under their banner. This strengthening was inimical to English interests. The publication of Luis de Avila y Zuñiga's *Comentario de la guerra de Alemania* in 1550 in Antwerp caused a violent reaction even among partisans of Charles, for enhancing Spain's part in the suppression of the heretical revolt and seemingly confirming their military superiority and domination. Roger Ascham recorded that Albert, marquis of Brandenburg, had been so 'chafed' by the book 'wherein the honour of Germany and the princes thereof, and by name Marquis Albert, who was in the first wars on the emperor's side, was so defamed to all the world... [that] he offered the combat with Luis de Avila, which the emperor, for good will and wise respects, would in no case admit'.[128] It can be no accident that this text was published in English translation five years later in 1555 in London, the only significant translation of any Spanish text undertaken in connection with Philip and his entourage's visit.

Roger Ascham was a potentially important conduit for the Germanic version of the Black Legend. Most famous for his treatises on archery, *Toxophilus* (1545), and teaching Latin, *The Scholemaster* (1570), he had left England in September 1550 as secretary to Sir Richard Morison, ambassador to Charles V, and did not return until August 1553. While at the imperial court he befriended the emperor's physician Vesalius, studied the histories of Herodotus, Polybius, Machiavelli and Paolo Giovio with Morison and learned Italian from and some German from his employer. He corresponded with Johannes Sleiden, historian of the Reformation, as well as delegates at Trent, including Johann Sturm.[129] He began his *A Report and Discourse of the Affairs and State of Germany* in mid-May 1552, a pragmatic political history based on his observations of day-to-day events following Charles' flight from Innsbruck, portraying the emperor as 'blinded with the over-good opinion of his own wisdom, liking only what himself listed, and contemning easily all advice of others'.[130] No doubt it was intended as a piece of intelligencing for Edward's Privy Council. After Ascham's return to England in August 1553, despite having been Elizabeth's Latin tutor and being associated with prominent Reformers like John Cheke, he was eventually appointed the queen's Latin secretary on 7th May 1554 against the vociferous objections of Mary's strongly Catholic intimate Sir Francis Englefield; no doubt in part through the good offices of former patrons, like Gardiner or Paget, and others like Sir William Petre, to whom Ascham initially offered his services as tutor to his children, or Mary Clarke, a lady-in-waiting of Queen Mary.[131] He dined with Pole and inspected his *Pro ecclesiasticae unitatis defensione*, which was republished at Strasbourg in 1555. Ascham offered in his manuscript report an especially unflattering picture of Pedro de Toledo, the duke of Alba's uncle and viceroy of Naples, who

> used himself with much cruelty over the people of Naples, by exactions of money without measure, by inquisition of men's doings without order, and not only of men's doings, but also of men's outward lookings and inward thinkings, using the least suspicion for a sufficient witness to spoil and to kill whomsoever he listed... men's suits were pulled from common law to private will, and were heard not in places open to justice, but in private parlours, shut up to all that came not in by favour or money.[132]

This individual study in tyranny, drawn from the experience of Italy, might be seen as personal and particular to a corrupt nobleman; however, Ascham went on to cite Albert of Brandenburg's book for 'sore envying against the pride of the Spaniards, and the authority of strangers, which had now in their hands the seal of the empire... compelling the Germans in their own country to use strange tongues for their private suits' and concluded that Maurice of Saxony had tried to obtain help from 'as many as hated the Spaniards, that is to say, almost all protestants and papists too in Germany'.[133] There is an early, indirect allusion to the Spanish Inquisition in his reference to 'inward thinkings'. Ascham's purpose in his history, though – to analyse the partialities, family ties, factional interests and financial motives behind the political struggles that had led the empire back into crisis by 1552 – turns on the concept of *unkindness*; personal relationships betrayed, slights and dishonours, that compelled subjects to fall away from Charles. The *topos* of Turkish cruelty imitated by Christians, invoked in an anecdote at the outset, underlies his critique of those uncommitted to God's word, both those he refers to as papists and those uninterested in religion, like the king of France.[134] In his story, a gentleman of the king of the Romans captured in battle is sliced up in front of the delegation sent to ransom him and fed to dogs. In symmetrical revenge, three Turkish captives have 'collops' of their flesh cut off and are fed to pigs by the 'Christian men' rather than being ransomed. Ascham was 'not so angry with the Turks... as I am sorry for the Christian men that follow them'.[135] This incident becomes for him a synecdoche for Christianity's barbarous degradation. It underlines the urgent need for reform in Christendom and is at the heart of his providential understanding of history. By 1570, looking back on the time when 'Papistrie, as a standyng poole, couered and ouerflowed all England', he inveighed against 'bookes of Cheualrie' written by 'idle Monkes, or wanton Channons', whose pleasure lay in 'open mans slaughter, and bold bawdrye', vices that threatened the youth; with the most dangerous books of all being those 'made in Italie, and translated in England'.[136] Here, where one might expect him to look to Spain, instead it is the Italianate that stands for the contaminating, morally suspect and culturally toxic.

Notes

1 *Cal. Scot.*, Vol. 1, no. 416. The fifth Earl of Westmoreland, Henry Neville, was responsible for crushing the Stafford revolt in April 1557 and by May had been named general of the horse in northern England. His wooden effigy, along with ones of two of his wives, can still be seen in Staindrop church in County Durham.

2 So expressed in Joan Thomas, 'Before the Black Legend: sources of anti-Spanish sentiment in England, 1553–1558', unpublished PhD thesis (University of Illinois, Urbana, 1972), p. 1.

3 E. H. Harbison, *Rival Ambassadors at the Court of Queen Mary* (New York: Books for Libraries Press 1940, repr. 1970), p. 330.

4 David Loades, *The Reign of Mary Tudor: Politics, Government and Religion, 1553–1558* (2nd edn, London: Longman, 1991), pp. 69–70.

5 A. M. Kinghorn, *The Chorus of History: Literary-Historical Relations in Renaissance Britain 1485–1558* (London: Blandford Press, 1971), p. 77.

6 John Skelton, *The Complete English Poems*, ed. John Scattergood (Harmondsworth: Penguin, 1983), pp. 231–2. On these lines see Greg Walker, *John Skelton and the Politics of the 1520s* (Cambridge: Cambridge University Press, 1988), pp. 78–9.

7 David Loades, *Mary Tudor: The Tragical History of the First Queen of England* (Richmond: The National Archives, 2006), p. 126.

8 Susan Doran, *Monarchy and Matrimony: The Courtships of Elizabeth I* (London: Routledge, 1996), p. 23.

9 Alluded to by John Edwards, *Mary I: England's Catholic Queen* (London: Yale University Press, 2011), p. 217.

10 John Gough Nichols, ed., *The Diary of Henry Machyn, Citizen and Merchant Taylor of London 1550–1563* (London: Camden Society, 1848), p. 74 and see Miranda Kaufman, 'Africans in Britain, 1500–1640', unpublished PhD thesis (Oxford, 2011), pp. 125–6.

11 Edwards, *Mary I*, pp. 165–6.

12 David Loades, 'Literature and national identity' in David Loewenstein and Janel Mueller, eds, *The Cambridge History of Early Modern English Literature* (Cambridge: Cambridge University Press, 2002), 201–28, p. 201.

13 Philip Schwyzer, *Literature, Nationalism, and Memory in Early Modern England and Wales* (Cambridge: Cambridge University Press, 2004), p. 1.

14 On the compexity of loyalties within the guilds in this period see Joseph Ward, *Metropolitan Communities: Trade Guilds, Identity, and Change in Early Modern London* (Palo Alto, Cal.: Stanford University Press, 1997), pp. 3*ff.* and 144–6.

15 Scott Oldenburg, 'Toward a multicultural mid-Tudor England: the Queen's royal entry *circa*

1553, *The Interlude of Weath and Health*, and the question of strangers in the reign of Mary I', *English Literary History* 76 (2009), 99–129, p. 100.

16 Oldenburg, 'Toward a multicultural mid-Tudor England', p. 122.

17 See Richard Helgerson, *Forms of Nationhood: The Elizabethan Writing of England* (Chicago: University of Chicago Press, 1992).

18 *English Historical Documents*, Vol. V, *1485–1558*, ed. C. H. Williams, p. 196. See Nigel Goose, '"Xenophobia" in Elizabethan and early Stuart England: an epithet too far' in Nigel Goose and Lien Luu, eds, *Immigrants in Tudor and Early Stuart England* (Brighton: Sussex Academic Press, 2005), 110–35, p. 112. This kind of attitude frequently finds expression in the cautious correspondence of the imperial ambassador Simon Renard.

19 Goose, '"Xenophobia" in Elizabethan and early Stuart England', p. 113. From Fynes Moryson, *An Itinerary written by Fynes Moryson Gent. etc.* (London: John Beale, 1617), Part 3, pp. 35 and 151.

20 Andrew Pettegree, *Foreign Protestant Communities in Sixteenth-Century London* (Oxford: Clarendon Press, 1986), p. 14. On the riot see Martin Holmes, 'Evil May Day, 1517: the story of a riot', *History Today* 15 (1965), 642–50.

21 Steve Rappaport, *Worlds within Worlds: Structures of Life in sixteenth-century London* (Cambridge: Cambridge University Press, 1989), pp. 45 and 104.

22 Rappaport, *Worlds within Worlds*, pp. 83 and 276.

23 Rappaport, *Worlds within Worlds*, p. 277.

24 Oldenburg, 'Toward a multicultural mid-Tudor England', p. 112.

25 Foxe, *TAMO*, Book 11, p. 2134.

26 Foxe, *TAMO*, Book 12, p. 2265 and Oldenburg, 'Toward a multicultural mid-Tudor England', p. 111 and note 57.

27 Alastair Hamilton, *The Family of Love* (Cambridge: James Clarke, 1981), pp. 115–41.

28 Ian Archer, *The Pursuit of Stability: Social Relations in Elizabethan London* (Cambridge: Cambridge University Press, 1991), p. 133. See LMA, Repertory of the Court of Aldermen 13, fols 427, 432, 444, 445 and 451.

29 See William Page, ed., *Letters of Denization and Acts of Naturalization for Aliens in England, 1509–1603*, 59 vols (Lymington: Publications of the Huguenot Society of London, 1893), vol. 8, p. xxxi.

30 Oldenburg, 'Toward a multicultural mid-Tudor England', p. 107.

31 Rappaport, *Worlds within Worlds*, p. 89.

32 James Walvin, *The Black Presence: A Documentary History of the Negro in England, 1555–1860* (London: Orbach and Chambers, 1971). On the repercussions of these ideas for evolving twenty-first century ideas about Englishness and British national identity, see Yasmin Alibhai-Brown, *Who do We Think we Are? Imagining the New Britain* (London: Penguin, 2000), pp. 47–50 and Peter Fryer, *Staying Power: The History of Black People in Britain* (London: Pluto Press, 1984). The bibliography on this topic has recently been added to by Miranda Kaufmann's definitive consideration of *Black Tudors: The Untold Story* (London: Oneworld, 2017).

33 On the play's topical allusions to Mary and Pole see T. W. Craik, 'The political interpretation of two Tudor Interludes: *Temperance and Humility* and *Wealth and Health*', *Review of English Studies* n. s. 14 (1953), 98–108.

34 John Christopherson, *An exhortation to all menne to take hede and beware of rebellion* (London: John Cawood, 24th July 1554), sigs Ni v–Nii r.

35 John Proctor, *The historie of wyates rebellion* (London: Robert Caly, 10th January 1555), sig. Civ v. Both examples are discussed by Oldenburg, 'Toward a multicultural mid-Tudor England', pp. 107 and 121.

36 Oldenburg, 'Toward a multicultural mid-Tudor England', p. 100.

37 Figures from Lien Bich Luu, *Immigrants and Industries of London, 1500–1700* (Aldershot: Ashgate, 2005), pp. 36 and 92.

38 Rappaport, *Worlds within Worlds*, chapter 2, 'The Nature and Extent of Citizenship', 23–60, p. 42.

39 Luu, *Immigrants and Industries*, p. 102.

40 Andrew Borde, *The fyrst boke of the introduction of knowledge. The whych dothe teache a man to speake parte of all maner of languages, and to know the usage and fashion of all maner of countreys. And for to know the moste parte of all maner of coynes of money, the whych is currant in euery region* (London: William Copeland, 1549; repr. 1555?), sigs A3v and L1r. The reprinting at the outset of Mary's reign of a work originally dedicated to her is significant, although it is not exactly flattering about many kingdoms that fell within the purview of Philip and Mary's empire. See Yolanda Rodríguez Pérez, *The Dutch Revolt through Spanish Eyes: Self and Other in historical and literary texts of Golden Age Spain (c. 1548–1673)* (Bern: Peter Lang, trans. and rev. 2008), pp. 48–9.

41 Borde, *The fyrst boke*, sig. F2v.

42 Vicente Alvarez, 'Relación del camino y buen viaje que hizo el príncipe de España…1551', in Juan Christóbal Calvete de Estrella, *El felicissimo viaje del muy alto y muy poderoso Príncipe don Phelippe*, ed. José María de Francisco Olmos and Paloma Cuenca (Madrid: Sociedad Estatal para la Conmemoración de los Centenarios de Felipe II y Carlos V, 2001), p. 666: 'algunos se paran tales con la cervesa doble que no se pueden levantar y allí se mean… Entre la gente commún no tienen por afrenta emborracharse.'

43 See my '"Last thought upon a windmill"?: Cervantes and Fletcher' in John Ardila, ed., *The Cervantean Heritage: Reception and Influence of Cervantes in Britain* (London: Legenda, 2009), 223–33 and 'Lazarillo de Tormes and the picaresque in early modern England' in Andrew Hadfield, ed., *Oxford Handbook of English Prose 1500–1640* (Oxford: Oxford University Press, 2013), 121–36.

44 Borde, *The fyrst boke*, sigs K3v–L3r.

45 John Ponet, *An Apologie fully answeringe by Scriptures and aunceant Doctors a blasphemose Book gatherid by D. Steph. Gardiner of late Lord Chancelar, D. Smyth of Oxford, Pighius, and other Papists* ([Strasbourg: heirs of W. Köpfel?], 1556), sigs C8v–D1r, pp. 48–9.

46 Stephen Gardiner, *A traictise declaringe and plainly prouying, that the pretensed marriage of prestes, and professed persons, is no marriage… Herewith is comprised in the later chapitres, a full confutation of Doctour Poynettes boke entitled a defence for the marriage of prestes. By Thomas Martin* (London: Robert Caley, May 1554).

47 Ponet, *An Apologie*, sigs Avi v and Avii v.

48 Thomas Wilson's *The Arte of Rhetorique for the vse of all suche as are studious of eloquence* (London: Richard Grafton, January 1553; London: John Kingston, 1560), sigs Aaiii r and M3r–v. See Mark Sanchez, 'Anti-Spanish sentiment in English literary and political writing, 1553–1603', unpublished PhD thesis, (University of Leeds, 2004), p. 71.

49 See Sverker Arnoldsson, *La leyenda negra: estudios sobre sus orígenes* (Gothenburg: Gothenburg University Press, 1960), p. 67.

50 Sanchez, 'Anti-Spanish sentiment', p. 20.

51 Thomas Cooper and Thomas Lanquet, *Coopers Chronicle, conteininge the whole discourse of the histories as well of this realme, as all other countreis* (London: Thomas Berthelet, 1560), sigs Bii v and Biii v. The same text is repeated verbatim in Richard Grafton, *An Abridgement of the Chronicles of England* (London: Richard Tottel, 1562), sig. X iv r, fol. 164.

52 Paulina Kewes, 'The exclusion crisis of 1553 and the Elizabethan succession', in Susan Doran and Thomas Freeman, eds, *Mary Tudor: Old and New Perspectives* (New York: Palgrave Macmillan, 2011), p. 49.

53 Susan Doran, 'A "sharp rod" of chastisement: Mary I through Protestant eyes during the reign of Elizabeth I', in *ibid.*, p. 26.

54 See Edwards, *Mary I*, pp. 295–304.

55 M. J. Rodríguez Salgado and Simon Adams, eds and trans., 'The Count of Feria's Dispatch to Philip II of 14 November 1558', *Camden Miscellany* XXVIII, 4th ser. (London: Royal Historical Society: 1984), 302–44, esp. p. 313.

56 Thomas Brice, *A compendious Register in metre, containing the names and patient sufferings of the members of Jesus Christ, and the tormented, and cruelly burned within England* (London: John

Kingston for Richard Adams, 1559) repr. in Edward Arber, *An English Garner: Tudor Tracts, 1532–1588*, intro. by A. F. Pollard (Westminster: Archibald Constable and Co., Ltd, repr. 1903), pp. 264 and 267. See also Sanchez, 'Anti-Spanish sentiment', p. 86.

57 Foxe, *TAMO*, Book 11, p. 1553.

58 'Hanc tamen vexationem haeretici formidantes, ut se ab illa eripere valerent astutia serpentina docuerunt ilicitam esse haereticorum punitionem, tyrannosque potius quam Reges esse dixerunt eos, qui haereticos puniunt, aut poenis, & cruciatibus illos ad fidem tenendam cogunt. Hac enim via putarunt Christianorum Principum animos ab ipsorum punitione deterrere, & prorsus revocare: ut vel sic impetrata, aut potius extorta impunitate liberius quotquot vellent, possent verbis, & scripturis haereses docere.' Alfonso de Castro, *De justa haereticorum punitione* (Antwerp: repr. John Stelsius, 1568), sig. a4r.

59 Eamon Duffy, *Fires of Faith: Catholic England under Mary Tudor* (London: Yale University Press, 2009), p. 113.

60 *Comentarios del Reverendissimo Señor Frai Batholome Carrança de Miranda, Arçobispo de Toledo, &ç. sobre el Catechismo Christiano* (Antwerp: Martin Nucio, 1558) [BL 476.e.5]. On the trial see José Ignacio Tellechea Idígoras, *El arzobispo Carranza y su tiempo*, 2 vols (Madrid: Ediciones Guadarrame, 1968) and *El proceso Romano del Arzobispo Carranza (1567–1576)* (Rome: Iglesia Nacional Española, 1988). His time in England is dealt with in *Fray Bartolomé Carranza y el Cardenal Pole: Un navarro en la restauración católica de Inglaterra (1554–1558)*, 2 vols (Pamplona: Editorial Aranzadi, 1977), esp. p. 51 and more recently in John Edwards and Ron Truman, eds, *Reforming Catholicism in the England of Mary Tudor: The Achievement of Friar Bartolomé Carranza* (Aldershot: Ashgate, 2005).

61 See Teodoro Olarte, *Alfonso de Castro (1495–1558): Su vida, tiempo y sus ideas –filológico-jurídicas* (San Jose: Facultad de Fiosofía y Letras, 1946), p. 252: 'Est alia poena de qua nihil prorsus hucusque Ecclesia statuit, quia per ecclestiasticas sanctiones illam statuit non conveniebat. Talis est mors.' I would like to recognise the indispensable help of my brilliant colleague Professor Gesine Manuwald with this and the Latin translations below.

62 AGS Indiferente 858. A translation with a useful introduction and other material was printed in Martin Austin Nesvig, ed., *Forgotten Franciscans: Works from an Inquisitorial Theorist, a Heretic and an Inquisitorial Deputy*, Latin American Originals (Pennsylvania: Pennsylvania State University Press, 2011).

63 BNE, MSS 9936 (covering the period 1521–49) and 9937 (1550–58).

64 Nesvig, *Forgotten Franciscans*, pp. 7–8.

65 On Ocampo, see Introduction: text relating to notes 73–7.

66 Reginaldus Gonsalvius Montanus, *A Discovery and playne Declaration of the sundry subtill practices of the Holy Inquisition of Spayne* (London: John Day, 1568).

67 A. Gordon Kinder, *Casiodoro de Reina: Spanish Reformer of the Sixteenth Century* (London: Tamesis, 1975), p. 47, footnote 40.

68 Montanus, *A Discovery and playne Declaration*, sig. Aiv v.

69 Montanus, *A Discovery and playne Declaration*, sig. Aiii r.

70 Montanus, *A Discovery and playne Declaration*, sig. Aii r.

71 Montanus, *A Discovery and playne Declaration*, sig. *Biiii r.

72 Montanus, *A Discovery and playne Declaration*, sigs *Bi r and *Bii r.

73 Montanus, *A Discovery and playne Declaration*, sig. *Biiii r.

74 Foxe, *TAMO* (1570), Book 12, p. 2338.

75 Foxe, *TAMO* (1570), Book 12, p. 2338.

76 Foxe, *TAMO*, Book 12, p. 2072.

77 Christopher Lever, *The Historie of the Defendors of the Catholique Faith; discoursing the State of Religion in England, and the care of the politique state for Religion during the reignes of King Henry 8, Edward 6, Queene Marie, Elizabeth, and... King James* (London: G. M. for N. Fussell and H. Moseley, 1627), title page: 'non natura sed pontificorum arte ferox'.

78 See the excellent discussion in Doran, 'A "sharp rod" of chastisement', pp. 28–31 and 35 on which this paragraph is based.

79 Victor Houliston, 'Mary Tudor and the Elizabethan Catholics', in Doran and Freeman, eds, *Mary Tudor: Old and New Perspectives*, pp. 43–4.

80 John Foxe, *Two Latin Comedies*, ed. J. H. Smith (Ithaca, NY and London: Cornell University Press, 1973), p. 349 and footnotes 2–4. Linen and wool were not supposed to be mixed together according to the Old Testament. On the play see Andreas Höfele, 'John Foxe, *Christus Triumphans*' in Thomas Betteridge and Greg Walker, eds, *The Oxford Handbook of Tudor Drama* (Oxford: Oxford University Press, 2012), pp. 123–43.

81 Found at lines 125–8.

82 Arnoldsson, *La leyenda negra*, p. 59: 'li chiamasse eretici, scismatici et maledetti da Dio, seme di giudei e di marrani, feccia del mondo; deplorando la miseria d'Italia, che fosse astretta a servire gente cosi abietta e cosi vile'. See *Cal. Ven.* VI, I, pp. 520–2, note 546 and 514–5, note 541.

83 Anon., *La Vida de Lazarillo de Tormes, y sus fortunas y aduersidades* (Antwerp: Martin Nucio, 1554). The exact date of this edition is not known but the earliest extant from Alcala had been published on 26th February.

84 Francisco López de Gómara, *La historia general de las Indias* (Antwerp: Juan Steelsio, 1554), sig. Nn7 r, fol. 287: 'todos quantos han hecho morir Indios assi [en las minas, en la pesqueria de perlas, y en las cargas], que han sido muchos, y casi todos, han acabado mal: en lo cual pareceme, que Dios ha castigado sus grauissimos peccados por aquella via. Yo escriuo sola, y breuemente, la conquista de Indias: quien quisiere ver la justificacion della, lea al doctor Sepulueda Coronista del Emperador.' On the status of López de Gómara's account in debates about the justice and licitude of Spanish imperialism, see Cristián Roa de la Carrera, *Histories of Infamy: Francisco López de Gómara and the Ethics of Spanish Imperialism*, trans. Scott Sessions (Boulder: University of Colorado Press, 2005), chapter 4, 'Gómara and the Destruction of the Indies'.

85 J. N. Hillgarth, *The Mirror for Spain, 1500–1700: The Formation of a Myth* (Ann Arbor: University of Michigan Press, 2000), Chapter 8, 'The Low Countries: The Origins of the Black Legend', pp. 309–27.

86 Pietro Martire d'Anghiera, *The Decades of the newe worlde or west India, conteynyng the navigations and conquestes of the Spanyards*, trans. Richard Eden (London: William Powell, 1555), sig. aii r–v.

87 Arnoldsson, *La leyenda negra*, p. 115

88 Martire d'Anghiera, *The Decades of the newe worlde*, sig. Eii v.

89 *Tower Chronicle*, pp. 38–9.

90 *A Faithful Admonition of a certeyne true Pastor and Prophete... translated with a Preface by M. Philip Melancthon*, trans. John Bale[?] (Greenwich: Conrad Freeman, May 1554), sig. Giii. See Chapter 3, text relating to note 43.

91 *The Copye of a letter, sent by John Bradforth to the right honourable lordes the Erles of Arundel, Darbie, Shrewsburye, and Pembroke, declaring the nature of Spaniardes, and discovering the most detestable treasons, which thei have pretended most falselye agaynste our moste noble kingdome of Englande* (Wesel?: J. Lambrecht, June–December, 1556), sig. Bii.

92 Sebastian Münster, *A treatyse of the newe India, with other new founde landes and Ilandes*, trans. Richard Eden (London: Stephen Mierdman for Edward Sutton, 1553), sig. Hv v.

93 *A Shorte Treatise of politike pouuer, and of the true Obedience which subiectes owe to kynges and other ciuile Gouernours, with an Exhortacion to all true naturall Englishe men* (Strasburg: heirs of W. Köpfel, 1556), sigs Fvii.r–v. This passage was taken from Ponet's reading of Richard Eden's translation of the Italian historian Peter Martyr Anglerius' *Decades of the New World* (1555).

94 See George Kubler, *Mexican Architecture of the Sixteenth Century*, 2 vols (New Haven, Conn.: Yale University Press, 1948), vol. 1, p. 78.

95 John Hawkins's *A true declaration of the toublesome voyadge of M. John Haukins to the parties of Guynea and the west Indies, in the yeares of our Lord 1567 and 1568* (London: Thomas Purfoote for Lucas Harrison, 1569), sig. A4.

96 John Bale, *A declaration of Edmonde Bonners articles, concerning the cleargye of London dyocese*

whereby that execrable Antychriste, is in his righte colours reueled in the yeare of our Lord a. 1554 Newlye set fourth & allowed according to the order appointed in the Quenes Maiesties Iniunctions. Woo to them whiche builde in bloude & iniquity. Mich. iii. All thinges, whan they are rebuked of the lyght are manyfest. Ephe v. (London: John Tysdall for Frauncis Coldocke, 1561), sig. *iiiv.

97 Walter Howard Frere and William Kennedy, eds, *Visitation Articles and Injunctions of the Reformation Period* (London: Longmans, 1910), vol. 2: 1536–58, pp. 330–72.

98 Bale, *A declaration of Edmonde Bonners articles*, sig. Ci r.

99 Bale, *A declaration of Edmonde Bonners articles*, sigs Fiii r–v.

100 Bale, *A declaration of Edmonde Bonners articles*, sig. Hviii r.

101 Bale, *A declaration of Edmonde Bonners articles*, sig. Q7 r.

102 Sanchez, 'Anti-Spanish sentiment', p. 59. This notion reached fulsome expression later in the century in *The Coppie of the Anti-Spaniard* (London: John Wolf, 1590), which described Philip II as a 'demie Moore, demie Jew, yea demie Saracine', a 'Saracin Castilian', and the Spanish as a 'Mauritanian race', and stated that the rest of Europe should 'with one breath to goe and abate the pride and insolencie of these Negroes'; sigs B2r, D2v, E1r and F1r. See discussion of this in Barbara Fuchs, *Exotic Nation: Maurophilia and the Construction of Early Modern Spain* (Philadelphia: University of Pennsylvania Press, 2009), pp. 116ff., esp. p. 123. Further examples of this trope in later writing are cited in Christopher Highley, *Catholics Writing the Nation in Early Modern Britain and Ireland* (Oxford: Oxford University Press, 2008), chapter 6, 'Anglo-Spanish Relations and the Hispaniolized English Catholic', 151–87, pp. 162–3.

103 John Strype, *Ecclesiastical Memorials*, 7 vols (London: Samuel Bagster, 1816), vol. 7, 'Number LXXI. A proclamation set forth by Thomas Stafford; from Scarborow Castle; exciting the English to deliver themselves fro the Spanyards', pp. 376–7.

104 John Knox, *The First Blast of the Trumpet against the Monstruous regiment of women* Veritas temporis filia* (Geneva: Pierre-Jacques Poullain & Antoine Reboul, 1558), sig. G1r.

105 Knox, *The First Blast*, sig. G1r.

106 Discussed in my 'A fine romance: Anglo-Spanish relations in the sixteenth century', *Journal of Medieval and Early Modern Studies* 39 (2009), 65–94, pp. 68–9.

107 On this, see my article 'The *adelantamiento* of Cazorla, *converso* culture and Toledo's Cathedral chapter's 1547 *estatuto de limpieza de sangre*', *Bulletin of Spanish Studies* 84 (2007), 819–36.

108 An excellent discussion of the *juego de cañas* celebrated in London in 1554 is found in Fuchs, *Exotic Nation*, p. 98.

109 See the delightfully drawn scene in Fuchs, *Exotic Nation*, pp. 120–1.

110 See Erin Sadlack, *The French Queen's Letters: Mary Tudor Brandon and the Politics of Marriage in Sixteenth-Century Europe* (New York: Palgrave MacMillan, 2011), p. 8.

111 See Kenneth Bartlett, 'The English exile community in Italy and the political opposition to Queen Mary I', *Albion* 13 (1981), 223–41, p. 224 and especially notes 2 and 3.

112 Gonzalo Jiménez de Quesada, *El antijovio*, ed. Guillermo Hernández Peñalosa, 2 vols (Bogotá: Instituto Caro y Cuervo, 1991), vol. 1, chapter 2, p. 29: 'Sobre todas las naciones contadas y sobre todas las demás que hay derramadas por el mundo, tiene este odio particular que hemos dicho contra España los italianos'.

113 Tommaso Campanella, *De Monarchia Hispanica* (Amsterdam: Ludovicus Elzevirius, 1653), sig. M2 v, p. 180: 'In talibus insulis barones magis quam alibi supprimendi sunt; cum situs locorum illis majorem quam alibi ansam novandarum rerum praebeat, & ingenio ad tyrannidem proclives sint. Quare praestat barones ex aliis nationibus huc transmittere; ad id vero convenientiores reliquis sunt Hispani, cum sint sub eodem climate positi; illisque tam officia, quam negotiationes committendae; quibus & Transalpini adjungendi sunt, partim militaturi, partim suscipiendae proli.' My thanks again to Gesine Manuwald for her help with the translation of these lines.

114 Arnoldsson, *La leyenda negra*, pp. 27–38.

115 Nerida Newbigin, ed., *Gl'Ingannati (1537)* (fac. edn, Bologna: Arnaldo Forni, 1984), sig. Civ v, p. 95: 'GIGLIO. Guadagno? Giuro a Dios que piú guadagnarite con á mi que con el primo gentil ombre de esta tierra; y, aunque vos paresque cosí male aventurade, io son de los buenos

y bien nascidos ydalgos de toda Spagna. PASQUELLA. Un miracolo non ha detto signore o cavaliere! poi che tutti gli spagnuoli che vengon qua si fan signori. E poi mirate che gente!'

116 Francesco Guicciardini, *Opera Omnia*, 'Relazione di Spagna' (1514) reproduced at http://digilander.libero.it/il_guicciardini/guicciardini_relazione_di_spagna.html (Accessed: 22nd October 2012): 'che tutto el regno era pieno di giudei ed eretici, e la maggiore parte de' populi erano maculati di questa pravità; e si trovava in loro tutti li ufici e arrendamenti principali del regno, e con tanta potenzia e numero, che si vedeva, non vi riparando, che in pochi anni Ispagna tutta arebbe lasciata la fede cattolica'/'neri di colore e di statura piccola', 'sono ingegni punici'. I would like to thank Dilwyn Knox for his help with these translations and bibliography on Guicciardini.

117 Arnoldsson, *La leyenda negra*, p. 98: 'La familiaridad creciente con los usos y costumbres de los españoles durante el siglo XVI, facilitó el mejor conocimiento de la herencia oriental y africana de los mimsos, fortaleciendo así el concepto de que eran del mismo origen que los moros y los judíos'.

118 Francisco Delicado, *La lozana andaluza*, ed. Bruno Damiani (Madrid: Castalia, 1969), p. 101: 'en Roma no podrídes encontrar con hombre que mejor sepa el modo de cuántas putas hay, con manta o sin manta. Mirá, hay putas graciosas más que hermosas, y putas que son putas antes que mochachas. Hay putas apasionadas, putas estregadas, afeitadas, putas esclarecidas, putas reputadas, reprobadas. Hay putas mozárabes de Zocodover, putas carcaveras...'. Translation by Bruno Damiani, *Portrait of Lozana: the Lusty Andalusian Lady* (Potomac, Mary.: Scripta Humanistica, 1987), pp. 90–1.

119 Arnoldsson, *La leyenda negra*, p. 100.

120 Juan del Encina, *Teatro completo*, ed. Miguel Angel Pérez Priego (Madrid: Cátedra, 1991), p. 16: 'Si quantos virgos he fecho/tantos tuviesse ducados,/no cabrían hasta el techo'.

121 Thomas Dandelet, *Spanish Rome: 1500–1700* (London: Yale University Press, 2001), p. 218.

122 On Alfonso de Valdés and his family see Dorothy Donald and Elena Lázaro, *Alfonso de Valdés y su época* (Cuenca: Diputación Provincial, 1983).

123 Antonio del Corro, *Reglas gramaticales para aprender la lengua Espanola y Francesa, confiriendo la vna con la otra, segun el orden de las partes de la oration Latinas* (Oxford: Joseph Barnes, 1586).

124 A superb account of Juan de Valdés, his cultural context and courtly career is Daniel Crews, *Twilight of the Renaissance: The Life of Juan de Valdés* (Toronto: University of Toronto Press, 2008); see p. 153 on justification and Carafa. See also Angel Castellán, 'Juan de Valdés y el círculo de Nápoles', *Cuadernos de Historia de España* 36 (1962), 199–291.

125 See Miles Pattenden, *Pius IV and the Fall of the Carafa: Nepotism and Papal Authority in Counter-Reformation Rome* (Oxford: Oxford University Press, 2012), p. 8.

126 Hugh Thomas, *The Golden Age: The Spanish Empire of Charles V* (London: Allen Lane, 2010), chapter 12, 'The Germans at the Banquet: The Welsers', 150–8.

127 Arnoldsson, *La leyenda negra*, p. 120: 'Malo Turcam hostem quam Hispanum protectorem, qui extremam exercet crudelitatem'. My thanks to Gesine Manuwald for her help with the translation.

128 Roger Ascham, *The Whole Works of Roger Ascham*, 3 vols, ed. J. Giles (London: John Russell Smith, 1865), p. 29.

129 *ODNB*.

130 Ascham, *The Whole Works*, p. 19.

131 His letter book as Mary's Latin secretary is preserved as BL Add. MS 35840.

132 Ascham, *The Whole Works*, pp. 23–4.

133 Ascham, *The Whole Works*, pp. 28 and 53.

134 See Linda Bradley Salamon, 'Blackening "the Turk" in Roger Ashcam's *A Report of Germany*' in Margaret Greer, Walter Mignolo and Maureen Quilligan, eds, *Rereading the Black Legend, The Discourses of Racial and Religious Difference in the Renaissance Empires* (Chicago: University of Chicago Press, 2007), pp. 270–92, which argues that the text is precursor to England's version of the Black Legend. I am suggesting its legacy is even more direct, influencing the

anti-Marian propaganda below, not a reflection of the 'English anti-Hispanism aroused by Philip II', but one of the things that produced it.

135 Ascham, *The Whole Works*, p. 13.
136 Ascham, *The Scholemaster: Or plaine and perfite way of teachyng children... the Latin tong* (London: John Day, 1570), sigs Iii r–v.

7

Spanish Tudor / English Habsburg

The writing of historians on Mary's position and status after her marriage to Philip is characterised by contradiction and inconsistency, resonant with the tensions apparent in the couple's representation of themselves in the first few months of the reign. On one side of the debate concerning the reality of their co-monarchy, David Loades has argued that although Philip was not prevented inexorably by the marriage treaty, he 'was baffled at every turn in his search for an effective role in English government': as 'king of England there is no doubt that Philip was a failure'.[1] This conclusion follows despite his stated premise that Mary 'fully shared the universal conviction that government was not women's work'.[2] In a development of his thinking, he revised this assessment, recognising Philip's experience but ultimately 'it was only partly relevant; and their court was a curious hybrid with no very clear sense of either direction or identity'; by the end of Philip's second visit to England 'politically he had more or less given up on England'.[3] Other historians, on the grounds of the notion that gender expectations were ultimately more significant than treaties or laws, have reached opposite conclusions. Mary 'was… wife to the man she and her counsellors saw as the real ruler', for example, according to Carole Levin.[4] Similarly Constance Jordan has stated that, despite the attempt by parliament to guarantee her power constitutionally through the 'Act for the Queen's Regal Power', it 'did not prove workable in practice', 'largely due to the queen herself' who failed to curb Philip's 'efforts to gain control of the internal affairs of the realm': in reality he obtained 'actual power… to determine the course of events within the realm and with respect to foreign policy'.[5] Others still have argued that, by marrying and refusing the title of Supreme Head, Mary 'announced herself as subject in both her persons – as woman and as queen – to the authority of male superiors: her husband and king, Philip II of Spain; and the head of the universal church and vicar of Christ, the Pope'.[6] Harry Kelsey's 2011 biography of Philip, England's 'forgotten sovereign', promised to restore his reign as king of England to its proper place and while it does make an important contribution, foregrounding in particular crucial but underutilised sources such as the Privy Council's responses concerning the defence of Calais and Feria's correspondence with Philip,[7] in other ways it falls back on old interpretations and ultimately sees Philip as largely powerless, king in a 'limited sense', circumscribed by treaty and parliament from exercising true authority, although in concluding it suggests that he refused to accept this 'secondary role'.[8] The co-monarchy's problems are attributed in part to Mary's unrequited love for her husband: a decidedly anachronistic reading of a dynastic marriage concluded for economic and political reasons first and foremost, a union that would, had it endured, have had profound 'ramifications for the religious and military balance in Western Europe'.[9] Furthermore, in Kelsey's reading the co-rulers were religious traditionalists, ignoring the lively ferment of Catholic Reformation, the humanists, scientists and theologians who littered their intellectual trajectories, ignoring much recent work on the successes of Catholic restoration and spiritual renewal in England under Philip and Mary. Reviewers have pointed to the lack of reference to the plethora of new work that appeared in the context of the 500th anniversary of Mary's death in 2008, especially the three fresh biographies.[10] Nevertheless, it has pointed towards promising avenues for fresh research, especially in relation to finance, and has foregrounded a number of ignored European sources. The most fascinating study of money under Philip and Mary is Glyn Redworth's article analysing the accounts of Domingo de Orbea and Thomas Egerton, which underlines the huge commitment of treasure by Philip to the enterprise: brought with him and coined in the Tower in October 1554, it amounted to over £40,000, an increase in the total money supply of around 2.5 per cent.[11] These funds covered the costs of his household and expenditure during his time in England, given the ban on him dipping into English revenues.

Assessing the extent of Philip's influence and control over English affairs during their joint reign is complicated by the loss of his archive and chancery documents in a shipwreck in September 1559 en route back to Spain.[12] In addition, it is closely linked to questions about Mary's own role in governing England and whether she left many political decisions to a select group of favoured Privy Councillors or intervened more directly in ways that have not left direct traces in the archive. Before Philip's arrival, Mary had ordered that he be apprised of all relevant business, instructing the Lord Privy Seal '[f]urst to tell the kyng the whole state of this Realme, with all thyngs appartaynnyng to the same, as myche as ye knowe to be trewe. Seconde to obey hys comandment in all thynge, thyrdly in all thyngys he shall ask your advyse to declare your opinion as becometh a faythfull conceyllour to do.'[13] While in England, it has been suggested, he attended Privy Council meetings on Tuesdays and Fridays.[14] John Guy, however, has questioned this notion, suggesting it derived from Spanish confusion between the Privy Council and some other conciliar arrangement created by Philip.[15] This may explain why the duke of Alba believed business was being conducted in Spanish. On 13th August 1554, he wrote to the imperial secretary Eraso from Richmond that '[b]usiness as far as I understand will not be dealt with in any other language than our own and that is what is happening', concluding by saying that the king was 'very well and most beloved by all the people here; pray God it may continue'.[16] Two days after the wedding the Privy Council recorded that 'a note of all such matters of Estate as shuld passe from hence should be made in Laten or Spanyshe from hensfourth'; 'all matters of Estate passing in the King and Quenes name shuld be signed with both their hands'.[17] After leaving for Brussels, secretary Petre did send him regular digests of business being transacted in Council, which he duly minuted with his decisions and sent back. Philip left a memorandum concerning government business shortly before his departure, which contains some of the best evidence of how Marian government was conducted including the membership of his Council of England, the so-called 'Select Council'. The document begins by outlining that this select group had been formed for 'the better and more expeditious deliberation... about matters of state, finance and other causes pertaining to the kingdom'.[18] The undersigned counsellors are Pole, Gardiner, William Paulet, marquis of Winchester, Arundel, Paget, Pembroke, Thomas Thirlby, bishop of Ely, Rochester and Petre. This group were to refer all their deliberations and actions on matters of state, finance, debts and anything touching the honour of the crown for Philip's consideration and in particular the king wished to be apprised of the legislative programme proposed for the upcoming parliament: 'we wish to see all the business and proposals to be considered by the domestic parliament in writing before its meeting'.[19] Even a cursory glance through the state papers makes it clear that denying Philip was involved in government in England in this period is a wilful misrepresentation.[20] As the biographer of William Paget noted, in the first year he spent in England, Philip 'frequently exercised his influence in the government'.[21] His wishes concerning key political appointments such as the Lord Deputy of Ireland were respected, with Clinton remaining in England and Fitzwalter eventually being appointed in his stead, perhaps a reward for his services in the negotiation of the treaty and Philip's household.[22] Nevertheless the council did not always accede to his wishes, refusing for example to grant export licences for oak or remit customs duties to certain individuals who had presented suits to Philip.[23] By the same token, it is clear that Mary was also perfectly capable of following her own counsel and refusing to do his bidding. One of the most mysterious decisions of her reign was her refusal to countenance Elizabeth's marrying Manuel Philibert of Savoy or any other dynastic option considered from the summer of 1554 on.[24] Although such negotiations granted a dignity to her half-sister that Mary must have found difficult to accept, it would have realised the Habsburg's fundamental objective in the marriage, uniting England and the Low Countries under one Catholic ruler. Similarly, in relation to the war with France, Mary stuck to the provisions of the treaty, perhaps for as long as two years, before the Stafford raid made it impossible to remain on the sidelines any longer. The campaign for Philip to be crowned was ultimately scotched by domestic opposition. These kinds of tension between the monarch and his or her local representatives were a consistent feature of Philip's reign, from which we have the idea of *obedezco pero no cumplo*, i.e. royal officials obeying his intention by not carrying out the specific instructions given.

When the Habsburg court moved from Brussels to London in 1557, a huge number of powerful and glittering potentates, courtiers, ambassadors and soldiers followed in its wake. At Lent Mary entertained the duchesses of Lorraine and Parma at Whitehall. The duchess of Lorraine, formerly Christina of Denmark, who had famously turned down Mary's father's overtures of matrimony, had previously visited London in March 1555. Ferrante Gonzaga and his sons Cesare and Andrea were back, recalled to play a part in the forthcoming war with France; they had briefly visited London on 13th October 1554, shortly after the wedding, returning to Brussels by 6th November. Cesare danced at a ball at Whitehall and went hunting with the duchess of Lorraine a few days later. The Mantuan ambassador Annibale Litolfi presented his credentials to Mary on 4th May and reported that the queen was 'not at all ugly as in her portraits, and that her lively expression, white skin and air of *gratia*, even rendered her beautiful'.[25] Alvise Schivenoglia, secretary to Sir Thomas Tresham, whose famous rose garden alluding to the passion of Christ would recall his Catholic devotion in Elizabeth's reign,[26] described the departure of the ambassadors of the duke of Muscovy on 13th May 1557. This was a moment when 'sixteenth-century London truly became a major capital of Europe'.[27]

The government of Mary I

The biggest change in the structure of Tudor government under Mary, in contrast to the two previous male incumbents, was a reduction in the importance of the privy chamber, which functioned, as has been suggested under Elizabeth, as a '"barrier or cocoon" rather than a political cockpit'.[28] The exploitation of personal intimacy with the king for political ends inevitably came to an end when the body servants in royal service were all necessarily female. As John Murphy has argued:

The demise of the Privy Chamber did not mean the demise of a second centre in politics and administration, however. Mary's own formidable character saw to that. From the outset, over appointments, her marriage negotiations, in the establishment of the religious settlement, in the settling of financial policy and in the reform of the revenue courts, Mary showed a determination to be far more deeply and routinely involved in business than her father had ever been.[29]

Her privy chamber was not a political and factional hotbed, there was no attempt to form a 'petticoat' government, rather it was composed of women of 'irreproachable character', who had long-standing personal relationships with Mary. The gentlewomen who served Mary generally did well out of the relationship. Susan Clarencius, for example, received grants of Essex manors, including Loverdown, Thamberley Hall and Thundersley in 1553, Runwell, Rivenhall, Chingford St Pauls and Chingford earls in 1555. By the end of Mary's reign Clarencius was probably receiving annual rents of about £200 from her various properties, in addition to fees for her services at court. Soon after Elizabeth's accession she went abroad in the household of Jane Dormer, duchess of Feria. While she had supported Philip's candidacy, Renard alluding to her support in one of his despatches, there is no real evidence that any of Mary's most intimate servants and members of her household were recipients of the kind of largesse seen under her father and husband.[30] During her reign, to her favourites were added the wives and relations of her leading councillors although 'as the queen was neither a particularly withdrawn figure nor particularly susceptible to pressure from her female servants, these women did not play much part in procuring either patronage or favour for their menfolk'.[31] One surprising member of Mary's household was Anne Bacon, whose strongly Reformed religious sympathies did not seem to preclude her from serving the queen. She was the daughter of the humanist Sir Anthony Cooke, who had been raised by his stepmother Margaret Pennington, a lady-in-waiting to Catherine of Aragón. Anne had published a translation of Bernardino Ochino's *Sermons* in 1548 and interceded on behalf of both her husband, Nicholas Bacon, and William Cecil, her brother-in-law, both of whom were implicated in Northumberland's plot. Her home at Redgrave in East Anglia was close to a number of Mary's properties and estates and this may explain, along with her father's personal connection to Catherine, why she had originally entered the queen's household. Another highly educated member of Mary's household, one who abandoned his faith under pressure from the Edwardian regime, was the poet and translator Alexander Barclay, a former friar and her chaplain in 1551, who died probably at Cranmer's residence at Croydon in 1552.[32]

Giacomo Soranzo reported to the Venetian Senate, after his well known, slighting description of her physical attractions, that 'she rises at daybreak, when, after saying her prayers and hearing Mass in private, she transacts business incessantly, until after midnight, when she retires to rest; for she chooses to give audience not only to all the members of her Privy Council, and to hear from them every detail of public business, but also to all other persons who ask it of her'.[33] This picture of her assiduity in carrying out her duties seems to be in keeping with other evidence, such as the annotations on her household accounts, checking the totals from the time of her reinstatement to Henry's favour and restoration of her household from 1536.[34] Three days after Philip's departure, Cardinal Pole commented in a letter that it was good that Mary was kept busy, as she had been the previous day executing orders from her husband's letters.[35] A month later, however, he was writing again that she was working too hard, during most of the night despite it being bad for her health.[36] James Basset, originally a servant of Stephen Gardiner, became her private secretary, as well as the Chief Gentleman of Philip's privy chamber, linking the two royal households together. Philip was the godfather of Basset's son, who was named after him, as were the famous Elizabeth courtier and poet Philip Sidney and Philip Howard, son of the duke of Norfolk.[37] Philip and Mary also shared the bishop of Chichester, George Day, who was Almoner to both king and queen. Basset recorded in a letter to Paget on 14th November 1556 how he had been called into the queen's presence immediately after she had received letters from Paget at around six or seven at night. Mary perused the letters, especially one to Ruy Gomez da Silva, disliking in particular 'your so vehement persuasions to Sir Ruy Gomez... she was most parfightely assured that the kyngs maiestie dothe asmoche as in hym dothe possibilie lye for his lyfe to procure his most spedy retorne, and therfor her highnes cannot by any means endure that any person shold speake or thinke otherwise of his maiestie'.[38] Paget's letters to Mary from Brussels on 25th April 1556, in which he broached the subject of Philip 'coming homewardes', indicate Philip's awareness of Mary's health from other sources and while of course any state-ment in such communications needs to be taken with a large pinch of salt, he received Mary's gifts and letters 'very gladly and chearefully, not a little glad to heare your good estate, much inquisitiue how your maiestie did... [and] not a little sorry to haue had such occasion to tarry here' owing to the king of Bohemia's arrival.[39] While it is true that accredited ambassadors gravitated towards Brussels from London, when the court was not there, England's own foreign ambassadors remained at post reporting directly back to Mary and her Council. After an audience with the French king at Poissy, Dr Nicholas Wotton wrote on 27th January 1555 'I delyverid the queenes highnesses lettre' and after outlining the dangers of protectorates and minorities declared 'yf it shuld please God to take the queenes majeste er her children came to lawfull eage, yf God sende her highnesse anye (as is well hoped he will), that then the kinges majeste shulde have the government of the chyld and realme, accordinge to your lordshippes lettre, knowinge verye well that the father will neither seeke the hindraunce of his child nor yet of his countrey, but will do all he canne to keepe it and preserve it the best he canne for his sonnes use and commodite': the courier of the letter is named Francisco and Wotton asks at the end of the letter, presumably so he can pass it on to Henry II, about Ruy Gomez's return to England and Francisco de Mendoza's departure for Spain.[40] A long series of documents signed by the queen, beginning with Philip and Mary's instructions to their new appointee Thomas Radclyffe, Lord Fitzwalter, demonstrate that not only did Mary I sign important state papers but compose them too, a number in addition to her signature stating 'by the Quene'.[41] Some went out while Philip was in England and others did not. Two documents dated 13th May 1557 to the earl of Sussex, the first confirming his title and succession to his father and the second thanking him for his assiduous service and commending the earls of Pembroke and Derby to him, have both Philip and Mary's signatures on them, his illegible scrawl and her neat, functional autograph.[42] There are a number of other documents signed by both monarchs.

Monstrous regiment of women

The clearest statement on the functioning of Marian government suggests the extent to which the precedent established by Mary influenced her sister and built on established practice with some modifications forced on the queen by reason of her gender. There are

> clear parallels between Elizabeth's use of probouleutic groups and Marian practice, as recently reconstructed by John Guy. By integrating the State Papers with the Cotton manuscripts, he has demonstrated how Marian counselling was dominated by a small 'inner ring' of individuals, who had a special personal relationship with Mary or Philip II (the earl of Arundel and Pembroke; Stephen Gardiner, bishop of Winchester; bishop Thirlby of Ely; Sir Robert Rochester; Sir William Paget; Sir William Petre and Cardinal Pole) and which functioned as both a probouleutic and policy-making body on a wide range of issues. This 'inner ring' was not a committee of the privy council – Pole's membership precluded this – nor an institutionalised, bureaucratic body: its membership was based on personal relations with Mary and Philip and thus subsumed into the court. Established prior to Mary's marriage, its practices only became more structured when Philip's absence required Petre to commit its proceedings to paper as part of his correspondence with the king.[43]

It was a model in which trusted advisors acted as intermediaries between the queen and broader groups of councillors. The major offices of her household remained in the hands of those who had served her for a long time. Many of them were appointed in addition after her accession to Councils of State. On the other hand, experienced politicians, who had served her father or brother or both, also retained their positions in the vast majority of cases. There was considerable continuity in the apparatus of state throughout the mid-Tudor period. The notion that Mary was politically inexperienced and unprepared for rule has been roundly dismissed by Jeri McIntosh's fascinating study of the pre-accession households of Elizabeth and Mary. Between 1525 and 1528, Mary presided over a vice-regal household at Ludlow, whose lavish cost (around £4,500 a year), underlined its 'princely scale', with over 200 servants in damask liveries, ladies of the privy chamber in black velvet and a throne in the presence chamber.[44] Despite being a girl between 9 and 12 years old, when Juan Luis Vives dedicated his education treatise *Satellitium* to her, she was dubbed incongruously 'Princeps Walliae'. Although never formally invested with the title it was used in foreign despatches and attributed to her by some of her closest servants, including Jane Dormer.[45] Even if it was not true, the confusion is telling. The Welsh remained loyal to Mary throughout her life as a result of this period there.[46] The death of her father transformed Mary's fortunes and after 1547 she became the seventh-richest person in England after the king, Somerset, Warwick, Shrewsbury, Pembroke and Derby.[47] Not only did she possess vast landed estates and income, she also inherited many of the accoutrements of Tudor royalty from Henry, including tapestries, furniture, jewels and paintings.[48] In May 1553, Mary received the grants of Framlingham and Hertford Castles. It has been suggested that they were a bribe from the Council to buy her acquiescence in the devise that would disinherit her.[49] Whether this is true or not, the grants turned out to be a huge mistake, providing her with an ideal military base from which to launch her challenge for the throne two months later. Either way, in the light of grants that allowed her to consolidate her East Anglian holdings, the picture of Mary as uninformed, no more than a provincial magnate unschooled in the ins and outs of court life, an image derived in part from her own calculated representation of herself as a defenceless maiden in need of her 'father' Charles V's protection, demonstrates that she was in fact a subtle political operator. The suggestion that she exaggerated the weakness of her position in the negotiations with the imperialists, especially divisions within her council, parliament and the country at large, to wring further concessions from them, chimes in with the calculated way she used her household officers to represent her indecision to Jean Dubois in 1550, in the context of the plot to spirit her out of the country.[50] At other times Mary was represented as exercising full sovereign independence, as for example in her letter to Philip's sister and regent Juana of 14th January 1555, announcing the reunification with Rome, printed in Spain, and twinned with an account of Richard Chancellor's expedition which had led to the establishment of trade relations with Ivan the Terrible's Russia and the Muscovy Company in 1555, which compared the discovery to the Spanish discovery of the Indies.[51] The concatenation of the two texts links religious reform with providential discovery and England beginning to draw alongside Spain as a colonial power in its own right.

The notion that Mary received an inferior education to her sister Elizabeth derives from a blind acceptance of Roger Ascham's claim in correspondence with Johann Sturm that his pupil was 'the shining star' of erudite evangelical women, at a time when classical learning was the preserve of Reformers.[52] Ascham's talents were of course put to good use by Mary as her Latin secretary. His subsequent representation of Elizabeth's education in *The Scholemaster* consciously altered previous accounts of his programme to make it look as if he had been preparing her for rule. In an early draft, rather than her humanist accomplishments, Ascham drew attention to her skill at 'ridingge most trymlie, in dansing most comlye, in playing of Insturmments' and her chaste rejection of 'courtlye pleasing' and 'vayne delites'.[53] In his dedication to Mary of the *Satellitium animi* (1524), Juan Luis Vives had outlined that '[t]here is no greater or more faithful protection than innocence and the love of the people, which is not won by arms or terror; rather it is achieved through, love, loyalty and care, a constant preoccupation for the public good'.[54] The ninetieth aphorism in this educational treatise was chosen by Mary as her personal motto: 'Truth is the daughter of time... Cicero writes: Time destroys and erases the fictions of opinion and confirms the judgement of nature'.[55] Vives' treatise probably formed the basis for the educational programmes of both Edward and Elizabeth, alongside the *De ratione studii puerilis* (1523), 'a brief plan of study you [Catherine] ordered me to prepare for the praeceptor for the formation of your daughter Maria' and which recommended Erasmus' aphorisms, Josephus, Titus Livy, the Griselda tale in Boccaccio, Valerius Maximus as well as Cicero, Seneca, Plutarch, Plato, St Jerome, St Augustine, Erasmus' *Enchiridion* and *Paraphrases*, More's *Utopia*, Justinian and the New Testament.[56] As part of her preparation to become a royal bride to the French king Louis XII, her tutor Giles Duwes had composed *An Introductorie for to lerne to rede, to pronounce, and to speake Frenche trewly* (c. 1532?), which in addition to language-teaching contained a series of model dialogues in which the princess features as a character, providing intriguing evidence about Mary's early education and intellectual world in the Welsh marches. In one dialogue she discourses with her servant Giles on the nature of the soul and in another discusses the reception of the Mass with her Almoner, asking 'what we shall do at the masse yf we praye not... and what shall do they whiche understande it not'?[57] The treatise, if it was printed in 1533, controversially described Mary as Lady Mary, princess of England, and demonstrates her discoursing about the sacrament that would be central to her restoration of the church.

In addition to these treatises, the *De institutione feminae Christianae* (1524), again written under the patronage of Catherine of Aragón for the instruction of Mary, although it considers female education more generally, was first published after Henry's suit for divorce had begun in 1527. Vives' dedication in Richard Hyrde's 1529 translation, to 'princes Katharine quene of Englande' was therefore already risqué.[58] By 1541 the dedication had been censored, referring merely to 'the most gratious princesse Katharine of Englande'.[59] Hyrde's fulsome praise of 'the moste excellent prynces quene Catharine, the most gratious Wyfe unto the moste noble and myghty prince kynge Henry the.viii.' was omitted entirely after 1531. Isabel of Castile's daughters were described in the 1529 and 1531 editions as 'quenes of Portugal, the thyrde of Spayne, mother unto Carolus Cesar: & the fourth moost holy and devout wyfe unto the most gratious kyng Henry', although by the 1541 edition Catherine had become 'wyfe unto the most noble prince Arthure'.[60] This rewriting was retained surprisingly in the 1557 edition of Mary's reign and it was not until the 1585 and 1592 editions, by the Protestant printers Robert Waldegrave and John Danter, that Catherine became sufficiently depoliticised for the wording to revert to the original of 1529. Mary's bastardisation and the repudiation of her mother by Henry VIII were the *sine qua non* of political developments in England from the 1530s, a changing political climate that can be traced in the publication history of the *Instruction of a Christen Woman* (London: Thomas Berthelet, editions 1529, 1531, 1541, 1547, 1557 and 1567). Her accession, therefore, invited a rewriting of history.[61] The Pilgrimage of Grace rebels had been particularly interested in Mary's succession rights. Aske believed Mary was necessary to avert the possibility of a Scottish succession (of James V). Even leaving religious motivations aside, Mary had been regarded as England's next sovereign and as the king's only legitimate offspring for seventeen years, before the Reformation parliament of 1533 and then Edward's birth four years later.

The second tract Vives wrote on women and marriage, *The Office and duetie of an husband* (Latin edn, 1529), contained a further eulogy to his patron despite the divorce proceedings that had forced him to leave England and a quarrel he had had with Catherine. It was only printed in English in 1555 during Mary's reign. Its translator Thomas Paynell addressed it to Sir Anthony Browne, later Viscount Montagu, who was then contemplating remarriage, explaining its value in choosing a spouse in order to avoid any occasion 'of breache, or of divorsement, the which (O lorde) is nothynge in these oure dayes regarded: for why? to have many wives at once, or to refuse her by some cautell or false interpretation of gods most holy worde, that myslyketh, is at this present but (as men call it) a shifte of descante'.[62] The oblique, critical reference to Henry VIII, possible only after the accession of Mary, demonstrates the historiographical shift, which was licensing the resurrection of Catherine as 'the type of pious, learned, and domesticated woman'. William Powell published an oration of 'Leonhard Goretti' in 1554, which compared Anne Boleyn to Salome.[63] Despite this, Judith Richards has argued that:

> [t]he vilification of Katherine became a foundation tenet of early English Protestantism. When her daughter Mary became first queen regnant of England she asserted the legitimacy of her parents' marriage but did nothing more to rehabilitate her mother's reputation. Rather, it remained one more weapon in the ongoing religious struggles in England, until Katherine's identity underwent a striking if partial rehabilitation by Tudor public opinion, later in the century.[64]

Although Mary banned Edward Hall's chronicle, which succinctly expressed the view that Katherine had been 'wedded and bedded' despite her insistence that she went to bed with Henry a virgin, Nicholas Harpesfield's *The Pretended Divorce between Henry VIII and Catharine of Aragon*, written during Mary's reign, was not published and remained in manuscript until the nineteenth century.[65] Another text explicitly on Catherine, *The history of Grisild the second* by Mary's chaplain William Forrest and presented to the queen in June 1558 made no mention of Philip and staged fictional scenes of closeted private grief, a gesture that passes over more complicated political history in favour of praising her as a maid rather than a queen.[66] His *A newe ballade of the marigolde* (1554) from the outset of the reign invoked fealty to Mary to offset discontent with royal policy and national sensitivity to the Spanish marriage by figuring the reader's identification at the level of the personal.

In spite of the highly political nature of his dedications of a series of educational treatises for royal women, Vives celebrated Isabel of Castile predominantly because she 'taught her doughters to spynne, sowe, and peynt' ('I wolde in no wyse that a woman shuld be ignorant in those feates, that must be done by hande: no nat though she be a princes or a quene'). Isabel of Castile had been a regnant queen in her own right and a military commander, while her daughter Catherine had acted as Henry's regent during his first campaign in France and for a time was the accredited Spanish ambassador in England. Even in a work commissioned by a powerful queen consort, Vives could assert women's unfitness for public life. Attitudes towards female rule were profoundly ambiguous even among humanist advocates of female education. In these treatises, the first piece of recommended reading for the young princess Mary was the New Testament. She would of course translate the lengthy section from the *Paraphrases* of Erasmus on the gospel of St John, for an edition overseen by Nicholas Udall, while she formed part of Catherine Parr's household. Udall's dedication praised Mary, who England may 'neuer bee hable (as hir desertes require) enough to praise and magnifie the moste noble, the moste vertuous, the moste wittie, and the moste studious Ladie Maries Grace... for takyng suche great studie, peine & trauail in translatyng this paraphrase of the said Erasmus upon the ghospell of Jhon': she was a 'pierlesse floure of virginitie... who in the middes of Courtly delices, & emiddes the enticements of worldly vanities, hath by hir owne choise & eleccion so vertuously, & so fruictefully passed hir tendre youth, to the publique conforte... she doeth now also conferre vnto the same the unestimable benefite of fertheryng both us & our posteritee in the knowelage of Goddes worde, & to the more clere understandyng of Christes ghospell'.[67] The dedication recounts that her chaplain Francis Mallett, who had originally served Parr, completed the translation as a result of Mary being sick. While it is impossible to be certain how much of it was the princess's sole work, the evidence of a letter from Parr suggests that Mallett was brought in merely to correct and emend. Aysha Pollnitz's analysis of the translation points out that the *Paraphrases* were orthodox in relation to the Mass and that although Nicholas Harpesfield removed copies from certain parishes during his 1557 visitations, no official action against the book was taken, because in fact the Marian church was in many ways Erasmian: his did not figure on the list of prohibited books in June 1555 and a defence by him of the sacrament was printed at the outset of the reign.[68] According to Pollnitz's analysis Mary's translation is deferentially literal, but sensitive at the same time to philological subtlety, handling technical and rare lexis well, even displaying some stylistic flair and in doctrinal terms the emphasis on faith and charity, the importance of Grace and the word of God, 'sacrament and sacrifice embodied in the mass' chimed perfectly with 'two authoritative statements of Marian Church doctrine: Bishop Edmund Bonner's *Profitable and necessary doctrine* (1555) and Bishop Thomas Watson's *Wholesome and Catholic doctrine* (1558)'.[69] Udall probably provided Mary with the first courtly entertainments of her reign in the form of *Respublica*, a partial repudiation of the Reformation but more importantly a powerfully conciliarist view of constitutional monarchic government.[70] As Alice Hunt has argued the radical leap forward in constitutional thought often situated in Elizabeth's 'monarchical republic' actually had roots in Mary's reign and the succession crisis. Although she does not go so far as to suggest that Marian England was a monarchical republic with Mary's refusal to call a parliament before her sacred investiture in her coronation, nevertheless in the play:

> Respublica looks like a type of queen at the end of this play, touched by the fleeting divinity of Nemesis, accompanied by the heaven-sent virtues of Mercy, Truth, Peace, and Justice, and surrounded by councillors. Consequently,

as Nemesis devolves her power to Respublica, it is with Respublica that Queen Mary is finally identified in this play: the queen is collapsed into the 'commonwealth'.[71]

On 13th December 1554 Mary signed a warrant ordering Cawarden to provide 'our wellbelovid Nicholas Udall [who] hath at sondry seasons convenient hertofore shewid and myndeth herafter to shewe his diligence in setting forthe of dialogwes and entreludes before vs for our Regall disport and recreacion' with such costumes as he required.[72] The Queen's Players 1553–6 included John Birch, Richard Cooke and Thomas Southey, who are associated with Udall's plays *Roister Doister*, *Respublica* and *Wealth and Health*. Cawarden received a warrant for another play titled *Humanum Genus*, a religious allegory perhaps dating back to the fifteenth century.[73]

Lords and Commons described themselves in 1554 in the act repealing the Statute of Proclamations as 'representing the whole body of the Realme of Englande and the Dominions of the same, In the name of our selves particularly, and also of the said bodye universally'.[74] This notion of representation was crucial in justifying the jurisdiction of parliament, as outlined in a discourse from the early 1570s: '[a]n alyene ys not bounde by our estatues, & so I saie of those of Irelande or those of ancient demesne, for they come not to the Parlyament. But thoughe those of Ireland be not bounden by our Parliament because they have a Parliament of their owne, yet notwithstandinge when they are in Englande, as they subiecte to the kynge, so are they subiect unto his laws'.[75] In 1604, the first chapter of James I's first statute restated the doctrine of parliament as a high court, 'where all the whole Bodie of the Realme, and everie particular Member thereof, either in person or by Representation (upon their free Elections) are by the Laws of this Realme deemed to be personallie presente'.[76] It was in Mary's reign that the rule of law was first conceptualised in these terms. The augmentation and strengthening of the political law heralded a nascent constitutionalism. Attacks upon Mary's government were directed predominantly at its unconstitutionality, at the illegality of her authority, which was more than ever referred and subjected to parliamentary approval in response.

There is no doubt Mary was exposed to the currents of early sixteenth-century humanism and her piety certainly does not seem to have reflected a conservative Henrician Catholicism, but rather one based on preaching and sermons, an interest in the pastoral aspects of the church and clerical education. Mary was heavily involved in the religious politics of Restoration. The first set of articles concerning the reformation of religion were sent by Mary to her bishops on 4th March 1554.[77] One of the few state papers from her reign to survive in an autograph copy are the instructions she sent to the London

convocation convened to consider the nature of the Marian church.[78] Even
after the repeal of the Supremacy, she did not shrink from involving herself
in ecclesiastical affairs. She cultivated a specifically English Catholicism which
shared many features of the Henrician programme of religious reform in the
1530s: 'the Marian authorities consistently sought to promote a version of
traditional Catholicism which had absorbed whatever they saw as positive in
the Edwardine and Henrician reforms, and which was subtly but distinctively
different from the Catholicism of the 1520s'.[79] We know from the trial records
of Bartolomé Carranza that Mary discussed religious ideas with Pole, according to the testimony of the count of Feria, who in the context of a search for an
Apologia written by Pole in response to the revocation of his legatine authority
by Paul IV, testified that 'the said Pole wrote certain colloquies that passed
between him and the queen on matters of the faith'.[80] Eamon Duffy has insisted
that 'a convincing account of the religious history of Mary's reign has yet to
be written'.[81] But much recent work has vastly expanded our understanding
of the Marian church and religious politics of the reign, not least Duffy's own
brilliant *Fires of Faith*.

The ritual calendar incorporated Henry VIII's excisions and Bonner's *A
Profytable and necessary doctryne, with certayne homelies adioyned* (1555) was largely
based on the *King's Book* (1543). The importance of evangelism was underlined. The Marian *Homilies* produced for this purpose included versions of
Thomas Cranmer's homilies, and prayers written by Thomas Becon also found
their way into Marian primers. There was an emphasis on redemption through
the passion of Christ in the devotional literature of the period and no allusion
to indulgences or miraculous legends.[82] This new picture has not gone unnoticed. Mary 'did not show enthusiasm for saints, relics, shrines, pilgrimages'
and 'before 1547,... was not noted for distinctive piety, but rather praised for
the acceptable qualities of learning, virtue and piety – by conservatives and
reformers'.[83] In the following reign, with the ascendance of the Marian exiles
in ecclesiastical affairs, there was a vested interest in representing the regime
as out of touch with popular sentiment, perpetrating a bloody persecution to
enforce conformity. Figuring the Reformist cause as a patriotic imperative,
built on consensus, forged the link between unabrogated English sovereignty
and anti-papal nationalism. This connection, defined by the religious opponents of Mary after the event, has tended to obscure the evidence that she in
fact extended and developed the notion of English *imperium* further and in ways
more radical than her predecessors. The issue of ecclesiastical jurisdiction had
been damaging to England's international standing for Catholic kings since
John's submission to the papacy in the thirteenth century, as much as it was
for Elizabeth I.

As time passed the assiduous precedence of Mary over Philip began to change and by 1556–57, he began to assume, in representational terms in particular, the role of king. A portrait vignette incorporated on a grant of 2nd September 1557 to the widow and son of Sir Adrian Fortescue of the manors of Barton Abbots, Chipping-Sodbury, Codrington and Washbourne in Gloucester shows Philip in the dominant position, his motto on the left as we face the image, Mary's on the right, the seated pair on a sort of double throne reminiscent of a modern sofa (see Plate 12).[84] The king looks out of the picture while Mary glances in his direction, a feature common to many of the images of the royal pair, including the great seal and coinage. Nevertheless, the secretary of the Council of State in the Low Countries, Josse de Courteville, who accompanied Philip from Brussels on his return to England, noted, however, that in the magnificent banquet to entertain the duchesses of Lorraine and Parma 'the king [was seated] on the left hand side and the queen on the right'.[85] In the context of the war in France, Philip's desperation to lead the English contingent into battle in person is clear from letters he wrote begging Emmanuel Philibert of Savoy not to enter battle until his arrival. Although the issue of the succession would not go away, of course, anxieties about Mary's authority at least within the kingdom did subside. The fears constantly underlined by exiled Reformers, enshrined in the first state paper of the Elizabethan period, in which William Cecil declared that she 'professing herself a free Princess to direct all her actions by hir owne Ministers and with the aduice of her Council of England only meanethe in this matters to proceed and direct withoute anie participation towards the Spaniard or anie king otherwise', were not realised.[86] Wisely, despite having been thwarted in realising the Habsburg plan to create an Anglo-Netherlandish block, Philip did not interfere in the succession of Elizabeth. Instead, he sought to keep that dream alive by offering to marry her himself. Although gender expectations meant that Mary's political status was undermined by her sexual status, especially in marriage to a potent foreign prince, by the end of the reign it was clear that she had been more than capable of wielding both queenly and kingly authority. As John White, who had helped to welcome the newly married royal couple in Winchester, preached in the sermon at her burial in 1558, Mary had been 'a queen and by the same title a king also. She was a syster to her that by the like title and wryght is both king and quene at this present of this realme'.[87] Mary's political authority was in the end kingly and her legacy would be a precedent for female rule to her half-sister. Early in Elizabeth's reign the Scottish ambassador Melville told her he believed she would never marry since in doing so she would become merely a queen, whereas she was then 'both king and queen'.[88] Mary, however, had remained both king and queen whether willingly or not, despite her inability to occupy that most important of royal roles, producer of heirs.

Finally, two of the charges frequently laid at Mary's door to support the notion of her reign's failure also need to be challenged. Firstly, the loss of Calais being a result of the Spanish marriage, rather than the indecision and temporising of the English Privy Council. Feria wrote to Philip in despair at their delayed response to his offer of help to retake the city. Even after Mary's death, Philip sought to reverse the French victory, offering to renew hostilities in the spring of 1559. Feria accused Elizabeth of feigning anger when her commissioners agreed to the permanent cession of Calais to the French.[89] Secondly, the notion of Philip's indifference to Mary's death, derived from his alleged comment that 'he felt a reasonable regret for her death'. In mourning at the monastery of Grunenthal on 4th December, what he actually wrote to his sister Juana was that '[g]iven that the problem of Calais can not be negotiated so soon, especially given the death of the most serene Queen, my wife, may she rest in peace, which I have felt as deeply as one would expect, even in this she is most necessary to me, the continued suspension of hostilities seemed agreeable so as to not break off the negotiation which is still to come'.[90] The Victorian translation of this document ('I felt a reasonable regret for her death. I shall miss her, even on this account') has given rise to the idea that Philip did not mourn Mary's passing, particularly. The original underlines, however, that whatever Philip's most intimate feelings about his wife, he expressed sorrow to his sister and underlined Mary's practical importance to him in the context of the war with France.

There are two underexploited sources in understanding the co-monarchy and government of Mary I and her husband. Firstly, the letters of Reginald Pole and the role played by the legate himself in public life during the reign, as a nexus for a vast network of continental connections. A recent biography offers the clearest assessment of Pole's centrality as a conduit for European intellectuals and theologians, such as Carranza, operating at the highest level of European religious politics. A few details underline the way in which this linked Marian England to the world of European politics, from Pole's regular correspondence with Ignatius Loyola, to the fact that the Spanish humanist Juan Ginés de Sepúlveda sent him a copy of his *De rebus gestisque Caroli Quinti* for correction, book 29 of which contained a paraphrase of the oration Pole had made to parliament bringing the schism to an end.[91] Detailed consideration of the correspondence between Mary and Pole as well as his importance in Marian government have been fleshed out in a recent biography that concludes 'it is extraordinary how much he achieved, and although Protestant efforts to undo his work began as soon as he was dead, his faith and achievement lived on, through his own followers, through the model for the church set out in his synod and amplified by the Council of Trent, and in the Catholic recusant and missionary movements of the decade after his death'.[92] Secondly, there is the trial record of Bartolomé Carranza, in which many individuals provided testimony about the role of Spanish courtiers and ecclesiastics in England under Philip and Mary. One witness asserted that Philip 'wanted Carranza to remain in England to participate in the councils of the kingdom and Legatine mission, so much did he esteem his wisdom and zeal in the service of God, that through his works and solicitude in that kingdom, reduced to the way of truth, it might be hoped the better to augment and confirm the Catholic faith. He never disappointed Philip's good opinion of him. He with all his efforts directed to the eradication of heresy and outrages converting the imprisoned, convicted and stubborn, and amongst them Thomas Cranmer.'[93] In the dedication of his *Comentarios del Reverendissimo Señor Frai Batholome Carrança de Miranda, Arçobispo de Toledo, &c. sobre el catechismo Christiano* (1558) to Philip II, Carranza alluded to a Latin edition designed 'especially for England', which 'I know... will be well received by the most serene Queen, our Lady, to whom that nation owes its life, the health of its bodies souls and I perpetual service'.[94] This testimony from one of the principal architects of the Catholic restoration in England, along with the other evidence discussed in this section concerning Mary's involvement in ecclesiastical affairs, underlines how deeply engaged Mary and her husband Philip were in governing England, whether pushing forward reform or prosecuting the war with France. England's Spanish king mourned his wife appropriately, whatever his personal feelings might have been. Their glittering and magnificent court, far from being without direction or identity, was a vibrant and dynamic sounding board for Catholic reform, a powerful offensive alliance, a conscious marrying of English and Spanish cultural elements that aimed to become the centre of an emerging global empire and offer a solution to the religious divisions of the period.

Although the reign has not generally been associated with significant cultural or intellectual achievements, Philip and Mary were well aware of the importance of print, incorporating the Stationer's Company, as well as seeing the earliest printing of vernacular poetry. There was a revival of printings of the romances of chivalry as well as important pedagogical and theological material. Drama and court culture also flourished and, while there was only one direct translation from Spanish into English, there is no doubt that the transnational nature of Philip's servants and sovereignty led to significant cultural translation.[95]

The earliest vernacular bilingual language-teaching treatise published for English can be related to the Spanish marriage. Although of uncertain date and provenance it seems highly likely that two texts were produced to capitalise on the newly created market for an English–Spanish bilingual language-teaching manual, with hundreds of courtiers and perhaps thousands of clingers-on, servants, artisans, factors, merchants and others attempting to capitalise on the wedding of the century. *A very profitable boke to lerne the maner of redyng, writyng, speakyng English* (London: John Kingston and Henry Sutton for John Wight, 1554) contained sample dialogues in parallel columns, while *The boke of Englysshe and Spanysshe* (London: Robert Wyer, 1554?) was a vocabulary and phrase book. These publications are fascinating because of the way they envisage the types of exchange and dialogues most useful to travellers. Unfortunately, their specific content cannot be wholly related to the marriage. *The boke of Englysshe and Spanysshe* was extracted and reordered from the polyglot *Sex linguarum, Latinae, Gallicae, Hispanicae, Italicae, Anglicae, et Teutonice* (Venice: Marchio Sessa, 1541),[96] while *A very profitable boke* is an adaptation of a German work entitled *Vocabulaer in vier spraken Duytsch, Francois, Latijn, ende Spaensch, profiteliick allen den ghenen die dese spraken leeren willen* (Louvain: Batholome de Grave, 1551) compiled by Noel van Barlement, using the Spanish and adding English translations.[97] The latter book was divided into four; giving examples of conversation 'at meate', of 'fashions of buiyng and sellyng', of '[h]ow to call upon debitours', and of 'how to write epistles, obligacions, and quittances', which included sections on 'how to admonish Debitoures' and '[t]he maner of paieyng debte to any with an excuse'.[98] In the third section 'How to call upon debitours' we find the following exchange:

M. Wote you why I come to you.
G. No verely, who are you?
M. What means this haue you forgotten that of late you bought some of our Marchandize?[99]

The sample dialogues imagine conviviality as well as some of the difficulties implicit in being a foreigner involved in mercantile exchange, such as negotiating the exact exchange rate for foreign coinage. One section details a disagreement as to whether a coin is worth 36½ *stuphers*, translated as *placas* in Spanish. A number of mistakes are apparent in the Spanish translations, suggesting that the anonymous adapter was not a native speaker, but probably a Habsburg subject from the Low Countries. The first epistle is a familiar letter addressed to a father, Peter Barlemon, dwelling significantly in Antwerp. It ends with an alphabetical vocabulary list and the Lord's Prayer.[100] Bruges and Ghent are also alluded to in the sections on debt. 'Come in' is rendered *Entradad aqui*, 'overcome' as *vencidado*, while 'brown' is translated *moron* and *buen paño y buen lienço* is simplified as 'good wollen clothe' as opposed to cloth and linen. At times there are some well-chosen idiomatic equivalents, '[g]ood wife what is the price of' being rendered *[s]eñora quanto pedis por la vara*, although there is additional information included in the Spanish, i.e. the qualification, 'by the yard'. Parts deal with days of the week, names, forms of address and 'many dayly facions of speakyng, whiche we use when we sytte at meate'.[101] As well as idiomatic phrases for post-prandial conversation, both texts possess a significant religious content, including translations of the Pater Noster, Ave Maria, articles of faith, the ten commandments and 'Grace at the table' in *A very profitable boke* and God and the trinity, seven works of mercy, seven deadly sins, the Devil, hell and purgatory in *The boke of Englysshe and Spanysshe*.[102] In addition to pragmatic economic interchanges, they also model violent confrontations ('I am euyll plesed/*Yo soy mal contento*. Thou lyest/*Tu mientes*. I am begyled/*Soy agañado*...Of a knave/*De un bellaco*'), as well as more intimate situations such as sharing a bed: '[f]or thou doest no Thynge all nyght but snore/*Por que toda la noche no hazes sino roncar*'.[103] The main intention of these two modern language-teaching books, according to the subject matter, hovers between the mercantile and everyday life, eating and religious worship. The publisher of the *A Very Profitable Boke*, John Wyght/Whyte, went on to become one of the city of London's sheriffs in 1556.[104]

Despite the potential for language teaching that these two little phrase books/vocabularies supposed, there was no notable increase in translation activity from Spanish to English under Philip and Mary. The only literary text translated from Spanish in the first half of the sixteenth century was of course John Rastell's version of *La Celestina*, 'an attempt to chasten and domesticate an international best-seller for a refined, morally-minded audience'.[105] Vives famously referred to Celestina as 'pestiferis libris' in his *De institutione foeminae Christianae*, dedicated to Catherine and Mary, in Hyrde's translation 'Celestina, the baude, mother of noughtynes'.[106] Elsewhere, however, he praised the morality of its tragic ending. It seems probable that Vives' friend Thomas More was the link to Rastell and Hyrde, tutor to More's daughters.[107] Ellis Heywood, eldest son of John Heywood, published a fictitious dialogue with Thomas More in Florence in 1556. He later became a Jesuit, having fled England after 1552, joining the entourage of Cardinal Pole, with whom he probably returned to England given that he was presented with the prebend of Eccleshall in Lichfield in 1554. Ellis' youngest sister, Elizabeth, was the mother of John Donne. John Heywood's wife was Joan Rastell, More's niece, the daughter of his sister Elizabeth. Ellis was principal heir in his uncle William Rastell's will made at Antwerp in 1564.[108]

The unique translation from Spanish into English from the Marian period was *The comentaries of Don Lewes de Auela, and Suniga, great Master of Acanter, which treateth of the great wars in Germany* (1555), a translation of the treatise that had so angered Albert of Brandenburg.[109] Dedicated by John Wilkinson to Edward Stanley, the earl of Derby, around the time of his son Henry's marriage to Lady Cumberland, Margaret Clifford, the granddaughter of Charles Brandon and Henry VIII's sister Mary Tudor, it underlined 'what hath folowed the doctrine of Martin Luther'.[110] The commentary described Germany as plagued by Lutherans, except in regions like Cleves where 'catholiques yet they tempered so with the Lutherans in shewing of frendship to the one, and the other part in such sort, that they might called rather newters, then catholiques'.[111] The agenda of this publication, like the Tunis tapestries, is concerned with the religious politics of schism and the fight back against heresy. Its relevance in Marian England was all too clear. The publisher Tottel would of course go on to publish his *Miscellany* in 1557, the first printed collection of contemporary poetry, predominantly works by Henry Howard, the earl of Surrey, and Sir Thomas Wyatt the elder. Its popularity saw a second edition six weeks after the first, which also included poems by John Heywood and Thomas Vaux, who had retired to his estates in 1534, presumably unhappy at the religious changes of that parliament.

John Heywood, who as we saw played a prominent role in welcoming Mary to London in 1553 and had been responsible for providing her with theatrical entertainments in the 1530s, produced a long allegorical poem about the religious divisions of the period and also an opaque parable about Mary's reign entitled *The Spider and the Fly* in 1556. On an obvious level, the flies represent Catholics and the spiders Protestants, with the maid of the house, intended to represent Mary, entering the room at the last minute to save the fly:

> The spider toward the flie, furiouslie drawse.
> And being stept to the flie: staying his stop,
> As he wold haue perst the flies hed: with his pawse,
> The maide of the house, to the window did chop.
> Setting her brome, hard to the copwebs top.
> Where: at one stroke with her brome: striken rounde,
> The copweb and spider, she strake to the grounde.[112]

The maid, about to tread the spider underfoot, grants it a stay of execution but having listened to its case alleges custom and eventually crushes it to death, in the face of woe on all sides, brought into relief through a touching conversation between the fly and its son. This symbolic and unique victim gives way to the resolution of the contention between spiders and flies, with the maid whose master is Christ and mistress, holy Church 'Setting flies at liberte: in their right rate:/Plasing spiders likewise in accustumd state'.[113] This fantasised resolution is followed by Heywood's key to the parable, that the window is a figure for the world:

> Ye se also: that this fygure here implies,
> For strife in windowes: betwene spiders and flies,
> The plat of all the world, and people therin.
> In which world: which people: if all now begin:
> And hensforth: endeuer them deuring theyr liues:

> By counsell of those two: to cut of all striues:
> By cutting of: all cause of strife: in all parties:
> As they both: (eche in his last tale) did deuise.[114]

This utopian resolution of 'sectarian' strife might have been seen in 1556 as a reference to and possible criticism of the burnings and a call for ecumenical resolution. However, in the conclusion, Heywood claimed he had not worked on the poem for nineteen years, suggesting that the context of its original was very different. Various interpretations have been offered, from seeing it as a reflection on the ultimately sterile controversies of the Henrician and Edwardian reformations, a criticism of political intrigue at Westminster and Rastell's entrapment by Cromwell or Heywood's by Cranmer, debates about tenure and commoners' rights (the fly calls itself a 'yeoman', the spiders are 'gentlemen' and addressed by the fly as 'sir', where the fly is merely 'thee'), to being a criticism of Mary's belated housekeeping in relation to England.[115] As Hunt argues, while it is clear that we find in the poem 'debates about ownership, property and rights, the hangings and threat of executions, the trials and spirit of rebellion', which can be related 'to real moments of political unrest', it collapses several political issues into one making it impossible for one single religious or other reading to be definitive.[116] The dedication to Philip and Mary may well have been an afterthought, but it filters the poem's take on contemporary religious controversies through the particular lens of Catholic restoration and Heywood's particular vision of healing sectarian divisions:

> And also our suffrayne Lord: Philip: to her brought:
> By god: as god brought her to us. Which twaine:
> Conioyned one: in matrimoniall trayne:
> Both one also: in auctorite regall:
> These two thus made one: bothe one here we call.
> Which two thus one, reioyce we eueriechone.
> And these two thus one, obey we all as one.
> Effectuallie: as those spiders and flies,
> Figuratiuelie, that one recongnies,
> Beseching god that brought the, to keepe them here.[117]

The somewhat crass repetition of 'one' through the dedication, underlining the unified nature of their joint authority, blends into its call for religious unity brought about through the recognition of their oneness by everyone. The providential marriage is figured as that which will reduce spiders and flies to unity and peace. Heywood's bizarre text blends idealistic fantasy and sharp social critique, wilfully obfuscating the ground of its allegorical significance. But it is an indication of the fluidity of religious identities, allegiances and perceptions of Philip and Mary's reign and achievements.

Often easy assumptions about what religious affiliations might mean for political outlook or personal ethos have clouded an appreciation of mid-Tudor literary culture, which the pioneering work of a number of scholars has gone some way to disperse.[118] Henry Parker, Lord Morley, made a New Year's gift to Mary in January 1537, the servant being rewarded with 10s. The future queen also received New Year's gifts from two Morley daughters, Jane, widow of George Boleyn, and Margaret Shelton (Mary acted as godmother to Shelton's child, giving £1 to the midwife and nurse).[119] These exchanges suggestive of friendship did not preclude Morley's connections with the Boleyns or even Thomas Cromwell, to whom he sent annotated copies of Machiavelli's *History of Florence* and *The Prince* on 13th February 1537.[120] Morley's translation of Petrarch's *Trionfi*, originally dedicated to Henry VIII, was printed in Mary's reign with a dedication to the earl of Arundel's son Lord Maltravers.[121] One of the most radical pieces of political writing of the reign, dedicated to Philip in Italian, is the so-called *Machiavellian Treatise*, which Gabriel Harvey believed had been penned by Stephen Gardiner, although generally attributed to George Rainsford.[122] This piece of political advice sought to show Philip how to make himself absolute master of England and more than anything else is perhaps the closest thing to representing the fears and anxieties expressed in the propaganda of exiled evangelicals.

Gynocracy

Mary it has been argued was politically inexperienced and struggled to be effective in government.[123] The assumption that the commonplace misogyny of the period made her incapable of exercising royal authority underestimates the significance of royal blood and the profoundly stratified and hierarchical nature of early modern society. Female rule was commonplace in contexts from the household and business to states and kingdoms, big and small. Assessments of Mary have given too much credence to the explosion of gynophobic literature attacking her 'monstrous' regime. While, as we saw in Chapters 2 and 3, female rule provoked legitimate anxieties, this anomalous situation in England was soon regularised through statutes settling the political rights of queens. The radical polemic demonising women in power reflected both a shifting panorama of political ideas and the changing place of women in general. The following section reviews this literature, unpicking the philosophical ideas at the heart of these virulent denunciations, arguing that they were rooted in anti-Catholicism more than misogyny, and tainted by their radical, anti-monarchical stance.

The growing security of Marian rule by 1558 seems to have produced a last-gasp attempt to destabilise the regime, with some of the most virulent anti-monarchical and gynophobic writing of the sixteenth century appearing in the last year of the reign. Going beyond even the ideas expressed by John Ponet in his *A Shorte Treatise of Politike Power* (1556), these Protestant writers gave full expression to the idea that the regiment of women was an inherent form of tyranny and that violent resistance was justified and justifiable. These positions soon came to seem uncomfortably radical, when the woman they reviled was succeeded by someone of a more amenable religion.[124] The challenges of female rule in the period were crystallised in Agostino Nifo's 1523 rewriting of Machiavelli's *Il principe*, when he argued that a 'ruler is required to practise virtues which are in some sense contrary to those recommended to woman in general; how then should queens, princesses and other women who by their social status form part of public life behave?'[125] William Thomas, who was executed for his part in the Wyatt rebellion, had recorded his objections on learning about the Spanish marriage, resolving the contradiction of royal women's authority by seeking to exclude them from public life altogether: '[a]s it becometh neither the Man to be Governed of the Woman, nor the Master of the Servant, even so in al other Regiments it is not convenient the Inferior should have power to direct the Superior'.[126] Female government inverted natural order. The solution to the problem of female authority in the 'Act for the Queen's Regal Power' had been to annex 'kingly office' by statute to women and license Mary to rule 'as king'. As we have seen, John White, bishop of Winchester, declared in his sermon at Mary's burial that she had been 'a queen and by the same title a king also'.[127] Mary's political authority was gendered male in spite of the sex of her natural body, relying on the separation of the sovereign's natural and political persons. Elizabethan defenders of female rule similarly gendered sovereign authority male. John Leslie, in his defence of Mary Queen of Scots, claimed that *ex fratribus* from the biblical passage (Deuteronomy 29: 15 '*one* from among thy brethren shalt thou set king over thee'), frequently cited as a precedent to debar women from authority, had been widely misinterpreted, since in classical languages, '[a]gaine as in civill law the masculine gender comprehendethe the feminine' and 'the worde kinge by propertie of one and the same voice and signification expresethe the Quene bothe in scripture & in other tonges'.[128] He specifically referenced the 'Act for the Queen's Regal Power' as an example proving this point. Similarly, John Aylmer refuted John Knox's use of the same biblical passage in *The First Blast of the Trumpet Against the Monstrous regiment of women* (Geneva, 1558) by pointing out its misinterpretation of the Latin: it prohibited foreign rulers, not women.[129]

Paradoxically, acclaiming figures of feminine excellence in defence of women often reinforced gender stereotypes, since they were celebrated precisely for qualities which rendered them more 'virile': the 'regularity with which these exemplary women are labelled "manly" finally undermines their rhetorical purpose'.[130] A similar gender confusion seems to have influenced and been produced by the figure of regnant queens. We have already read the Scottish ambassador Melville's words to Elizabeth;[131] Sir Thomas Smith in the *De Republica Anglorum* (1583) sought to solve the problem of female authority, the biological accident of two female accessions in a row, by setting against the assertion of women's unsuitability for government an appeal to lineage:

> those whom nature hath made to keepe home and to nourish their familie and children... except it be in such cases as the authoritie is annexed to the bloud and progenie, as the crowne, a dutchie, or an erledome for there the blood is respected, not the age or the sexe... These I say have the same authoritie although they be women or children in that kingdom, dutchie or erledome, as they should have had if they had bin men of full age.[132]

The possibility of the transmissibility of political rights by women, who could not exercise them in their own persons, was confirmed, as we have seen, by the case of Katherine Willoughby and Richard Bertie, although he never came to exercise them. Despite Smith's claim that the 'same authoritie although they be women' applied in case of a kingdom, political and property rights were not generally exercised by women in baronies; although they were transmissible lineally, they were not generally transmissible laterally to non-blood relations, i.e. in the absence of male heirs. A notable exception was Margaret Pole, who was made countess of Salisbury, an earldom formerly held by her father and brother. In the twelfth century Henry I 'because he hadde none other issue male, ordeyned Maude [Matilda] the Empresse which was his daughter, to succede him in the kingdome'; however, Maude's claim was denied by her cousin Stephen, opening a period of civil strife, which ended only with the accession of her son Henry II and a return to legitimate succession. This vindicated posthumously her claim to have possessed those rights.[133] Torquato Tasso argued 'that the first duty of a princess is to her royal status... The princess is, as it were, a man by virtue of her birth, and hence the masculine standard of morality applies to her.'[134] These paradoxical views reflected the basic problem that monarchy as an extension of dynasticism often involved women occupying elevated positions of political authority, a practice particularly notable among the Habsburgs.

Under Mary, Thomas Becon, John Knox, Christopher Goodman and others published vitriolic attacks on gynocracy. These writers read gender as a uniquely determining condition, outweighing all other forms of social differentiation. Women were exclusively and solely defined by their gender, a 'natural' and divinely ordained subjection to men. The Pauline injunctions that 'women keep silence in the churches: for it is not permitted unto them to speak; but *they are commanded* to be under obedience' and 'I suffer not a woman to teache, neither yet to usurpe authoritie above man' (I Corinthians 14:34 and I Timothy 2:12), were frequently cited to make this case. These treatises have been read as representative of contemporary views on female author- ity and linked to the wider sixteenth-century humanist debate about women and female education. However, situating them in this way is problematic; firstly because reading from the rhetorical to the historical poses fundamental epistemological problems, and secondly because these authors had specific political agendas, served by destabilising Mary's regime. Literary attacks on or defences of women possessed generic conventions and were often no more than rhetorical, theoretical exercises, 'without any connection with real life at all'; a notion reinforced by the fact that there were authors 'who wrote formal essays on both sides of the woman question, damning and praising women with equal conviction'.[135] Edward Gosynhyll's *The Schole House of Women* (1541), for example, an anonymous satire and catalogue of misogynist commonplaces, was published as a refutation of Sir Thomas Elyot's *The Defence of Good Women* (1540), a vindication of women's claim to political equality, to be capable as citizens of full participation in civic life. Gosynhyll averred: 'A fole of late contryued a boke/And all in prayse of the femynye/Who so taketh laboure, it to out loke/Shal proue, all is but flaterye/Pehan he calleth it, it maye well be/The pecocke is prowdest, of his fayre tayle/And so be all women of theyr apparayle'.[136] A year later Gosynhyll retracted his former position in a poem *The Prayse of all Women* (1542), in which Venus appears to him in a dream, exhorting him to 'slepe not so fast./Consyder our grefe, and howe we be blamed/And all by a boke, that lately is past/Whiche by reporte by the was fyrst framed/The scole of women none auctour named/In prynte it is passed, lewdely compyled/All women wherby before revyled'.[137] Effectively, Gosynhyll had argued both sides of the argument, entering into a controversy with himself. In Elyot's dialogue Queen Zenobia figures as one of the three interlocutors, an icon of political womanhood invoked by Vives in *De institutione foeminae christianae* (1523), by Agrippa in *De Nobilitate & Praecellentia foeminei Sexus* (1529), by Chaucer in the 'Monk's Tale', by Lydgate in *Fall of Princes*, and twice by Boccaccio in 'De casibus virorum' and 'De claris mulieribus'. The intriguing argument has been made by Stanford Lehmberg that Queen Zenobia should be identified with Catherine of Aragón: 'the *Defence of Good Women* seems to be in fact a veiled defence of Katherine of Aragon'.[138] From 1532 to 1536, according to Garrett Mattingly, Elyot was aware of a conspiracy to welcome Charles V's forces into England, depose Henry and place Catherine on the throne as regent for her daughter Mary. His suggestion is that the *Defence* was written as a preliminary to the acceptance of Catherine's government.[139] The majority of his text was taken up with a refutation of the influential Aristotelian notion that women were less perfect than men, a refutation stressing the complementarity of their virtues finally making a case for female superiority.

The notion in the Renaissance of the predominance of cold and wet humours in women was commonplace: 'a combination of cold and moist produces a retentive memory because, like wax, impressions can be registered easily and remain fixed on cold and moist substances. The memory, which is sometimes described as *intellectus passibilis*, is also associated with woman (vs. man) as is passive (vs. active)'.[140] According to the Galenic model of biological sex difference female genitals were believed to be inverted versions of men's. The 'one-sex body' model understood women as male inverts: the 'vagina was an internal penis', as a result of insufficient heat during gestation.[141] The location of sexual difference on a continuum made any absolute differentiation of gender roles difficult to sustain other than on grounds of custom and acculturation. The presentation of rigid divisions between gender roles in the early modern period was problematised by the fact that a one-sex body made a notion of femaleness-in-itself, the female as distinct from the male, a difficult difference to maintain. The attribution of male qualities to powerful women, as the only possible mode of their celebration, followed from the opposition of masculine and feminine characteristics on a continuum, with one merely reflecting, or inverting, the other. The virago's assumption of male characteristics through her occupation of a social role at odds with her gender was the corollary of the effeminisation of men in assuming subordinate roles, under 'improper' female domination.

The accepted consecration of John Knox's *The First Blast of the Trumpet Against the Monstrous regiment of women* 'as representative of the "real" views of the age' and its attitudes towards women in authority, the belief that 'Knox's view of women was "commonplace"',[142] has shaded too easily into speculation about Mary's acceptance of her own subordination. Knox's attack, however, was not general, but directed at three specific women: Mary of Guise, regent of Scotland, Catherine de Medici and Mary I, 'whose persecution of Knox's fellow Protestants had forced him into exile'.[143] Before Mary's reign, Sir David Lindsay had attacked the Scottish regent, Mary of Guise: 'Ladyis no way I can commend,/Presumptuouslye quhilk doith pretend,/Tyll vse the office of ane kyng,/Or Realmes tak in governing'.[144] On Elizabeth's accession the same authors became silent on the issue of female rule or wrote of special dispensation, the mysterious providence which had set a 'godly princess' over them. Calls for open rebellion against the 'regiment of women' by polemical Reformers were engaged less with the issue of gender than obedience and false religion; the right of the people to overthrow ungodly rulers. In the context of religious persecution, sex was a useful adjunct to rhetorical strategies to discredit. Even after Mary's death Catholic apologists continued to defend female sovereignty from these attacks: John Fowler, for example, publishing a translation of Peter Frarin's *An Oration Against the Unlawfull Insurrections of the Protestantes* in 1566, which rebutted Knox and Goodman's denial of Mary's right to rule.[145]

Christopher Goodman was unique in excluding female rule on principle. Mary was disqualified not just because she was the 'ungodlie and vnlawful Gouernesse, wicked Iesabel' and 'in dede bastarde, and unlawfully begotten', but also because 'beit that she were no bastard, but the kinges daughter as law-fullie begotten as was her sister, that Godlie Lady, and meke Lambe, voyde of all Spanishe pride, and straunge bloude what woman you shulde crowne, if you had bene preferrers of Goddes glorie'.[146] Nevertheless Goodman sought entry to England within a year of Elizabeth's accession and before an ecclesiastical commission in 1571 recanted his former anti-feminine arguments. Calvin, in a letter to Cecil shortly after Elizabeth's accession, admitted having had discussions with Knox about the issue of female rule: 'Knox asked of me, in a private conversation, what I thought about the government of women' and Calvin had conceded 'it was a deviation from the original and proper order of nature'; however, 'I had no suspicion of the book, and for a whole year was ignorant of its publication'.[147] *The First Blast of the Trumpet*, on whose frontispiece is prominently printed Mary's motto *Veritas temporis filia*, ignored the complexity of issues surrounding inheritance and female succession, affirming that to 'promote a woman to beare rule, superioritie, dominion or empire aboue any realme, nation, or citie, is repugnant to nature, contumelie to God, a thing most contrarious to his reueled will and approved ordinance, and finalie it is the subuersion of good order, of all equitie and justice'.[148] The exile Thomas Becon lamented that 'in the stead of that virtuous prince [Edward VI] thou hast set to rule over us a woman, whom nature hath formed to be in subjection unto man, and whom thou by thine holy apostle commandest to keep silence and not to speak in the congregation', interpreting Mary's rule as providential retribution for the nation's unworthiness:

> Ah Lord! to take away the empire from a man and give it unto a woman, seemeth to be an evident token of thy anger towards us Englishmen. For by thy prophet thou, being displeased with thy people, threatenest to set women to rule over them, as people unworthy to have lawful, natural and meet governors... such as ruled and were queens were for the most part wicked, ungodly, superstitious, and given to idolatry and to all filthy abominations; as we may see in the histories of queen Jesebel, queen Athalia, queen Herodias, and such-like.[149]

In Thomas Stapleton's *Apologia pro Rege Catholico Philippo II* (1592), a response to the Elizabethan government's proclamation against 'Seminarie Priests and

Jesuits' (1591) in the aftermath of the Armada, Elizabeth was labelled just as Mary was here, a Jezebel and unnatural stepmother.[150] Elizabeth I, it is suggested 'carefully developed the cult of the Virgin Queen' and cultivated her difference from other women in a post-Reformation world where the icon of the Virgin Mary was no longer available as a model for emulation.[151] However, the celebration of Elizabeth's physical autonomy was at odds with the insistence early in her reign that she marry, not least to assure a Protestant succession.[152] At the opening of Parliament in 1563, Alexander Nowell, Dean of St Paul's, preached that 'as the marriage of Queen Mary was a terrible plague to all England, and like in continuance to have proved greater; so now for the want of your marriage and issue is like to prove as great a plague'.[153] Even more radically, Philippa Berry has suggested that, while later representations of Elizabeth 'allied emphasis upon Elizabeth's combination of femaleness and physical autonomy', the recognition of her 'extensive powers in the political and spiritual spheres, [being] related to and overshadowed by another mode of power, one altogether more enigmatic and secretive, which was signified by the motif of chastity: a power over her own body', in fact 'reveal[s] a growing anxiety about this unorthodox image of the queen'.[154] There is no reason to believe therefore that Mary I's marrying was any more problematic than Elizabeth's virginity, although it posed a unique set of problems.

What kind of obedience did a ruling queen owe her husband? The apparent contradictions in the position of a married queen between a wife's subordination and the necessary 'autonomy' of her political role, in exercising justice and political power, were confronted head on by Aylmer:

> if he breake any lawe, if it were capitall, she myghte strike with the sword, and yet be a wife good inought for the dutye that she oweth to him, is not omitted in that she obserueth, that she oweth to the common weale, wherein he is as a member conteyned. But if for her wedlocke dutie to him, she will neglect the commonwealth: Then is she a loving wife to him and an euel head to the countrye.[155]

Theoretically, a wife might exercise her authority as head of the commonwealth without abrogating her duty to her husband.[156] However, pragmatically, as Aylmer's last clause recognised, to be 'a loving wife' implied the 'neglect [of] the commonwealth'. In declaring the terms of the marriage Gardiner had deliberately emphasised that Philip undertook it as a 'subject', confronting precisely this tension between queenly authority and female subjection.

One way of gauging the progress towards a less fraught acceptance of Mary's female authority are the appearance and waning of rumours of a revenant king. The archetype for the popular belief in revenant kings was the myth of King Arthur's return prophesied by the dying Cadwallader, last of the

British kings. The scepticism of French monks visiting Bodmin in 1113, who denied Arthur was still alive, provoked a riot. Both the usurpers, Edward IV and Henry VII, traced their lineage back to Cadwallader, deliberately enlisting his symbolic support to bolster their shaky lineal claims to legitimacy. This link was underlined by Henry VII naming his eldest son Arthur; a moment which had marked a brief renaissance of interest in the Arthurian cult and Geoffrey of Monmouth's *British History*.[157] The unease surrounding Henry IV's unauthorised dynastic supplanting of Richard II and the problems of Lancastrian legitimation were addressed by Henry V in his decision to reinter Richard in Westminster Abbey after thirteen years at Langley Abbey. In 1402, in spite of the very public funeral procession accorded to Richard through London with his face uncovered and on display to the crowds, Henry IV had been forced to proclaim that the 'said Richard is dead and buried'.[158] Before the Battle of Shrewsbury in 1403 Henry Percy was so incensed by the credulousness of some Welsh volunteers, who appeared at muster wearing Ricardian livery of white harts in the mistaken belief that Richard was still alive and that they were fighting for him, that he claimed to be personally responsible for the king's murder. The Scottish court offered long-term sponsorship to a Richard imitator, Thomas Ward of Trumpington, while the rumours that he was alive were fuelled by both William Serle, the former Chancellor who forged and sent out letters under the king's seal, and Maud de Vere, who fabricated and distributed Ricardian white hart badges. But the persistence of the belief in his miraculous return went beyond a manipulation of malcontents. The rumours and invocation of Ricardian allegiance were a focus for dissidence. Handbills claiming him to be alive were still being circulated in 1417 and Sir John Oldcastle at his trial that year claimed that Henry's courts 'had no power amongst them, their true liege lord being alive in the kingdom of Scotland'.[159] Similar rumours and pretenders plagued queen Isabella and her lover Roger de Mortimer after Edward II's murder.

Within a month of Mary I's coronation rumours were circulating that Edward VI was not dead and would imminently return. During her reign, these rumours functioned as a displacement of anxieties related to her gender; what would happen on her marriage, or in childbirth, or as a mother to a Catholic heir? They cropped up at moments when her gender was politically foregrounded, sublimating and projecting anxieties attaching to female rule. They surfaced in November 1553 with the first gossip about her intentions in marriage; then in the summer of 1555 as her pregnancy was due to come to term; and in 1556 with the inception of plans to crown Philip. In November 1553 three men, Robert Tayler, Edmonde Cole and Thomas Wood, were questioned in Star Chamber concerning their 'lewde reportes' that Edward VI was still alive.[160] In January a member of Mary's own household, Robert

Robotham 'of the wardrobe of the robes', was committed to the Fleet for 'his lewde talke that the kinges majestie deceased shulde by yet lyving' and a certain Joan Wheler was imprisoned in the Marshalsea 'for her devellishe sayeng that King Edward was styll lyving'.[161] At the crucial moment in the summer of 1555, with the hopes of Mary bearing the heir who would resolve the constitutional difficulties surrounding Philip's regency at their zenith, two men were apprehended in Essex for spreading rumours of Edward's survival and another two men were arrested for claiming to be him. One, William Cunstable, an 18-year-old 'the wyche sayd he was kyng Edward the vj[th],[162] had been arrested and examined at Hampton Court on 10th May 1555. According to the Venetian ambassador, after being 'believed to be such, both in the country and here [in London]... he raised a tumult amongst the populace'.[163] He also came to the attention of the London diarist Machyn. This particular impersonator achieved considerable notoriety, before his arrest and committal to the Marshalsea. On the 'xxij day of May one William, sum tyme a lake, rod in a care from the Marsalsey thrugh London unto Westmynster and in-to the Hall, and ther he had ys jugement to be wypyd be-caws he sayd he cam as a messynger from kyng Edward the vj[th]'.[164] By January 1556 handbills were circulating in London and the countryside, inciting rebellion and insinuating that Edward VI was living in France, awaiting a demonstration of popular support to herald his return to reclaim the crown.[165] Laurence Trymmyng was imprisoned for possessing a bill, allegedly given to him by associates of William Cunstable, who was rearrested. William Cockes, an officer of the Pantry in Mary's own household, was dismissed after someone found in his possession 'a lewde bill surmysing that King Edward was still lyving'.[166] The pretender's supporters were linked to at least some of these leaflets and after the rearrest he and his co-conspirators were hanged.[167] These rumours did not die with Mary; Edward remained a persistently troubling figure well into the reign of his other sister, Elizabeth. In 1581 Robert Blosse, another Essex man, was executed after first disseminating rumours of Edward's being alive and then impersonating him himself. Six years later history repeated itself: another Essex inhabitant, the smith William Francis, was arrested for asserting Edward was alive. In 1589 a soldier returning from the Low Countries similarly claimed that Edward was living in Spain or France.[168]

The examination of the demons conjured by female dominion and the threat of a foreign prince unscrupulously appropriating her power dynastically must be counterbalanced by the perspective of pro-Marians, who could celebrate precisely those consequences of the marriage treaty's ratification rehearsed as malevolent and fearful by anti-Marian propagandists to promote opposition within the political estate. In his account of the treaty's passage the Catholic Robert Wingfield, unperturbed by the 'patriotic' doubts of exiled

Reformers, praised Mary's subordination of herself to a foreign king as exemplary piety, a return to natural and divine order:

> In this session, *under particular pressure from the queen*, they discussed the question of granting the title of the threefold kingdom, that is, England, France and Ireland, to the Spaniard, to the end that *the queen's conjugal love for the king might be made clearer to everyone*. Immediately, therefore, this title which from ancient times has been solely reserved and deemed fitting for the kings of England, was by the decision of parliament granted to the Spaniard, *conferring on him the queen's hereditary honour during the life of his most puissant consort*. This was indeed an uncommon proof, not to say extremely uncommon, and *by far the most renowned token of obedience which such a princess might show to her husband*, against the innate character of ordinary women, who are almost universally believed to be rather greedy for honour and for a leading role. Through the sharing of the famous title of such mighty kingdoms, everyone might see more clearly than daylight that *the subjection of wives to their menfolk so often ordered and emphasized by St Paul and the other Apostles was held in high esteem in the queen's sacred conscience.*[169]

Wingfield recognised the resistance to the bill and the reasons for it: it has been 'solely reserved and deemed fitting' for the natural-born of the realm from 'ancient times'. Nevertheless, the granting of the title to Philip and the conferral of Mary's 'hereditary honour' on him are to be celebrated as a sign of the queen's 'conjugal love', and 'a token of obedience'. Remarkable is the description of Mary as Philip's consort. Robert Wingfield apparently interpreted the position of Mary after her marriage, as envisaged in the treaty, as being that of queen consort to Philip's king: the very problem Renard had reported no doubt as an opportunity to the emperor in January and which had sparked off the events culminating in its submission to the authority of parliament in the first place for statutory ratification. Mary is conceptualised as a model of piety in respecting the very Pauline injunctions which Reformers were repeatedly to turn against her and the legitimacy of her government for the rest of the reign. Wingfield returns to the notion of obedience, the 'subjection of wives to their menfolk', to situate the marriage and the concessions it represented within the context of righting the gender relations thrown off-balance by the accession of a woman even though of more 'than womanly daring'.[170] Wingfield's 'Life' draws to a close with an expression of the hopes and expectations underlying this position:

> I use all my energy to pray, beseech and implore God the Greatest and Best that this prince, the eldest son of the most powerful monarch in the whole world, may obtain a happy and safe landing with all his people, and very soon will enter the beloved and long-sought embraces of our most honourable queen; and that some say, God willing, that pure and fertile womb will be made fruitful through the most noble seed of all Europe, and will render her the joyful mother of a

manifold progeny, so that from the marriage bed of such parents there will spring forth a native prince who will match the praises of his ancestors, and will rule over the men of England, France and the Low Countries with the utmost felicity; for all that the king of France turns to his accustomed wiles and stirs up his allies the Scots.[171]

The birth of an heir would have effected a unification of Mary's subjects and Philip's interest in retaining the Low Countries as part of his patrimony.

Power sharing

Writing on Philip and Mary's power-sharing arrangements has been overshadowed by the negative reputations of both monarchs; the Habsburg prince's image rooted in the Black Legend and that of the first English queen regnant unfavourably compared to her successor's and embodied in her epithets of bloody and tragic.[172] Early modern European government needs to be understood not only through its documentary remains, but also in terms of material culture. The historiographical tendency to view the marriage of Philip and Mary negatively needs to be offset by consideration of factors such as the display of courtly magnificence, an area where the marriage enjoyed considerable success.[173] Their entries, entertainments, luxurious clothing, priceless jewels, gifts, as well as conjoined arms and style were disseminated globally, from a church dedicated to the pair in Argentina in 1555, to the stained glass window of them in Gouda of 1557 commemorating the victory of San Quentin. Their joint arms are also found above the Via Maggiore in Milan, symbol of an offensive alliance holding back the French tide in Italy.[174] Indirect forms of influence and favour can be more useful in nuancing our understanding of how royal government translated into political action. The idea that Philip's power was compromised by the absence of a personal patrimony in England ignores firstly that he had one of the largest pools of personal patrimony from which to draw in western Europe. Secondly, it has recently been persuasively argued that in Spanish royal government of the period 'clientage was an ineffective administrative tool'.[175] Our relatively poor understanding of Marian government reflects to some extent the invisibility of high politics in documentary terms under a queen regnant; an invisibility that may be more characteristic of the *modus operandi* of queen consorts, whose influence worked in more informal, less public ways, and through signs of favour, intercession, endowments and gift-giving.

Although we know Mary apparently applied herself assiduously to matters of state, co-monarchies hover between the personal and the political, the conspicuous and the invisible, the familial and the international. An instructive comparison is Philip IV's favourite, the duke of Lerma, who bequeathed very little documentary evidence as a political actor, as a symptom not of disengagement but rather astuteness. It allowed him to disavow creatures and clients when policies proved unpopular, failed or fell foul of royal disapproval.[176] This final section asks how might Philip have been seen at the time, in the context of a historicised understanding of their co-monarchy, with particular reference to Spanish precedents.

Early modern monarchies were ruled neither by one person, nor by a political structure. Instead they consisted of dominant kinship groups forging themselves into dynasties, at whose central axis lay the politics of marital alliances, crucially between king and queen. The corporatist nature of monarchy meant that a range of different power-sharing arrangements were common. Most typical, though, was a contract between king, grandees and urban elites. This 'corporational character'[177] underpinned the political authority of queen regents, which was an extension of their maternal rights as guardians of their (normally) male children, especially when many leading courtiers were also close kin. The distinctive nature of Spanish queenship made royal women in the Iberian peninsula far more likely to participate actively in the governance of the realm than their northern counterparts, effectively forming 'political partnerships' with their husbands.[178] Close dynastic ties between the kingdoms of the Iberian peninsula, as well as the on-going struggle of the *reconquista*, had led to frequent female regencies and regnancies in pre-modern Iberia.[179] In Aragón, although women were barred from inheriting the crown, some seven queen consorts governed for varying lengths of time during the fourteenth and fifteenth centuries.[180]

The English opposition to the Spanish match on the eve of the Wyatt rebellion in January 1554 seems to have ignored such reassuring precedents of female sovereign independence and active participation in government. More familiar contemporary regencies, such as those of Charles V's sister Mary of Hungary and Philip II's recently widowed sister Juana, also went unheeded. Mary's most obvious role model, however, as for her mother Catherine of Aragón, was her grandmother Isabella of Castile, who had ruled much of Spain in her own right for three decades, despite marrying Ferdinand V of Aragón in 1469. Ferdinand's irritation when Isabella declared herself queen and had herself crowned in his absence in Segovia in 1474, was mollified to some extent by a subsequent agreement about their representational equality and his precedence in their joint style (identical to the case of Philip and Mary). Like Philip and Mary and many other dynasts, Ferdinand and Isabella required a dispensation to marry because of consanguinity.[181] The document was drawn up in 1475 by Pero Gónzalez de Mendoza and Alonso Carrillo, archbishop of Toledo after fraught negotiations between the two camps; the

'Concordia entre los señores Reyes Catolicos D. Fernando, y Doña Isabel, a cerca del regimiento de sus Reynos; y el poder que dio la Reyna al Rey, año M.CCCCLXXV. con lo que han dicho sobre esto algunos Historiadores' asserted that 'the style on letters patent, proclamations and the coinage, on seals shall be common to both the said lords, king and queen, being present or absent; but the said king's name shall take precedence although the arms of Castile and León shall go before those of Sicily and Aragón'.[182] The compromise was that, while his name preceded hers, the royal arms of Castile came first. Of course, the government of the Catholic monarchs only effectively began at the back-end of civil war, with the death of Isabella's brother Henry IV in 1474 and the eventual defeat of the rival claimant Juana la Beltraneja, supported by Alfonso V of Portugal, at the battle of Toro in 1476. While Ferdinand and the Aragónese party managed to secure some concessions after their arrival in Segovia, ultimately Isabella remained sole proprietary ruler and Ferdinand enjoyed limited powers in the Castilian kingdoms.

Philip's success in conforming to native customs on his arrival in England, in accordance with his intention to consider English ways his own, was reflected by the assertion of his English servants that 'he is English'. As the Spanish observer noted, '[t]he English spread abroad their great happiness at having seen and worked with the king and accordingly they say that he is English and not Spanish'.[183] The utopian sensibility feeding Habsburg dynastic politics was both vindicated and exposed by this appropriation of Philip as 'Ingles y no español'. Their universalist aspirations depended on the possibility of such negotiations of regional particularities. However, the dark underside to this internationalist ideology was the *de facto* tension between his two households, which produced a struggle for control and possession of his person. The definition of Philip's identity as king of England externalised problems implicit in the conceptualisation of the treaty. The difficulties the treaty gestured towards resolving, inherent in the inconvenience of a 'diversity of nations', were played out as a symbolic household drama, with stabbings taking place within the confines of the court itself. The resulting deaths and seriousness of the situation led Philip to set up a special commission headed by Sir Thomas Holcroft and Briviesca de Muñatones to investigate incidents and impose the death penalty should there be any recurrences.[184] The discontent among Philip's followers over the English servants 'waiting for us at Southampton who did not wish to let us serve', had provoked 'enormous confusion'.[185] In spite of the assertion that 'with the intercession' of Philip it was being assuaged and that 'all would be contented', the approach adopted discriminated between his 'Spanish' and English households.[186] By relegating the latter for the most part to service exclusively in the outer chambers, he underlined the hierarchy of trust and confidence which favoured his 'Spanish' intimates over *outsiders* who, in not possessing the same access to and intimacy with him, could not claim to represent him as fully. Philip's approach might have been divisive, moving Azevedo from Lord Chamberlain to Master of the Horse, but it is difficult to see what other compromise was possible. Azevedo made way for men like James Basset, who as we saw had originally been one of Gardiner's secretaries and divided his time between being Mary's private secretary and Chief Gentleman of Philip's privy chamber. Similarly, the bishop of Chichester, George Day was Almoner in both Philip and Mary's households, while Anthony Kempe as well as being a Gentleman of both privy chambers seems to have acted as their go-between.[187]

Although Philip's attempts to blend distinctive cultural forms like the joust and Spanish *juego de cañas* gave rise to slighting comments, the reality is that court culture under Philip and Mary demonstrated an unrivalled magnificence and sophistication not seen for decades in England, nor seen again. The *juego de cañas* occurred no fewer than three times, and this and other martial tourneys and jousts were a common feature of Philip's time in England. All bar one of these events occurred while Philip was in England: 4th December 1554 at Greenwich, 18th December 1554 also at Greenwich, 24th January 1555 at Whitehall, 12th February 1555 for the wedding of Lord Strange and Lady Cumberland, 19th March 1555, 25th March 1555 at Whitehall, Shrovetide 1556 and 29th December 1557 at Hampton Court.[188] Philip came second for most gallant entry and first in the combat with foils in the first tourney of his reign. Importantly, in another example of his use of sartorial codes to win acceptance, he wore the Tudor colours of blue and yellow with the blue cloak of the Order of the Garter, as opposed to the Habsburg colours red, yellow and white.[189] Two weeks later another foot tournament was held in which he also participated, then in February a meal to celebrate the marriage of Lord Strange and Lady Cumberland was rounded off with a *juego de cañas* or cane game.[190] The first *juego de cañas*, which took place in November 1554, saw Philip pay out 1.3 million *maravedis* to the merchant Juan Bautista de Sanvitores on 13th December for 'silk, silver, gold and other merchandise purchased from him for the *juego de cañas* which I caused to take place in the said city of London in the said month of November'.[191] The student Francisco Sanchez, in his poem celebrating the conversion of the English Lutherans, described how '[f]or fifteen days they ordered celebrations in which they wore costumes not ceasing to go abroad night and day. Many bulls were run, they ran at the ring, triumphal carts paraded forth, there were *juego de cañas*, everyone celebrates.'[192] The sumptuousness of these events underlines their huge importance at the Anglo-Spanish court. Soon enough, defending Habsburg dominions provided significant opportunities for the English nobility to test their mettle in a continental war for which they were later to feel nostalgia.

The rehabilitation of Robert Dudley through participation in the chivalric culture of the court paved the way for his service alongside his brothers during the St Quentin campaign in which one of them was killed.[193] Despite being subjects of the Tudor state 'between 1586 and 1610 "roughly 20,000 Irish soldiers saw service in Flanders"'.[194] Many English Catholic soldiers continued to fight for Philip on the continent long into Elizabeth's reign.[195]

The duke of Alba encouraged Philip to appoint his own choice as Lord Chancellor after the death of Gardiner and the king vetoed appointments not to his liking, contrary to the stipulations of the marriage contract.[196] Alba's observed in April 1555 that Philip's

> way of negotiating and dispatching business is very good: may Your Majesty, for the love of God, want to be lord of that kingdom, nothing is lacking for you to become it, the most absolute that it has ever had, that loving it and showing them that is it and that it must be so, because that is what they all want apart from that handful of ill-favoured contradictors of your will.[197]

In spite of the distrust of Philip's intentions and the rumours disseminated by anti-Marian propagandists, his attitude in a letter to his father written on 16th November 1554 was far from Machiavellian: 'I am anxious to show the whole world by my actions that I am not trying to acquire other peoples' states, and your Majesty I would convince of this not by my actions only, but by my very thoughts'.[198] Philip's behaviour in England as king exemplified that of the ideal courtier and the trope of courtesy surfaces constantly in the accounts. One of his early biographers claimed that Philip 'won them over with his wisdom, affability, honours and favour... With these things and the courtesy of his family'.[199] This reception did not weaken over time. On 13th April 1557 he wrote to his father about the good will he found on his return there: 'I arrived here well and thus have I found the Queen thanks be to God, and I have begun to despatch the business that corresponds to me and I find such good will in all those in this kingdom that they do not differ from anything that I desire'.[200] This was not simply wishful thinking on his part about his own popularity, according to the secretary to the Council of State for the Low Countries, Josse de Courteville, who travelled with him: '[y]ou understand there was no lack of spectators nor honour. In my judgement the people are well pleased about his return and have received him with happiness.'[201] Two weeks later Philip continued in similar vein: 'the Queen and I are well, and the business here all goes very well'.[202] If there was implacable opposition to his authority or his attempts to govern were ineffectual, it does not show in the accounts he wrote to his father or in those of others.

In his 1619 history of Philip, Luis Cabrera de Córdoba reflected a feature shared by contemporary and later Spanish accounts of the co-monarchy: a detailed understanding of the precise nature of its terms and what it enshrined in relation to Philip's power, a grudging understanding that foreigners were 'intolerable to any nation' and could 'tyrannise', despite their necessity in the face of a queen regnant because 'it was unhappy and dangerous for a kingdom to come into gynaecocracy against natural law'.[203] Cabrera de Córdoba knew that 'Philip and Mary are equal and of one quality: but the queen solely and alone enjoys supreme authority over those kingdoms, without the Prince being able to enjoy it by means of the courtesy of England'.[204] This recognition of the exact status Philip had enjoyed in English law, even half a century after Mary's death, reflects the nuanced political understanding in Spain — one it is hard to believe Philip did not share.

While expressions of anti-Spanish sentiment in the Elizabethan period generally focused on the 'insufferable lust', pride, arrogance and cruelty of the Spanish, the surprisingly popular and cryptic anonymous poem of 1594, *Willobie His Avisa*, contains an allegorical commentary on Philip's courtship of Elizabeth even before the death of Mary in 1558. The poem viewed Philip in contradistinction to Spanish-style seduction. The heroine Avisa (a mask for Elizabeth if we accept that the poem refers to 1558), at first a 'modest maide' then 'chast and constant wife', is the subject of five attempted seductions. Her second suitor — the significantly named Caveilero — argues that she can not 'fare so well at home' for although a 'stranger' he can offer 'great store of wealth': she spurns his advances, telling him to spend his cash on his 'queanes', for '[y]our wannie cheekes, your shaggy lockes,/Would rather move my mind to grudge,/To feare the piles, or else the pockes'.[205] In the preface, the pseudonymous Hadrian Dorrell asserts that the author of the poem had 'out of Cornelius Agrippa, drawen the several dispositions of the Italian, the Spanyard, the Frenchman, the German, and the English man, and how they were affected in love', the Spaniard being according to Agrippa 'unpatient in burning love, very mad with troubled lasciviousnesse, hee runneth furiously, and with pittyful complaintes, bewailing his fervent desire, doth call upon his Lady, and worshippeth her, but having obtained his purpose maketh her common to all men'.[206] The figure Caveilero, taken to represent Philip, does not exemplify these qualities, however; rather, they are embodied by her final suitor, an Italo-Spaniard, while Caveilero is courteous, calculating and forlorn even, despite Avisa's accusations about his wenching. Alternative views of Philip to those peddled initially by anti-Marian propagandists and later under Elizabeth by the anti-Spanish party went on surfacing into James' reign.[207] Two years later, in 1596, Sir John Harrington referred to Philip in his *Apology* as 'a beggerly, thridbare Kavalliero, like Lazorelloes maister'.[208] The wealth that Philip had brought to England in 1554, like so much else, had dissipated in the face of constantly having 'new warres in hand', as Avisa says in her opening lines to him.[209]

The most common image of Philip and Mary's co-monarchy is perhaps typified by Sir Francis Hastings' *A Watchword to all religious true hearted Englishmen* of 1598, the content of which derived in large part from John Bradford's contemporary work of propaganda, *The Copye of a letter, sent by John Bradforth to the right honourable lordes the Erles of Arundel, Darbie, Shrewsburye, and Pembroke, declaring the nature of Spaniardes, and discovering the most detestable treasons, which thei have pretended most falselye agaynste our moste noble kingdome of Englande* (1556). Hastings described how

> the plots and practices, layed, and pursued by the Spanish King, had made a wofull proofe to England of a further marke shotte at (which was discovered in a letter to some of our nobles from a true harted Englishman in Spaine) had not God almightie, in his rich mercie, prevented their purposes.[210]

He mixed attacks on Mary's reintroduction of Catholicism with misplaced blame on the 'proude and bloodie monster' Stephen Gardiner, for 'he and his complices never rested, till they had brought in the *Spaniard*, and had matched him in marriage with the Queene; by which they betrayed God, her, and the whole realme': he also accused the Spanish of seeking only to win the crown, alter the laws of England and introduce the Inquisition, and declared that the marriage 'could not drawe the least sparke of true love from him to this noble Queene, who so lovingly made choice of him to be her husband'.[211] The episode came to represent the stereotype of the proud, tyrannical and lust-driven Spaniard that became iconic after the beginnings of the Dutch Revolt and William of Orange's *Apology*. As we saw, while this is the image that has come to dominate historiography of the marriage, the reality of the Marian interlude was of a more nuanced and delicate balancing act between competing factional, national and personal interests. The notion that Philip failed to forge an effective role for himself as king of England ignores two crucial factors: firstly, the corporatist nature of monarchy itself, its implication in some form of power sharing, a fact to which he was well used in Catalunya, for example, where regal authority was hemmed in by *fueros* or rights of subjects far beyond those enjoyed in England and secondly – and perhaps more importantly – the extent to which power was exercised symbolically, ceremonially and ritualistically, through intimacy, clientage, courtly exchange, festival, tournaments, religious observance and music. Philip clearly influenced major policy decisions and participated in important debates. Getting his way, however, was not a foregone conclusion, despite expectations of Mary's submission to his will. However, he was effective in 'aiding' his wife in the administration of her dominions, a task he assiduously carried out, leading both countries in war when eventually, following the Stafford raid, the English council finally agreed to support him against the French. Mary's bad press owes much to the unfortunate coincidence of her reign with a more general loss of control over the medium of print and break-down of the royal monopoly on public discourse, as religiously oppositional voices exploited the international nature of print culture more and more effectively to undermine her regime.[212] These voices echoed down through the Elizabethan period although they never altogether silenced those who saw the co-monarchy as a limited success, despite its failure to resolve the most pressing issue of all, the succession.

Portraying Philip and Mary

In addition to the literary culture associated with the match, there were also portraits and prints celebrating the marriage which carefully constructed each spouse in relation to domestic and European audiences. The Anthonis Mor portrait of Mary is emblematic of the way understandings of her and her reign have been materialised visually (see Plate 9). These aesthetic judgements reflect ideological assumptions. One discussion is tempted to suggest that Mor has attempted to 'to get over a powerful impression of fanaticism hinted at in other ways: the rod-like backbone, the pursed lips, the chisel-like chin, the meaty facial muscles, a stare more reminiscent of a gargoyle than of a woman of thirty-seven. The picture is positively frightening.'[213] Mary's lack of interest in image-making is paradoxically related to her 'obsessive devotion to Catholicism', and the portrait is understood in the context of a marriage that was 'barren in every sense'.[214] There is no doubt that the uncompromising lighting in the Mor portrait creates a stark image, but her look is not of fury, but redolent with dignity, authority and power. Her gaze is intense, transfixing the viewer with its determined and unflinching directness. Mor, painter to Cardinal Granvelle, had become acquainted with Philip in Antwerp in 1549 and frequented his apartments in Brussels between 1549 and 1550, before travelling to Spain to carry out commissions for the royal family there. He was appointed Philip's official court painter on 20th December 1554 in London. An earlier portrait of María de Portugal, the princess jilted by Philip for Mary, employed an identical composition, seated posture, gloves in one hand and even the division of the pictorial space, underlining that Mary is being framed in accordance with a Habsburg iconography of royal wives. The image was reused in 1555 by Hieronymous Cock, when it was cropped and used with text in a pair of prints by Frans Huys (see Plate 13).

Karel van Mander described how, when Mor was sent to England by the emperor to portray Mary, '[h]e copied the face of this Queen, who was a very beautiful Woman, several times on face panels that he gave to great Men'.[215] Mor allegedly received 'a gold chain, a hundred pounds sterling and a hundred pounds sterling as an annual pension' from the queen for the portrait.[216] The version in the Isabella Stewart Gardner Museum was probably Mary's own copy. It was sold from the Jerningham collection, Costessy Hall, Norfolk and was probably a gift from Mary to Sir Henry Jerningham, Captain of the Guard, vice-Chamberlain and master of her household. Other versions of the portrait include one in the Cathedral of Durham (see Plate 14). This suggests that at least Mary did not appear to have been displeased by the image. As well as Hans Eworth, Mary also patronised other artists, including the female painter Lievine Teerlinc, whose representations of her on the Coram Rege roll adapted work done by her father Simon for Dom Fernando of Portugal, for an elaborate genealogical tree of the royal houses of Iberia.[217]

Philip also used portraiture to project his role as king of England. There is a large group of portraits from the 1550s depicting him in black and yellow with gold buttons and a black cap, sometimes with the Lesser George of the Order of the Garter around his neck as opposed to the more usual Order of the Golden Fleece. These portraits self-consciously frame Philip as king of England. Hans Eworth's portrait of Philip from 1557 (the whereabouts of which are unknown, but twinned with an extant one of Mary) was one of very few surviving of the royal couple, the other being the strange image now at Woburn Abbey.[218] The cultivation of these images underlines how deeply invested Philip was in the public projection of himself as an English king, an example of what Daniel Nexon has dubbed 'polyvalent signalling'. The most surprising image of all from this period, however, may be the print of Philip II produced in 1555 by Jan Cornelisz Vermeyen. It titles him simply king of England and prince of Spain. The gloves and other aspects of the composition, costume and so on, make it part of the series of images discussed by Matthews, but here the subject seems to literally morph into the figure of Henry VIII himself, an appropriate visual emblem of the symbolic, ideological and political importance of the union of England and Spain and Philip's identity as king of England and Prince of the Spains (see Plate 15).

Notes

1 David Loades, 'Philip II and the government of England' in Claire Cross, David Loades and J. J. Scarisbrick, eds, *Law and Government under the Tudors* (Cambridge: Cambridge University Press, 1988), p. 194.

2 David Loades, *The Reign of Mary Tudor: Politics, Government and Religion, 1553–1558* (2nd edn, London: Longman, 1991), p. 219.

3 David Loades, *Intrigue and Treason: The Tudor Court 1547–1558* (London: Pearson, 2004), pp. vii and 207.

4 Carole Levin, 'Queens and claimants: political insecurity in sixteenth century England' in Janet Sharistanian, ed., *Gender, Ideology, and Action: Historical Perspectives on Women's Public Lives* (New York: Greenwood Press, 1986), p. 42.

5   Constance Jordan, 'Woman's rule in sixteenth century British political thought', *Renaissance Quarterly* 40 (1987), 421–51, pp. 426–9.

6   Anne MacLaren, *Political Culture in the Reign of Elizabeth I: Queen and Commonwealth 1558–1585* (Cambridge: Cambridge University Press, 1999), p. 16.

7   BL Cotton Titus B II, fols 59–60 and AGS E 811.

8   Harry Kelsey, *Philip of Spain, King of England: The Forgotten Sovereign* (London: I. B. Tauris, 2012), pp. 161–2.

9   Daniel Nexon, *The Struggle for Power in Early Modern Europe: Religious Conflict, Dynastic Empires and International Change* (Princeton, NJ: Princeton University Press, 2009), p. 185.

10 See for example the review on http://mary-tudor.blogspot.com/ [Accessed: 30th January 2019].

11 Glyn Redworth, 'Philip I of England, embezzlement and the quantity theory of money', *Economic History Review* 55 (2002), 248–61, p. 258. Orbea's accounts are at AGS, Contaduría Mayor de Cuentas, 1ª Epoca, Leg. 1345, fol. 6 *et seq.*

12 Geoffrey Parker, 'Guide to the archives of the Spanish institutions in or concerned with the Netherlands (1556–1706)', *Archives de Bibliothèque de Belgique* 3 (1971), p. 26. Original at AGS E 813, fols 23–4, 37.

13 BL Cottton MS Vespasian F III, no. 23.

14 His attendance at Privy Council meetings on Tuesdays and Fridays is recorded in 'Relación de las cosas de Inglaterra en tiempo de sus reyes Enrique VIII y Maria, su hija', Real Biblioteca del Monasterio de San Lorenzo de El Escorial V.ii.3, fols 486–7. See also MS V.ii.4, fol. 456. See also *Acts of the Privy Council*, V, p. 53.

15 John Guy, 'The Marian court and Tudor policy making' at www.tudors.org/undergraduate/the-marian-court-and-tudor-policy-making/ [Accessed 27th October 2014].

16 *Epistolario del III Duque de Alba*, ed. 17th duke of Alba, 3 vols (Madrid: Real Academia de la Historia, 1952), pp. 64–5.

17 *APC*, V, p. 53. Winchester, 27th July 1554.

18 BL Cotton MS Titus B II, item 79, fol. 176. This volume contains numerous other items relating to Marian government: see nos 50–86, fols 113–82. A number of these memoranda have the signatures of both Philip and Mary. Item 57 is a draft of Mary's first letter to Philip in French, subject of a chapter by Rayne Allinson and Geoffrey Parker, 'A king and two queens: the holograph correspondence of Philip II with Mary I and Elizabeth I' in Helen Hackett, ed., *Early Modern Exchanges: Dialogues between Nations and Cultures, 1500–1800* (Farnham: Ashgate, 2015), 95–118. Item 72 is an autograph letter from Mary to the marquis of Winchester requesting he approve a grant of lands to Edmund Peckham. Mary's deference in the letter is notable: 'I made you a promys not to determyne the gyfte of any lande, wythowte your consent'.

19 BL Cotton MS Titus B II, item 79, fol. 176: 'et quae agenda et proponenda uidebuntur in parlamento in scriptis redigi nolumns ante parlamenti mitium'.

20 For example National Archives SP11/14 no. 4, SP11/6 nos 16, 18, 21, 28, 30, 51, 78, 82, 83, SP11/7 nos 5, 10, 20, 22, SP11/8 nos 50, 71, SP11/9 nos 10, 12, 28, 30, 32, 33, 34, 39, 42, 47, 50, 53.

21 Samuel Gammon, *Statesman and Schemer: William, First Lord Paget Tudor Minister* (Newton Abbot: David & Charles, 1973), pp. 221–2.

22 National Archives SP11/6 no. 20 and SP11/9 no. 35.

23 National Archives SP11/9 no. 10.

24 Savoy had first been in England at Christmas 1554, presumably in the context of a prospective marriage to Elizabeth; see Charles Wriothesley, *A Chronicle of England during the Reigns of the Tudors*, ed. William Hamilton, Camden Series 20 (London: J. B. Nichols, 1877), p. 125.

25 D. S. Chambers, 'A Mantuan in London 1557: further research on Annibale Litolfi' in Edward Chaney and Peter Mack, eds, *England and the Continental Renaissance: Essays in Honour of J. B. Trapp* (Woodbridge: Boydell and Brewer, 1990), 73–99, p. 86.

26 Paula Henderson, 'Medievalism in the English "Renaissance" garden', in *Locus Amoenus: Gardens*

and Horticulture in the Renaissance, ed. Alexander Samson (Chichester: Wiley-Blackwell, 2012), p. 51.

27 Chambers, 'A Mantuan in London 1557', p. 83 and see Mariagrazia Bellorini, 'Da Londra a Mantova. Immagini di vita e cultura inglese nella corrispondenza di Aloisio Schivenoglia (1556–1560)', in *Studi di Letteratura Inglese e Americana*, ed. S. Rossi (Milan: Pubblicazioni dell'Università Cattholica del Sacro Cuore, 1980), pp. 57–92.

28 Natalie Mears, 'Politics in the Elizabethan privy chamber: Lady Mary Sidney and Kat Ashley', in James Daybell, ed., *Women and Politics in Early Modern England, 1450–1700* (Aldershot: Ashgate, 2004), 67–82, p. 67. The inset quote is from Pam Wright, 'A change in direction: the ramifications of a female household, 1558–1603' in David Starkey, D. A. L. Morgan, John Murphy, Pam Wright, Neil Cuddy and Kevin Sharpe, eds, *The English Court: from the Wars of the Roses to the Civil War* (London: Longman, 1987), pp. 147–72.

29 John Murphy, 'The illusion of decline: the Privy Chamber, 1547–1558', in Starkey *et al.*, *The English Court*, p. 141.

30 On Susan Clarencius see Jennifer Rowley-Williams, 'Image and reality: lives of aristocratic women in early Tudor England', unpublished PhD thesis (Bangor University, 1998), chapter 7, pp. 218–45.

31 Murphy, 'The illusion of decline', p. 140. Robert Rochester's reissued household ordinances are at *APC* IV, p. 421.

32 Anna Whitelock and Diarmaid MacCulloch, 'Princess Mary's household and the succession crisis, July 1553', *The Historical Journal* 50 (2007), 265–87, p. 274.

33 *Cal. Ven.*, V (1553–4), p. 533. Giacomo Soranzo to Senate, 18ᵗʰ August 1554.

34 BL Royal MS 17 B XXVIII, fols 6, 19–20, 22, 25. See Jeri McIntosh, *From Heads of Household to Heads of State: The Preaccession Households of Mary and Elizabeth Tudor, 1516–1558* (New York: Columbia University Press, 2009), pp. 46–7 and 80, and Frederick Madden, *Privy Purse Expenses of the Princess Mary* (London: William Pickering, 1831), pp. 1*ff.*

35 Thomas F. Mayer and Courtney Walters, eds, *The Correspondence of Reginald Pole*, 4 vols (Aldershot: Ashgate, 2002–8), vol. 3, p. 160.

36 Mayer and Walters, *The Correspondence of Reginald Pole*, vol. 3, p. 176. Their mutual concern for Mary is apparent in subsequent letters between them, with Philip's letter to Pole about his concern to make 'her know she is loved', e.g. p. 183.

37 Sarah Duncan, '"He to be intituled Kinge": King Philip of England and the Anglo-Spanish court' in Charles Beem and Miles Taylor, eds, *The Man Behind the Queen: Male Consorts in History*, Queenship and Power Series (New York: Palgrave Macmillan, 2014), 55–80, p. 69.

38 Barret Beer and Sybil Jack, eds, *The Letters of William Lord Paget of Beaudesert, 1547–63*, in *Camden Miscellany XXV*, 4th ser. (London: Royal Historical Society, 1974), p. 140.

39 *The Letters of William Lord Paget of Beaudesert, 1547–63*, p. 116.

40 Sheila Richards, ed., *Secret Writings in the Public Records: Henry VIII–George II* (London: HMSO, 1974), pp. 12–13.

41 BL Cotton MS Titus BXI no. 241. Instructions of Philip and Mary to Thomas Radclyffe, Lord Fitzwalter, their deputy in Ireland, 28ᵗʰ April 1556, fol. 442: it assigned Fitzwalter £1,000 sterling on various rents – farms, castles and other houses and mansions. No. 243 contains six letters from Mary to successive Lord Deputies in Ireland (Fitzwalter, Sir Anthony St Leger and the Earl of Sussex): dated 18ᵗʰ July 1554; 22ⁿᵈ September 1555; 30ᵗʰ April 1556; 13ᵗʰ May 1556; and 1ˢᵗ June 1558, fol. 458.

42 BL Cotton MS Titus BXI, fols 466*ff.*

43 Natalie Mears, *Queenship and Political Discourse in the Elizabethan Realms* (Cambridge: Cambridge University Press, 2005), pp. 82–3. Guy, 'The Marian court and Tudor policy-making'.

44 McIntosh, *From Heads of Household to Heads of State*, pp. 29–32. Original 'Instructions' for Mary's household on going to Wales in 1525 are at BL Cotton Vitellius CI, fols 7–18.

45 Again, see the discussion in McIntosh, *From Heads of Household to Heads of State*, pp. 34–6.

46 See Glanmor Williams, 'Wales and the reign of Queen Mary I', *Welsh History Review* 10 (1981), pp. 334–58.

47 See David Loades, *The Tudor Court* (2nd edn: Oxford: Davenant Press, 2003), p. 137.

48 Alistair Hawkyard, David Starkey and Philip Ward, eds, *The Inventory of King Henry VIII: The Transcript*, vol. 1 (London: Harvey Miller, 1998), pp. 376–80.

49 McIntosh, *From Heads of Household to Heads of State*, pp. 149–61.

50 See Elizabeth Russell, 'Mary Tudor and Mr Jorkins', *Historical Research* 63 (1990), 263–276 and McIntosh, *From Heads of Household to Heads of State*, Appendix C.

51 *Dos cartas la vna de la serenissima reyna de Inglaterra, embiada a la Serenissima princesa de Portugal, de la reducion de los Ingleses a la obediencia de la yglesia Romana. Y la otra de vn cauallero haziendo saber como los Ingleses han hallado vans nueuas Indias* (Toledo?: Borbon librero del Duque de Maqueda y marques Delche, 1555?).

52 Aysha Pollnitz, 'Christian women or sovereign queens? The schooling of Mary and Elizabeth' in Alice Hunt and Anna Whitelock, eds, *Tudor Queenship* (New York: Palgrave Macmillan, 2010), pp. 136–8.

53 In Aysha Pollnitz, 'Humanism and court culture in the education of Tudor royal children' in Thomas Betteridge and Anna Riehl, eds, *Tudor Court Culture* (Selinsgrove, Penn.: Susquehanna University Press, 2010), 42–58, p. 56.

54 Juan Luis Vives, *Obras completas*, trans. Lorenzo Riber, 2 vols (Madrid: Aguilar, 1948), vol. 1, p. 1177: 'No hay guardia más segura ni más fiel que la innocencia propia y el amor de los pueblos, que no se gana con las armas ni con el terror; consíguese con el amor, con la lealtad, con el desvelo, con la preocupación constante del bien público'.

55 Vives, *Obras completas*, vol. 1, p. 1189: '*Veritas, temporis filia*... Dice Cicerón: *El tiempo destruye y borra las ficciones de la opinión y confirma los juicios de la Naturaleza*'.

56 Vives, *Obras completas*, vol. 2, pp. 317, 323 and 326: 'Mandasteme escribir un breve plan de estudios, del cual pudiese usar su preceptor en la formación de tu hija María'. See Judith Richards, 'Public identity and public memory: case studies of two Tudor women', in Stephanie Tarbin and Susan Broomhall, eds, *Women, Identities and Communities in Early Modern Europe* (Aldershot: Ashgate, 2008), 195–210, p. 195.

57 Giles Duwes, *An Introductorie for to lerne to rede, to pronounce, and to speake Frenche trewly* (London: Nicholas Bourman for John Keyns, c. 1540?, first edn. 1533?), sigs Bb iv r, Dd ii v.

58 Foster Watson, ed. and trans., *Vives and the Renascence Education of Women* (London: Edward Arnold, 1912), p. 29.

59 Betty S. Travitsky, 'Reprinting Tudor history: the case of Catherine of Aragon', *Renaissance Quarterly* 50 (1997), pp. 167–9, 171–2.

60 Travitsky, 'Reprinting Tudor history', pp. 167–9, 171–2.

61 A useful survey of historical writing under Mary is included in Thomas Betteridge, *Tudor Histories of the English Reformations, 1530–83* (Aldershot: Ashgate, 1999), chapter 3, '"Making New Novelties Old": Marian Histories of the Reformation', 120–60.

62 Travitsky, 'Reprinting Tudor history', pp. 171–2.

63 Loach, 'The Marian establishment and the printing press', p. 144.

64 Richards, 'Public identity and public memory', p. 196.

65 Richards, 'Public identity and public memory', pp. 206–7.

66 See Thomas Betteridge, 'Maids and wives: representing female rule during the reign of Mary Tudor', in Susan Doran and Thomas Freeman, eds, *Mary Tudor: Old and New Perspectives* (New York: Palgrave MacMillan, 2011), pp. 145–52.

67 *The first tome or volume of the Paraphrase of Erasmus upon the newe testamente* (London: Edward Whitchurch, 1548), sig. ¶ii r. See Pollnitz, 'Christian women or sovereign queens?', p. 132.

68 There is a brilliant essay on this by Aysha Pollnitz, 'Religion and translation at the court of Henry VIII: Princess Mary, Katherine Parr and the *Paraphrases* of Erasmus', in Doran and Freeman, *Mary Tudor: Old and New Perspectives*, 123–36, pp. 135–6.

69 Pollnitz, 'Religion and translation at the court of Henry VIII', p. 135.

70 On the play see Sarah Carpenter, '*Respublica*' in Thomas Betteridge and Greg Walker, eds, *The Oxford Handbook of Tudor Drama* (Oxford: Oxford University Press, 2012), 514–30; Michael Winkelman, '*Respublica*: England's trouble about Mary', *Comitatus* 33 (2002), 77–98;

Alice Hunt, 'Legitimacy, ceremony and drama: Mary Tudor's coronation and *Respublica*', in *Interludes and Early Modern Society*, ed. Peter Happé and Wim Husken (Amsterdam: Rodopi, 2007), 331–51; Gordon Kipling, *Enter the King* (Oxford: Clarendon Press, 1998), pp. 347–8; and Howard Norland, *Drama in Early Tudor Britain: 1485–1558* (Lincoln: University of Nebraska Press, 1995), chapter 14, '*Respublica*', 199–209.

71 Alice Hunt, 'The monarchical republic of Mary I', *Historical Journal* 52 (2009), 557–72, p. 570.

72 Albert Feuillerat, *Documents relating to the Revels at Court in the time of King Edward VI and Queen Mary* (Louvain: Uystpruyst, 1914, repr. 1963), p. 159.

73 See W. R. Streitberger, *Court Revels, 1485–1559* (Toronto: Toronto University Press, 1994), pp. 417 and 417.

74 1 & 2 Philip and Mary, c. 8, s. 1. See *A Discourse upon the Exposicion & Understandinge of Statutes with Sir Thomas Egerton's Additions* (c. 1557–1571), ed. Samuel E. Thorne (California: Huntington Library, 1942); T. F. T. Plucknett, 'Ellesmere on statutes', *Law Quarterly Review* 60 (1944), 242–9; and Max Radin, 'Early statutory interpretations in England', *Illinois Law Review* 38 (1943–4), 16–40.

75 *A Discourse upon the Exposicion*, pp. 110–11.

76 1 James I, c. 1.

77 Full details of these and other visitation articles from her reign are reprinted in Walter Frere and William Kennedy, eds, *Visitation Articles and Injunctions of the Period of the Reformation*, vol. 2: *1536–58*, Alcuin Club Collections XX (London: Longman, 1910), pp. 322–426.

78 BL Cotton Titus CVII, fol. 120.

79 Eamon Duffy, *The Stripping of the Altars: Traditional Religion in England c. 1400–c. 1580* (London: Yale University Press, 1992), pp. 525–6.

80 José Ignacio Tellechea Idigoras, *Fray Bartolomé Carranza: Documentos historicos* (Madrid: Real Academia de la Historia, 1963), vol. II, p. 897: 'el dicho Cardenal Polo escrevía unos colloquios que pasavan entre el dicho Cardenal e la Reyna sobre cosas de la fe'.

81 Quoted in Michael Hutchings, 'The reign of Mary Tudor: a reassessment', *History Review* 23 (1999), 20–25, p. 20.

82 Duffy, *The Stripping of the Altars*, chapter 16, 'Mary', 524–64.

83 Jenny Wormald, 'The usurped and unjust empire of women', *Journal of Ecclesiastical History* 42 (1991), 283–92, pp. 288–9.

84 BL Additional Ch. 62464.

85 *Relations Politiques des Pays-Bas et de l'Angleterre: sous le Règne de Philippe II*, ed. Kervyn de Lettenhove and J. M. B. Constantin, 11 vols (Brussels : F. Hayez, 1882–1900), vol. 1, p. 67 (Letter no. LXXII, Josse de Courteville to President Viglius, 28th April 1557): 'le roi au costel gauche, et la royne au droiet'.

86 BL Cotton MS Titus CX, fol. 77v, 'The First Paper or Memorial/of Sir William Cecil Anno/ primo Elizabethae'.

87 John Strype, *Ecclesiastical memorials, relating chiefly to religion, and the reformation of it: and the emergencies of the Church of England, under King Henry VIII. King Edward VI. and Queen Mary I* (Oxford: Clarendon Press, 1822), vol. 3, 'Catalogue of Originals' no. LXXXI, 277–87, p. 284. Original is at BL Cotton Vesp. D XVIII x, fol. 104.

88 Levin, 'Queens and claimants', p. 43.

89 AGS E 811, fols 25*ff.*, 28*ff.* and 812, *CODOIN*, vol. 87, pp. 83–157. 144 and 154.

90 AGS, E 516, fol. 86: 'Visto que lo de calés no se podía negoçiar tan presto, espeçialmente con ser Muerta la ser[enísi]ma reyna, mi muger, que aya Gloria, que lo he sentido quanto es razón que aun para esto me hará mucha falta, me ha paresçido de venir en lo de la dicha suspensión por no romper la plática y que quede todavía pendiente'. Discussed in a paper by Gonzalo Velasco Berenguer, 'An uncomfortable presence: the Black Legend applied to reign of Philip and Mary 1554–2014', at *The Black Legend Then and Now*, Institute of Historical Research, 27th September 2014, who I would like to thank for sharing this reference with me. The translation in the Calendar reads: 'The Calais question cannot be settled so soon, now

that the Queen, my wife, is dead. May God have received her in His glory! I felt a reasonable regret for her death. I shall miss her, even on this account. I have given my agreement to the prolongation of the truce, in order not to break off with the French, and I shall seek to induce the English to agree to terms making it possible to conclude a peace for the general good', *Cal. Span.* XIII, p. 440.

91   Mayer and Walters, ed., *The Correspondence of Reginald Pole*, vol. 3, p. 172.

92   John Edwards, *Archbishop Pole* (Farnham: Ashgate, 2014), p. 267.

93   José Ignacio Tellechea Idigoras, *El proceso Romano del Arzobispo Carranza (1567–1576)* (Rome: Iglesia Nacional Española, 1988), p. 203: 'voluit Caranzam in Anglia remanere, particpem consiliorum Reginae et Legati, tantique aestimavit prudentiam atque zelum servi Dei, ut illius opera speraret tem catholicam posse confirmari et in melius augeri in eo Regno, eiusdem solicitudine in viam veritatis reducto. Neque fefellit opinionem Philippi Caranza. Is enim ad eradicandam funditus haeresim toto conatu conversus, comples eius flagitii nomine comprehensos, convictos, contumaces, et inter eos Thomam Cranmerum.'

94   *Comentarios del Reverendissimo Señor Frai Batholome Carrança de Miranda, Arçobispo de Toledo, &c. sobre el catechismo Christiano* (Antwerp: Martin Nucio, 1558), sig. iiii r: 'particularmente a Ingaterra'/'se que sera bien recebido de la serenissima Reyna nuestra señora, a quien deue aquella nacion la vida, y salud de sus cuerpos, y de sus almas: y yo perpetua seruidumbre'.

95   See my 'Culture under Philip and Mary I', in Sarah Duncan and Valerie Schutte, eds, *The Birth of a Queen: Essay on the Quincentenary of Mary I* (New York: Palgrave MacMillan, 2016), 155–78.

96   British Library, English Short Title Catalogue S771. Available at http://estc.bl.uk/.

97   This identification was made by Hannah Crumme, 'The politics of Spanish in Elizabethan England', unpublished PhD thesis (King's College London, 2015).

98   *A Very Profitable boke to lerne the maner of redyng, writyng, & speackyng english & Spanish* (London: John Kingston and Henry Sutton for John Wight, 1554), sig. Cv.

99   *A Very Profitable boke*, sig. Cv.

100   *A Very Profitable boke*, sig. Di v.

101   *A Very Profitable boke*, sigs Aii, Cii and Di.

102   *The boke of Englysshe and Spanysshe* (London: Robert Wyer, 1554?), sigs Aii–iii, Ci and Dii.

103   *The boke of Englysshe and Spanysshe*, sigs Aiii and Biii.

104   See the table at the back of Richard Grafton, *A Chronicle at large* (London: Henry Denham, 1568), sig. b.vii.v.

105   Richard Axton, ed., *Three Rastell Plays: Four Elements, Calisto and Melebea, Gentleness and Nobility* (Cambridge: Brewer, 1979), Introduction, pp. 15–20, and text, pp. 16 and 69–96.

106   *The very fruteful and plesant boke calle the Instruction of a Christen Woman*. trans. Richard Hyrde (London: Thomas Berthelet, 1541), sig. E4.

107   Axton, *Three Rastell Plays*, p. 16. On *La Celestina* in England see Gustav Ungerer, *Anglo-Spanish Relations in Tudor Literature* (Bern: Francke Verlag, 1956), pp. 9–41; J. Brault, 'English translations of the *Celestina* in the sixteenth century', *Hispanic Review* 27 (1960), 301–12; and H. D. Purcell, 'The *Celestina* and the *Interlude of Calisto and Melebea*', *Bulletin of Hispanic Studies* 44 (1967), 1–15.

108   Dennis Rhodes, '*Il Moro*: an Italian view of Sir Thomas More' in Chaney and Mack, eds, *England and the Continental Renaissance*, 67–71, pp. 68 and 70.

109   Luis de Avila y Zúñiga, *The comentaries of Don Lewes de Auela, and Suniga, great Master of Acanter, which treateth of the great wars in Germany made by Charles the fifth Maximo Emperoure of Rome, king of Spain, against John Frederike Duke of Saxon, and Philip the Lantgraue of Hesson with other gret princes and Cities of the Lutherans, wherin you may see how god hath preserued this worthie and victorious Emperor, in al his affayres against his enemies translated out of Spanish into English* (London: Richard Tottel, 1555).

110   *The comentaries of Don Lewes de Auela*, tp verso.

111   *The comentaries of Don Lewes de Auela*, sig. Aiii v.

112   John Heywood, *The Spider and the Fly* (London: Thomas Powell, 1556), sig. Nn iv v.

113   Heywood, *The Spider and the Fly*, sig. Ss iii v.
114   Heywood, *The Spider and the Fly*, sig. Ss iii r.
115   These views are summarised in the brilliant essay on the poem by Alice Hunt, 'Marian political allegory: John Heywood's *The Spider and the Fly*', in Mike Pincombe and Cathy Shrank, eds, *The Oxford Handbook of Tudor Literature, 1485–1603* (Oxford: Oxford University Press, 2009), pp. 337–55. See Richard Axton and Peter Happé, *The Plays of John Heywood* (Cambridge: Brewer, 1991), Introduction; Judith Henderson, 'John Heywood's *The Spider and the Fly*: educating queen and country', *Studies in Philology* 96 (1999), 241–74; and James Holstun, '*The Spider and the Fly* and the commonwealth: merrie John Heywood and agrarian class struggle', *English Literary History* 71 (2004), 53–88.
116   Hunt, 'Marian political allegory', p. 341.
117   Heywood, *The Spider and the Fly*, sig. Ss iv r.
118   See the invaluable collection by Pincombe and Shrank, *The Oxford Handbook of Tudor Literature, 1485–1603*.
119   Marie Axton and James Carley, eds, *'Triumphs of English' Henry Parker, Lord Morley Translation to the Tudor Court: New Essays in Interpretation* (London: British Library, 2000), p. 14.
120   Axton and Carley, *'Triumphs of English'*, p. 77.
121   Kenneth Bartlett, 'The occasion of Lord Morley's translation of the *Trionfi*: The Triumph of Chastity over Politics', in *Petrarch's Triumphs. Allegory and Spectacle*, ed. Konrad Eisenblicher and Amilcare A. Iannucci (Ottawa: Dovehouse, 1990), 325–34. The suggestion it was part of a conspiracy to put Maltravers on the throne with Elizabeth as his wife seems to me unlikely.
122   Sydney Anglo, 'Crypto-Machiavellism in early Tudor England: the problem of *ragionamento dell'advenimento...*', *Renaissance et Reforme*, n. s. 2 (1978), 182–93 and P. S. Donaldson, 'George Rainsford's *Ritratto d'Inghiterra* (1556)', *Camden Miscellany* 27 (London: Royal Historical Society, 1979), 49–111.
123   David Loades, *Intrigue and Treason: The Tudor Court 1547–1558* (London: Pearson, 2004), p. vii.
124   Gerry Bowler, 'Marian Protestants and the idea of violent resistance to tyranny' in Peter Lake and Maria Dowling, eds, *Protestantism and the National Church in Sixteenth Century England* (London: Croom Helm, 1987), 124–43, and Jane Dawson, 'Revolutionary conclusions: the case of the Marian exiles', *History of Political Thought* 11 (1990), 257–72.
125   See Ian Maclean, *The Renaissance Notion of Woman: A Study in the Fortunes of Scholasticism and Medical Science in European Intellectual Life*, Cambridge Monographs on the History of Medicine (Cambridge: Cambridge University Press, 1980), p. 61.
126   William Thomas, 'A Second Discourse made by the Same Person for the Kings use' in John Strype, ed., *Memorials especially Ecclesiastical and such as concern Religion*, 3 vols (London: S. Richardson, 1721), vol. II, Appendix S, p. 65. The suggestion has to be made that Edward was being primed by this material to exclude his sisters from the succession.
127   Strype, *Memorials especially Ecclesiastical*, vol. 3, 'Catalogue of Originals' no. LXXXI, 277–87, p. 284. Original is at BL Cott. Vesp. D XVIII x, fol. 104.
128   John Leslie, *Defence of the Honour of Marie Queen of Scots* (Rheims: J. Foigny, 1569), sigs rvi v and rvii v, pp. 136 and 137.
129   See Paula Louise Scalingi, 'The scepter or the distaff: the question of female sovereignty, 1516–1607', *The Historian* 41 (1978), 59–75, p. 70.
130   Constance Jordan, 'Feminism and the humanists: the case of Sir Thomas Elyot's *Defence of Good Women*', *Renaissance Quarterly* 36 (1983), 181–201, p. 191.
131   Levin, 'Queens and claimants', p. 43; see text relating to note 89 above.
132   Sir Thomas Smith, *De Republica Anglorum* (1583), ed. Mary Dewar (Cambridge: Cambridge University Press, 1982), pp. 64–5.
133   Richard Grafton, *An Abridgement of the Chronicles of England* (London: Richard Tottel, 1562), cited by Judith Richards, '"To promote a woman to beare rule": talking of queens in mid-Tudor England', *Sixteenth Century Journal* 28 (1997), 101–21, p. 105.
134   In Maclean, *The Renaissance Notion of Woman*, p. 62. See Torquato Tasso, *Discorso della virtù*

feminile e donnesca (1582) in *Le prose diverse*, ed. Cesare Guasti (Florence: Successori Le Monnier, 1875), II, pp. 203*ff*.

135 Linda Woodbridge, *Women and the English Renaissance: Literature and the Nature of Womankind, 1540–1620* (Chicago: University of Illinois Press, 1984), pp. 5 and 17.

136 Edward Gosynhyll, *The Schole House of Women: wherein euery man may read a goodly prayse of the condicyons of women* (London: John King, 1541), sig. Ai v. See Scalingi, 'The scepter and the distaff', p. 63.

137 Edward Gosynhyll, *The Prayse of All Women Called Mulierum Pean. Very Fruytfull and delectable unto all the reders* (London: Wylyam Myddylton, 1542), sig. Aii r.

138 Stanford E. Lehmberg, *Sir Thomas Elyot: Tudor Humanist* (Austin: Univeristy of Texas Press, 1960), p. 176.

139 Garrett Mattingly, *Catherine of Aragon* (London: Jonathan Cape, 1944), p. 322. See Jordan, 'Feminism and the humanists', pp. 198–200.

140 Maclean, *The Renaissance Notion of Woman*, p. 42.

141 Thomas Laqueur, *Making Sex: Body and Gender from the Greeks to Freud* (Cambridge, Mass.: Harvard University Press, 1990), pp. 35, 52, 96, 108 and 124.

142 Richards, 'To promote a woman to beare rule', p. 116 and note 45.

143 Patricia-Ann Lee, 'A bodye politique to governe: Aylmer, Knox, and the debate on queenship', *The Historian* 52 (1990), 242–61, p. 243.

144 Sir David Lindsay, *The Monarchie* (1st edn, 1552, repr. 1560), Book II, ll. 3247–9, in *The Works of Sir David Lindsay of the Mount (1490–1555)*, ed. Douglas Hamer, 4 vols (London: The Scottish Text Society, William Blackwood and Sons Ltd, 1931), vol. 1, p. 295.

145 Scalingi, 'The scepter and the distaff', p. 73.

146 Christopher Goodman, *How Superior Powers oght to be obeyd of their subiects: and wherin they may lawfully by Gods Worde be disobeyed and resisted* (Geneva: John Crispin, 1st January 1558), pp. 34 and 53–4.

147 *The Zurich Letters*, 2nd ser., ed. Hastings Robinson, The Parker Society, 2 vols (Cambridge: Cambridge University Press, 1845), vol. 2, pp. 34–6.

148 John Knox, *The First Blast of the Trumpet Against the Monstruous regiment of women* Veritas temporis filia* (Geneva: Pierre-Jacques Poullain & Antoine Reboul, 1558), p. 9.

149 Thomas Becon, *An Humble Supplication unto God for the Restoring of His Holy Word Unto the Church of God* (1554) in *Prayers and Other Pieces of Thomas Becon*, ed. Rev. J. Ayre (Cambridge: Parker Society, 1844), p. 227.

150 Jan Machielson, 'The lion, the witch, and the king: Thomas Stapleton's *Apologia pro Rege Catholico Philippo II* (1592)', *English Historical Review* 129 (2014), 19–46, p. 36.

151 Levin, 'Queens and claimants', p. 43.

152 Susan Doran, 'Juno versus Diana: the treatment of Elizabeth I's marriage in plays and entertainments, 1561–1581', *The Historical Journal* 38 (1995), 257–74. See also Helen Hackett, *Virgin Mother, Maiden Queen: Elizabeth and the Cult of the Virgin Mary* (Basingstoke: Macmillan, 1995), esp. pp. 1–37.

153 Cited by Annaliese Connolly, 'Evaluating virginity: *A Midsummer Night's Dream* and the iconography of marriage', in Lisa Hopkins and Annaliese Connolly, eds, *Goddesses and Queens: the Iconography of Elizabeth I* (Manchester: Manchester University Press, 2007) 136–53, p. 145.

154 Philippa Berry, *Of Chastity and Power: Elizabethan Literature and the Unmarried Queen* (London: Routledge, 1989), p. 78.

155 John Aylmer, *An Harborowe for Faithful and Trewe Subiectes Agaynst the late blowne Blaste, concerninge the Gouernment of Wemen* (Strasbourg [London]: John Day, 26th April 1559), sig. Giii.

156 See on this question Margaret Sommerville, *Sex and Subjection: Attitudes to Women in Early Modern Society* (London: Arnold, 1995), pp. 58–9.

157 Keith Thomas, *Religion and the Decline of Magic: Studies in Popular Beliefs in Sixteenth and Seventeenth Century England* (London: Penguin, repr. 1991), pp. 494–501.

158 See Paul Strohm, 'The trouble with Richard: the reburial of Richard II and Lancastrian symbolic strategy', *Speculum* 71 (1996), 87–111, p. 94.

159 Strohm, 'The trouble with Richard', pp. 94–108: 'se non habere judicem inter eos, vivente ligeo domino sui in regno Scotiae'.

160 *APC*, n. s. IV (1552–4), pp. 363–4 and 367.

161 *APC*, n. s. IV, pp. 383–4.

162 *Machyn's Diary*, pp. 86–7. The other, Edward Fetherstone, is mentioned by Strype, *Memorials especially Ecclesiastical*, vol. 3, p. 286.

163 *Cal. Ven.*, VI, pt. I (1555–6), p. 85. Giovanni Michiel to Doge and Senate, 27th May 1555.

164 *Machyn's Diary*, p. 88.

165 *Cal. Ven.*, VI, pt. I (1555–6), p. 324. Giovanni Michiel to Doge and Senate, 21st January 1556.

166 *APC*, n. s. V (1554–6), pp. 221 and 228.

167 *Cal. Ven.*, VI, pt. I (1555–6), p. 339. Giovanni Michiel to Doge and Senate, 5th February 1556. Extant manuscripts prophesying Edward's return are at BL Sloane 2578, fols 18v, 20, and 32.

168 Thomas, *Religion and the Decline of Magic*, p. 499. On this section see Levin, 'Queens and claimants', pp. 50–55.

169 Diarmaid MacCulloch, ed. and trans., 'The *Vitae Mariae Angliae Reginae* of Robert Wingfield of Brantham', in *Camden Miscellany XXVIII*, Camden Society 4th ser., XXIX (London: Royal Historical Society, UCL, 1984), pp. 291–2: 'eo reginae haereditorio honore insigniendo, durante vita dignissimae reginae suae consortis', p. 242. My italics.

170 Macculloch, 'The *Vitae Mariae Angliae Reginae* of Robert Wingfield of Brantham', p. 252.

171 Macculloch, 'The *Vitae Mariae Angliae Reginae* of Robert Wingfield of Brantham', p. 293.

172 The continuities between the reigns of Mary and Elizabeth, in terms of the language and conceptualisation of Elizabeth's authority and government, owe more to the example of Mary than has previously been acknowledged. See Paulina Kewes, 'Two queens, one inventory: the lives of Mary and Elizabeth Tudor' in Kevin Sharpe and Steven Zwicker, eds, *Writing Lives: Biography and Textuality, Identity and Representation in Early Modern England* (Oxford: Oxford University Press, 2008), 187–207.

173 A recent consideration of this aspect of the marriage is found in Jesús Pascual Molina, '"Porque vean y sepan cuánto es el poder y grandeza de nuestro Príncipe y Señor": Imagen y poder en el viaje de Felipe II a Inglaterra y su matrimonio con María Tudor', *Reales Sitios* 197 (2013), 6–26.

174 See the lavish collection of essays on the window, analysing its heraldic significance and political importance, in Wim de Groot, ed., *The Seventh Window: The King's Window Donated by Philip II and Mary Tudor to Sint Janskerk in Gouda (1557)* (Hilversum: Verloren, 2005) and Corinna Streckfuss, '"Spes maxima nostri": the marriage of Mary Tudor and Philip of Spain in its European propaganda context' in Hunt and Whitelock, eds, *Tudor Queenship*, 145–58. The window is alluded to in Judith Richards, *Mary Tudor* (Abingdon: Routledge, 2008), p. 239.

175 J. B. Owens, *'By My Absolute Royal Authority': Justice and the Castilian Commonwealth at the Beginning of the First Global Age* (Rochester, NY: University of Rochester Press, 2005), p. 215.

176 Patrick Williams, *The Great Favourite: The Duke of Lerma and the court and government of Philip III of Spain* (Manchester: Manchester University Press, 2006). He leapt from 57th in the list of aristocratic incomes before 1598 to double the next closest grandee, the duke of Medina Sidonia.

177 Ernst Kantorowicz, *The King's Two Bodies: A Study in Medieval Political Theology* (Princeton, NJ: Princeton University Press, 1957), p. 381.

178 Theresa Earenfight, ed., *Queenship and Political Power in Medieval and Early Modern Spain* (Aldershot: Ashgate, 2005), Preface by editor, pp. xiii–xiv. For interesting Spanish views of queenship in the pre-modern period, see the proscriptive ideas found in Alfonso X's *Siete partidas* and *Espéculo*, and the descriptive one in Jaume II of Aragón's *Llibre dels Feyts*. A digital edition of the manuscript of the *Siete partidas* is available through the Biblioteca Digital Hispánica [http://bdh.bne.es/bnesearch/detalle/2700287], the *Espéculo* can be viewed here [www.boe.es/publicaciones/biblioteca_juridica/publicacion.

php?id=PUB-LH-2018-92_OP%C3%9ASCULOS_DEL_REY_SABIO_EL_ESP%C3 %89CULO&tipo=L&modo=1], while the *Llibre dels Feyts* is available on Cervantes Virtual [www.cervantesvirtual.com/portales/clasicos_en_la_biblioteca_nacional/obra-visor/llib re-dels-feits-del-rei-en-jacme-manuscrit--0/html/].

179   From Ormisinda, the daugher of Pelayo in the eighth century, to Sancha of León, Elvira of Castile, Urraca of León and Berenguela of Castile, in the twelfth and thirteenth centuries, María de Molina in the thirteenth and early fourteenth century, Catalina of Lancaster in the fifteenth, there are numerous examples of co-ruling, regent and regnant queens in medieval Iberia.

180   See Theresa Earenfight, 'Absent kings: queens as political partners in the medieval crown of Aragon' and Ana Echevarria-Asuaga, 'The queen and the master: Catalina of Lancaster and the military orders', in Earenfight, *Queenship and Power*, pp. 34, 96. A number of these precedents were cited by the chronicler Hernando de Pulgar in the context of Ferdinand and Isabella's marriage: see Peggy Liss, *Isabel the Queen: Life and Times* (2nd edn, Philadelphia: University of Pennsylvania Press, 2004), p. 114.

181   Issued by Paul II on 23rd June 1469.

182   Diego Dormer, *Discursos varios de historia; con muchas escrituras reales antiguas, y notas a algunas dellas* (Zaragoza: Herederos de Diego Dormer, 1683), pp. 296–7. All translations are my own, unless otherwise noted.

183   BNE MS 9937: Florián de Ocampo, *Sucesos Acaecidos, 1550–1558 and 1521–1549*, fol. 126v.

184   Andrés Muñoz, *Viaje de Felipe Segundo a Inglaterra* (Zaragoza, 1554), 'Tercera Carta', p. 118. See also Loades, *The Tudor Court*, p. 26.

185   *CODOIN*, vol. 3, p. 530.

186   *CODOIN*, vol. 3, p. 530.

187   Murphy, 'The illusion of decline: the Privy Chamber, 1547–1558', p. 141.

188   See Jennifer Wollock, 'Medieval England and Iberia: a chivalric relationship', in María Bullón-Fernández, ed., *England and Iberia in the Middle Ages, 12th–15th Centuries* (New York: Palgrave Macmillan, 2007), 11–28, on continuities and mutual influences through chivalry.

189   Pascual Molina, 'Porque vean y sepan', p. 14.

190   Alan Young, *Tudor and Jacobean Tournaments* (London: George Philip, 1987), pp. 30–2, 201. The challenge of Lord Strange has two small drawings of foot combat at barriers with swords and then staves, on pp. 32 and 82. Original at BL Cotton MS Vitellius F. v.

191   Pascual Molina, 'Porque vean y sepan', p. 13: 'sedas plata oro e otras mercaderías que del se tomaron para el juego de cañas que yo hize en esta dicha ciudad de Londres en el dicho mes de noviembre'. Original is at AGS CMC, 1a epoca, leg. 1184.

192   Francisco Sanchez, *Relacion muy verdadera de la bienauenturada nueua de la conuersion de los Ingleses luteranos, hechas por Francisco Sanchez estudiante, natural de la villa de Orgaz* (Salamanca: Juan de Cánova, 1555), sig. aiii r: 'Por quinze dias mandaron/que se hagan alegrias/en los quales se sacaron/disfraces que no cesaron/de salir noches y dias. [next stanza] Muchos toros se corrieron/jugauan a la sortija/carros triumphales salieron/juegos de cañas se hizieron/ cada qual se regozija.'

193   Richard McCoy, 'From the Tower to the tiltyard: Robert Dudley's return to glory', *The Historical Journal* 27 (1984), 425–35.

194   Christopher Highley, *Catholics Writing the Nation in Early Modern Britain and Ireland* (Oxford: Oxford University Press, 2008), p. 153.

195   See the excellent monograph by Rory Rapple, *Martial Power and Elizabethan Political Culture: Military Men in England and Ireland, 1558–1594* (Cambridge: Cambridge University Press, 2009).

196   National Archives SP11/6, no. 20.

197   *Epistolario del III Duque de Alba*, p. 77.

198   AGS E 808, fol. 21. *Cal. Span.*, XIII, p. 97: 'Yo querria mucho justificar mis actiones para con todo el mundo de no pretender estados agenos y para con V. Mt. no solo las actiones mas aun los pensamientos'. Philip to Emperor, 16th November 1554.

199 Luis de Cabrera y Córdoba, *Felipe Segundo, Rey de España* (Madrid: Luis Sánchez, 1619; in modern edn, Aribau, 1876–7), p. 19.

200 Real Academia de Historia, Salazar y Castro A–52: *Cartas de Felipe II del Emperador, Principes y otras personas 1555 siguientes*, esp. fol. 53v.

201 *Relations Politiques Des Pays-Bas et de l'Angleterre*, vol. 1, p. 61 (Letter no. LXVI, Josse de Courteville to President Viglius, 25th March 1557): '[v]ous entendés bien qu'il n'y avoit faulte spectateurs, ni de honoy. A mon jugement, la commune s'en contenta bien et le receut allêrement'. I would like to thank Matthew Tibble for pointing out this reference and sharing his fascinating reseach on the period with me.

202 Real Academia de Historia, Salazar y Castro A–52, fol. 56v. 28th April 1557.

203 Cabrera y Córdoba, *Felipe Segundo*, p. 19.

204 Cabrera y Córdoba, *Felipe Segundo*, p. 19. See the section discussing 'Curtesie of England' in Thomas Edgar, *The Lawes Resolutions of Womens Rights: Or, the Lawes Provision for Woemen. A Methodicall Collection of such Statutes and Customes, with the Cases, Opinions, Arguments and points of Learning in the Law, as doe concerne Women* (London: John Moore, 1632).

205 *Willobie his Auisa. Or the true picture of a modest maid, and of a chast and constant wife* (London: John Windet, 1594), fols 15ʳ, 16ʳ⁻ᵛ.

206 *Willobie his Auisa*, fol. 3ᵛ. See Patricia Shaw, 'Philip II and seduction *à la española* in an Elizabethan *roman à clef*' in *Actas del II Congreso de la Sociedad Española de Estudios Renacentistas Ingleses*, ed. S. G. Fernández-Corugedo (Oviedo: Universidad de Oviedo, 1992), 289–302, pp. 292–3. Agrippa's *De Vanitate Scientarum* had been published in Latin in 1530 and translated into English in 1575.

207 See Sandra Clark, 'Spanish characters and English nationalism in English drama of the early seventeenth century', *Bulletin of Hispanic Studies* 84 (2007), 131–44.

208 Shakespeare referred to *caballeros* in 1597, through Shallow in *Henry IV, Part II*: 'I'll drink to Master Bardolph and to all his cavlieroes about London', 5.3.60 (Norton Shakespeare based on Oxford edition).

209 *Willobie his Auisa*, fol. 15v.

210 Sir Francis Hastings, *A watch-word to all religious, and true hearted English-men* (London: Felix Kingston for Ralph Jackson, 1598), p. 90.

211 Hastings, *A watch-word*, pp. 82–3, 101.

212 See Herbert Grabes, 'England or the Queen?: Public conflict of opinion and national identity under Mary Tudor', in his *Writing the Early Modern English Nation: The Transformation of National Identity in Sixteenth- and Seventeenth-Century England* (Amsterdam: Rodopi, 2001), 47–87.

213 David Howarth, *Images of Rule: Art and Politics in the English Renaissance, 1485–1649* (Basingstoke: Macmillan, 1997), p. 101.

214 Howarth, *Images of Rule*, p. 100.

215 On all of this see the excellent monograph by Joanna Woodall, *Anthonis Mor: Art and Authority* (Zwolle: Waanders Publishers, 2007), 199–293, p. 268.

216 Woodall, *Anthonis Mor*, p. 275.

217 Susan James, *The Feminine Dynamic in English Art, 1485–1603* (Farnham: Ashgate, 2009), chapter 7, 'The Queen's Painter: Lievine Teerlinc', 287–321, p. 298. See KB 27/1168/2, Coram Rege roll, Michaelmas 1553 and 'Binnick sheet', BL Add. MS 12531, fol. 4.

218 On these images see P. G. Matthews, 'Portaits of Philip II of Spain as King of England', *The Burlington Magazine* 142 (2000), pp.13–19.

Conclusion

A positive new vision of Mary I is emerging from the work of numerous scholars.[1] This book has sought to build on and extend these ideas, foregrounding evidence for the joint reign's importance from a constitutional, cultural, political and historical perspective. That England had a Spanish king in the sixteenth century still comes as a surprise to many, reflecting how resistant to revisionist history public and popular understandings of the period have proved. The argument has explored the dynamics of this exclusion, analysing why Mary and Philip have been persistently marginal in Tudor historiography. Versions of the Black Legend already established by this time in Italy and the German lands influenced the form taken by the polemic and propaganda of evangelical Marian exiles. Such vitriolic and intemperate attacks circulated largely among literate elites and did not form the basis for a more generalised Hispanophobia, something that would not be consolidated until after the Dutch Revolt and the Armada, and the essentialist, racialised readings of the Spanish that became commonplace in the literature and drama of the 1590s.[2] Understanding the Reformation as a movement of national liberation, a casting off of foreign tyranny and oppression, has occluded the huge complexity of the ways in which ordinary people responded to religious change, but more importantly underlies the pernicious sense of the Marian period as un-English, a time when not only was the pope restored, but the kingdom was subject to a foreign prince.

As we have seen, this notion rests on the mistaken assumption that a small group of radicals represented England, when in fact Catholic restoration was popularly welcomed and a reinvigorated church and spirituality transformed the religious landscape through clerical education, an insistence on preaching and theological innovations. This was not a wholesale reversal; rather, it built on the experiments and innovations of the previous two decades. If relations between England and Spain have been mischaracterised by reading them through the lens of the Armada rather than two major dynastic marriages, religious conflict has equally been flattened out by simplistic and anachronistic readings of difference. It is important to attend to the fluidity of religious positions, in a reign straddled by the Council of Trent. While a savage persecution of heresy led to the deaths of more than 300 people, many committed evangelicals not only survived but were close participants in the regime from Edward Underhill to Anne Bacon and Thomas Geminus; whether their conformity represented an incipient Nicodemism or acceptance of a state's right to determine forms of worship regardless of distinct individuals' beliefs. This is not to suggest that emergent or traditional theological positions did not have vociferous and sometimes violent proponents. Conflicts between faith and secular allegiances sharpened as the sixteenth century wore on and Europe became embroiled in religious wars.

Related to this Manichean simplification of religious differences is under-estimating the complexity of the political arrangement marrying Tudor England and Habsburg Spain. On one hand, there is the inadequacy of identifying groups as Spanish or English. Philip's entourage was multinational, multilingual and while dominated by Iberians, included Dutch, Germans, Italians and others; each of these labels in turn a generalisation involving further simplification. On the other, the Hispanic monarchy, house of Austria or the Spains dub a con-glomeration of polycentric, internally divided states over which Philip ruled, held together by personal fealty to the monarch. England's insular, peripheral status in the period has generated an expectation of greater homogeneity than pertained in imperial states like his. The notion that he harboured sinister intentions towards England makes little sense in this context and is easily disproved by correcting the distortions produced in the nineteenth century *Calendars*. Iberian kings 'were far from theocratic and... worked closely with their queens as political partners'.[3] This expectation is apparent in the Spanish sources. For many commentators though, the contradiction for a ruling queen between her monarchical role and enjoined subservience to her husband 'made Mary I miserable and kept Elizabeth I celibate'.[4] I hope that the foregoing pages have shown that the marriage did not make Mary miserable. The failure to pro-duce an heir cannot have been anything other than painful and difficult and no matter how well understood by them, the demands of empire took their toll on both partners. However, from the actual evidence it is clear the marriage was a huge success, incorporating England into the heart of a global empire, a forerunner of its own, and producing considerable and lasting contributions in music, painting, poetry, political philosophy, court and print culture. Far from lacking identity, the Anglo-Spanish world's hybridity and heterogeneity produced a ferment of creativity and innovation from cartography to theology, exploration and enterprise; the earliest copperplate maps printed in England, the Tunis tapestries, portraits by Antonis Mor and Titian, Stephen Borough's visit to the Casa de Contratación, the foundation of the Muscovy Company in 1555 (the first chartered joint stock company) and establishment of links with the court of Ivan the Terrible, and the incorporation of the Stationer's Company by Royal Charter.

Their marriage is a unique case for gender history. Anxieties about the marriage exacerbated by English inexperience of female regnancies have too easily been conflated with broader misogynist assumptions common in the period and since. A fundamental misunderstanding of the intersectional relationship between gender and blood has seen Mary cast as a tragic, stupid or cowed figure. Nothing could be further from the truth. Formidable and sophisticated, the stability of her regime despite famine induced by two years of harvest failure and an influenza epidemic that reduced the population by as much as 6 per cent and may have ultimately killed Mary herself, are testament to these political abilities, of which the marriage itself is another example.[5] She reformed the coinage, successfully reintroduced traditional religion and laid the constitutional changes that would allow her sister to rule.[6] In Anna Whitelock's pithy judgement, far from being 'a weak-willed and easily influenced woman distant from politics and policy-making, Mary can be understood as a determined and resolute monarch who ultimately proved to be very much her own woman'.[7] If Mary has been fundamentally misjudged, Philip's active and highly public participation in jousting and martial tourneys underlines how far this figure is from the Counter-Reformation fundamentalist of legend. According to her confessor, one of Mary's ladies in waiting, Madgalena Dacre, was accosted while washing herself by Philip reaching in through an open window. She repelled the assault with blows from a stick, something the king did not take badly.[8] Philip's womanising, despite slanderous and nasty gossip such as that in *The Lamentacion of England* (1557) – 'his spanierds have blasid abrode in other contres saieng what shall the king do with such an old bich, also affirmeing that she may be his mother, a yonger is more meter for him' – can hardly be taken as evidence of his dislike of the marriage itself.[9]

The sources themselves have presented a considerable barrier to research on the reign, dispersed across multiple archives, countries and languages. In the same way that this complexity has bolstered the persistence of certain myths about Mary and Philip, it has also hampered recognising the co-monarchy's cultural achievements. The period witnessed some of the earliest vernacular stirrings – Tottel's *Miscellany* in England, and *Lazarillo de Tormes* in Spain – but most culture of the period cannot be read or understood according to the national categories through which we have corralled its study since the nineteenth century. Reflecting on Francis Bacon's 'Certain Articles or Considerations Touching the Union of the Kingdoms of Scotland and England' that created Britain ('none can be an Alien but he that is of another allegiance'), Willy Maley comments that 'the British project is, on one level, an alternative to the continent, an attempt to establish "another Europe". The fact that we can still speak of British *and* European history is one measure of the success of that project.'[10] The Marian period was probably the last time that we were all Europeans. In the original version of a recent government's publication *Life in the United Kingdom: a Journey to Citizenship*, it was claimed that Mary I 'came to the throne with Spanish support', rather than through the defeat of Northumberland in a well-prepared counterattack that relied on her popularity and the religious sympathies of the majority in England.[11] While this particular publication was produced under considerable time pressure and full of mistakes, *this* mistake is telling, foregrounding the extraordinary persistence of sectarian and providentialist Anglican history, informed by parochial, anti-Catholic assumptions that go on obscuring the true legacy of Mary and her Spanish husband. While presentist comparisons can be reductive as much as illuminating, the frequent invocation of the Reformation as the original Brexit by politicians, journalists and schools forces Mary into the unexpected role of Bloody Remainiac. The oddity of this comparison reminds us how much our history turns on the connections and disconnections out of which we fabricate it.

At Charles II's Restoration in 1661, the Spanish ambassador's coach was 'escorted by a crowd, which came out of all the shops, applauding the event with words and cries, showing great affection for Spain, even ringing bells in some places, and followed the coach to the very embassy'.[12] Robert Persons' vision of historic Anglo-Spanish harmony in *Newes from Spayne and Holland* culminates in the narrator's visit to the English Church of St George in Sanlúcar, Seville, whose existence reminds the reader of:

> larger patterns of commercial, religious, and political/dynastic exchange that have historically bound the two countries together... notions of an essential incompatibility between the two people and of a threat of contamination to English visitors in Spain are simply Protestant fictions.[13]

The significance of the reign of Philip and Mary lies in what its historiographical misfortunes say about the nature of and writing of history itself. Its marginalisation bears a direct relationship to a particular version of English identity and reflects how big a part confessional difference has gone on playing in that historiography. The acceptability of Mary's foreign marriage will no doubt continue to inflect the evolving relationship between Britain and Europe, and its cultural politics. While there is no major monument to Mary I in England, her tomb lying below that of her half-sister in Westminster Abbey, in Madrid a tube station was named María Tudor after her in 2007, on a street of the same name. Although there have been a wealth of new publications on Mary, it feels as if we are at the start rather than their marking a new consensus about her and her reign. Many avenues remain unexplored, from manuscript sources like the Granvelle papers or Ogden manuscripts, to accounts from other witnesses and observers such as the French doctor Étienne Perlin who wrote a description of England and Scotland published in 1559.[14] It feels as though the field of Marian studies is only just opening up.

Notes

1 Glyn Redworth, Judith Richards, Anna Whitelock, John Edwards, Linda Porter, Sarah Duncan, Thomas Freeman, Susan Doran and Eamon Duffy amongst others have all built on the interest in mid-Tudor England renewed by Jennifer Loach and Robert Tittler in 1980.

2 On this see both Eric Griffin, *English Renaissance Drama and the Specter of Spain: Ethnopoetics and Empire* (Philadelphia: University of Pennsylvania Press, 2009) and Barbara Fuchs, *The Poetics of Piracy: Emulating Spain in English Literature* (Philadelphia: University of Pennsylvania Press, 2013).

3 Theresa Earenfight, 'Without the persona of the Prince: kings, queens and the idea of monarch in late medieval Europe', *Gender and History* 19 (2007), 1–21, p. 6.

4 Lucy Hughes-Hallett, review of Maureen Waller, *Sovereign Ladies*, 'How ridiculous!', *Times Literary Supplement*, 23rd March 2007, p. 36.

5 John Moore, 'Jack Fisher's flu: a visitation revisited', *Economic History Review* 46 (1993), 280–307; Michael Zell, 'Fisher's flu and Moore's probates: quantifying the mortality crisis, 1556–60', *Economic History Review* 47 (1994), 354–8; John Moore, 'Jack Fisher's flu: a virus still virulent', *Economic History Review* 47 (1994), 359–61.

6 On finance see J. Alsop, 'Nicholas Brigham (*d.* 1558): scholar, antiquary and crown servant', *Sixteenth Century Journal* 12 (1981), 49–67 and Christopher Coleman, 'Artifice or accident? The reorganization of the Exchequer of Receipt, *c.* 1554–1572' in Coleman and David Starkey, eds, *Revolution Reassessed: Revisions in the History of Tudor Government and Administration* (Oxford: Clarendon Press, 1986), esp. pp. 176–7.

7 Anna Whitelock, 'A woman in a man's world: Mary I and political intimacy, 1553–1558', *Women's History Review* 16 (2007), 323–34, p. 328 and 'Mary Tudor: the first queen of England', in Liz Oakley-Brown and Louise Wilkinson, eds, *The Rituals and Rhetoric of Queenship: Medieval to Early Modern* (Dublin: Four Courts, 2009), 59–73, p. 70.

8 Geoffrey Parker, *Felipe II: La biografía definitiva* (Madrid: Planeta, 2010), p. 500. See also Harry Kelsey, *Philip of Spain, King of England: The Forgotten Sovereign* (London: I. B. Tauris, 2012), p. 129.

9 *The Lamentacion of England* (Germany?: n. p., 1557), sig. A7 r.

10 *The Letters and the Life of Francis Bacon*, ed. James Spedding (London: Longman, 1868), vol. 4, pp. 218–34. Willy Maley, '"Another Britain"?: Bacon's certain considerations touching the plantation in Ireland (1609)', *Prose Studies* 18 (1995), 1–18, p. 10.

11 Lee Glendinning, 'Citizenship guide fails its history exam', *The Guardian*, 29th April 2006: available from www.theguardian.com/uk/2006/apr/29/immigration.immigrationpolicy [Accessed: 3rd September 2015].

12 Nigel Goose, '"Xenophobia" in Elizabethan and early Stuart England: an epithet too far' in Nigel Goose and Lien Luu, eds, *Immigrants in Tudor and Early Stuart England* (Brighton: Sussex Academic Press, 2005), 110–35, p. 128.

13 Christopher Highley, *Catholics Writing the Nation in Early Modern Britain and Ireland* (Oxford: Oxford University Press, 2008), p. 175

14 For example, Sir Henry Bedingfield's papers at Oxburgh Hall or the cache of papers from the Marian period now in UCL's Special Collections, Ogden MS 7/1. There are also exciting contributions from early-career scholars like Gonzalo Velasco Berenguer, María Pascual Ortega and Matthew Tibble. Étienne Perlin is cited in Isabelle Fernandes, *Marie Tudor: La souffrance du pouvoir* (Paris: Tallandier, 2016), p. 183.

Bibliography

Manuscripts

Archivo General de Protocolos, Madrid
    Protocolo No. 5
Archivo General de Simancas
    CJH 23, 29, 30
    E 98, 103, 112, 114, 117, 119, 120, 121, 131, 139, 306, 322, 510, 512, 516,
    807, 808, 811, 812, 1492, 1498
    Indiferente 858
Real Biblioteca del Monasterio de San Lorenzo de El Escorial
    V.ii.3 and V.ii.4
Biblioteca del Palacio Real, Madrid
    II 2318, II 255, II 2285 and 2286: *Correspondencia de Granvela*
Biblioteca Nacional de España, Madrid
    430, 638, 706, 721, 764, 765, 815, 907, 912, 1013, 1029, 1080, 1088, 1167,
    1181, 1293, 1305, 1317, 1443, 1517, 1723, 1750, 1751, 1778, 1881, 1890,
    1922, 2349, 9936, 9937, 13267, 18408
Bibliothéque National, Paris
    Map Room, Réserve Ge B 2112, Ge C 5177
Bodleian Library
    Tanner 84
    Wood F33
British Library
    Additional: 12531, 28449, 29546, 34320, 35840, 38135, 62135, Ch. 62464,
    71009
    Cotton: Galba CIII, Titus CVII, Titus CX, Titus BII, Titus BXI, Titus FII,
    Vespasian CVII, CXII, CXIII and F III, Vitellius CI
    Egerton: 415, 763, 1832, 1888
    Harleian: 353, 419, 540, 559, 6166, 6234, 6807
    Lansdowne: 3, 103, 156, 1236
    Royal: 12 AXX, 17 B XXVIII, Appendix 89

College of Arms
    WB, I 7 and I 18
Corpus Christi College Library, Cambridge
    127
Lambeth Palace Library, Manuscript 285
London Metropolitan Archives
    Repertory of the Court of Aldermen 13
    Mercers' Company, Acts of Court, ii
    Drapers' Company, MB 6
The National Archives
    SP 10/1, 11/1, 2, 3, 6 and 9, 69/4
    E 159/334
    KB8/37
Real Academia de Historia, Madrid
    Salazar y Castro, F–17 and A–52
University College London Special Collections
    Ogden MS 7/1
Winchester College Archives, Liber Albus 22992

State papers

Bain, Joseph (ed.), *Calendar of State Papers, Scotland*, vol. 1, *1547–63* (London: HMSO, 1898)

Brown, Rawdon, ed., *Calendar of State Papers and Manuscripts, Relating to English Affairs etc., Venetian*, vols V–VII (London: Longman & Co. 1873–90)

Calendar of Letters, Despatches, and State Papers, Relating to the Negotiations Between England and Spain, vol. 1, ed. G. Bergenroth (London: Longman, Green, Longman & Roberts, 1862), vols 11–13, ed. Royall Tyler (London: HMSO, 1916–54)

Calendar of Patent Rolls: Philip and Mary, 4 vols (London: HMSO, 1936–9)

Calendar of State Papers, Domestic: Edward VI, Mary, Elizabeth I, and James I, 12 vols (London: 1856–72)

Calendar of State Papers, Foreign: Edward VI, Mary, Elizabeth I, 25 vols (London: 1861–1950)

Letters and Papers, Foreign and Domestic, Henry VIII, 21 vols (London: HMSO, 1864–1920)

Navarete, Fernando (ed.), *Colección de Documentos Inéditos para la Historia de España*, 113 vols (Madrid: 1842–95)

Roche Dasent, John (ed.), *Acts of the Privy Council*, New Series, vols 4–6 (London: HMSO, 1892–3)

Statutes of the Realm, 11 vols (London: Dawsons of Pall Mall, repr. 1963)

Primary sources

Anonymous works and collections

Ambassades de Messieurs de Noailles en Angleterre, ed. R. A. Vertot, 5 vols (Leyden: Dessaint & Saillant, Durand, 1763)

A very profitable boke to lerne the maner of redyng, writyng, speakyng english & spanish (London: John Kingston and Henry Sutton for John Wight, 1554)

Boke of Englysshe and Spanysshe, The (London: Robert Wyer, 1554?)

Chronicle of the Grey Friars of London, Camden Society 1st ser., LIII (London: J. B. Nichols and Son, 1851)

Comentarios del Reverendissimo Señor Frai Batholome Carrança de Miranda, Arçobispo de Toleod, &c. sobre el catechismo Christiano (Antwerp: Martin Nucio, 1558)

Copia d'una lettera scritta all'illustriss. S. Francesco Taverna Crancanz etc. (Milan: F. and S. Moscheni, 1554)

Coppie of the Anti-Spaniard, The (London: John Wolf, 1590)

Discourse upon the Exposicion & Understandinge of Statutes with Sir Thomas Egerton's Additions, A (c. 1557–1571), ed. Samuel E. Thorne (California: Huntington Library, 1942)

Dos cartas la vna de la serenissima reyna de Inglaterra, embiada a la Serenissima princesa de Portugal, de la reducion de los Ingleses a la obediencia de la yglesia Romana. Y la otra de vn cauallero haziendo saber como los Ingleses han hallado vans nueuas Indias (Toledo?: Borbon librero del Duque de Maqueda y marques Delche, 1555?)

Fourth Report of the Deputy Keeper of the Public Records (London: William Clawes and Sons for HMSO, 1843)

La solemne et felice intrata delli Serenissimi Re Philippo, et Regina Maria d'Inghilterra, nella Regal città di Londra (Rome?: 1554)

La Vida de Lazarillo de Tormes, y sus fortunas y aduersidades (Antwerp: Martin Nucio, 1554)

Lamentacion of England, The (Germany: n. p., 1557)

Procesos Inquisitoriales contra la familia judia de Juan Luis Vives. I. Proceso contra Blanquina March (1528–9), madre del Humanista, transcribed by Miguel de la Pinta Llorente and José María de Palacio y de Palacio (Madrid: Instituto Arias Montano, 1964)

Supplicacyon to the quenes Maiestie, A (Strasbourg: W. Rihel, 26th January 1555)

Willobie his Auisa. Or the true picture of a modest maid, and of a chast and constant wife (London: John Windet, 1594)

Other

Alba, Third Duke of, *Epistolario del III Duque de Alba Don Fernando Alvarez de Toledo*, ed. 17th duke of Alba, 3 vols (Madrid: Real Academia de la Historia, 1952)

Apocrypha, The (Cambridge: Cambridge University Press, 1895)

Arber, Edward, ed., *A Transcript of the Company of Stationers of London, 1554–1640*, 5 vols (London: Privately printed, 1875)

——, *An English Garner: Tudor Tracts, 1532–1588*, intro. by A. F. Pollard (Westminster: Archibald Constable and Co., Ltd, repr. 1903)

Ascham, Roger, *The Scholemaster: Or plaine and perfite way of teachyng children... the Latin tong* (London: John Day, 1570)

——, *The Whole Works of Roger Ascham*, 3 vols, ed. J. Giles (London: John Russell Smith, 1865)

Augustine, Saint, *A Select Library of the Nicene and Post-Nicene Fathers of the Christian Church*, Vol. V: *Anti-Pelagian Writings*, ed. Philip Schaff (Michigan: Wm. B. Eerdmans Publishing Co., 1956)

Avila y Zúñiga, Luis de, *The comentaries of Don Lewes de Auela, and Suniga, great Master of Acanter, which treateth of the great wars in Germany made by Charles the fifth Maximo Emperoure of Rome, king of Spain, against John Frederike Duke of Saxon, and Philip the Lantgraue of Hesson with other gret princes and Cities of the Lutherans, wherin you may see how god hath preserued this worthie and victorious Emperor, in al his affayres against his enemies translated out of Spanish into English* (London: Richard Tottel, 1555)

Aylmer, John, *An Harborowe for Faithful and Trewe Subjectes Agaynst the late blowne Blaste, concerninge the Gouernment of Wemen* (Strasbourg [London]: John Day, 26th April 1559)

Bale, John, attr., *An Admonishion to the Bishoppes of Winchester, London and others &c. Ecclesia, v. Make no tariying to turne vnto the Lord and put not of from daie to daie, for sodenly shal his wrath come, & in time of vengeance he shall destroye the. ¶ From Roane by Michael wood, Anno. M. D. Liii. the first of October* (London: John Day, 1553)

——, attr., *The Communication betwene my Lord Chauncelor and iudge Hales, being among other iudges to take his oth in Westminster hall. Anno. M. D. Liii. Vi. of October* (London: John Day[?], 1553)

——, *The uocacyon of Johan Bale to the bishiprick of Ossorie in Irelande his persecucions in the same & finall delyueraunce* (Rome [Wesel?]: [J. Lambrecht for Hugh Singleton?], 1554)

——, *A declaration of Edmonde Bonners articles, concerning the cleargye of London dyocese whereby that execrable Antychriste, is in his righte colours reueled in the yeare of our Lord a. 1554 Newlye set fourth & allowed according to the order appointed in the Quenes Maiesties Iniunctions. Woo to them whiche builde in bloude & iniquity. Mich. iii. All thinges, whan they are rebuked of the lyght are manyfest. Ephe v.* (London: John Tysdall for Frauncis Coldocke, 1561)

——, *The Dramatic Writings of John Bale Bishop of Ossory*, ed. J. S. Farmer (fac. edn of Early English Text Society's 1907 edn,, Guildford: Charles Traylen, 1966)

Ball, Rachael and Geoffrey Parker, eds, *Como ser rey. Instrucciones del Emperador Carlos V a su hijo Felipe. Mayo de 1543* (New York: HSA, CEEH, CSA, 2014)

Bansley, Charles, *A Treatyse Shewing and Declering The Pryde and Abuse of Women Now A Dayes* (c. 1550), ed. John Payne Collier (London: repr. from a unique copy [Thomas Raynalde, 1550], 1841)

Baskerville, E. J., *A Chronological Bibliography of Propaganda and Polemic Published in England between 1553 and 1558 From the Death of Edward VI to the Death of Mary I* (Philadelphia: American Philosophical Society, 1979)

Becon, Thomas, *Prayers and Other Pieces of Thomas Becon*, ed. Rev. J. Ayre (Cambridge: Parker Society, 1844)

Beem, Charles and Dennis Moor, eds, *The Name of a Queen: William Fleetwood's Itinerarium ad Windsor* (New York: Palgrave Macmillan, 2013)

Beer, Barrett and Sybil Jack, eds, *The Letters of William Lord Paget of Beaudesert, 1547–1563, Camden Miscellany*, xxv, Camden 4th ser., XIII, 1974

Bland, A. E., P. A. Brown and R. H. Tawney, eds, *English Economic History: Select Documents* (London: Bell, 2nd edn, 1915)

Boccaccio, Giovanni, *Tutte le Opere*, vol. X, ed. Vittore Branca (Verona: Arnoldo Mondadori Editore, 2nd edn, 1970)

Boemius, Johann, *The fardle of facions conteining the aunciente maners, customes, and lawes, of the peoples enhabiting the two partes of the earth, called Affrike and Asie*, trans. William Watreman (London: John Kingston and Henry Sutton, 1555)

———, *El libro de las costumbres y maneras de vivir de todas las gentes, el qual traduzia y copilaua el Bachiller Thamara Cathedratico de Cadiz*, ed. Francisco de Tamara (Antwerp: Martin Nutius, 1556)

Bonner, Edmund, *An honest godlye instruction and information for the tradynge, and bringinge vp of children, set furth by the Bishoppe of London commaundyng all scholemaisters and other teachers of youthe within his diocese, that they neither teach, learne reade, or vse anye other maner of A B C, catechisme or rudimentes, then this made for the first instruction of youth. Mense Ianuarij. 1556. Cum priuilegio ad imprimendum solum* (London: Robert Caly, 1555)

———, *A profitable and necessarye doctrine with certayne homelies adioyned thervnto / set forth by the reuerend father in God, Edmunde Bishop of London* (London: John Cawood, 1555)

Borde, Andrew, *The fyrst boke of the introduction of knowledge. The whych dothe teache a man to speake parte of all maner of languages, and to know the usage and fashion of all maner of countreys. And for to know the moste parte of all maner of coynes of money, the whych is currant in euery region* (London: William Copeland, 1549; repr. 1555?)

Bradford, John, *The Copye of a letter, sent by John Bradforth to the right honourable lordes the Erles of Arundel, Darbie, Shrewsburye, and Pembroke, declaring the nature of Spaniardes, and discovering the most detestable treasons, which thei have pretended most falselye agaynste our moste noble kingdome of Englande* (Wesel?: J. Lambrecht, June–December, 1556)

Brice, Thomas, *A compendious Register in metre, containing the names and patient sufferings of the members of Jesus Christ, and the tormented, and cruelly burned within England* (London: John Kingston for Richard Adams, 1559)

Brinklow, Henry, *The Complaint of Roderick Mors sometime a gray fryre unto the parlement house of Englande his naturall countrye* (Geneva: Myghell Voys, 1546)

Cabrera y Córdoba, Luis de, *Felipe Segundo, Rey de España* (Madrid: Luis Sánchez, 1619; in modern edn, Aribau, 1876–7)

Calvete de Estrella, Juan Christóbal, *El Felicissimo Viaie D'el Mvy Poderoso Principe Don Phelippe, Hijo d'el Emperador Don Carlos Quinto Maximo, desde Espana a sus tierras dela baxa Alemana: con la descripcion de todos los Estados de Brabante y Flandes* (Antwerp: Martin Nucio, 1552)

——, *El felicissimo viaje del muy alto y muy poderoso Príncipe don Phelippe*, ed. José María de Francisco Olmos and Paloma Cuenca (Madrid: Sociedad Estatal para la Conmemoración de los Centenarios de Felipe II y Carlos V, 2001)

Camões, Luís, *Obras Completas*, ed. Hernâni Gidade (Lisbon: Livraria Sá da Costa, 2nd edn. 1955)

Campanella, Tommaso, *De Monarchia Hispanica* (Amsterdam: Ludovicus Elzevirius, 1653)

Canons and Decrees of the Council of Trent, The, trans. H. J. Schroeder (1st pub. 1941; London: Tan Books and Publishers Inc., 1978)

Carmeliano, Petro, *The solempnities & triumphes doon & made at the spousells and mariage of the kyngs doughter the Ladye Marye to the Prynce of Castile Archeduke of Austrige* (London: Richard Pynson, 1508)

Carranza y Miranda, Bartolomé, *Comentarios del Reverendissimo Señor Frai Batholome Carrança de Miranda, Arçobispo de Toleod, &c. sobre el catechismo Christiano* (Antwerp: Martin Nucio, 1558)

Cartagena, Alfonso de (García de Santa Maria), *Doctrinal de los caballeros* (Burgos [Al fuego del capellan mayor de la capilla de la sancta visitacion]: Fadrique Aleman, 20th June 1487)

Castrillo, Alonso de, *Tractado de república [Con otras Hystorias y antiguedades: intitulado at muy reverendo senor fray Diego de gayangos Maestro en sancta theologia Provincial de la Orden de la sanctissima Trinidad de la redemption de los captivos, en estos reynos de Castilla. Nuevamente compuesto por el reverendo padre fray Alonso de Castrillo frayle de la dicha Orden...]* (Burgos: Alonso de Melgar, 21st April 1521), Colección Civitas (Madrid: Instituto de Estudios Politicos, 1958)

Castro, Alfonso de, *De justa haereticorum punitione* (Antwerp: repr. John Stelsius, 1568)

Christopherson, John, *An exhortation to all menne to take hede and beware of rebellion: Wherein are set fourth the causes, that commonlye move men to rebellion, and that no cause is there, that ought to move any man thereunto* (London: John Cawood, 24th July 1554)

Churchyard, Thomas, *A generall rehearsall of warres called Churchyardes Choise: wherein is fiue hundred seuerall seruices of land and sea* (London: Edward White, 1579)

Cieça, Pedro de, *Parte Primera de la Chronica del Peru, Que tracta la demaracion de sus prouinicias, la descripcion dellas, las fundanciones de las nuevas ciudades, los ritos y costumbres de los Indios, y otras cosas estrañas dignas de ser sabidas* (Anvers: Juan Bellero a la enseña del Salmon, 1554)

Clemencín, Diego, *Elogio de la reina Católica Doña Isabel, al que siguen varias illustraciones sobre su reinado* (Madrid: I. Sancha, 1821)

Cobbett, William, *Complete Collection of State Trials*, vol. 1 (London: T. Hansard, 1809)

Cochayne, G. E., *The Complete Peerage of England, Scotland and Ireland, Great Britain and the United Kingdom*, 6 vols (Gloucester: Alan Sutton, repr. 1982)

Coke, John, *The debate betwene the heraldes of Englande and Fraunce, compyled by Ihoñ Coke, clarke of the kynges recognysaunce, or vulgerly, called clarke of the statutes of the staple of Westmynster, and fynyshed the yere of our Lorde. M.D.L* (London: Robert Wyer for Richard Wyer, 1550)

Cooper, Thomas and Thomas Lanquet, *Coopers Chronicle, conteininge the whole discourse of the histories as well of this realme, as all other countreis* (London: Thomas Berthelet, 1560)

Corro, Antonio del, *Reglas gramaticales para aprender la lengua Espanola y Francesa, confiriendo la vna con la otra, segun el orden de las partes de la oration Latinas* (Oxford: Joseph Barnes, 1586)

Davies, Norman, ed., *Paston Letters and Papers of the Fifteenth Century*, 2 vols (Oxford: Clarendon Press, 1971)

Dekker, Thomas and John Webster, *The Famouse History of Sir Thomas Wyat*, ed. John Farmer (Amersham: Tudor Facsimile Texts, 1914)

Delicado, Francisco, *La lozana andaluza*, ed. Bruno Damiani (Madrid: Castalia, 1969)

——, *Portrait of Lozana: the Lusty Andalusian Lady*, trans. Bruno Damiani (Potomac, Mary.: Scripta Humanistica, 1987)

Díaz Plaja, Fernando, *La historia de España en sus documentos: El siglo XVI* (Madrid: Instituto de Estudios Politicos, 1958)

Dickens, A. G., ed., 'Robert Parkyn's Narrative of the Reformation', *English Historical Review* 52 (1947), 58–83

Digges, Leonard, *A Prognostication of Right Good Effect, fructfully augmented etc.* (London: Thomas Geminus, 1555)

Diodorus of Sicily, Loeb edn, trans. C. H. Oldfather (London: William Heinemann Ltd., 1935)

Donaldson, P. S., 'George Rainsford's *Ritratto d'Inghiterra* (1556)', *Camden Miscellany* 27 (London: Royal Historical Society, 1979), 49–111

Dormer, Diego, *Discursos varios de historia; con muchas escrituras reales antiguas, y notas a algunas dellas* (Zaragoza: Herederos de Diego Dormer, 1683)

Duwes, Giles, *An Introductorie for to lerne to rede, to pronounce, and to speake Frenche trewly, compyled for the ryghte hygh excellent & moste vertuous lady, the lady Mary of England doughter to our moste gracious souerayne Lorde kyng Henry the eyghte* (London: Nicholas Bourman for John Reyns, 1540)

Edgar, Thomas, *The Lawes Resolutions of Womens Rights: Or, the Lawes Provision for Woemen. A Methodicall Collection of such Statutes and Customes, with the Cases, Opinions, Arguments and points of Learning in the Law, as doe concerne Women* (London: John Moore, to be sold by John Grove, 1632)

Elder, John, *Copie of a Letter Sent into Scotlande (1555)* (Amsterdam: Theatrum Orbis Terrarum, fac. edn, 1971) also reproduced as Appendix X of *Tower Chronicle*

Ellis, Henry, *Original Letter Illustrative of English History; Including Numerous Royal Letters: From Autographs in the British Museum and one or two other Collections*, 2nd ser., 4 vols (London: Harding and Lepard, 1827)

Elton, Geoffrey, ed., *The Tudor Constitution: Documents and Commentary* (Cambridge: Cambridge University Press, 1965)

Elyot, Sir Thomas, *The Boke Named the Gouernour* (London: Thomas Berthelet, 1531)

Encina, Juan del, *Teatro completo*, ed. Miguel Angel Pérez Priego (Madrid: Cátedra, 1991)

Erasmus, Desiderius, *The first tome or volume of the Paraphrase of Erasmus upon the newe testamente* (London: Edward Whitchurch, 1548)

——, *The Education of a Christian Prince*, trans. and intro. L. K. Born, Records of Civilization Sources and Studies No. XXVII (New York: Columbia University Press, 1934)

——, *The Collected Works of Erasmus*, vol. 34, trans. R. A. B. Mynors and vol. 66, trans. J. W. O'Malley (Toronto: University of Toronto Press, 1988 and 1992)

Eymerich, Nicolau, *Le Manuel des Inquisiteurs* (Avignon: 1376) (Rome: 1578, 1st edn, with commentary of Peña), trans. and intro. Louis Sala-Moulins (Paris: Mouton Editeur, 1973)

Farmer, J., ed., *Anonymous Plays, Recently Recovered 'Lost' Tudor Plays and The Dramatic Writings of John Bale, Bishop of Ossory*, Early English Dramatists (fac. of Early English Drama Society edn, 1906; Guildford: Charles Traylen, 1966)

Fernández Álvarez, Manuel, ed., *Corpus Documental de Carlos V*, 5 vols (Salamanca: Ediciones Univerdidad de Salamanca, 1973–81)

Feuillerat, Albert, *Documents relating to the Revels at Court in the time of King Edward VI and Queen Mary* (Louvain: Uystpruyst, 1914, repr. 1963)

Fish, Simon, *A Supplicacyon for the Beggers* (London: n.p., n.d., 1529?)

Forrest, William, *A newe ballade of the marigolde* (London: Richard Lant: 1554)

——, *The History of Grisild the Second*, ed. William Macray (London: Roxburgh Club, 1875)

Fortescue, Sir John, *The Governance of England: otherwise called The Difference between an Absolute and a Limited Monarchy*, ed. Rev. Charles Plummer (Oxford: Clarendon Press, 1885)

——, *De Laudibus Legum Anglie*, ed. and trans. S. B. Chrimes (Cambridge: Cambridge University Press, 1942)

Foxe, John, *Acts and Monuments*, ed. Rev. Stephen Reed Cattley, vol. V (London: R. B. Seeley and W. Burnside, 1838)

——, *The Acts and Monuments*, ed. Rev. J. Pratt, vol. VI (London: The Religious Tract Society, 4th edn)

——, *Two Latin Comedies by John Foxe the Martyrologist: Titis et Gesippus / Christus Triumphans [1556]*, ed. with intro. and trans. John Hazel Smith (Ithaca, NY and London: Cornell University Press, 1973)

——, *The Unabridged Acts and Monuments Online* or *TAMO* (1563 edition) (Sheffield: HRI Online Publications, 2011). Available from: www.johnfoxe.org [Accessed: 26th September 2016]

Frere, Walter and William Kennedy, eds, *Visitation Articles and Injunctions of the Period of the Reformation*, vol. 2: 1536–58, Alcuin Club Collections XX (London: Longman, 1910), 322–426

Gachard, Louis, ed., *Collections des Voyages des Souverains des Pays-Bas*, 4 vols (Brussels: F. Hayez, 1874–82)

Gardiner, Stephen, *De vera obedientia[:] An Oration made in Latine by the ryghte Reuerend father in God Stephan B. of Winchestre, nowe lord Chauncellour of england, with the preface of Edmunde Boner, somtime Archdeacon of Leicestre, and the kinges maiesties embassadour in Denmarke, & sithence B. of London, touchinge true Obedience. Printed at Hamburgh in Latine. In officina Francisci Rhodi. Mense Ia. M. D. xxxvi. And nowe translated into english and printed by Michael Wood: with the Preface and conclusion of the traunslator. ¶From Roane. xxvi of Octobre. M. D. liii. In Readinge marke the Notes in the margine. A double mynded man, is inconst[an]t in al his Waies. Iac.i.* (London: John Day[?], 1553)

————, *A traictise declaringe and plainly prouying, that the pretensed marriage of prestes, and professed persons, is no marriage... Herewith is comprised in the later chapitres, a full confutation of Doctour Poynettes boke entitled a defence for the marriage of prestes. By Thomas Martin* (London: Robert Caley, May 1554)

————, *Obedience in Church and State: Three Political Tracts by Stephen Gardiner*, ed. and trans. Pierre Janelle (Cambridge: Cambridge University Press, 1930)

————, *The Letters of Stepehen Gardiner*, ed. James Arthur Muller (Cambridge: Cambridge University Press, 1933)

————, *De Vera Obedientia*, 1st edn, 1535, trans. John Bale (?) (fac. edn, of 2nd Roane edn, October 1553, Leeds: Scolar Press, 1966)

————, *A Machiavellian Treatise*, ed. and trans. P. Donaldson (London: Cambridge University Press, 1975)

Garnett, R., ed., *The Accession of Queen Mary: Being the Contemporary Narrative of Antonio de Guaras, a Spanish Resident in London* (1st pub. Medina del Campo: Matheo y Francisco del Canto, 23rd March 1554; London: Lawrence and Bullen, 1892)

Gayangos, Don Pascual de, *Catalogue of the Manuscripts in the Spanish Language in the British Museum*, 3 vols (London: 1st edn, 1875–81; repr. British Museum Publications Ltd, The Scolar Press, 1976)

Geminus, Thomas, *Compendiosa totius Anatomie Delineatio* (London: Nicholas Hill, 1545)

————, *Compendiosa totius Anatomie Delineatio* (fac. edn, of 1st English edn of 1553 by Nicholas Udall, London: Dawson's of Pall Mall, 1959)

Geoffrey of Monmouth, *The British History*, trans. A. Thomson (London: William Stevens, 1842)

Gilby, Anthony, *Admonition to England and Scotland to call them to repentance* (Geneva: [J. Poullain and A. Rebul?], 1558)

Giles Godet, *Brief Abstract of the Genealogie and Race of All the Kinges of Englande* (1560?)

Goodman, Christopher, *How Superior Powers oght to be obeyd of their subiects: and wherin they may lawfully by Gods Worde be disobeyed and resisted* (Geneva: John Crispin, 1st January 1558)

Gosynhyll, Edward, *The Schole House of Women: wherein euery man may read a goodley prayse of the condicyons of women* (London: John King, 1541)

————, *The Prayse of All Women Called Mulierum Pean. Very Fruytfull and delectable unto all the reders* (London: Wylyam Myddylton, 1542)

Grafton, Richard, *An Abridgement of the Chronicles of England* (London: Richard Tottel, 1562)

——, *A Chronicle at large* (London: Henry Denham, 1568)

——, *This Chronicle of Briteyn, beginning at William the Conquerour, endeth wyth our moste dread and soueraigne Lady Queene Elizabeth* (London: Richard Grafton, 1568)

Greffier, Cornille Grapheus, *Le triumphe d'Anuers, faict en la susception du Prince Philips, Prince d'Espaign[e]* (Antwerp: P. de Lens, 1549)

Guaras, Antonio de, *Relacion muy verdadera de Antonio de Guaras: criado de la Serenissima y Catholica reyna de Inglaterra: al Illustre S. Duque de Alburquerque: Visorrey y Capitan General del Reyno de Nauarra &c. En la qual se trata en que miserias y calamidades y muertes de grandes ha estado el reyno tantos años ha Como doña Maria fue proclamada por Reyna y de todos obedescida y de su coronacion &c.* (Medina del Campo: Mateo and Francisco del Canto, 1554)

Guevara, Antonio de, *The Diall of Princes*, trans. Sir Thomas North (London: 1557), ed. K. Colvile, The Scholar's Library No. 1 (London: Philip Allan & Co., 1919)

Guicciardini, Francesco, *Maxims and Reflections of a Renaissance Statesman (Ricordi)*, trans. Mario Domandi (Gloucester, Mass.: Peter Smith, 1970)

——, *Opera Omnia*, 'Relazione di Spagna' (1514) repr. http://digilander.libero.it/il_guicciardini/guicciardini_relazione_di_spagna.html [Accessed: 22nd October 2012]

Harpesfield, Nicholas, *Concio quaedam admodum elegans, docta, salubris, & pia magistri Iohannis Harpesfeldi, sacre Theologiae baccalaurei, habita coram patribus & clero in Ecclesia Paulina Londini 26 Octobris. 1553* (London: John Cawood, 1553)

Harrington, Sir John, *Nugae Antiquae, Being a Miscellaneous Collection of Original Papers*, 2 vols (London: J. Wright, 1804)

Hastings, Sir Francis, *A Watchword to all religious, and true hearted English-men* (London: Felix Kingston for Ralph Jackson, 1598)

——, *An apologie or defence of the watch-word against the virulent and seditious ward-word published by an English-Spaniard* (London: Felix Kingston for Ralph Jackson, 1600)

Hawkins, John, *A true declaration of the toublesome voyadge of M. John Haukins to the parties of Guynea and the west Indies, in the yeares of our Lord 1567 and 1568* (London: Thomas Purfoote for Lucas Harrison, 1569)

Hawkyard, Alistair, David Starkey and Philip Ward, eds, *The Inventory of King Henry VIII: The Transcript*, vol. 1 (London: Harvey Miller, 1998)

Hayward, Sir John, *The Life and Raigne of K. Edward the Sixth* (London: for John Partridge, 1630)

Herodotus, *The History*, trans. David Greene (London: University of Chicago Press, 1987)

Herrera, Alonso de, *Agricultura general que trata de la labranza del campo y sus particular-idades* (Madrid: viuda de Alonso Martin, 1620)

Heywood, John, *The Spider and the Fly* (London: Thomas Powell, 1556)

——, *The Proverbs, Epigrams, and Miscellanies of John Heywood*, ed. J. S. Farmer, Early

English Dramatists (fac. edn, of 1906 Early English Drama Society, Guildford: Charles Traylen, 1966)

Heywood, Thomas, *If you know not me, you know no bodie: or, the Troubles of Queene Elizabeth* (London: Thomas Purfoot for Nathaniel Butter, 1605)

——, *Englands Elisabeth: her life and troubles, during her minoritie, from the cradle to the crown, historically laid open and interwoven with such eminent passages of state, as happened under the reigne of Henry the eight, Edward the sixt, Q. Mary; all of them aptly introducing to the present relation* (London: John Beale, 1631)

Hogherde, Myles, *Certayne questions demaunded and asked by the Noble Realme of Englande of her true naturall chyldren and Subiectes of the same* (London: 1555)

Holinshed, Ralph, *Chronicles of England, Scotland and Ireland*, 6 vols (London: J. Johnson, 1808)

Homem, Diogo, *The Queen Mary Atlas* (London: Folio Society, 2005)

Hughes, Paul and James Larkin, eds, *Tudor Royal Proclamations:* Vol. 2, *The Later Tudors (1553–1587)* (London: Yale University Press, 1969)

Hume, Martin A. S., ed., *Chronicle of King Henry VIII of England* (London: George Bell and Sons, 1889)

Jiménez de Quesada, Gonzalo, *El antijovio*, ed. Guillermo Hernández Peñalosa, 2 vols (Bogotá: Instituto Caro y Cuervo, 1991)

Kingsford, Charles Lethbridge, ed., *Two London Chronicles from the Collections of John Stow*, Camden Miscellany XII, 3rd ser. (London: Camden Society, 1910)

Kipling, Gordon, ed., *The Receyt of the Ladie Katheryne*, Early English Text Society no. 296 (Oxford: Oxford University Press, 1990)

Knox, John, *The First Blast of the Trumpet Against the Monstruous regiment of women* Veritas temporis filia* (Geneva: Pierre-Jacques Poullain & Antoine Reboul, 1558)

——, *The History of the Reformation of Religion within the Realm of Scotland* (Glasgow: J. Galbraith and Co., 1761)

Kramer, Heinrich and James Sprenger, *The Malleus Maleficiarum*, trans. Rev. Montague Summers (New York: Dover Publications Inc., 1971)

Laguna, Andrés de, *Anotationes in Discoridem Anazarbeum, per Andream Lacunam Segobiensem, Medicum* (Venice: Gulielmum Rouillium, 1554)

——, *Pedacio Dioscorides Anazarbeo, acerca de la materia medicinal, y de los venenos mortiferos, traduzido de lengua Griega, en la vulgar Castellana, & illusrado con claras y substantiales Annotationes, y con las figuras de innumeras plantas exquisitas y raras por el Doctor Andres de Laguna, Medico* (Antwerp: Juan Latio, 1555)

Laiglesia, Francisco de, *Estudios históricos (1515–1555)* (Madrid: Clásica Española, 1918)

Latimer, Hugh, *Sermons*, ed. Rev. George Elwes Corrie, Parker Society, 2 vols (Cambridge: Cambridge University Press, 1845)

Leslie, John, *Defence of the Honour of Marie Queen of Scots* (Rheims: Jean Foigny, 1569)

Lettenhove, Kervyn de and J. M. B. Constantin, eds, *Relations Politiques Des Pays-Bas et de l'Angleterre: Sous Le Règne de Philippe II*, 11 vols (Brussels: F. Hayez, 1882–1900)

Lever, Christopher, *The Historie of the Defendors of the Catholique Faith; discoursing the*

State of Religion in England, and the care of the politique state for Religion during the reignes of King Henry 8, Edward 6, Queene Marie, Elizabeth, and... King James (London: G. M. for N. Fussell and H. Moseley, 1627)

Lindsay, Sir David, *The Works of Sir David Lindsay of the Mount (1490–1555)*, ed. Douglas Hamer, 4 vols (London: The Scottish Text Society, William Blackwood and Sons Ltd., 1931)

Loades, David, ed., *The Papers of George Wyatt*, Camden Society 4th ser., V (London: Camden Society, 1968)

López de Gómara, Francisco, *La historia general de las Indias* (Antwerp: Juan Steelsio, 1554)

Luther, Martin, *A Faithful Admonition of a certeyne true Pastor and Prophete... translated with a Preface by M. Philip Melancthon*, trans. Eusebius Pamphilus [John Bale?] (Greenwich [London]: Conrad Freeman [John Day?], May 1554)

Machiavelli, Niccolò, *Discourses on the First Ten Books of Titus Livy*, ed. B. Crick, trans. L. J. Walker and rev. B. Richardson (London: Penguin, repr. 1983)

Madden, Frederick, *Privy Purse Expenses of the Princess Mary* (London: William Pickering, 1831)

Malfatti, Cesare, ed. and trans., *The Accession, Coronation and Marriage of Mary Tudor as related in Four Manuscipts of the Escorial* (Barcelona: Sociedad Alianza de Artes Graficas y Ricardo Fontá, 1956)

Martire d'Anghiera, Peter, *The Decades of the newe worlde or West India, conteynyng the navigations and conquestes of the Spanyards*, trans. Richard Eden (London: William Powell, 1555)

Matienzo, Juan, *Dialogus Relatoris et Advocati Pinciani Senatus* (Valladolid: Sebastianus Martinez, 1558)

Mendoza, Diego Hurtado de, *Poesía*, ed. Luis Díaz Larios and Olga Gete Carpio (Madrid: Cátedra, 1990)

Mexía, Pedro, *Historia imperial y cesarea: en la qual en suma se contiene las vidas y hechos de todos los emperadores de Roma: desde Julio Cesar hasta el emperador Maximiliano* (Seville: Juan de Leon, 30th June 1545)

Montanus, Reginaldus Gonsalvius (Casiodoro de Reina?), *A Discovery and playne Declaration of the sundry subtill practices of the Holy Inquitision of Spayne* (London: John Day, 1568)

Morysine, Richarde, *An Exhortation to styre all Englyshe men to the defence of theyr countrye* (London: Thomas Berthelet, 1539)

Munday, Anthony and Henry Chettle, *Sir Thomas More*, ed. John Jowett (London: Methuen, 2011)

Muñoz, Andrés, *Sumario y verdadera relación del buen viaje que el invictissimo Príncipe de las Españas don Felipe hizo a Inglaterra, y recibimiento en Vincestre donde caso y salio para Londres* (Zaragoza: Esteban Nagera, 1554)

——, *Viaje de Felipe Segundo a Inglaterra y Relaciones Varias Relativas Al Mismo Suceso*, ed. Pacual de Gayángos and Manuel Zarco del Valle (Madrid: La Sociedad de Bilbiófilos Españoles, 1877)

Münster, Sebastian, *A treatyse of the newe India, with other new founde landes and*

Ilandes, trans. Richard Eden (London: Stephen Mierdman for Edward Sutton, 1553)

Myers, A. R., ed., *The Household of Edward IV: The Black Book and the Ordinance of 1478* (Manchester: Manchester University Press, 1959)

Nebrija, Elio Antonio de [Aelii Antonii Nebrissensis], *La gramatica que nuevamente hizo sobre la lengua castellana* (Salamanca: n. p., 1492)

——, *Rerum a Fernando & Elisabe Hispaniarum foelicissimus Regibus gestar. Decadas Duas.* (Granada: Inclyta, October 1545)

——, *Gramática Castellana*, Introducción y notas Miguel Ángel Esparza Ramón Sarmiento (Madrid: Fundación Antonio de Nebrija, 1992)

Newbigin, Nerida, ed., *Gl'Ingannati (1537)* (fac. edn, Bologna: Arnaldo Forni, 1984)

Nichols, John Gough, ed., *The Diary of Henry Machyn, Citizen and Merchant Taylor of London 1550–1563* (London: Camden Society, 1848)

——, *The Chronicle of Queen Jane and of two years of Queen Mary and especially of the Rebellion of Sir Thomas Wyat*, Camden Society XLVIII (London: The Camden Society, 1850) [Known and cited as *Tower Chronicle*]

Ocampo, Florian de, *Los Cinco Libros primeros de la Cronica general de España* (Medina del Campo: Guillermo de Millis, 1553) [BNE: R – 6369]

Orléans, Charles d' (?), *Le debat des heraulx darmes de frãnce et d'engleterre* (Rouen: Richard Azoult for Thomas Iaisne, 1515?)

Page, William, ed., *Letters of Denization and Acts of Naturalization for Aliens in England, 1509–1603*, The Publications of the Huguenot Society of London, vol. 8 (Lymington: 1893)

Palsgrave, John, *Lesclarcissement de la Langue Francoyse* (London: John Hawkins, 1530)

Peele, George, *The Stukeley Plays*, ed. Charles Edelman, Revels Plays Companion Library (Manchester: Manchester University Press, 2005)

Peele, James, *The maner and fourme how to kepe a perfecte reconyng, after the order of the moste worthie and notable accompte, of Debitour and Creditour, set forthe in certain tables...* (London: Richard Grafton, 1553)

Persons, Robert, *A temperate ward-word, to the turbulent and seditous Wach-word of Sir Francis Hastinges knight* (Antwerp: Arnout Conincx, 1599)

Pole, Reginald, *Epistolarum Reginaldi Poli*, ed. J. M. Rizzardi (Brescia: 1744)

Pollard, A. and Redgrave, G., eds, *A Short Title Catalogue of Books Printed in England Scotland and Ireland and of English books printed abroad 1475–1640*, 2 vols (London: Bibliographical Society, 2nd rev. edn, 1986)

Ponet, John, attr., *A Warnyng for Englande Conteynyng the horrible practices of the kyng of Spayne in the kyngs dome of Naples and the miseries whereunto that noble Realme is brought. Wherby all Englishe men may understand the plage that shall light upon them if the kyng of Spayn obteyne the Dominion in Englande* (Emden: E. van der Erve, 15–20th November 1555)

——, *An Apologie fully answeringe by Scriptures and aunceant Doctors a blasphemose Book gatherid by D. Steph. Gardiner of late Lord Chancelar, D. Smyth of Oxford, Pighius, and other Papists* ([Strasbourg: heirs of W. Köpfel?], 1556)

——, *A Shorte Treatise of politike pouuer, and of the true Obedience which subiectes owe to kynges and other ciuile Gouernours, with an Exhortacion to all true naturall Englishe men* (Strasbourg: heirs of W. Köpfel, 1556)

Power, Eileen and Richard Tawney, eds, *Tudor Economic Documents*, 3 vols (London: Longman, 1953)

Pownall, Robert, *An admonition to the towne of Callays* (Wesel?: P. A. de Zutere?, 1557)

Prayer Books of Edward VI, The First and Second, ed. E. C. S. Gloucester (London: J. M. Dent and Sons Ltd, 1910)

Proctor, John, *The historie of wyates rebellion, with the order and maner of resisting the same, wherunto in the ende is added an earnest conference with the degenerate and sedicious rebelles for the serche of the cause of their daily disorder* (London: Robert Caly, 10th January 1555)

Ptolemaei, Claudii Alexandrii, *Geographiae*, Libro VIII, trans. Balibaldo Pirckheymero, corr. Sebastian Münster (Basle: Henry Pierre, June 1552)

Puttenham, George, *The Arte of English Poesie*, ed. Gladys Doidge Willcock and Alice Walker (Cambridge: Cambridge University Press, repr. 1970)

Rabelais, François, *Gargantua and Pantagruel*, trans. J. M. Cohen (London: Penguin, 1995)

Reynolds, John, *Vox Coeli, or, Newes from Heaven, or, A Consultation there held by the High and Mighty Princes, King Hen. 8 King Edw. 6. Prince Henry, Queene Mary, Queene Elizabeth and Queene Anne; wherein Spaines ambition and treacheries to most Kingdomes and free Estates of Evrope, are vnmask'd and truly represented, but more particularly towards England, and now more especificaly vnder the pretended match of Prince Charles, with the Infanta Dona Maria. Whereunto is annexed two Letters written by Queene Mary from Heauen, the one to Count Gondomar, the Ambassadour of Spaine, the other to all the Romane Catholiques of England. Written by S. R. N. I.* (Elisium [London]: n. p., 1624)

Robinson, Hastings, ed., *The Zurich Letters*, 2nd ser., The Parker Society, 2 vols (Cambridge: Cambridge University Press, 1845)

——, ed., *Original letters relative to the English Reformation*, 2 vols (Cambridge: Cambridge University Press, 1846)

Roca de Togores, Mariano, Marqués de Molina, *Crónica del Rey Enrico Otavo de Inglaterra* (Madrid: Alfonso Durán, 1874)

Rodrigo de Yepes, F., profesor y predicador del monasterio de S. Hieronymo el Real de Madrid, *Historia de la muerte y glorioso martyrio del Sancto Innocente, que llaman de la Guardia, natural de la ciudad de Toledo. Con las cosas procuradas antes por ciertos Iudios, hasta que al Sancto Inocente crucificaron: y lo succedido despues* (Madrid, S. Hieronymo Real: Impreso por Iuan Yñiguez de Lequerica, 1583)

Rodríguez de Montalvo, Garci, *Amadís de Gaula*, ed. Juan Manuel Cacho Blecua, 2 vols (Madrid: Cátedra, SA, 1991)

Rodríguez Salgado, M. J. and Simon Adams, eds and trans., 'The Count of Feria's Dispatch to Philip II of 14 November 1558', *Camden Miscellany* XXVIII, 4th ser. (London: Royal Historical Society: 1984), 302–44

Rojas, Fernando de, *La Comedia de Calisto y Melibea/La Celestina* (1st edn, Burgos: Fadrique de Basilea, 1499)

Salinero, Fernando García, ed., *Viaje de Turquía* (Madrid: Cátedra, 1980)

Sanchez, Francisco, *Relacion muy verdadera de la bienauenturada nueua de la conuersion de los Ingleses luteranos, hechas por Francisco Sanchez estudiante, natural de la villa de Orgaz* (Salamanca: Juan de Cánova, 1555)

Sandoval, Fray Prudencio de, *Historia de la Vida y Hechos del Emperador Carlos V Máximo, fortísimo, Rey Católico de España y de las Indias, Islas y Tierrra firme del mar Océano*, 3 vols, Biblioteca de Autores Españoles (Madrid: Atlas Ediciones, 1955–56)

Shakespeare, William, *The Sonnets and A Lover's Complaint*, ed. John Kerrigan (London: Penguin, 1986)

Skelton, John, *The Complete English Poems*, ed. John Scattergood (Harmondsworth: Penguin, 1983)

Smith, Sir Thomas, attr., *A Discourse of the Commonweal of this Realm of England* (written *c.* 1549, 1st pub. 1581), ed. Mary Dewar, Folger Documents of Tudor and Stuart Civilization (Charlottesville: University of Virginia Press, 1969)

——, *De Republica Anglorum*, ed. Mary Dewar (1583; repr. Cambridge: Cambridge University Press, 1982)

Spedding, James (ed.), *The Letters and the Life of Francis Bacon* (London: Longman, 1868)

Standish, John, *A discourse wherin is debated whether it be expedient that the scripture should be in English for al men to read that wyll* (London: Robert Caly, December 1554)

Starkey, Thomas, 'A Dialogue between Pole and Lupset', ed. T. F. Mayer, Camden Society 4th ser., XXXVII (London: Royal Historical Society and UCL, 1989)

Stopes, Leonard, *An Ave Maria in Commendation of oure most vertuouse Queene* (London: Richard Lant, 1553?)

Strype, John, *Memorials especially Ecclesiastical and such as concern Religion*, 3 vols (London: S. Richardson, 1721)

——, *Ecclesiastical Memorials*, 7 vols (London: Samuel Bagster, 1816)

——, *Ecclesiastical memorials, relating chiefly to religion, and the reformation of it: and the emergencies of the Church of England, under King Henry VIII. King Edward VI. and Queen Mary I* (Oxford: Clarendon Press, 1822)

Tasso, Torquato, *Le prose diverse*, ed. Cesare Guasti (Florence: Successori Le Monnier, 1875)

Taverner, Richard, *An oration gratulatory made upon the ioyfull proclayming of the moste noble princes Quene Mary Quene of Englande* (London: John Day, 1553)

Torre, Felipe de la, *Institución de un Rey Christiano* (Antwerp: 1556), ed. R. Truman, Exeter Hispanic Texts XXIII (Exeter: Exeter University Printing Unit, 1979)

Tunstall, Cuthbert, *Sermon... made upon Palme sondaye laste past* (London: Thomas Berthelet, 1539)

Tyndale, William, 'The Obedience of a Christen Man, and how Christen rulers ought to gouerne' (2nd October 1528) in *Doctrinal Treatises*, The Parker Society, ed. Rev. H. Walker (Cambridge: Cambridge University Press, 1848)

Udall, Nicholas, attr., *Respublica*, ed. W. W. Greg, Early English Text Society no. 226 (London: Oxford University Press, 1952)

Valdés, Alfonso de, *Dialogo de las cosas acaecidas en Roma* (1529), ed. Rosa Navarro Durán (Madrid: Cátedra, 2001)

Valdés, Juan de, *Diálogo de la Lengua*, ed. Cristina Barbolani (Madrid: Cátedra, 1982)

Vega, F. Andreas de, *Opusculum de iustificatione, gratia et meritis* (1st pub. Venice: 1548; this edn: Complutum [Alcala de Henares]: Andrea de Angulo, 1564)

Vicary, Thomas, *The anatomie of the bodie of man* (1548 edn, reissued by Surgeon of St Bartholomew's 1577), ed. F. J. and Percy Furnivall, Early English Text Society Extra Series, No. LIII (2nd edn, London: Oxford University Press, 1930)

Vigo, Johannes de, *Libro o pratica en Cirurgía del muy famoso y experto Doctor Juan de Vigo: medico que fue y cirurgiano del sanctissimo padre Julio Segundo* trans. Dr Migual Juan Pascual (Valencia: 15th May 1537)

Vives, Juan Luis, *The very fruteful and plesant boke calle the Instruction of a Christen Woman*, trans. Richard Hyrde (London: Thomas Berthelet, 1541)

——, *Opera Omnia*, ed. Gregorio Majansio, 8 vols (Valentiae Edetcenorum, 1782–90)

——, *Vives and the Renascence Education of Women*, ed. and trans. Foster Watson (London: Edward Arnold, 1912)

——, *Vives: On Education. A Translation of the De Tradendis Disciplinis of Juan Luis Vives*, trans. Foster Watson (Cambridge: Cambridge University Press, 1913)

——, *Obras completas*, trans. Lorenzo Riber, 2 vols (Madrid: Aguilar, 1948)

——, *The Education of a Christian Woman*, ed. Charles Fantazzi (Chicago: Chicago University Press, 2000)

Watson, G. *et al.*, *The New Cambridge Bibliography of English Literature*, 5 vols (Cambridge: Cambridge University Press, 1969–77)

Weiss, Charles, ed., *Papiers d'état du Cardinal de Granvelle*, 9 vols (Paris: Imprimerie Royale, 1843)

Williams, C. H., ed., *English Historical Documents:* Vol. V, *1485–1558*, 12 vols (London: Eyre and Spottiswoode, 1967)

Wilson, Thomas, *The Arte of Rhetorique for the vse of all suche as are studious of eloquence* (London: Richard Grafton, January 1553; London: John Kingston, 1560)

Wingfield, Robert of Brantham, '*Vitae Angliae Reginae*', ed. and trans. Diarmaid MacCulloch, in *Camden Miscellany XXVIII*, Camden Society 4th ser., XXIX (London: Royal Historical Society, UCL, 1984)

Wriothesley, Charles, *A Chronicle of England during the Reigns of the Tudors*, ed. William Hamilton, Camden Series 20 (London: J. B. Nichols, 1877)

Wyatt, Sir Thomas, *Complete Poems*, ed. R. A. Rebholz (London: Penguin, 1978)

Secondary Sources

Achinstein, Sharon, 'Audiences and authors: ballads and the making of English Renaissance literary culture', *Journal of Medieval and Renaissance Studies* 22 (1992), 311–26

Ahnert, Ruth, *The Rise of Prison Literature in the Sixteenth Century* (Cambridge: Cambridge University Press, 2013)

Alibhai-Brown, Yasmin, *Who do We Think we Are? Imagining the New Britain* (London: Penguin, 2000)

Allan, David, 'Anti-Hispanicism and the construction of late eighteenth-century British patriotism: Robert Watson's *History of the Reign of Philip the Second*', *Bulletin of Hispanic Studies* 77 (2000), 423–49

Allinson, Rayne and Geoffrey Parker, 'A king and two queens: the holograph correspondence of Philip II with Mary I and Elizabeth I' in Helen Hackett, ed., *Early Modern Exchanges: Dialogues between Nations and Cultures, 1500–1800* (Farnham: Ashgate, 2015), 95–118

Alsop, J. D., 'Nicholas Brigham (*d.* 1558): scholar, antiquary and crown servant', *Sixteenth Century Journal* 12 (1981), 49–67

——, 'The Act for the Queen's Regal Power, 1554', *Parliamentary History* 13 (1994), 261–76

Amezúa y Mayo, Agustín de, *Opúsculos Histórico-Literarios*, 3 vols (Madrid: Consejo Superior de Investigaciones Científicas, 1951–3)

Anglo, Sydney, 'The *British History* in early Tudor propaganda', *Bulletin of the John Rylands Library* 44 (1961), 17–48

——, *Spectacle, Pageantry and Early Tudor Policy* (Oxford: Clarendon Press 1969)

——, 'Crypto-Machiavellism in early Tudor England: the problem of *ragionamento dell'advenimento...*', *Renaissance et Reforme*, n. s. 2 (1978), 182–93

Aram, Bethany, *Juana the Mad: Sovereignty and Dynasty in Renaissance Europe* (Baltimore, Mary.: Johns Hopkins University Press, 2005)

Archer, Ian, *The Pursuit of Stability: Social Relations in Elizabethan London* (Cambridge: Cambridge University Press, 1991)

Archer, Jayne, 'The Queens' *arcanum*: authority and authorship in *The Queens Closet Opened* (1655)', *Renaissance Journal* 1 (2002), 14–26

Arens, William, *The Man-Eating Myth: Anthropology and Anthropophagy* (New York: Oxford University Press, 1979)

Armstrong, Adrian, 'The manuscript reception of Jean Molinet's *Trosne d'honneur*', *Medium Aevum* 74 (2005), 311–28

Armstrong, C. A. J., *England, France and Burgundy in the Fifteenth Century* (London: Hambledon Press, 1983)

Arnoldsson, Sverker, *La leyenda negra: estudios sobre sus orígenes* (Gothenburg: Gothenburg University Press, 1960)

Atkins, Sinclair, 'Charles V and the Turks', *History Today* 30 (December, 1980), 13–18

Attreed, Lorraine and Alexandra Winkler, 'Faith and forgiveness: lessons in statecraft for Queen Mary Tudor', *Sixteenth Century Journal* 36 (2005), 971–89

Auerbach, Erna, *Tudor Artists: A Study of Painters in the Royal Service and of Portraiture on Illuminated Documents from the Accession of Henry VIII to the Death of Elizabeth I* (London: The Athlone Press, 1954)

Axton, Marie, *The Queen's Two Bodies: Drama and the Elizabethan Succession* (London: Royal Historical Society, 1977)

—— and James Carley, eds, *'Triumphs of English' Henry Parker, Lord Morley Translation to the Tudor Court: New Essays in Interpretation* (London: British Library, 2000)

Axton, Richard, ed., *Three Rastell Plays: Four Elements, Calisto and Melebea, Gentleness and Nobility* (Cambridge: Brewer, 1979)

—— and Peter Happé, *The Plays of John Heywood* (Cambridge: Brewer, 1991)

Aylmer, G. E., 'The meaning and definition of "property" in seventeenth century England', *Past and Present* 86 (1980), 87–97

Baelde, Michael, 'Financial policy and the evolution of the demesne in the Netherlands under Charles V and Philip II (1530–1560)' in H. J. Cohn, ed., *Government in Reformation Europe 1520–1560* (London: MacMillan, 1971), 203–24

Bakhtin, Mikhail, *Rabelais and His World*, trans. Hélène Iswolsky (Cambridge Mass.: MIT, 1968)

Barber, Peter, 'England II: monarchs, ministers, and maps, 1550–1625', in *Monarchs, Ministers and Maps: The Emergence of Cartography as a Tool of Government in Early Modern Europe*, ed. David Buisseret (Chicago and London: University of Chicago Press, 1992), 57–98

——, 'The British Isles' in Marcel Watelet, ed., *The Mercator Atlas of Europe: Facsimile of the maps by Gerardus Mercator contained in the Atlas of Europe, circa 1570–1572* (Pleasant Hill, Oreg.: Walking Tree Press, 1998), 43–77

——, 'The Copperplate Map in context', in *Tudor London: A Map and a View*, ed. Ann Saunders and John Schofield (London: Topographical Society, 2001), 16–32

——, 'Court and country: English cartographic initiatives and their derivatives under Henry VIII and Philip and Mary', in *Actas. XIX Congreso Internacional de Historia de la Cartografía* (Madrid: Ministerio de Defensa, 2002), 1–12

——, *The Queen Mary Atlas: Commentary* (London: Folio Society, 2005)

——, 'Putting Musselburgh on the map: two recently-discovered cartographic documents from the "Rough Wooing"', in *Mappae Antiquae Liber Amicorum Günter Schilder*, ed. Paula van Gest-van het Schip and Peter van der Krogt (Amsterdam: Hes & De Graaf, 2007), 327–38

Baroja, Julio Caro, *Los Judíos en la España moderna y contemporánea*, 3 vols, vol. 3 (Madrid: Ediciones Arion, 1961)

Bartlett, Kenneth R., 'The English exile community in Italy and the political opposition to Queen Mary I', *Albion* 13 (1981), 223–41

——, 'The occasion of Lord Morley's translation of the *Trionfi*: The Triumph of Chastity over Politics', in *Petrarch's Triumphs. Allegory and Spectacle*, ed. Konrad Eisenblicher and Amilcare A. Iannucci (Ottawa: Dovehouse, 1990), 325–34

Bataillon, Marcel, 'Sur Florian Docampo', *Bulletin Hispanique* 25 (1923), 33–59

——, *Erasmo y España: estudios sobre la historia espiritual del siglo xvi*, trans. Antonio Alatorre (Mexico: Fondo de Cultura Economica, Segunda Reimpresión en España, 1988)

Baudrillard, Jean, *Selected Writings*, ed. Mark Poster (Cambridge: Polity Press, 1988)

Beem, Charles, *The Lioness Roared: The Problems of Female Rule in English History*, Queenship and Power Series (New York: Palgrave Macmillan, 2006)

—— and Miles Taylor, eds, *The Man Behind the Queen: Male Consorts in History*, Queenship and Power Series (New York: Palgrave Macmillan, 2014)

Bellorini, Mariagrazia, 'Da Londra a Mantova. Immagini di vita e cultura inglese nella corrispondenza di Aloisio Schivenoglia (1556–1560)', in *Studi di Letteratura Inglese e Americana*, ed. S. Rossi (Milan: Pubblicazioni dell'Università Cattholica del Sacro Cuore, 1980), 57–92

Beltrán, Antonio and Pío, 'Numismatica de los Reyes Católicos' and Pío Beltrán Villagrasa, 'Bibliografia numismatica de los Reyes Catolicos' in J. Vicens Vives *et al.*, eds, *Instituciones economicas sociales y politicas de la epoca Fernandina* (Zaragoza: Institución 'Fernando el Católico', n. d.), 223–42

Benner, Erica, *Really Existing Nationalisms: A Post-Communist View from Marx and Engels* (Oxford: Clarendon Press, 1995)

Bérenger, Jean, *A History of the Habsburg Empire 1273–1700*, trans. C. Simpson (London: Longman, 1994)

Berenguer, Gonzalo Velasco, 'An uncomfortable presence: the Black Legend applied to reign of Philip and Mary 1554–2014', at *The Black Legend Then and Now*, IHR, 27th September 2014

Bernard, G. W., *The Power of the Early Tudor Nobility: A Study of the 4th and 5th Earls of Shrewsbury* (Sussex: Harvester Press, 1985)

Berry, Philippa, *Of Chastity and Power: Elizabethan Literature and the Unmarried Queen* (London: Routledge, 1989)

Bertomeu Masiá, M. J., 'Relaciones de sucesos italianas sobre la boda de Felipe II con María Tudor', *Cartaphilus* 5 (2009), 6–17

Betteridge, Thomas, *Tudor Histories of the English Reformations, 1530–83* (Aldershot: Ashgate, 1999)

—— and Greg Walker, eds, *The Oxford Handbook of Tudor Drama* (Oxford: Oxford University Press, 2012)

Bindoff, S. T., *Tudor England* (London: Penguin, 1950)

——, *The Fame of Sir Thomas Gresham*, Neale Lecture in English History (London: Jonathan Cape, 1973)

Birchwood, Matthew and Matthew Dimmock, 'Popular xenophobia' in Andrew Hadfield, Matthew Dimmock and Abigail Shinn, eds, *The Ashgate Companion to Early Modern Popular Culture* (Amersham: Ashgate, 2014), 207–20

Birnbaum, Marianna D., 'The Fuggers, Hans Dernshcwam, and the Ottoman Empire', *Südost-Forschungen* 50 (1991), 119–44

Bishop, Jennifer, 'Currency, conversation and control: political discourse and the coinage in mid-Tudor England', *English Historical Review* 131 (2016), 763–92

Bock, G., Quentin Skinner and M. Viroli, eds, *Machiavelli and Republicanism* (Cambridge: Cambridge University Press, 1990)

Bolgar, R. R., ed., *Classical Influences on European Culture* AD *1500–1700*, Proceedings of an International Conference at Cambridge, 1974 (Cambridge: 1976)

Borges, Jorge Luis, *Ficciones* (Buenos Aires: Emecé Editores, 1967)

Bossy, J., *The English Catholic Community 1570–1850* (London: Darton, Longman and Todd, 1976)

Bourdieu, Pierre, *The Field of Cultural Production: Essays on Art and Literature*, ed. and intro. Randal Johnson (Cambridge: Polity Press, 1993)

Boutcher, Warren, 'A French dexterity, & an Italian confidence: new documents on John Florio, learned strangers and Protestant humanist study of modern languages in Renaissance England *c.* 1547 to *c.* 1625', *Reformation* 2 (1997), 39–109

Bowler, Gerry, 'Marian Protestants and the idea of violent resistance to tyranny' in Peter Lake and Maria Dowling, eds, *Protestantism and the National Church in Sixteenth Century England* (London: Croom Helm, 1987), 124–43

Braden, Gordon, *Renaissance Tragedy and the Senecan Tradition: Anger's Privilege* (London: Yale University Press, 1985)

Brady, Ciaran, *James Anthony Froude: An Intellectual Biography of a Victorian Prophet* (Oxford: Oxford University Press, 2014)

Brandi, Karl, *The Emperor Charles V: The Growth and Destiny of a Man and of a World-Empire*, trans. C. V. Wedgwood (Sussex: Harvester Press, 1970)

Braudel, Fernand, *Civilization and Capitalism 15th–18th Century*, trans. Siân Reynolds, 3 vols, Vol. II, *The Wheels of Commerce* (London: Collins, 1982)

———, *The Mediterrranean and the Mediterranean World in the Age of Philip II*, trans. Siân Reynolds, 2 vols (2nd rev. edn, 1966, trans.1972, London: Fontana Press)

Brault, J., 'English translations of the *Celestina* in the sixteenth century', *Hispanic Review* 27 (1960), 301–12

Braunmuller, A. and M. Hattaway, eds, *The Cambridge Companion to English Renaissance Drama* (Cambridge: Cambridge University Press, 1990)

Brenner, Robert, *Merchants and Revolution: Commercial Change, Political Conflict, and London's Overseas Traders, 1550–1653* (Victoria: Cambridge University Press, 1993)

Brigden, Susan, *London and the Reformation* (Oxford: Clarendon Press, 1989)

———, *Thomas Wyatt: The Heart's Forest* (London: Faber and Faber, 2012)

Brotton, Jerry, *Trading Territories: Mapping the Early Modern World* (London: Reaktion Books, 1997)

Buchanan, Jane, *Mary Tudor: Courageous Queen or Bloody Mary?* (New York: Franklin Watts, 2008)

Buckley, H., 'Sir Thomas Gresham and the foreign exchanges', *Economic Journal* 34 (1924), 589–601

Bullón-Fernández, María, ed., *England and Iberia in the Middle Ages, 12th–15th Centuries* (New York: Palgrave Macmillan, 2007)

Burke, Peter, *Popular Culture in Early Modern Europe* (Aldershot: Scolar Press, rev. repr. 1994)

Bush, M. L., ed., *Serfdom and Slavery: Studies in Legal Bondage* (London: Longman, 1996)

Bushnell, David F., Richard E. Webb and Jane C. Widseth, 'Tiresias and the breast: thinking of Lacan, interpretation, and caring', *International Journal of Psychoanalysis* 74 (1993), 597–612

Campbell, Lorne, *Renaissance Portraits: European Portrait-Painting in the 14th, 15th and 16th Centuries* (London: Yale University Press, 1990)

Carande, Ramon, *Carlos V y sus Banqueros: La Vida Económica de España en una Fase de su Hegemonia 1516–1556 / La Hacienda Real de Castilla*, 3 vols (Madrid: Revista de Occidente, 1943–9)

Carter, Alison J., 'Mary Tudor's wardrobe', *Costume: The Journal of the Costume Society* 18 (1984), 9–28

Carter, Patrick, 'Mary Tudor, Parliament and the renunciation of first fruits, 1555', *Historical Research: The Bulletin of the Institute of Historical Research* 69 (1996), 340–6

Castellán, Angel, 'Juan de Valdés y el círculo de Nápoles', *Cuadernos de Historia de España* 36 (1962), 199–291

Cave, Terence, *The Cornucopian Text: Problems of Writing in the French Renaissance* (Oxford: Clarendon Press, 1979)

——, '"Or donne par donne": échanges metaphoriques et matériels chez Rabelais', paper given at the conference 'Or, monnaie, échange dans la culture de la Renaissance', Lyons, September 1991

Chabod, Federico, '¿Milán o los Países Bajos? Las discusiones sobre la "alternativa" de 1544', in Homenaje de la Universidad de Granada, *Carlos V (1500–1558)* (Granada: Urania, 1958)

——, *Carlos V y su imperio*, trans. Rodrigo Ruza (Mexico: Fondo de Cultural Económica, 1992)

Challis, C. E., *The Tudor Coinage* (Manchester: Manchester University Press, 1978)

Chaney, Edward and Peter Mack, eds, *England and the Continental Renaissance: Essays in Honour of J. B. Trapp* (Woodbridge: Boydell and Brewer, 1990)

Chatterjee, Partha, *Nationalist Thought and the Colonial World: A Derivative Discourse* (London: Zed Books, 1986)

Childs, Wendy, *Anglo-Castilian Trade in the Later Middle Ages* (Manchester: Manchester University Press, 1978)

Cirot, Georges, 'Florian de Ocampo, chroniste de Charles-Quint', *Bulletin Hispanique* XVI (1914), 307–36

Clark, Peter, *English Provincial Society from the Reformation to the Revolution: Religion, Politics and Society in Kent, 1500–1640* (Sussex: The Harvester Press, 1977)

Clark, Sandra, 'Spanish characters and English nationalism in English drama of the early seventeenth century', *Bulletin of Hispanic Studies* 84 (2007), 131–44

Clavería, Carlos, *Le Chevalier Délivré de Olivier de la Marche y sus versiones españolas del siglo XVI* (Zaragoza: Institute Fernando el Católico, C. S. I. C., 1950)

Clifford, Henry, *The Life of Jane Dormer, Duchess of Feria (1643)*, transcribed E. Estcourt and ed. J. Stevenson (London: Burns and Oates Ltd, 1887)

Clot, André, *Suleiman the Magnificent: The Man, His Life, His Epoch* (London: Saqui Books, 1992)

Coleman, Christopher and David Starkey, eds, *Revolution Reassessed: Revisions in the History of Tudor Government and Administration* (Oxford: Clarendon Press, 1986)

Conklin, James, 'The theory of sovereign debt and Spain under Philip II', *Journal of Political Economy* 106:3 (1998), 483–513

Connell-Smith, Gordon, *Forerunners of Drake: A Study of English Trade with Spain in the Early Tudor Period* (Westport, Conn.: Greenwood Press, repr. 1975)

——, 'The ledger of Thomas Howell', *Economic History Review* 2nd ser. 3:3 (1951), 363–70

Cooper, Edward, 'La revuelta de las comunidades. Una visión desde la sacristía', *Hispania* 56 (1996), 467–95

Craik, T. W., 'The political interpretation of two Tudor interludes: *Temperance and Humility* and *Wealth and Health*', *Review of English Studies* n. s. 14 (1953), 98–108

Crehan, J. H., 'The return to obedience: new judgement on Cardinal Pole', *The Month* n. s. 14 (1955), 221–29

Crews, Daniel, *Twilight of the Renaissance: The Life of Juan de Valdés* (Toronto: University of Toronto Press, 2008)

Croft, Pauline, *The Spanish Company* (Chatham: London Record Society, 1973)

Cross, Claire, David Loades and J. J. Scarisbrick, eds, *Law and Government Under the Tudors* (Cambridge: Cambridge University Press, 1988)

Hannah Crumme, 'The politics of Spanish in Elizabethan England', unpublished PhD thesis (King's College London, 2015)

Cummings, Brian, *The Literary Culture of the Reformation: Grammar and Grace* (Oxford: Oxford University Press, 2002)

——, 'Conscience and the law in Thomas More', *Renaissance Studies* 23 (2009), 463–85

Dalton, Heather, 'Roger Barlow: Tudor trade and the Atlantic world' (unpublished doctoral thesis, University of Melbourne, 2008)

——, 'Fashioning new worlds from old worlds: Roger Barlow's *A Brief Summe of Geographie, c.* 1541', in *Old Worlds, New Worlds: European Cultural Encounters c. 1000–1750.* eds Lisa Bailey, Lindsay Diggelmann and Kim Phillips (Turnhout: Brepols, 2008), 75–97

——, 'Negotiating fortune: English merchants in early sixteenth-century Seville', in *Bridging the Early Modern Atlantic World: People, Products and Practices on the Move.* ed. Caroline Williams (Farnham: Ashgate, 2009), 57–73

——, '"Into speyne to selle for slavys": English, Spanish, and Genoese merchant networks and their involvement with the "Cost of Gwynea" trade before 1550' in Toby Green, ed., *Brokers Of Change: Atlantic Commerce and Cultures in Pre-Colonial Western Africa*, British Academy Proceedings Series (Oxford: Oxford University Press, 2012), 91–123

——, *Merchants and Explorers: Roger Barlow, Sebastian Cabot and Networks of Atlantic Exchange, 1500–1560* (Oxford: Oxford University Press, 2016)

Dandelet, Thomas, *Spanish Rome: 1500–1700* (London: Yale University Press, 2001)

Davies, Glyn, *A History of Money: From Ancient Times to the Present Day* (Cardiff: University of Wales Press, 1994)

Dawson, Jane, 'Revolutionary conclusions: the case of the Marian exiles', *History of Political Thought* 11 (1990), 257–72

Deleuze, Gilles, *Masochism: Coldness and Cruelty* (New York: Zone Books, 1989)

Deyermond, Alan, ed., *Historical Literature in Medieval Iberia*, Papers of the Medieval Hispanic Research Seminar 2 (London: Department of Hispanic Studies, Queen Mary and Westfield, 1996)

Diccionario Biográfico Español (Madrid: Real Academia de la Historia, 2009–13) – online versión available at www.dbe.rah.es

Dickens, A. G., *The Courts of Europe: Politics, Patronage and Royalty 1400–1800* (New York: Crown Pub., 1984)

Oxford Dictionary of National Biography, (Oxford: Oxford University Press) – online versión available at www.oxforddnb.com/

Dietz, Frederick, C., *English Government Finance 1485–1558*, University of Illinois Studies in the Social Sciences, vol. 9, no. 3 (Illinois: University of Illinois Press, 1921)

Dillon, Anne, *The Construction of Martyrdom in the English Catholic Community, 1535–1603* (Aldershot: Ashgate, 2002)

——, *Michelangelo and the English Martyrs* (Farnham: Ashgate, 2012)

Dollinger, Philippe, *The Emergence of International Business, 1200–1800*. Vol. I. *The German Hansa* (London: Routledge, repr. 1990)

Domínguez Ortiz, Antonio, *Los Judeoconversos en España y América* (Madrid: Ediciones ISTMO, 1971)

Donald, Dorothy and Elena Lázaro, *Alfonso de Valdés y su época* (Cuenca: Diputación Provincial, 1983)

Donaldson, Peter, 'George Rainsford's *Ritratto d'Inghiterra* (1556)', *Camden Miscellany* 27 (London: Royal Historical Society, 1979), 49–111

——, 'Bishop Gardiner, Machiavellian', *The Historical Journal* 23 (1980), 1–16

Doran, Susan, 'Juno versus Diana: the treatment of Elizabeth I's marriage in plays and entertainments, 1561–1581', *The Historical Journal* 38 (1995), 257–74

——, *Monarchy and Matrimony: The Courtships of Elizabeth I* (London: Routledge, 1996)

—— and Thomas Freeman, eds, *Mary Tudor: Old and New Perspectives* (New York: Palgrave MacMillan, 2011)

Duffy, Eamon, *The Stripping of the Altars: Traditional Religion in England c. 1400–c. 1580* (London: Yale University Press, 1992)

——, *The Voices of Morebath: Reformation and Rebellion in an English Village* (London: Yale University Press, 2001)

——, 'Rolling back the Reformation', *London Review of Books* 30 (7th February 2008), 27

——, *Fires of Faith: Catholic England under Mary Tudor* (London: Yale University Press, 2009)

—— and David Loades, eds, *The Church of Mary Tudor* (Aldershot: Ashgate, 2006)

Duncan, Sarah, *Mary I: Gender, Power, and Ceremony in the Reign of England's First Queen* (New York: Palgrave MacMillan, 2012)

—— and Valerie Schutte, eds, *The Birth of a Queen: Essay on the Quincentenary of Mary I* (New York: Palgrave MacMillan, 2016)

Dunham, William Huse, Jr, 'Regal power and the rule of law: a Tudor paradox', *Journal of British Studies* 3 (1963–4), 24–56

Dupire, Noel, *Jean Molinet: La vie – Les oeuvres* (Paris: Droz, 1932)

——, *Jean Molinet: Les Faictz et les dictz*, 3 vols (Paris: Société des anciens textes françaises, 1936–9)

Earenfight, Theresa, ed., *Queenship and Political Power in Medieval and Early Modern Spain* (Aldershot: Ashgate, 2005)

Edwards, John, 'Without the persona of the Prince: Kings, Queens and the idea of monarch in late medieval Europe', *Gender and History* 19 (2007), 1–21

——, *Mary I: England's Catholic Queen* (London: Yale University Press, 2011)

——, *Archbishop Pole* (Farnham: Ashgate, 2014)

——, *Mary I: The Daughter of Time* (London: Allen Lane, 2016)

—— and Ronald Truman, eds, *Reforming Catholicism in the England of Mary Tudor: The Achievement of Friar Bartolomé Carranza* (Aldershot: Ashgate, 2005)

Edwards, Peter, *The Horse Trade in Tudor and Stuart England* (Cambridge: Cambridge University Press, 1988)

Ehrenberg, Richard, *Capital and Finance in the Age of the Renaissance: A Study of the Fuggers and their Connections*, trans. H. M. Lucas (London: Jonathan Cape, 1928)

Eisenstadt, S. N., and Louis Roniger, 'Patron–client relations as a model of structuring social exchange', *Society for Comparative Study of Society and History* 22 (1980), 42–77

Elliott, J. H., *Imperial Spain 1469–1716* (1st pub. 1963; London: Penguin repr. 1975)

——, *Spain and Its World 1500–1700* (London: Yale University Press, 1989)

Elton, Geoffrey, *England under the Tudors* (London: Longman, 1964)

——, 'Reform by statute: Thomas Starkey's *Dialogue* and Thomas Cromwell's policy', *Proceedings of the British Academy* 54 (1968), 165–88

——, *Reform and Reformation: England 1509–1558* (London: Edward Arnold, 1977)

Emmison, F. G., *Tudor Secretary: Sir William Petre at Court and at Home* (London: Longmans, 1961)

Esclapez, Raymond, 'La parodie des *Antiquités* chez Rabelais', *Nouvelle Revue du Seizième Siècle* 7 (1989), 25–36

Escudero, José Antonio, *Los Secretarios de Estado y del Despacho (1472–1724)*, 4 vols, Vol. 1. *El Desarrollo Historico de la Institución* (2nd edn, Madrid: Instituto de Estudios Administrativos, 1976)

Fabel, Kirk M., 'Questions of numismatic and linguistic signification in the reign of Mary Tudor', *Studies in English Literature* 37 (1997), 237–55

Fenlon, Dermot, *Heresy and Obedience in Tridentine Italy: Cardinal Pole and the Counter Reformation* (Cambridge: Cambridge University Press, 1972)

Fernandes, Isabelle, *Marie Tudor: La souffrance du pouvoir* (Paris: Tallandier, 2016)

Fernández Álvarez, Manuel, *La España del emperador Carlos V (1500–1558; 1517–1556)*, Vol. XVIII de *La Historia de España*. ed. R. Menéndez Pidal (Madrid: Espasa-Calpe, SA, 1966)

——, *Felipe II y su tiempo* (Madrid: Espasa-Calpe, SA, 1998)

Fernández-Santamaria, J. A., *The State, War and Peace: Spanish Political Thought in the Renaissance 1516–1559* (Cambridge: Cambridge University Press, 1977)

Fernández y Fernández de Retana, Luis P., *Historia de España,* Vol. XIX. *España en tiempo de Felipe II (1556–1598)* (Madrid: Espasa-Calpe, SA, 1958)

Ferrer Valls, Teresa, *La Práctica Escénica Cortesana* (London: Tamesis, 1993)

——, *Nobleza y Espectáculo Teatral (1535–1622): Estudio y Documentos* (Valencia: Uned, Uinversidad de Sevilla/Universitat de València, 1993)

Fichtner, Paula Sutter, *Emperor Maximilian II* (London: Yale University Press, 2001)

Fisher, F. J., 'Influenza and inflation in Tudor England', *Economic History Review* 2nd ser. XVIII (1965), 120–9

Fletcher, Anthony, *Tudor Rebellions*, Seminar Studies in History (London: Longmans 1968)

Fontaine, Marie Madeleine, 'Olivier de la Marche and Jen Lemaire de Belges: the author and his female patron' in Dagmar Eichberger, ed., *Women of Distinction: Margaret of York/Margaret of Austria* (Leuven: Brepols, 2005), 221–9

Foster, G. M., 'Peasant society and the image of limited good', *American Anthropologist* 67 (1965), 293–315

Foster, Steven, 'The reception of Romans 13:1–7 during the English Reformation', unpublished PhD thesis (University of Leeds, 2017)

Foucault, Michel, *The Order of Things: An Archaeology of the Human Sciences* (London: Routledge, repr. 1994)

Fox, Alistair, and John Guy, eds, *Reassessing the Henrician Age* (Oxford: Basil Blackwell, 1986)

Froude, James Anthony, *The Reign of Mary Tudor* (London: Continuum, 2009)

Fryer, Peter, *Staying Power: The History of Black People in Britain* (London: Pluto Press, 1984)

Fuchs, Barbara, *Exotic Nation: Maurophilia and the Construction of Early Modern Spain* (Philadelphia: University of Pennsylvania Press, 2009)

——, *The Poetics of Piracy: Emulating Spain in English Literature* (Philadelphia: University of Pennsylvavnia Press, 2013)

Gammon, Samuel, *Statesman and Schemer: William, First Lord Paget Tudor Minister* (Newton Abbot: David & Charles, 1973)

Garrett, Christina, *The Marian Exiles 1553–1559: A Study in the Origins of Elizabethan Puritanism* (Cambridge: Cambridge University Press, 1938)

Gelabert, Juan E., 'Intercambio y tolerancia: las Villas marineras de la fachada atlantica y el conflicto Anglo-Español (1559–1604)', *Revista de historia naval* 5 (1987), 57–68

Gil, Luis, 'Una petición de ayuda al Cardenal Granvela', *Sefarad* 52 (1992), 97–101

Gill, J., *The Council of Florence* (Cambridge: Cambridge University Press, 1959)

Glacken, Clarence J., *Traces on the Rhodian Shore: Nature and Culture in Western Thought From Ancient Times to the end of the Eighteenth Century* (London: University of California Press, repr. 1973)

Goose, Nigel, '"Xenophobia" in Elizabethan and early Stuart England: an epithet too far' in Nigel Goose and Lien Luu, eds, *Immigrants in Tudor and Early Stuart England* (Brighton: Sussex Academic Press, 2005), 110–35

Gordon Kinder, A., *Casiodoro de Reina: Spanish Reformer of the Sixteenth Century* (London: Tamesis Books Ltd, 1975)

Gordon Zeeveld, W., *Foundations of Tudor Policy* (Cambridge, Mass., Harvard University Press, 1948)

Grabes, Herbert, *Writing the Early Modern English Nation: The Transformation of National Identity in Sixteenth- and Seventeenth-Century England* (Amsterdam: Rodopi, 2001)

Graves, Michael A. R., *The House of Lords in the Parliaments of Edward VI and Mary I: an institutional study* (London: Cambridge University Press, 1981)

Grayzel, Solomon, *The Church and the Jews in the XIIIth Century* (New York: Hermon Press, 1966)

Grierson, Philip, 'The origins of the English sovereign and the symbolism of the closed crown', *British Numismatic Journal* 33 (1964), 118–34

Griffin, Eric, 'From ethos to ethnos: 'hispanizing' the Spaniard in the Old World and the New', *Centennial Review: the new Centennial Review* 2 (2002), 69–116

——, *English Renaissance Drama and the Specter of Spain: Ethnopoetics and Empire* (Philadelphia: University of Pennsylvania Press, 2009)

Griffiths, G., *Representative Government in Western Europe in the Sixteenth Century* (Oxford: Clarendon Press, 1968)

Groot, Wim de, ed., *The Seventh Window: The King's Window Donated by Philip II and Mary Tudor to Sint Janskerk in Gouda (1557)* (Hilversum: Verloren, 2005)

Guth, Delloyd and John McKenna, eds, *Tudor Rule and Revolution: Essays for G. R. Elton from his American friends* (Cambridge: Cambridge University Press, 1982)

Guy, John, 'Law, equity and conscience in Henrician juristic thought', in *Reassessing the Henrician Age*. eds Alistair Fox and John Guy (Oxford: Basil Blackwell, 1986)

——, *Tudor England* (Oxford: Oxford University Press, 1988)

——, *The Oxford History of the Tudors and Stuarts* (Oxford: Oxford University Press, 1996)

——, 'Conference style' review of *Talking Peace 1604* exhibition and Rosemary Mulcahy, *Philip II of Spain: Patron of the Arts*, *Times Literary Supplement*, 10th September 2004, 17

——, 'The Marian court and Tudor policy making' at www.tudors.org/undergradu ate/the-marian-court-and-tudor-policy-making/ [Accessed 27th October 2014]

Hackett, Helen, *Virgin Mother, Maiden Queen: Elizabeth and the Cult of the Virgin Mary* (Basingstoke: Macmillan, 1995)

Hadfield, Andrew, ed., *Amazons, Savages and Machiavels: Travel and Colonial Writing in English* (Oxford: Oxford University Press, 2002)

Haigh, Christopher, *English Reformations: Religion, Politics and Society under the Tudors* (Oxford: Clarendon Press, 1993)

Haliczer, Stephen, *The Comuneros of Castile: Forging a Revolution, 1475–1521* (London: University of Wisconsin Press, 1981)

Hall, A., 'Catholicism and drama', unpublished PhD thesis (Cambridge, 1994)

Hamilton, Alastair, *The Family of Love* (Cambridge: James Clarke, 1981)

——, *Heresy and Mysticism in Sixteenth Century Spain: The Alumbrados* (Cambridge: James Clarke, 1992)

Hansen, Mogens H., *The Athenian Democracy in the Age of Demosthenes: Structure, Principles and Ideology* (Oxford, Blackwell, repr. 1992)

Harbage, Alfred, ed., *Annals of English Drama 975–1700*, revised S. Schoenbaum (London: Methuen, 1964)

Harbison, E. H., *Rival Ambassadors at the Court of Queen Mary* (New York: Books For Libraries Press 1940, repr. 1970)

——, 'French intrigue at the court of Queen Mary', *American Historical Review* 45 (1940), 533–51

Harris, Barbara J., 'Marriage sixteenth century style: Elizabeth Stafford and the third Duke of Norfolk', *Journal of Social History* 15 (1982), 371–82

Hart, H., *The Concept of Law* (Oxford: Clarendon Press, 1961)

Harvey, Margaret, *England, Rome and the Papacy 1417–1464: The study of a relationship* (Manchester: Manchester University Press, 1993)

Hearn, Karen, ed., *Dynasties: Painting in Tudor and Jacobean England 1530–1630*, exhibition catalogue, 1997 (Peterborough: Tate Publishing, 1995)

Heath, Michael, 'Unholy alliance: Valois and Ottomans', *Renaissance Studies* 3 (1989), 303–18

Heesakkers, Chris, 'The ambassador of the republic of letters at the wedding of Prince Philip of Spain and Queen Mary of England: Hadrianus Junius and his *Philippeis*', in *Acta Conventus Neo-Latini Abulensis: Proceedings of the Tenth International Congress of Neo-Latin Studies*. gen. ed. Rhoda Schnur (Tempe: Arizona Centre for Medieval and Renaissance Studies, 2000), 325–32

Helgerson, Richard, *Forms of Nationhood: The Elizabethan Writing of England* (Chicago: University of Chicago Press, 1992)

——, *A Sonnet from Carthage* (Philadelphia: University of Pennsylvania Press, 2007)

Henderson, Judith, 'John Heywood's *The Spider and the Fly*: educating queen and country', *Studies in Philology* 96 (1999), 241–74

Henderson, Paula, 'Medievalism in the English "Renaissance" garden', in *Locus Amoenus: Gardens and Horticulture in the Renaissance*, ed. Alexander Samson (Chichester: Wiley-Blackwell, 2012)

Herrup, Cynthia, 'The patriarch at home: the trial of the 2nd Earl of Castlehaven for rape and sodomy', *History Workshop Journal* 41 (1996), 1–18

Highley, Christopher, *Catholics Writing the Nation in Early Modern Britain and Ireland* (Oxford: Oxford University Press, 2008)

Hill, Tracey, *Pageantry and Power: A Cultural History of the Early Modern Lord Mayor's Show, 1585–1639* (Manchester: Manchester University Press, 2010)

Hillgarth, J. N., *The Mirror for Spain, 1500–1700: The Formation of a Myth* (Ann Arbor: University of Michigan Press, 2000)

Himsworth, Sheila, 'The marriage of Philip II of Spain with Mary Tudor', *The Proceedings of the Hampshire Field Club and Archaeological Society* 22 (1962), 82–100

Hind, Arthur M., *Engraving in England in the 16th and 17th Centuries: A Descriptive Catalogue with Introductions*, 3 vols (Cambridge: Cambridge University Press, 1952)

Hoak, Dale, ed., *Tudor Political Culture* (Cambridge: Cambridge University Press, 1995)

———, 'The coronations of Edward VI, Mary I, and Elizabeth I, and the transformation of the Tudor monarchy', in *Westminster Abbey Reformed, 1540–1640*. eds C. S. Knighton and Richard Mortimer (Basingstoke: Ashgate, 2003), 114–51

Hobbes, Thomas, *Leviathan*, ed. R. Tuck, Cambridge Texts in the History of Political Thought (Cambridge: Cambridge University Press, 1991)

Hogrefe, Pearl, 'Legal rights of Tudor women and the circumvention by men and women', *Sixteenth Century Journal* 3 (1972), 97–105

Holdsworth, W. S., *A History of English Law*, 17 vols (7th edn, London: Methuen & Co., 1956–72)

Holmes, Martin, 'Evil May Day, 1517: the story of a riot', *History Today* 15 (1965), 642–50

Holmes, Peter, *Resistance and Compromise: The Political Thought of the Elizabethan Catholics* (Cambridge: Cambridge University Press, 1982)

Holstun, James, '*The Spider and the Fly* and the commonwealth: merrie John Heywood and agrarian class struggle', *English Literary History* 71 (2004), 53–88

Hope, Charles, *Titian* (London: Jupiter Books, 1980)

Hopkins, Lisa, *Queen Elizabeth I and her Court* (London: St Martin's Press, 1990)

——— and Annaliese Connolly, eds, *Goddesses and Queens: the Iconography of Elizabeth I* (Manchester: Manchester University Press, 2007)

Horn, H. J., *Jan Corneliz Vermeyen: Painter of Charles V and his Conquest of Tunis*, Actas Aurea, Monographs on Dutch and Flemish Painting VIII: Jan Cornelisz Vermeyen, 2 vols (Doornspijk, Netherlands: Davaco. 1989)

Houlbrooke, Ralph, 'Mid-Tudor polity', *Journal of Ecclesiastical History* 32 (1981), 503–7

Howarth, David, *Images of Rule: Art and Politics in the English Renaissance, 1485–1649* (Basingstoke: Macmillan, 1997)

Hudson, W. S., *John Ponet (1516?–1556): Advocate of Limited Monarchy* (Chicago: University of Chicago Press, 1942)

Hughes, Diane Owen, 'Distinguishing signs: ear-rings, Jews and Franciscan rhetoric in the Italian Renaissance city', *Past and Present* 112 (1986), 3–59

Hume, Martin A. S., 'The visit of Philip II', *English Historical Review* VII (1892), 253–80

Hunt, Alice, 'Legitimacy, ceremony and drama: Mary Tudor's coronation and *Respublica*', in *Interludes and Early Modern Society*, eds Peter Happé and Wim Husken (Amsterdam: Rodopi, 2007), 331–51

———, *The Drama of Coronation: Medieval Ceremony in Early Modern England* (Cambridge: Cambridge University Press, 2008)

———, 'The monarchical republic of Mary I', *Historical Journal* 52 (2009), 557–72

—— and Anna Whitelock, eds, *Tudor Queenship* (New York: Palgrave MacMillan, 2010)

Hunt, William, *The Puritan Moment: The Coming of Revolution in an English County* (London: Harvard University Press, 1983)

Hutchings, Michael, 'The reign of Mary Tudor: a reassessment', *History Review* 23 (1999), 20–25

Ife, Barry W., *Reading and Fiction in Golden-Age Spain: A Platonist critique and some picaresque replies* (Cambridge: Cambridge University Press, 1985)

Iñiguez Almech, Francisco, *Casas reales y jardines de Felipe II* (Madrid: Consejo Superior de Investigaciones Cientificas, 1952)

Iongh, Jane de, *Mary of Hungary: Second Regent of the Netherlands*, trans. Herter Norton (London: Faber & Faber, 1959)

Jagger, Meriel, 'Bonner's episcopal visitation of London, 1554', *Historical Research* 45 (1972), 306–11

James, Susan, *The Feminine Dynamic in English Art, 1485–1603* (Farnham: Ashgate, 2009)

Jansen, Sharon, *The Monstrous Regiment of Women: Female Rulers in Early Modern Europe*, Queenship and Power Series (New York: Palgrave Macmillan, 2002)

Jardine, Lisa, *Worldly Goods* (London: Macmillan, 1996)

—— and Jerry Brotton, *Global Interests: Renaissance Art between East and West* (London: Reaktion, 2000)

Jedin, H., *A History of the Coucil of Trent*, trans. D. Graf, 2 vols (Edinburgh: Thomas Nelson and Sons Ltd, 1961)

Jenkins, Michael, *Artful Eloquence: Jean Lemaire de Belges and the Rhetorical Tradition* (Chapel Hill: North Carolina Studies in the Romances Languages and Literatures, 1980)

Jerdan, William, 'Device for the coronation of Henry VII', *Rutland Papers*, Camden Society Old Series 21 (London: Camden Society, 1842)

Johnson, Hugh, *The Story of Wine* (London: Mitchell Beazley, 1989)

Jones, Edwin, *The English Nation: The Great Myth* (Thrupp: Sutton Publishing, 1998)

——, *John Lingard and the Pursuit of Historical Truth* (Brighton: Sussex Academic Press, 2001)

Jones, Emrys, *The New Oxford Book of Sixteenth-Century Verse* (Oxford: Oxford University Press, 1992)

Jones, Whitney, *William Turner: Tudor Naturalist, Physician and Divine* (London: Routledge 1988)

Jordan, Constance, 'Feminism and the humanists: the case of Sir Thomas Elyot's *Defence of Good Women*', *Renaissance Quarterly* 36 (1983), 181–201

——, 'Woman's rule in sixteenth-century British political thought', *Renaissance Quarterly* 40 (1987), 421–51

Jordan, W. K., *Edward VI: The Threshold of Power. The Dominance of the Duke of Northumberland* (London: George Allen and Unwin Ltd, 1970)

Juderías, Julián, *La Leyenda Negra: Estudios acerca del concepto de España en el extranjero* (Madrid: Editora Nacional, 1960)

Kagan, Richard L., 'Philip II and the art of cityscape', *Journal of Interdisciplinary History* 17 (1986), 115–35

——, *Spanish Cities of the Golden Age: The Views of Anton van den Wyngaerder* (London: University of California Press, 1989)

——, 'Clio and the crown: writing history in Habsburg Spain' in Richard Kagan and Geoffrey Parker, eds, *Spain, Europe and the Atlantic World: Essays in Honour of John H. Elliot* (Cambridge: Cambridge University Press, 1995), 73–99

Kamen, Henry, *Inquisition and Society in Spain in the Sixteenth and Seventeenth Centuries* (London: Weidenfeld and Nicolson, 1985)

——, *Spain 1469–1714: A Society of Conflict* (2nd edn, London: Longman, 1991)

——, *Felipe de España*, trans. Patricia Escandón (Madrid: Siglo Venitiuno de España Editores, SA, 1997)

——, *The Spanish Inquisition: An Historical Revision* (London: Weidenfeld & Nicolson, 1997)

Kantorowicz, Ernst, *The King's Two Bodies: A Study in Medieval Political Theology* (Princeton, NJ: Princeton University Press, 1957)

Karrow, Robert W., *Mapmakers of the 16th Century and Their Maps* (Chicago: Speculum Orbis Press, 1993)

Katz, D., *The Jews in the History of England 1485–1850* (Oxford: Clarendon Press, 1994)

Kaufman, Miranda, 'Africans in Britain, 1500–1640', unpublished PhD thesis (Oxford, 2011)

——, *Black Tudors: The Untold Story* (London: Oneworld, 2017)

Kelley, D. R., *Foundations of Modern Historical Scholarship: Language, Law and History in the French Renaissance* (New York: Columbia University Press, 1976)

Kelsey, Harry, *Philip of Spain, King of England: The Forgotten Sovereign* (London: I. B. Tauris, 2012)

Kerridge, Eric, *Trade and Banking in Early Modern England* (Manchester: Manchester University Press, 1988)

Kewes, Paulina, 'Two queens, one inventory: the lives of Mary and Elizabeth Tudor' in Kevin Sharpe and Steven Zwicker, eds, *Writing Lives: Biography and Textuality, Identity and Representation in Early Modern England* (Oxford: Oxford University Press, 2008), 187–207

King, John, *Tudor Royal Iconography: Literature and Art in an Age of Religious Crisis* (Princeton, NJ: Princeton University Press, 1989)

Kingdon, John Abernethy, *Richard Grafton: Citizen and Grocer of London* (London: Rixon & Arnold, 1901)

Kinghorn, A. M., *The Chorus of History: Literary-historical relations in Renaissance Britain 1485–1558* (London: Blandford Press, 1971)

Kipling, Gordon, *The Triumph of Honour: Burgundian Origins of the Elizabethan Renaissance* (Leiden: Leiden University Press, 1977)

——, *Enter the King* (Oxford: Clarendon Press, 1998)

Klein, Melanie, *Envy, Gratitude and Other Works, 1946–1963*, The International

Psychoanalytic Library No. 104, ed. Melanie Klein (London: Hogarth Press and Institute of Psychoanalysis, 1975)

——, *Love, Guilt and Reparation and Other Works 1921–1945*, The International Psychoanalytic Library No. 103, ed. Melanie Klein (London: Hogarth Press and Institute of Psychoanalysis, 1975)

Knight, Stephen, *Arthurian Literature and Society* (London: Macmillan, 1983)

Koenigsberger, H. G., *The Government of Sicily under Philip II of Spain: A Study in the Practice of Empire* (London: Staples Press, 1951)

Kristeva, Julia, *Strangers to Ourselves*, trans. Leon S. Roudiez (London: Harvester Wheatsheaf, 1991)

Kubler, George, *Mexican Architecture of the Sixteenth Century*, 2 vols (New Haven, Conn.: Yale University Press, 1948)

Laqueur, Thomas, *Making Sex: Body and Gender from the Greeks to Freud* (Cambridge, Mass.: Harvard University Press, 1990)

Laslett, Peter, W. G. Runciman and Quentin Skinner, eds, *Philosophy, Politics and Society*, 4th ser. (Oxford: Basil Blackwell, 1972)

Lea, Henry Charles, *Chapters from the Religious History of Spain* (Philadelphia, Penn.: Lea Brothers & Co., 1890)

——, 'Él Santo Niño de la Guardia', *English Historical Review* 4 (1889), 229–50

——, *A History of the Inquisition of Spain*, 4 vols (London: MacMillan & Co. Ltd, 1907)

Leadam, I. S., 'A narrative of the pursuit of English refugees in Germany under Queen Mary', *Transactions of the Royal Historical Society* n. s. XI (1897), 113–31

Leader, Damian Riehl, *A History of the University of Cambridge*. Vol. I, *The University to 1546* (Cambridge: Cambridge University Press, 1988)

Lee, Patricia-Ann, 'A bodye politique to governe: Aylmer, Knox, and the debate on queenship', *The Historian* 52 (1990), 242–61

Lehmberg, Stanford E., *Sir Thomas Elyot: Tudor Humanist* (Austin: Univeristy of Texas Press, 1960)

Leland, John, *De rebus Britannicis collectanea* (1774: repr. Farnborough, fac. edn 1970)

Levin, Carole, 'Queens and claimants: political insecurity in sixteenth-century England' in Janet Sharistanian, ed., *Gender, Ideology and Action: Historical Perspectives on Women's Public Lives* (London: Greenwood Press, 1986)

——, *Propaganda in the English Reformation: Heroic and Villainous Images of King John* (Lewiston, Maine: Edwin Mellen Press, 1988)

Levine, Mortimer, *Tudor Dynastic Problems, 1460–1571*, Historical Problems Studies and Documents no. 21, ed. G. R. Elton (London: George Allen and Unwin Ltd, 1973)

Lévi-Strauss, Claude, *The Elementary Structures of Kinship*, trans. James Harle Bell and Richard von Sturmer and ed. Rodney Needham (London: Eyre & Spottiswoode, 1970)

Lewis, Elizabeth, 'A sixteenth century painted ceiling from Winchester College', *Proceedings of the Hampshire Field Club Archaeological Society* 51 (1995), 137–65

Liss, Peggy, *Isabel the Queen: Life and Times* (2nd edn, Philadelphia: University of Pennsylvania Press, 2004)

Lloyd, Terence, *England and the German Hanse, 1157–1611: A Study of their Trade and Commercial Diplomacy* (Cambridge: Cambridge University Press, 1991)

Loach, Jennifer, 'Pamphlets and politics 1553–1558', *Bulletin of the Institute of Historial Research* 98 (1975), 31–45

—— *Parliament and Crown in the Reign of Mary Tudor* (Oxford: Clarendon Press, 1986)

—— 'The Marian establishment and the printing press', *English Historical Review* 101 (1986), 135–48

—— and Robert Tittler, eds, *The Mid-Tudor Polity c. 1540–1560* (London: Macmillan, 1980)

Loades, David, 'The authorship and publication of *The Copye*', *Transactions of the Cambridge Bibliographical Society* 3 (1960), 155–60

——, 'The Essex Inquisitions of 1556', *Bulletin of the Institute of Historical Research* 35 (1962), 87–97

——, *Two Tudor Conspiracies* (Cambridge: Cambridge University Press, 1965)

——, *The Oxford Martyrs* (London: B. T. Batsford Ltd, 1970)

——, 'The Netherlands and the Anglo-Papal reconciliation of 1554', *Nederlands Archief voor Kerkgeschiedenis* 60:1 (1980), 39–53

——, *The Tudor Court* (Totowa, NJ: Barnes & Noble Books, 1987) (2nd edn: Oxford: Davenant Press, 2003)

——, 'The reign of Mary Tudor: historiography and research', *Albion* 21 (1989), 547–58

——, *Politics, Censorship and the English Reformation* (London: Pinter Publishers, 1991)

——, *The Reign of Mary Tudor: Politics, Government and Religion, 1553–1558* (2nd edn, London: Longman, 1991)

——, *Politics and the Nation 1450–1660: Obedience, Resistance and Public Order* (1st pub. 1974, London: Fontana, repr. 1992)

——, *Mary Tudor: A Life* (Oxford: Basil Blackwell, 1992)

——, *Power in Tudor England* (London: Macmillan, 1997)

——, 'Literature and national identity' in David Loewenstein and Janel Mueller, eds, *The Cambridge History of Early Modern English Literature* (Cambridge: Cambridge University Press, 2002), 201–28

——, *Intrigue and Treason: The Tudor Court 1547–1558* (London: Pearson, 2004)

——, *Mary Tudor: The Tragical History of the first Queen of England* (Richmond: The National Archives, 2006)

——, *The Life and Career of William Paulet (c. 1475–1572)* (Aldershot: Ashgate, 2008)

——, *The Religious Culture of Marian England* (London: Pickering & Chatto, 2010)

—— and Katherine Walsh, *Faith and Identity: Christian Political Experience*, Studies in Church History Subsidia 6 (Oxford: Basil Blackwell, 1990)

Lovett, A. W., *Early Habsburg Spain 1517–1598* (Oxford: Oxford University Press, 1986)

Loyola, Ignatius, *The Spiritual Exercises*, trans. W. H. Longbridge (4th edn, London: A. R. Mawbry and Co. Ltd., 1950)

Lucian, *The Works of Lucian*, trans. K. Kilburn, Loeb Classical Library 430, 8 vols (Cambridge Mass.: Harvard University Press, 1959)

Luu, Lien Bich, *Immigrants and Industries of London, 1500–1700* (Aldershot: Ashgate, 2005)

MacCulloch, Diarmaid, 'Two dons in politics: Thomas Cranmer and Stephen Gardiner, 1503–1533', *The Historical Journal* 37 (1994), 1–22

——, *Thomas Cranmer: A Life* (London: Yale University Press, 1996)

Macfarlane, Alan, *The Origins of English Individualism: The Family, Property and Social Transition* (Oxford: Basil Blackwell, 1978)

Machielson, Jan, 'The lion, the witch, and the king: Thomas Stapleton's *Apologia pro Rege Catholico Philippo II* (1592)', *English Historical Review* 129 (2014), 19–46

MacKay, Angus, 'Popular movements and pogroms in fifteenth-century Castile', *Past and Present* 55 (1972), 33–67

Mackie, J. D., *The Earlier Tudors 1485–1558*, The Oxford History of England VII (Oxford: Clarendon Press, 1952)

Anne MacLaren, *Political Culture in the Reign of Elizabeth I: Queen and Commonwealth 1558–1585* (Cambridge: Cambridge University Press, 1999)

Maclean, Ian, *The Renaissance Notion of Woman: A Study in the Fortunes of Scholasticism and Medical Science in European Intellectual Life*, Cambridge Monographs on the History of Medicene (Cambridge: Cambridge University Press, 1980)

Maley, Willy, '"Another Britain"?: Bacon's certain considerations touching the plantation in Ireland (1609)', *Prose Studies* 18 (1995), 1–18

——, 'Spenser and Scotland: the view and the limits of Anglo-Irish identity', *Prose Studies* 19 (1996), 1–18

Maltby, William, *The Black Legend in England* (Durham, NC: Duke University Press, 1971)

Marland, Hilary, ed., *The Art of Midwifery: Early Modern Midwives in Europe* (London: Routledge, 1993)

Marshall, Rosalind K., *Mary I* (London: HMSO, 1993)

Martin, Colin and Geoffrey Parker, *The Spanish Armada* (London: Hamish Hamilton, 1988)

Martin, J. W., 'The Marian regime's failure to understand the importance of printing', *Huntington Library Quarterly* 44 (1981), 231–47

——, 'Miles Hogharde: artisan and aspiring author in sixteenth-century England', *Renaissance Quarterly* 34 (1981), 359–83

Martínez Millán, José, 'Élites de poder en tiempos de Felipe II (1539–1572)', *Hispania* 49 (1989), 111–49

Martz, Linda, 'Converso families in fifteenth and sixteenth century Toledo: the significance of lineage', *Sefarad* 48 (1988), 117–96

——, 'Pure blood statutes in sixteenth century Toledo: implementation as opposed to adoption', *Sefarad* 54 (1994), 83–106

Marx, Karl, *Selected Writings*, ed. David McLellan (Oxford: Oxford University Press, repr. 1988)

Matthews, P. G., 'Portaits of Philip II of Spain as King of England', *The Burlington Magazine* 142 (2000), 13–19

Mattingly, Garrett, *Catherine of Aragon* (London: Jonathan Cape, 1944)

———, *Renaissance Diplomacy* (London: Jonathan Cape, 1955)

Maurer, Gretchen, *Mary Tudor: 'Bloody Mary'* (Foster City, Cal.: Goosebottom Books, 2011)

Mayer, Thomas F. and Courtney Walters, eds, *The Correspondence of Reginald Pole*, 4 vols (Aldershot: Ashgate, 2002–8)

McCoy, Richard C., 'From the Tower to the tiltyard: Robert Dudley's return to glory', *The Historical Journal* 27 (1984), 425–35

McGrath, Patrick, 'Winchester College and the old religion in the sixteenth century' in Roger Custance, ed., *Winchester College: Sixth Centenary Essays* (Oxford: Oxford University Press, 1982), 229–80

McIntosh, Jeri, *From Heads of Household to Heads of State: The Preaccession Households of Mary and Elizabeth Tudor, 1516–1558* (New York: Columbia University Press, 2009)

McKendrick, Melveena, *Theatre in Spain 1490–1700* (Cambridge: Cambridge University Press 1989)

Mears, Natalie, 'Politics in the Elizabethan Privy Chamber: Lady Mary Sidney and Kat Ashley', in *Women and Politics in Early Modern England, 1450–1700*, ed. James Daybell (Aldershot: Ashgate, 2004), 67–82

———, *Queenship and Political Discourse in the Elizabethan Realms* (Cambridge: Cambridge University Press, 2005)

Medvei, V. C., 'The illness and death of Mary Tudor', *Journal of the Royal Society of Medicine* 80 (1987), 766–70

Mély, F. de, 'Les primitifs et leurs signatures: Quinten Matsys et Marinus', *Gazette des Beaux-Arts* (1908), 135–47

Mercer, Eric, *English Art 1533–1625*, The Oxford History of Art, 11 vols (Oxford: Clarendon Press, 1962)

Merton, Charlotte, 'The women who served Queen Mary and Queen Elizabeth: ladies, gentlewomen and maids of the Privy Chamber, 1553–1603', unpublished PhD thesis (Cambridge University, 1992)

Metzger, Marcia Lee, 'Controversy and "correctness": English chronicles and the chroniclers, 1553–1568', *Sixteenth Century Journal* 27 (1996), 437–51

Monter, William, 'Heresy executions in Reformation Europe, 1520–65' in Ole Peter Grell and Bob Scribner, eds, *Tolerance and Intolerance in the European Reformation* (Cambridge: Cambridge University Press, 1996), 48–64

Moore, John, 'Jack Fisher's flu: a visitation revisited', *Economic History Review* 46 (1993), 280–307

———, 'Jack Fisher's flu: a virus still virulent', *Economic History Review* 47 (1994), 359–61

Morales Folguera, José Miguel, 'El arte al servicio del poder y de la propaganda imperial. La boda del príncipe Felipe con María Tudor en la catedral de Winchester y la solemne entrada de la pareja real en Londres', *Potestas: Revista del Grupo Europeo de Investigación Histórica* 2 (1999), 165–89

Muir, Kenneth, *Life and Letters of Sir Thomas Wyatt* (Liverpool: Liverpool University Press, 1963)

Muldrew, Craig, 'Interpreting the market: the ethics of credit and community relations in early modern England', *Social History* 18 (May 1993), 1
63–83

Mullaney, Stephen, 'Lying like truth: riddle, representation and treason in Renaissance
England', *English Literary History* 47 (1980), 32–47

Muller, James Arthur, *Stephen Gardiner and the Tudor Reaction* (London: Macmillan,
1926)

Mulvey, Laura, *Visual and Other Pleasures* (London: Macmillan, 1989)

Nader, Helen, *Liberty in Absolutist Spain: The Habsburg Sale of Towns, 1516–1700*
(London: Johns Hopkins University Press, 1990)

Necipo_lu, Gülru, 'Süleyman the Magnificent and the representation of power in
the context of Ottoman–Habsburg–Papal rivalry', *Art Bulletin* LXXI (1989),
401–27

Nesvig, Martin Austin, ed., *Forgotten Franciscans: Works from an Inquisitorial Theorist,
a Heretic and an Inquisitorial Deputy*, Latin American Originals (Pennsylvania:
Pennsylvania State University Press, 2011)

Nexon, Daniel, *The Struggle for Power in Early Modern Europe: Religious Conflict, Dynastic
Empires and International Change* (Princeton, NJ: Princeton University Press,
2009)

Noreña, Carlos G., *Studies in Spanish Renaissance Thought*, International Archives of the
History of Ideas 82 (The Hague: Martinus Nijhoff, 1975)

Norland, Howard, *Drama in Early Tudor Britain 1485–1558* (Lincoln: University of
Nebraska Press, 1995)

Novalín, José Luis G., *El inquisidor general Fernando de Valdés (1483–1568)* (Oviedo:
Universidad de Oviedo, 1971)

Oakley-Brown, Liz and Louise Wilkinson, eds, *The Rituals and Rhetoric of Queenship:
Medieval to Early Modern* (Dublin: Four Courts, 2009)

Olarte, Teodoro, *Alfonso de Castro (1495–1558): Su vida, tiempo y sus ideas – filolófi-
co-jurídicas* (San Jose: Facultad de Fiosofía y Letras, 1946)

Oldenburg, Scott, 'Toward a multicultural mid-Tudor England: the Queen's royal
entry circa 1553, *The Interlude of Weath and Health*, and the question of strangers
in the reign of Mary I', *English Literary History* 76 (2009), 99–129

Ollero, Julio, ed., *Los Austrias: Grabados de la Biblioteca Nacional* (Madrid: Biblioteca
Nacional, 1993)

Outhwaite, R. B., 'The trials of foreign borrowing: the English crown and the
Antwerp money market in the mid-sixteenth century', *Economic History Review*
2nd ser. XIX (1966), 289–305

Owens, J. B., *'By My Absolute Royal Authority': Justice and the Castilian Commonwealth
at the Beginning of the First Global Age* (Rochester, NY: University of Rochester
Press, 2005)

Páez Ríos, Elena, *Iconografía britana: catálogo de los retratos grabados de personajes ingleses
de la Biblioteca Nacional* (Madrid: Blass, S.A, 1948)

——, *Repertorio de grabados españoles en la Biblioteca Nacional*, 4 vols (Madrid:
Ministerio de Cultura, 1985)

Page, William, ed., *The Victoria County History of Hampshire and the Isle of Wight*, vol. 5 (London: Constable and Co. Ltd, 1912)

Painter, Sidney, *Studies in the History of the English Feudal Barony* (Baltimore, Mary.: Johns Hopkins University Press, 1943)

Palliser, D. M., *The Age of Elizabeth 1547–1603* (London: Longman, 1983)

Parker, Geoffrey, 'Guide to the archives of the Spanish institutions in or concerned with the Netherlands (1556–1706)', *Archives de Bibliothèque de Belgique* 3 (1971), 26–7

——, *The Dutch Revolt* (London: Penguin, 1977)

——, *Philip II* (1st pub. 1979; London: Sphere Books Ltd. 1988)

——, 'Maps and ministers: the Spanish Habsburgs' in David Buisseret, ed., *Monarchs, Ministers and Maps: The Emergence of Cartography as a Tool of Government in Early Modern Europe* (Chicago and London: University of Chicago Press, 1992), 124–52

——, *Felipe II: La biografía definitiva* (Madrid: Planeta, 2010)

——, *Imprudent King: A New Life of Philip II* (London: Yale University Press, 2014)

Parker, Patricia, and David Quint, eds, *Literary Theory/Renaissance Texts* (Baltimore, Mary.: Johns Hopkins University Press, 1986)

Parmelee, Lisa Ferraro, *Good Newes from Fraunce: French Anti-League Propaganda in Late Elizabethan England* (New York: University of Rochester Press, 1996)

Pascual Molina, Jesús, '"Porque vean y sepan cuánto es el poder y grandeza de nuestro Príncipe y Señor": Imagen y poder en el viaje de Felipe II a Inglaterra y su matrimonio con María Tudor', *Reales Sitios* 197 (2013), 6–26

Pascual Ortega, María, 'El matrimonio entre Felipe II y María Tudor en la correspondencia de Granvela: Edición filológica de documentos inéditos y notas', unpublished PhD thesis (University of Valencia, 2017)

Pattenden, Miles, *Pius IV and the Fall of the Carafa: Nepotism and Papal Authority in Counter-Reformation Rome* (Oxford: Oxford University Press, 2012)

Paz, Octavio, *El Laberinto de la Soledad* (México: Fondo de cultura económica, 1959)

Peardon, Barbara, 'The politics of polemic: John Ponet's *Short Treatise of Politic Power* and contemporary circumstance 1553–1556', *Journal of Bristish Studies* 22 (1982), 35–49

Pérez Martín, María Jesús, *María Tudor: La gran reina desconocida* (Madrid: Rialp, 2008)

Pettegree, Andrew, *Foreign Protestant Communities in 16th Century London* (Oxford: Clarendon Press, 1986)

——, 'Humanism and the Reformation in Britain and the Netherlands', in N. Scott Amos, Andrew Pettegree and Henk van Nierop, eds, *The Education of a Christian Society: Humanism and the Reformation in Britain and the Netherlands* (Aldershot: Ashgate, 1999), 1–18

——, *Marian Protestantism: Six Studies* (Aldershot: Scolar Press, 1996)

Pietschmann, Horst, 'El problema del "nacionalismo" en España en la edad moderna. La resistencia de Castilla contra el Emperador Carlos V', *Hispania* 52 (1992), 83–106

Pincombe, Mike and Cathy Shrank, eds, *The Oxford Handbook of Tudor Literature, 1485–1603* (Oxford: Oxford University Press, 2009)

Pineas, Rainer, 'William Turner and Reformation politics', *Bibliothéque d'Humanisme et Renaissance* 37 (1975), 193–200

——, 'William Turner's polemical use of ecclesiastical history and his controversy with Stephen Gardiner', *Renaissance Quarterly* 33 (1980), 599–608

Plucknett, T. F. T., 'Ellesmere on statutes', *Law Quarterly Review* 60 (1944), 242–9

Pollard, A. F., *The History of England From the Accession of Edward VI to the Death of Elizabeth (1547–1603)*, The Political History of England, 12 vols (London: Longmans, Green and Co., 1915)

Pollnitz, Aysha, 'Humanism and court culture in the education of Tudor royal children' in Thomas Betteridge and Anna Riehl, eds, *Tudor Court Culture* (Selinsgrove, Penn.: Susquehanna University Press, 2010), 42–58

Pollock, Sir Frederick and Frederic Maitland, *The History of English Law before the Time of Edward I*, 2 vols (Cambridge: Cambridge University Press, repr. 1968)

Popham, A. E., 'The authorship of the drawings of Binche', *Journal of the Courtauld and Warburg Institute* 3 (1940), 55–7

Porter, Linda, *Mary Tudor: The First Queen* (London: Portrait, 2007)

Prescott, H. F. M., *Mary Tudor* (London: Eyre & Spottiswoode, 1953)

——, *Mary Tudor: The Spanish Tudor* (London: Phoenix, 1952 repr. 2003)

Purcell, H. D., 'The *Celestina* and the *Interlude of Calisto and Melibea*', *Bulletin of Hispanic Studies* 44 (1967), 1–15

Rabb, Felix, *The English Face of Machiavelli: A Changing Interpretation 1500–1700* (London: Routledge & Kegan Paul, 1965)

Radin, Max, 'Early statutory interpretations in England', *Illinois Law Review* 38 (1943–4), 16–40

Rady, Martin, *The Emperor Charles V*, Seminar Studies in History (London: Longman, 1988)

Rancière, Jacques, *The Ignorant Schoolmaster: Five Lessons in Intellectual Emancipation*, trans. Kristin Ross (Palo Alto, Cal.: Stanford University Press, 1991)

Rappaport, Steve, *Worlds within Worlds: Structures of Life in sixteenth-century London* (Cambridge: Cambridge University Press, 1989)

Rapple, Rory, *Martial Power and Elizabethan Political Culture: Military Men in England and Ireland 1558–1594* (Cambridge: Cambridge University Press, 2009)

Redworth, Glyn, *In Defence of the Church Catholic: The Life of Stephen Gardiner* (Oxford: Basil Blackwell Ltd, 1990)

——, 'Nuevo mundo u otro mundo?: conquistadores, cortesanos, libros de caballerías y el reinado de Felipe el Breve de Inglaterra', in *Actas del I Congreso Anglo-Hispano*, 3 vols (Madrid: 1994)

——, 'Matter impertinent to women: male and female monarchy under Philip and Mary', *English Historical Review* 112 (1997), 597–613

——, 'Philip I of England, embezzlement and the quantity theory of money', *Economic History Review* 55 (2002), 248–61

——, 'A family at war? King Philip I of England and Habsburg dynastic politics' in

Franz Bosbach, ed., *Prinz-Albert-Gesellschaft / Prince Albert Society* (Coburg: Prinz-Albert-Gesellschaft, 2008), 1–20

—— and Fernando Checa, 'The courts of the Spanish Habsburgs 1500–1700', in John Adamson, ed., *The Princely Courts of Europe: Ritual, Politics and Culture under the Ancien Regime, 1500–1750* (London: Weidenfeld and Nicolson, 1998), 43–66

Reed, A., *Early Tudor Drama* (London: Methuen, 1926)

Richards, Judith, '"To promote a woman to beare rule": talking of queens in mid-Tudor England', *Sixteenth Century Journal* 28 (1997), 101–21

——, 'Mary Tudor as "sole quene"? Gendering Tudor monarchy', *The Historical Journal* 40 (1997), 895–924

——, 'Renaissance queen' in Carole Levin, Jo Carney and Debra Barrett-Graves, eds, *'High and Mighty Queens' of Early Modern England: Realities and Representations* (Basingstoke: Palgrave Macmillan, 2003)

——, 'Public identity and public memory: case studies of two Tudor women', in Stephanie Tarbin and Susan Broomhall, eds, *Women, Identities and Communities in Early Modern Europe* (Aldershot: Ashgate, 2008), 195–210

——, *Mary Tudor* (London: Routledge, 2008)

Richards, Sheila, ed., *Secret Writings in the Public Records: Henry VIII–George II* (London: HMSO, 1974)

Riordan, Michael and Alec Ryrie, 'Stephen Gardiner and the making of a Protestant villain', *Sixteenth Century Journal* 34 (2003), 1039–63

Roa de la Carrera, Cristián, *Histories of Infamy: Francisco López de Gómara and the Ethics of Spanish Imperialism*, trans. Scott Sessions (Boulder: University of Colorado Press, 2005)

Robison, William B., 'The national and local significance of Wyatt's rebellion in Surrey', *The Historical Journal* 30 (1987), 769–90

Rodríguez Pérez, Yolanda, *The Dutch Revolt through Spanish Eyes: Self and Other in historical and literary texts of Golden Age Spain (c. 1548–1673)* (Bern: Peter Lang, trans. and rev. 2008)

Rodríguez Salgado, María José, *The Changing Face of Empire: Charles V, Philip II and Habsburg Authority, 1551–1559*, Cambridge Studies in Early Modern History (Cambridge: Cambridge University Press, 1988)

Root, Deborah, 'Speaking Christian: orthodoxy and difference in sixteenth century Spain', *Representations* 23 (1988), 118–34

Roover, Raymond de, *Gresham on Foreign Exchange: An Essay on Early English Mercantilism with the Text of Thomas Gresham's Memorandum for the Understanding of the Exchange* (Cambridge, Mass.: Harvard University Press, 1949)

Roper, Lyndal, *The Holy Household: Women and Morals, in Reformation Augsburg* (Oxford: Clarendon Press, repr. 1991)

——, *Oedipus and the Devil: Witchcraft, Sexuality and Religion in Early Modern Europe* (London: Routledge, 1994)

Rorty, Richard, J. B. Shneewind and Quentin Skinner, eds, *Philosophy in History: Essays on the historiography of philosophy* (London: Cambridge University Press, 1984)

Round, J. Horace, *Peerage and Pedigree Studies in Peerage Law and Family History*, 2 vols (London: J. Nisbet and Co. Ltd, 1910)

Rowley-Williams, Jennifer, 'Image and reality: lives of aristocratic women in early Tudor England', unpublished PhD thesis (Bangor University, 1998)

Rubin, Miri, *Corpus Christi: The Eucharist in Late Medieval Culture* (Cambridge: Cambridge University Press, 1991)

Ruddock, Alwyn, 'The earliest records of the High Court of Admiralty (1515–1558)', *Bulletin of the Institute of Historical Research* 22 (1949), 139–49

Ruiz, Teofilo, *A King Travels: Festive Traditions in Late Medieval and Early Modern Spain* (Princeton, NJ: Princeton University Press, 2012)

Russell, Elizabeth, 'Mary Tudor and Mr Jorkins', *Historical Research* 63 (1990), 263–76

Russell, Jocelyn, *Diplomats at Work: Three Renaissance Studies* (Stroud: Alan Sutton Publishing Ltd, 1992)

Rutledge, Douglas F., '*Respublica*: rituals of status elevation and the political mythology of Mary Tudor', *Medieval and Renaissance Drama in England* 5 (1991), 55–68

Sadlack, Erin, *The French Queen's Letters: Mary Tudor Brandon and the Politics of Marriage in Sixteenth-Century Europe* (New York: Palgrave MacMillan, 2011)

Salamon, Linda Bradley, 'Blackening "the Turk" in Roger Ashcam's *A Report of Germany*' in Margaret Greer, Walter Mignolo and Maureen Quilligan, eds, *Rereading the Black Legend, The Discourses of Racial and Religious Difference in the Renaissance Empires* (Chicago: University of Chicago Press, 2007), 270–92

Samson, Alexander, 'Changing places: the marriage and royal entry of Philip, Prince of Austria, and Mary Tudor, July–August 1554', *Sixteenth Century Journal* 36 (2005), 761–84

———, 'Florián de Ocampo, imperial chronicler, Habsburg propagandist and historical commentator: the uses of history in early modern Spain', *Forum for Modern Language Studies* 42 (2006), 339–54

———, ed., *The Spanish Match: Prince Charles's Journey to Madrid, 1623* (Basingstoke: Ashgate, 2006)

———, 'The *adelantamiento* of Cazorla, *converso* culture and Toledo's Cathedral chapter's 1547 *estatuto de limpieza de sangre*', *Bulletin of Spanish Studies* 84 (2007), 819–36

———, 'Mapping the marriage: Thomas Geminus's *Britanniae Insulae Nova Descriptio* and *Nova Descriptio Hispaniae* (1555)', *Renaissance and Reformation* 31 (2008), 95–115

———, 'A fine romance: Anglo-Spanish relations in the sixteenth century', *Journal of Medieval and Early Modern Studies* 39 (2009), 65–94

———, 'English travellers in Spain, 1604–1625: writing, politics and identity', *Studies in Travel Writing* 13 (2009), 111–24

———, '"Last thought upon a windmill"?: Cervantes and Fletcher' in John Ardila, ed., *The Cervantean Heritage: Reception and Influence of Cervantes in Britain* (London: Legenda, 2009), 223–33

———, 'Power sharing: the co-monarchy of Philip and Mary', in Anna Whitelock and

Alice Hunt, eds, *Tudor Queenship: The Reigns of Mary and Elizabeth* (New York: Palgrave MacMillan, 2010), 159–72

———, 'Images of co-monarchy in the London entry of Philip and Mary (1554)', in Jean Andrews, Marie-France Wagner and Marie-Claude Canova-Green, eds, *Writing Royal Entries in Early Modern Europe* (Turnhout: Brepols, 2013), 113–28

———, 'Lazarillo de Tormes and the picaresque in early modern England' in Andrew Hadfield, ed., *Oxford Handbook of English Prose 1500–1640* (Oxford: Oxford University Press, 2013), 121–36

———, 'Culture under Philip and Mary I', in Sarah Duncan and Valerie Schutte, eds, (*The Birth of a Queen: Essay on the Quincentenary of Mary I* New York: Palgrave MacMillan, 2016), 155–78

Sanchez, Mark, 'Anti-Spanish sentiment in English literary and political writing, 1553–1603', unpublished PhD thesis (University of Leeds, 2004)

Sánchez González, Antonio, *Documentación de la Casa de Medinaceli: El Archivo General de los Duques de Segorbe y Cardona* (Madrid: Archivos Estatales, 1990)

Sánchez Jiménez, Antonio, *Leyenda negra: la batalla sobre la imagen de España en tiempos de Lope de Vega* (Madrid: Cátedra, 2016)

Sanders, N. and R. Southern, eds, *Revels History of Drama in English*. Vol. 2, *1500–1576* (London: Methuen, 1980)

Scalingi, Paula Louise, 'The sceptre or the distaff: the question of female sovereignty, 1516–1607', *The Historian* 41 (1978), 59–75

Scarisbrick, J. J., *Henry VIII* (London: Eyre & Spottiswoode, 1968)

Schäfer, Ernesto, *El Consejo Real y Supremo de las Indias: Su historia, organización y labor administrativa hasta la terminación de la Casa de Austria*, Vol. I. *Historia y organización del Consejo y de la Casa de la Contratación de las Indias* (Seville: M. Carmona, 1935)

Schilder, Günter, *Monumenta Cartographica Neerlandica*, 5 vols (Alphen aan den Rijn: Uitgeverij 'Canaletto', 1987)

Schramm, Percy Ernst, *A History of the English Coronation*, trans. L. G. Wickham Legg (Oxford: Clarendon Press, 1937)

Schutte, Valerie, 'Queen Mary I's books at Lambeth Palace library', *Journal of the Early Book Society* 17 (2014), 348–51

———, *Mary I and the Art of Book Dedications: Royal Women, Power and Persuasion* (New York: Palgrave Macmillan, 2015)

Schwyzer, Philip, *Literature, Nationalism, and Memory in Early Modern England and Wales* (Cambridge: Cambridge University Press, 2004)

Scott Kastan, David, '"Holy wurdes" and "slypper wit": John Bale's *King Johan* and the poetics of propaganda' in Peter Herman, ed., *Rethinking the Henrician Era: Essays on Early Tudor Texts and Contexts* (Urbana: University of Illinois Press, 1994), 267–82

———, '"Shewes of honour and gladnes": dissonance and display in Mary and Philip's entry into London', *Research Opportunities in Renaissance Drama* 33 (1994), 1–14

Seyssel, Claude de, *The Monarchy of France*, trans. J. H. Hexter, ed. Donald Kelley (London: Yale University Press, 1981)

Shaw, Patricia, 'Philip II and seduction à la española in an Elizabethan roman à clef' in S. G. Fernández-Corugedo, ed., *Actas del II Congreso de la Sociedad Española de Estudios Renacentistas Ingleses* (Oviedo: Universidad de Oviedo, 1992), 289–302

Shell, Alison, *Oral Culture and Catholicism in Early Modern England* (Cambridge: Cambridge University Press, 2007)

Shippey, Tom, 'Macho man's nightmare', *Times Literary Supplement*, 15th January 1999

Shirley, Rodney W., *Early Printed Maps of the British Isles 1477–1650* (East Grinstead: Antique Atlas Publications, repr. 1991)

Sicroff, Albert A., *Les Controverses des Statuts de "Pureté de Sang" en Espagne du Xve au XVIIe Siècle* (Paris: Didier, 1960)

Silver, Larry, *The Paintings of Quinten Massys with Catalogue Raisonné* (Oxford: Phaidon, 1984)

Simon, Bruno, 'Contribution à l'étude du commerce Vénetien dans l'Empire Ottoman au milieu du XVIe siècle (1558–1560)', *Mélanges de l'école Française de Rome. Moyen Age–Temps Moderne* 96 (1984), 973–1020

Skinner, Quentin, *The Foundations of Modern Political Thought*. Vol. 1, *The Renaissance*, Vol. 2, *The Age of Reformation* (Cambridge: Cambridge University Press, 1978)

——, 'Moral ambiguity and the Renaissance art of eloquence', *Essays in Criticism* 94 (1994), 267–92

Smith, A. G. R., *The Emergence of a Nation State: The Commonwealth of England, 1529–1600* (London: Longman, 1984)

Smith, Paul Julian, *Writing in the Margin: Spanish Literature of the Golden Age* (Oxford: Clarendon Press, 1988)

Smuts, R. M., 'Public ceremony and royal charisma: the English royal entry in London, 1485–1642', in A. L. Beier, D. Cannadine and J. Rosenheim, eds, *The First Modern Society. Essays in English History in Honour of Lawrence Stone* (Cambridge: The Past and Present Society, 2005), 65–94

Snow, Vernon, 'Proctorial representation and conciliar management during the reign of Henry VIII', *The Historical Journal* 9 (1966), 1–26

——, 'Proctorial representation in the House of Lords during the reign of Edward VI', *Journal of British Studies* 2 (1969), 1–27

Sommerville, Margaret, *Sex and Subjection: Attitudes to Women in Early Modern Society* (London: Arnold, 1995)

Stallybrass, Peter, 'Patriarchal territories: the body enclosed', in Margaret W. Ferguson, Maureen Quilligan and Nancy J. Vickers, ed., *Rewriting the Renaissance: The Discourse of Sexual Difference in Early Modern Europe* (London: University of Chicago Press, 1986)

Starkey, David, 'Representation through intimacy: a study in the symbolism of monarchy and court office in early modern England', in Ioan Lewis, ed., *Symbols and Sentiments: Cross-cultural Studies in Symbolism* (London: Academic Press, 1977)

——, *The Reign of Henry VIII: Personalities and Politics* (London: Collins & Brown, 1991)

——, D. A. L. Morgan, John Murphy, Pam Wright, Neil Cuddy and Kevin Sharpe, eds, *The English Court: from the Wars of the Roses to the Civil War* (London: Longman, 1987)

Stern, Virginia F., *Gabriel Harvey: A Study of His Life, Marginalia and Library* (Oxford: Clarendon Press, 1979)

Streckfuss, Corinna, 'England's reconciliation with Rome: a news event in early modern Europe', *Historical Research* 82 (2009), 62–73

Streitberger, W. R., *Court Revels, 1485–1559* (Toronto: University of Toronto Press, 1994)

Strickland, Agnes, *Lives of the Queens of England from the Norman Conquest*, 8 vols, vol. 3 (London: Henry Colbourn, 1854)

Strohm, Paul, 'The trouble with Richard: the reburial of Richard II and Lancastrian symbolic strategy', *Speculum* 71 (1996), 87–111

Strong, Roy, 'From manuscript to miniature', in John Murdoch, Jim Murrell, Patrick Noon and Roy Strong, eds, *The English Miniature* (London: Yale University Press, 1981)

——, *The English Renaissance Miniature* (London: Thames and Hudson, 1983)

Sulzberger, Suzanne, 'Considération sur le chef-d'oeuvre de Quentin Metsys: Le prêteur et sa femme', *Bulletin des Musees Royaux des Beaux-Arts de Belgique* 42 (1965), 27–34

Surtz, Ronald, 'Cardinal Juan Martínez Silíceo in an allegorical *entremés* of 1556', in Sylvia Molloy and Luis Fernández Cifuentes, eds, *Essays on Hispanic Literature in Honour of Edmund L. King* (London: Tamesis, 1983)

Tanner, Marie, *The Last Descendant of Aeneas: The Habsburgs and the Mythic Image of the Emperor* (London: Yale University Press, 1993)

Tazón, Juan, *The Life and Times of Thomas Stukeley (c. 1525–78)* (Aldershot: Ashgate, 2003)

Tellechea Idígoras, José Ignacio, *El arzobispo Carranza y su tiempo*, 2 vols (Madrid: Ediciones Guadarrame, 1968)

——, *Fray Bartolomé Carranza: Documentos historicos* (Madrid: Real Academia de la Historia, 1963)

——, *Fray Bartolomé Carranza y el Cardenal Pole: Un navarro en la restauración católica de Inglaterra (1554–1558)*, 2 vols (Pamplona: Aranzadi, 1977)

——, *El proceso Romano del Arzobispo Carranza (1567 – 1576)* (Rome: Iglesia Nacional Española, 1988)

The National Gallery of Art, Washington (Fetham: Hamlyn Publishing Group Ltd, 1968)

Thirsk, Joan, *Horses in Early Modern England: for Service, for Pleasure for Power*, The Stenton Lecture 1977 (Reading: University of Reading, 1978)

Thomas, Hugh, *The Golden Age: The Spanish Empire of Charles V* (London: Allen Lane, 2010)

Thomas, Joan M., 'Before the Black Legend: sources of anti-Spanish sentiment in England 1553–1558', unpublished PhD thesis (University of Illinois, Urbana, 1972)

Thomas, Keith, *Religion and the Decline of Magic: Studies in Popular Beliefs in Sixteenth and Seventeenth Century England* (London: Penguin, 1971 repr. 1991)

Thomson, Patricia, *Sir Thomas Wyatt and His Background* (Palo Alto, Cal.: Stanford University Press, 1964)

Thorp, Malcolm R., 'Religion and the Wyatt rebellion of 1554', *Church History* 47 (1978), 363–80

Tibble, Matthew C. 'Nicolaus Mameranus: poetry and politics at the court of Mary Tudor', unpublished PhD thesis (University of Edinburgh, 2019)

Tittler, Robert and Susan L. Battley, 'The local community and the crown in 1553: the accession of Mary Tudor revisited', *Bulletin of the Institute of Historical Research* 57:136 (1984), 131–9

——, *The Reign of Mary I* (London: Longman, repr. 1991)

Took, Patricia, 'Government and the printing trade, 1540–1560', unpublished PhD thesis (University of London, 1978)

Tooley, Marian J., 'Bodin and the medieval theory of climate', *Speculum* 28 (1953), 64–83

Towler, Jean and Joan Bramall, eds, *Midwives in History and Society* (London: Croom Helm, 1986)

Tracy, James D., *A Financial Revolution in the Habsburg Netherlands: Renten and Renteniers in the County of Holland, 1515–1565* (London: University of California Press, 1985)

——, *Holland under Habsburg Rule, 1506–1566: The Formation of a Body Politic* (London: University of California Press, 1990)

——, 'Herring wars: the Habsburg Netherlands and the struggle for control of the North Sea, ca. 1520–1560', *Sixteenth Century Journal* XXIV:2 (1993), 249–73

Trapp, J. B., and Hubertus Schulte Herbrüggen, *'The King's Good Servant': Sir Thomas More 1477/8–1535* (London: National Portrait Gallery exhibition catalogue, 1977)

Travitsky, Betty S., 'Reprinting Tudor history: the case of Catherine of Aragon', *Renaissance Quarterly* 50 (1997), 164–74

Trevor-Roper, Hugh, *Princes and Artists: Patronage and Ideology at four Habsburg Courts 1517–1633* (London: Thames and Hudson, 1976)

Tudor, Philippa, 'Protestant books in London in Mary Tudor's reign', *London Journal* 15 (1990), 19–28

Tully, James, ed. and intro., *Meaning and Context: Quentin Skinner and his Critics* (Cambridge: Polity Press, 1988)

Turner, Gerard L'E., *Elizabethan Instrument Makers: The Origins of the London Trade in Precision Instrument Making* (Oxford: Oxford University Press, 2000)

——, *Renaissance Astrolabes and Their Makers* (Basingstoke: Ashgate Variorum, 2003)

Tytler, P. T., *England under the Reigns of Edward VI and Mary*, 2 vols (London: Richard Bentley, 1839)

Ullman, Walter, 'On the influence of Geoffrey of Monmouth in English history' in C. Bauer, L. Boehm and M. Muller, eds, *Speculum Historiale: Geschichte Im Spiegel Von Geschichtsschreibung und Geschichtdeutung* (Munich: Verlag Karl Alber Freiburg, 1965)

——, 'This realm of England is an empire', *Journal of Ecclesiastical History* 30 (1979), 175–204

Ulloa, Modesto, *La Hacienda Real de Castilla en el Reinado de Felipe II* (3rd edn, Madrid: Fundación Universitaria Española, 1986)

Ungerer, Gustav, *Anglo-Spanish Relations in Tudor Literature* (Bern: Francke Verlag, 1956)

——, 'The printing of Spanish Books in Elizabethan England', *The Library* 5th ser. 20 (1965), 177–229

——, 'The Earl of Southampton's donation to the Bodleian in 1605 and its Spanish books', *Bodleian Library Record* 16 (1997), 17–41

——, *The Mediterranean Apprenticeship of British Slavery* (Madrid: Verbum, 2008)

Uriol, José I., 'Viajes de Carlos V por España', *Historia y Vida* 19 (1986), 36–49

Van de Put, Albert, 'Two drawings of the *fêtes* at Binche for Charles V and Philip II, 1549', *Journal of the Courtauld and Warburg Institute* 3 (1940), 49–55

Velasco Berenguer, Gonzalo, 'Philip I, King of England and Ireland: Spanish influence under Habsburg-Tudor rule', unpublished PhD thesis (University of Bristol, 2017)

Venn, John, *The Works of John Caius, MD, Second Founder of Gonville and Caius College and Master of the College 1559–1573*, ed. E. S. Roberts (Cambridge: Cambridge University Press, 1912)

Vidmar, John, *English Catholic Historians and the English Reformation, 1585–1954* (Brighton: Sussex Academic Press, 2005)

Villacorta, Antonio, *Las cuatro esposas de Felipe II* (Madrid: Rialp, 2011)

Vogelstein, Ingeborg, 'Johann Sleiden's Commentaries: new insights from an old history', *Storia della Storiografia* 11 (1987), 5–21

Vos, Dirk de, *Rogier van der Weyden: The Complete Works* (New York: Harry Abrams, 1999)

Walker, Greg, *John Skelton and the Politics of the 1520s* (Cambridge: Cambridge University Press, 1988)

——, *Plays of Persuasion: Drama and Politics at the Court of Henry VIII* (Cambridge: Cambridge University Press, 1991)

——, *The Politics of Performance in Early Renaissance Drama* (Cambridge: Cambridge University Press, 1998)

Wallerstein, Immanuel, *The Modern World-System: Capitalist Agriculture and the Origins of the European World-Economy in the Sixteenth Century* (London: Academic Press, 1974)

Walsham, Alexandra, '"Domme preachers"?: Post-Reformation English Catholicism and the culture of print', *Past and Present* 168 (2000), 72–123

——, 'Translating Trent? English Catholicism and the Counter Reformation', *Historical Research* 78 (2005), 288–310

——, *Catholic Reformation in Protestant Britain* (London: Ashgate, 2014)

Walvin, James, *The Black Presence: A Documentary History of the Negro in England, 1555–1860* (London: Orbach and Chambers, 1971)

Ward, Joseph, *Metropolitan Communities: Trade Guilds, Identity, and Change in Early Modern London* (Palo Alto, Cal.: Stanford University Press, 1997)

Warnicke, Retha M., 'Lord Morley's statements about Richard III', *Albion* 15 (1983), 173–8

——, 'Queenship: politics and gender in Tudor England', *History Compass* 4 (2006), 203–27

Watanabe-O'Kelly, Helen and Anne Simon, eds, *Festivals and Ceremonies: A Bibiliography of Works Relating to Court, Civic and Religious Festivals in Europe 1500–1800* (London: Mansell, 2000)

Waters, David, *The Art of Navigation in English in Elizabethan and Early Stuart Times* (London: Hollis and Carter, 1958)

Watson, Robert, *The History of the Reign of Philip the Second*, 2 vols (London: W. Strathan and T. Cadell, 1777)

Watt, Tessa, *Cheap Print and Popular Piety 1550–1640* (Cambridge: Cambridge University Press, 1991)

Weber, Max, *The Protestant Ethic and the Spirit of Capitalism*, trans. Talcott Parsons (London: Routledge, 1992)

Wernham, Robert, *The Growth of English Foreign Policy 1485–1588* (London: Jonathan Cape, 1966)

Whitelock, Anna, 'In opposition and in government: the household and affinities of Mary Tudor, 1516–1558', unpublished PhD thesis (Cambridge University, 2004)

——, 'A woman in a man's world: Mary I and political intimacy, 1553–1558', *Women's History Review* 16 (2007), 323–34

——, *Mary Tudor: England's First Queen* (London: Bloomsbury, 2009)

—— and Diarmaid MacCulloch, 'Princess Mary's household and the succession crisis, July 1553', *The Historical Journal* 50 (2007), 265–87

Willan, T. S., *Studies in Elizabethan Foreign Trade* (Manchester: Manchester University Press, 1959)

Willard, Charity Cannon, 'The concept of true nobility at the Burgundian court', *Studies in the Renaissance* 14 (1967), 33–48

Williams, Glanmor, 'Wales and the reign of Queen Mary I', *Welsh History Review* 10 (1981), 334–58

Williams, N. J., *The Maritime Trade of the East Anglian Ports 1550–1590* (Oxford: Clarendon Press, 1988)

Williams, Patrick, *The Great Favourite: The Duke of Lerma and the court and government of Philip III of Spain* (Manchester: Manchester University Press, 2006)

Williams, Penry, *Tudor Regime* (Oxford: Clarendon Press, 1979)

——, *The Later Tudors* (Oxford: Clarendon Press, 1996)

Williams, R. B., *The Staging of Plays in the Spanish Peninsula Prior to 1555*, ed. R. House, University of Iowa Studies in Spanish Language and Literature (Iowa City: University of Iowa 1930)

Winkelman, Michael, '*Respublica*: England's trouble about Mary', *Comitatus* 33 (2002), 77–98

Wizeman, William, *The Theology and Spirituality of Mary Tudor's Church* (Aldershot: Ashgate, 2006)

Wolff, Philippe, 'The 1391 pogrom in Spain. Social crisis or not?', *Past and Present* 50 (1971), 4–18

Wollman, David H., 'The Biblical justification for resistance to authority in Ponet's and Goodman's polemics', *Sixteenth Century Journal* 13 (1982), 29–41

Woodacre, Elena, 'The Queen's marriage: matrimonial politics in premodern Europe', in Jacqueline Murray, ed., *Marriage in Premodern Europe: Italy and Beyond* (Toronto: Centre for Reformation and Renaissance Studies, 2012), 29–48

Woodall, Joanna, 'An exemplary consort: Antonis Mor's portrait of Mary Tudor', *Art History* 14 (1990), 192–224

——, *Anthonis Mor: Art and Authority* (Zwolle: Waanders Publishers, 2007)

Woodbridge, Linda, *Women and the English Renaissance: Literature and the Nature of Womankind, 1540–1620* (Chicago: University of Illinois Press, 1984)

Wordie, J. R., 'Deflationary factors in the Tudor price rise', *Past and Present* 154 (1997), 32–70

Wormald, Jenny, 'The usurped and unjust empire of women', *Journal of Ecclesiastical History* 42 (1991), 282–92

Alan Young, *Tudor and Jacobean Tournaments* (London: George Philip, 1987)

Yungblut, Laura, *Strangers Settled Here Amongst Us: Policies, Perceptions and the Presence of Aliens in Elizabethan England* (London: Routledge, 1996)

Zell, Michael, 'Fisher's flu and Moore's probates: quantifying the mortality crisis, 1556–60', *Economic History Review* 47 (1994), 354–8

Zemon Davies, Natalie, *Society and Culture in Early Modern France* (London: Duckworth, 1975)

Index

INDEX